D1521910

WHEN BLAME
BACKFIRES

WHEN BLAME BACKFIRES

Syrian Refugees and Citizen Grievances
in Jordan and Lebanon

Anne Marie Baylouny

CORNELL UNIVERSITY PRESS **ITHACA AND LONDON**

First published 2020 by Cornell University Press

Library of Congress Cataloging-in-Publication Data

Names: Baylouny, Anne Marie, author.
Title: When blame backfires : Syrian refugees and citizen grievances in Jordan and
    Lebanon / Anne Marie Baylouny.
Description: Ithaca [New York] : Cornell University Press, 2020. | Includes
    bibliographical references and index.
Identifiers: LCCN 2020007272 (print) | LCCN 2020007273 (ebook) |
    ISBN 9781501751516 (hardcover) | ISBN 9781501751530 (pdf) |
    ISBN 9781501751523 (epub)
Subjects: LCSH: Political refugees—Syria—Public opinion. | Political refugees—
    Jordan—Public opinion. | Political refugees—Lebanon—Public opinion. |
    Political refugees—Syria—Economic conditions—21st century. | Political
    refugees—Jordan x Economic conditions—21st century. | Political refugees—
    Lebanon x Economic conditions—21st century. | Syria—History—Civil War,
    2011——Refugees—Jordan. | Syria—History—Civil War, 2011——Refugees—
    Lebanon. | Jordan—Economic conditions—21st century. | Lebanon—
    Economic conditions—21st century.
Classification: LCC HV640.5.S97 B395 2020 (print) | LCC HV640.5.S97 (ebook) |
    DDC 956.9104/231—dc23
LC record available at https://lccn.loc.gov/2020007272
LC ebook record available at https://lccn.loc.gov/2020007273

To the Syrian refugees . . . May they find peace, acceptance, and housing.

Contents

Acknowledgments

Gratitude goes first to my local posse, my colleagues and friends Anshu Chatterjee, Michael Malley, and Rodrigo Nieto-Gomez. They supported me through the process, by variously listening, lighting a fire under me when I needed it, and giving feedback. I owe a special debt to Anshu, who motivated and pushed me in just the right ways at different points from beginning to end. Mike gave me an initial push and discussed the ideas with me until the research was well underway. Rodrigo's friendship and academic feedback then took over and saw me into the writing process. They gave short pieces of advice or listened to my long monologues as I worked out the material. Invariably, it was exactly what I needed at the time.

Many people supported me and discussed my developing ideas. Early on, I was encouraged by positive feedback and long conversations with Jill Schwedler, Joel Beinin, Fred Lawson, and Harold Trinkunas. Mohammed Hafez and later Clay Moltz, in their roles as colleagues and chairs of my department, provided feedback and supported my ability to devote time to writing. Julie Chernov Hwang helped me with the initial organizing of the book, and continued to listen when I needed to work things out. Dianna Beardslee was a supportive friend throughout, brain-storming with me at times. Productive discussions with Roger Haydon at Cornell University Press helped shape and improve the book. I am grateful also to the two book reviewers, who provided timely comments, helping to improve the book.

Aysar Hammoudeh was a fabulous, tireless researcher helping me to compile and translate primary sources. My former student, Stephen Klingseis, researched the effects of the refugees on water, which we subsequently published as an article. I draw from our findings in chapter 2. My research benefited from the wonderful Greta Marlatt at the Dudley Knox library, who helped me generously in searching and citation advice. Rachel Templer edited my chapters and kept me to a tight schedule. Her skill in catching errors and suggesting improvements was invaluable. The Minerva Research Initiative funded other research before the book that helped to feed ideas for this work. The Abbasi Program in Islamic Studies at Stanford provided me with an institutional affiliation, for which I am grateful.

Many Jordanians and Lebanese generously spoke with me, provided networks, aid, and hospitality. Some prefer to remain nameless; others I anonymize due to the intensely political climate. In Lebanon I owe many thanks to Rabih Shibli, who helped me with networks and contacts. Special thanks go to Omar Tantawi and Omar El Maadarani for their time and connections, taking me to far-flung areas of Lebanon and arranging interviews. My husband's relatives, Samira and Rabih Dabbous, provided my second home while I was in Beirut. They made me feel welcome, helping whenever I needed anything or just taking me to dinner. In Jordan, Lillian Frost provided contacts, connecting me to May Shalabieh and others. May, in turn, introduced me to more people and accompanied me to many research appointments. I benefited from her presence and friendship. Jumana Kawar conducted seed interviews and made connections for me during her trip to Jordan. My friends in Amman, Kolthoum Abdelhaq and her wonderful daughters, Sarah and Farah, provided my home-away-from-home in Amman, complete with great meals, coffee, and companionship during all my trips to Jordan. I miss them whenever I return to the United States.

Finally, a debt goes to my husband, Amer Saleh, my daughter, Zahra, my father, Raymond Baylouny, and my late mother-in-law, Janan Saleh. They supported me continuously, taking over my family duties when I traveled or needed to write. I will miss the drunken conversations with my mother-in-law, who deserved an easier life than that of a refugee from Palestine, and who was later forced to leave her home in Kuwait along with so many others. My daughter was patient and helpful while I was writing or away on research. Being away from her was the hardest part of fieldwork, and I am grateful for family and friends who stepped in while I was away. My father's faith in me, his support, and his pride in my accomplishments have remained solid during my journey from graduate school through today. My apologies to anyone I have forgotten to mention; it truly takes a community of scholars, friends, and family.

All opinions expressed here are my own, and should not be interpreted as statements of official U.S. Navy, Department of Defense policy, or any other institutional affiliation.

An early account of some of the research for portions of chapter 2 appeared as Anne Marie Baylouny and Stephen Klingseis, "Water Thieves or Political Catalysts? Syrian Refugees in Jordan and Lebanon," *Middle East Policy* 25, no. 1 (Spring 2018).

Abbreviations

EDL	Électricité du Liban
EU	European Union
GDP	gross domestic product
GSO	General Security Office (Lebanon)
ILO	International Labour Organization
IMF	International Monetary Fund
INGO	international nongovernmental organization (including Mercy Corps and the plethora of UN organizations, such as UNICEF)
IOM	International Organization for Migration
IRC	International Rescue Committee
ISIS	Islamic state of Iraq and Syria
ITS	informal tented settlements
JD	Jordanian dinars
LAF	Lebanese Armed Forces
MOI	Ministry of the Interior (Jordan)
MoIM	Ministry of Interior and Municipalities (Lebanon)
MOPIC	Ministry of Planning and International Cooperation
MOU	Memoranda of Understanding
MP	Municipal Police (Lebanon)
NGO	nongovernmental organization (referring to local unless specified)
NSA	nonstate actor
PRS	Palestinian refugees from Syria
TPS	temporary protected status
UN	United Nations
UNHCR	United Nations High Commissioner for Refugees
UNRWA	United Nations Relief and Works Agency
USD	United States dollars
VAT	value-added tax

Note on Transliteration

I use a simplified version of the *International Journal of Middle East Studies* guidelines for writing Arabic words in the Latin alphabet. I omit the diacritical marks. Proper nouns and place names are not italicized.

WHEN BLAME BACKFIRES

SCAPEGOATS OR SOLUTIONS?

Four-year-old Sanad stood waiting in court with his seven-year-old sister and their mother in Mafraq, northern Jordan. The widow Um Sanad and her small family had been evicted, a direct result of the influx of Syrian refugees in Jordan. Um Sanad had been paying 75 Jordanian dinars (JD) a month for their apartment, around USD 100, for the previous nine years. Her landlord increased the rent by close to 70 percent, and the new cost would leave her with only JD 10 (USD 14) to live on per month. Hundreds of families were similarly threatened with eviction across Mafraq, as their rent increased by as much as 300 percent. Syrians were flooding across the border looking for shelter at this time in 2013, a condition that landlords exploited to charge far more rent. The situation pit son against father, brother against brother, and ultimately, Jordanian against Syrian.

Abu Mohammad joined the growing protests against this injustice. His rent had tripled because of the Syrians. Unable to pay, he bought a tent and, together with some twenty families, took part in one of the first tent protests. These Jordanians, made homeless in their own country due to refugees from neighboring Syria, set up their own camp, the Jordanian Displaced People's Camp #1 (Mukhayyam an-Naziheen al-Urduniyyin, Raqm 1) in Mafraq. Their tents bore the United Nations High Commissioner for Refugees (UNHCR) logo, ironically having been purchased from Syrian refugees. The evicted families demanded that the authorities intervene and help them solve the problem of high rents. Local and national Jordanian government officials called on the protesters to disband. The protesters responded with a threat to escalate the open-ended protest to hunger strikes until their problem was fixed. "We protesters responded to them that there

1

is no way to stop the protest unless our demands are met. If the police interfere [to force them to disband], we will go on a hunger strike, with no food or water, and Mafraq city will become a city of tents," one organizer said. These protesting Jordanians were not historically part of opposition to the government. On the contrary, they formed the regime's base of support. But they needed a solution. Their situation could not continue as it was, they declared.[1]

Half an hour down the road from Mafraq, Hamda Masaeed sat in her self-made tent, timeworn and frayed. The seventy-year-old grandmother watched as aid trucks and charities alike passed her ten-member family by to deliver help across the road in Za'atari, the newly established Syrian refugee camp. A Jordanian citizen, Hamda envied the beautiful new tents of the Syrian refugees and lamented, "Don't they realize that we need help too?"[2]

Accounts of citizen suffering, presumably caused by the Syrian refugee influx, and the apparent neglect of local needs in favor of the refugees, caused immense resentment. By this time, two years into the Syrian war, there was no love lost on the Syrian refugees. Large swaths of society in Lebanon and Jordan had become overtly hostile to the Syrians after their initial welcome. The Syrian presence in these countries was overwhelming. Syrian refugee numbers far surpassed anything seen in the West. Syrians formed an average of 10 percent of the population in Jordan from 2014 to 2018, and in Lebanon the numbers were much higher: Syrians in Lebanon were at least one quarter of the population.[3] The sheer demographic impact of the Syrians overwhelmed institutions, services, and infrastructure. People of all social classes in both countries questioned what national identity meant. "What does it mean to be Jordanian when twenty percent of your country is Syrian or Iraqi?"[4]

As an unpopular minority group, Syrian refugees seemingly made the perfect scapegoats.[5] Scapegoats displace grievances against the state to an unpopular minority or immigrant group. These states tried at every turn to blame the Syrians for national problems, no matter how long those issues preceded the Syrians' arrival. In typical scapegoating fashion, state elites turned attention and hostility toward the Syrians. The state could have fixed electricity in Lebanon, but officials claimed the Syrians took five hours of power a day from households. Similarly, authorities in Jordan stated that Syrians drained national water resources and used far more than nationals, who conserve this resource.[6] These scapegoating discourses did not function as such tactics usually do. They did not divert attention from the state into anger at the minority or outsider group.

Crucial daily needs were affected by the demographic stress of the influx of Syrians, altering or threatening citizens' lives. These needs called out for solutions, not merely blame against a group unable to fix their situation. It is this aspect that distinguishes Jordan and Lebanon from other cases of attempted scapegoating. Citizens were—and are—angry at Syrians, but such anger does nothing to provide water, waste removal, or electricity. Indeed, electricity, housing, water, and waste—which have been long-standing national problems—are some of the basic issues that spurred protests by Jordanians and Lebanese against their governments. Anger against the Syrians, and hatred in many cases, did not displace protests or demands directed at the government. In tent protests like the one above, Jordanian protesters blamed the Syrian refugees for their predicament, and many wanted the Syrians to leave. However, their demands focused on concrete redress from the state. Large signs in the tent protests declared the inhabitants' patriotism and begged for housing from God and king.[7] During the same period in Lebanon, Lebanese demonstrated, burned tires, and blocked roads to protest the prolonged lack of electricity in Baalbek, an area with one of the highest Syrian refugee populations. There was widespread popular agreement that the Syrian refugees were at fault in draining electricity from nationals. Officials accused the refugees of stealing electricity and of simply overwhelming the electrical grid's capacity due to their large numbers. But instead of protests aimed at the Syrian refugees, the Lebanese attacked and targeted the Energy Ministry and other arms of the state, demanding more electricity.[8]

The arrival of the Syrian refugees stressed domestic fault lines, both calling attention to endemic problems and triggering protests against the states for remedies. Many of these fault lines were a lack of basic, daily needs, some crucial to survival. Citizens responded with dual blame. They faulted the Syrians for causing the problems but accused the states of responsibility for fixing those issues. Active protest, with a few exceptions, was focused on national and local state institutions and demanded solutions. When one Jordanian town ran out of water, they blamed Syrians for taking from Jordan's scarce national water supply. International aid organizations were providing water to the Syrian refugees, sometimes drawing from domestic supplies. No one seemed to consider Jordanian needs. Citizens' priorities for water were dramatically clear. The Jordanian protesters confronted their government—and, quite surprisingly, the king himself—with guns. "I have nothing to lose. If I don't drink water, I will die," a lead protester said.[9]

"It's the Syrians' fault," one man in Jordan of Palestinian heritage told me. "But the government has to do something about it."[10] Aid money received on behalf of the Syrians only exacerbated the criticisms. Before the Syrians, "People said the problem was Lebanese. Then the politicians blamed the Syrians for all the waste and using infrastructure. But the politicians were getting all this money for these problems. So people turned against the politicians. You say you are getting all this money and nothing is happening," a Lebanese man said.[11] "There are just too many Syrians for the population of Lebanon. We have to be humanitarian toward them—but the state and the UN do not help enough," another Lebanese said.[12]

A Jordanian city council member described, "We had tent protests here [northern Jordan, with a large refugee population] but not much anymore. They demanded help from the government, which is their right [as Jordanians] in the constitution, [the right] to work, to a house, and to health care."[13] A Lebanese UNICEF employee added, "In the back of their [Lebanese] minds they realize their government is failing. Sometimes they blame the Syrians, but more and more they realize this blame is used by the politicians for their own benefit."[14]

Scapegoating historically has worked as intended, displacing anger away from the state. In the case of Syrian refugees in Jordan and Lebanon, this tactic has failed. The difference here is that the grievances concern resources fundamental to life. In such cases, solutions can outweigh scapegoating. Scapegoats are rarely in a position to provide water, electricity, or housing, nor can they restructure a national waste system. In these cases, Jordanians and Lebanese ranked their basic needs over the psychological benefit of blame toward a presumed guilty group. The states' use of scapegoating to exempt themselves from scrutiny and fault for deep structural problems arguably backfired. Citizens in these refugee-hosting countries agreed that the Syrians were to blame, but levied responsibility to alleviate their grievances on the states.

This book examines changes in the states hosting the Syrian refugees and the citizens' relations to governance in these states.[15] What we see is a broadening of citizen demands on the states amid state austerity policies, in the context of mass refugee influx and concomitant aid to the states and the refugees. Jordan and Lebanon are among the countries most demographically burdened with refugees in the world. In the middle of one of the biggest refugee crises in the modern era, citizens have increasingly demanded and placed blame on their own states and, in some cases, international nongovernmental organizations (INGOs). While refugees are a humanitarian issue, they also generate a new structural situation for the host countries, presenting practical, social, and cultural challenges. Examining the direct effects of the refugees, in tandem with political mobilizing and oppositional changes, allows us to understand how the refugees' presence has echoed through society, catalyzing grievances against the states. The resulting national changes in discourses and mobilizing will affect these countries long after the refugees have gone.

The Failure of Scapegoating

Beginning in 2011, many Syrians fled on foot to neighboring states, like most refugees at the start of a war, mainly to Turkey, Lebanon, and Jordan. While Turkey has a large economy, population, and territory, Jordan and Lebanon have little to offer newcomers. These fellow Arabic-speaking countries originally greeted their cultural compatriots with open arms and aid, well before the international community began its humanitarian operations. Many citizens were related to Syrians or shared other commonalities with the refugees. The bulk of the new refugees, like the Iraqi refugees before them, chose to settle among the population rather than in camps, even where camps were allowed. The warm welcome for these self-settled or urban refugees quickly turned to animosity, however, as the numbers of Syrians substantially increased and economic circumstances in the countries worsened. During the time the Syrian refugees have been in Jordan and Lebanon, these states have experienced a range of resource and infrastructure problems that seriously affect daily life. The fact that aid organizations ignored lower-class citizens in areas of refugee concentration while doling out help to the refugees in their midst further fueled resentment against the refugees.

Opinions turned sharply against the refugees, with residents accusing them of causing numerous troubles in these countries. The refugees have, or are perceived to have, stressed garbage collection, water, electricity, roads, education, real estate, consumer price inflation, and jobs. "We had big problems already, then the Syrians came and increased them."[16] The condemnations include a range of social and economic issues: Syrians drive motorcycles that are noisy and disturb the neighbors; Syrian women act inappropriately in public (Jordan); Syrian men demonstrate lewd behavior toward women (Lebanon); Syrian refugees are taking local jobs because they work for less due to receiving international aid; Syrians get rich on aid while the country pays and goes into debt; Syrians increase crime; the refugees overuse and waste water and electricity without a care, creating scarcities since they do not pay; and Syrians increase the amount of waste and litter indiscriminately, causing pollution. Syrians even purportedly spread disease and use up the available vaccines.[17] "I feel for them, but don't ask me to kill myself for others," one Lebanese said.[18] These accusations betray clear cultural and class biases, and repeat stereotypes common of refugees in other regions as well.[19]

Political elites joined in on the blame, echoed by media and social media, scapegoating Syrians for the diverse ills of the states and their institutions. Such a discourse was expected, since these countries govern through identity divisions. Blame against an internal or external group is rampant. Sectarian war, much feared in Lebanon since the Syrians disrupted the existing precarious balance between the sects, has not occurred. Pervasive hostility toward the Syrians, however, dominates both states. Globally, right-wing and anti-immigrant movements, nativism and xenophobia, have risen with (perceived) large immigration flows. Scholars question whether the roots of such nationalist fervor lie with cultural fear or economic self-interest, and their research tracks when the hostility is more or less profound, but they do not doubt the central dynamic of scapegoating. Historically, scapegoating works. Blaming a minority or unpopular group diverts attention from the state and from demands on it. Given the widespread animosity, why has scapegoating of Syrians failed? Why has it not generated support for the state, a rally around flag and country, and support for the politicians who wield this weapon?

The question of who is blamed is intensely political and consequential for the future of political life. The object of popular blame is fought over by political elites, the media, and social movements. Blame creates an opponent or villain to serve as the focus of protest, and as such is integral to protest success. Diffuse or unfocused protest soon fizzles out and fails. Specifying blame not only frames conceptions of the enemy but also reflects legacies of animosity and concepts of history and agency. Differences of opinion, interpretations of causation, narratives, emotions, memory, and personal bias all play roles in determining which stories of blame resonate with the population.[20] Perception, often distinct from reality, heavily influences the target of blame. Confusion, uncertainty, or disagreement on specifying fault is common, and provides space for passivity or scapegoating.[21]

Although people seek to externalize blame and rationalize their own inaction,[22] there are times when psychological convenience falls before a practical reality. The nature of the grievances in Jordan and Lebanon explain the peculiar results, as citizens both faulted refugees and increased demands and expectations from their states. When the grievances that give rise to blame are experienced as threats to livelihood, people can prioritize solutions. Solutions can continue to be the focus of popular demands even though elites promote psychological diversion into anger at an unpopular group. This is particularly true when the grievance is pivotal to daily life. The particular attributes of grievances have long been recognized as affecting the ability, resonance, and duration of mobilizing in social movement studies. Workers' rights, taxation, and the price of bread have been powerful motivators of activism,[23] and for good reason. Obtaining food, water, and shelter is integral to survival, preceding concern over political representation and even rights.

Grievances that stand out as threats to livelihood increase the chances of activism. Psychologically, threats can be more motivating than opportunities, which have been central to the study of collective action, since people value what they have more than what they desire but do not yet have.[24] Abrupt scarcity or loss of goods that are integral to society's daily norms, its taken-for-granted routines, is one such threat. This has been called "disruption of the quotidian" or disturbances to daily life.[25] The particular resources or services at issue are important: They must be meaningful to shake up the stability of ordinary existence.[26] In such crisis situations, people's minds shift into action mode and collective organizing is quicker than in normal times. Community solidarity can rise rapidly in response, mobilizing latent networks. Grievances in these cases are more swiftly and simply recognized than long-term, gradual changes, and protest discourses arise seemingly without elite framing. The resulting protest events or movements of crisis may be more violent and less formally organized than organizing for political rights.[27] Austerity is one instance of a crisis that can threaten livelihood.[28] Past austerity crises have shown that mobilizing from crisis and threat can open the door to wider critiques of the system and status quo, in a process similar to developing oppositional consciousness.[29]

Focus on the State

Crises in basic livelihood goods call out for remedies, even if people simultaneously believe that a blamed group is at fault. The ancient ritual that spawned the term "scapegoating" entailed not only transferring blame, guilt, and sins from individuals in the community onto another body but also eliminating those problems. The goat escaped or was driven out, taking the troublesome issues as well. The modern usage of the term has lost this second component of solving problems, but it is similar relief that Jordanians and Lebanese seek. Blame is twofold, consisting of causal fault and responsibility to fix or prevent the situation. Both the immediate perpetrator and the more powerful institution or person(s) responsible for protecting society from the results can be blamed. As solutions have been found for many problems previously considered immutable, governance and regulatory bodies have been held increasingly responsible.[30] What were formerly considered acts of god(s) or mother nature, such as diseases and damaging weather, are now attributed to institutions that should have foreseen, contained, or fixed the problem. Environmental movements protest the state and its regulatory bodies, even when other people, companies, and institutions created the issues, or when the cause is unknown. Food safety is the responsibility of the state, not individual food producers. Disease control is laid at the feet of state institutions, although the cause may be unclear. While the existence of evildoers can seem inevitable, the authorities charged with protecting society against them are held particularly liable when they are perceived as being careless in those duties. The 9/11 widows accused the intelligence and justice communities of negligence that made them culpable and expected them to be held to account, in addition to the perpetrators of the 9/11 violence.[31]

Where do people look for remedies? Identifying the responsible body to resolve problems involves institutional authority, history, and popular ideas of ability. The institution or person making decisions and formally charged with fixing a problem is often the focal point of blame and protest demands. In a world structured around nation-states, the target of responsibility is frequently the state and its institutions. With jurisdiction over justice and security, the state is the embodiment

of the collective, entailing the necessary legal and punitive mechanisms to imple-
ment and enforce resolutions upon society as a whole. In Jordan and Lebanon,
the state has been popularly held responsible for negative outcomes, both pre-
existing and those believed to be caused by the refugees, despite the differing capacities of the two states. These states have been critiqued for not fulfilling their
duties, ignoring problems, and failing to protect the public from the negative effects of the refugees. State institutions in Jordan and Lebanon are not bureau-
cratically independent. Governing institutions are subject to the general elite
power structure, a rotation of the same faces and families between diverse positions from election to election. These intense linkages have generated a confluence between the terms "state," "regime," and "governance," lumped into the general designation of the state, or *dawla*, and that broad state is held responsible for
the failure of its constituent institutions.

The Jordanian state has been a powerful actor in the daily lives of citizens, and
few effective alternatives to state and local authorities exist for infrastructure and
resources. The turn of Lebanese toward their state is more surprising, as analysts
have long demonstrated the ineffectiveness of the Lebanese state contrasted with
the power and independence of civil society. Like Jordan, social services and welfare in Lebanon have been in the hands of civil society, along with political, and
kin, groups.[32] The legacy of the civil war furthered this trend in Lebanon, as the
country was split into mini-states performing statelike roles. Hizbollah alone
maintained such services after the war. Still, the lack of existing state services
should not be conflated with citizen satisfaction with this state of affairs.

Scholars have now successfully questioned stock notions of the Lebanese state's
irrelevance and of citizens' acceptance of its absence.[33] In their place, a more complex idea of the state and attitudes toward governance emerges. Idealized concepts of the state coexist with skepticism toward it. A dual attitude toward the
Lebanese state prevails, one an assessment of the current lack of state services,
and the other a vision of what people wish the state were.[34] Lebanese have an ideal
of the state in their minds, however rough and imprecise, that becomes apparent
in the frustrated daily complaints of Lebanese and routine comparisons of their
state with states in the West. "This would not happen in the United States or Europe," people say. The common phrase "*ma fi dawla*" (there is no state) is a lamented fact, not a desirable outcome. The Lebanese state does provide aid and
services, often through the mechanism of sectarianism, discussed further in chapter 1. Electricity and water are provided by Lebanese state institutions on a national basis. Waste processing is decentralized outside Beirut, but funding for it
comes mainly from the national state. Such services are considered to be in the
realm of state duties even when the state does not supply them well, as the protests discussed in this book attest.[35]

Humanitarianism and the State

The presence of Syrian refugees in these countries has increased the centrality of the state and local authorities and the popular idea that the state is—or should be—the relevant actor in fixing problems. In Jordan the state has taken the lead dealing with the refugees, while Lebanon initially allowed municipalities to act in its stead. Both levels of governance interact with donors and INGOs, and both receive the brunt of citizen demands and grievances in these countries. As time has gone on, the Lebanese state has taken a larger role in receiving this international donor money, passing it through state institutions and to citizens, developmental projects, or the refugees.

With refugees comes an intricate infrastructure of humanitarian aid. In camps, UN agencies provide for refugees' needs, leading to questions of sovereignty and whether UN provision decreases the purview and reach of the state. Aid routinely leaks out to surrounding areas, either in the form of goods or trade. When refugees reside outside camps, as the Syrians and others do currently, aid is given to the host states themselves in addition to the refugees directly. Resources provided to the states essentially pay for refugees' use of public goods and services. This presents opportunities for both host states and citizens. Humanitarian organizations can serve as an alternative form of governance for citizens to rely on. States also turn to them, finding they can obtain financing for their own projects, basically subcontracting state services to the aid organization. States attempt to direct aid to citizens in the guise of development assistance. For the states, this appears to be a win-win scenario, as they can continue to blame the refugees for all the ills of the state while taking credit for humanitarian aid.

The dynamics of the international humanitarian system have provided incentives for the Lebanese and Jordanian states to emphasize their centrality in citizens' lives, inadvertently promoting themselves as objects of demands for solutions in the process. After initially sidelining itself and being marginalized by international donors, the Lebanese state in 2014 began actively negotiating with the international community on behalf of its citizens. The states argued internationally that their people suffered due to the refugees, and they pleaded for aid money on these grounds. Jordan and Lebanon willingly interjected themselves between the international community's money and their own citizens. Massive amounts of aid and loans went to the states, accompanied by public statements to that effect, well covered in the press, by international NGOs and the humanitarian community. Weak though it may be, the Lebanese state has been the crucial intermediary between international aid money and the Lebanese people. In countless conferences and meetings with humanitarian organizations and donors, the state is the sole accepted representative of the country. The necessity of a national government was put in stark relief when Lebanese representatives failed to form a government for nine months after their election in 2018, leaving billions in aid money stalled, much of it intended to alleviate failures in essential services. Elite failure reinforced popular perception of the state's critical role in daily life, and the vulnerability of that life to state inefficiency, incapacity, and corruption.

Refugee host states with little capacity increase in importance not only through their role as intermediaries to global aid provisioning but also through the common desire of citizens to differentiate themselves from the refugees. Indeed, ideological attachment to the state can increase as citizens draw upon myths and ideas of themselves and their state in an effort to avoid association with the morally flawed refugees.[36] The prevalent boundary making of citizens versus refugees makes the state the referent and responsible party for citizens within the nation-state construct. The humanitarian community plays a role here also, helping to generate this identity distinction and reinforce a particular notion of state-citizen relations.

Concepts of national identity have been brought to the fore through mundane processes. In the practical course of aiding refugees and requesting aid money, INGOs and think tanks have produced statistical reports comparing the status of the refugee population with that of the average host citizen. This distinction and the term "citizen" have been repeated domestically, highlighting both an ideal relationship between citizens of host countries and their states, and a similarly idealized sharp delineation between refugees and those citizens. Humanitarian organizations have speculated on potential conflict in host-refugee relations and documented actual violence. The societal rumor mill has not been the only actor circulating stories about refugees. INGO reports have detailed child labor, prostitution, debt, and other negative coping strategies used by Syrians to survive.[37] To the international community, these reports have demonstrated the need for more funding. For host citizens, these stories have generated added impetus to distance themselves from this population, who act contrary to their own societal norms.

NGO actions have helped to increase citizen expectations. Through both the international community and the states, the refugees have received services that these states have not provided, or have provided badly, to their own citizens. These states have long pushed services and public goods outside formal state institutions, through kin networks or political parties. The provision of public goods to refugees, whose noncitizen status has continually and routinely been affirmed, contrasts with the inadequacy of such goods and services for nationals. Refugees receiving public goods deviates from the understood arrangement by which the states do not provide public goods to the populace, while kin groups and political parties subsidize public goods for themselves as club goods. "Maybe the UN thinks that the Lebanese state gives to Lebanese, like Europe, but it doesn't. This area is deprived [*hirman*]. All we are asking for is the same as the Syrians get," a group of female teachers in the Lebanese north told me. "Syrians get treated in the hospital without insurance. But if Lebanese do not have insurance, they are left to die."[38] Some citizens do receive significant benefits from the state—East Banker Jordanians have come to expect a decent livelihood in state employment and subsidy support. But economic reforms and hard times diminish the value of this aid. The well-publicized money flowing into the states from aid organizations puts the lie to the idea that lack of funds blocks solutions to fundamental infrastructure and service problems.

Simply put, citizens have begun to expect the same or better than the refugees receive. The presence of the Syrian refugees, together with the actions of the international community, has amplified historic grievances and created new expectations of governance. Services provided to the refugees, along with the large resources given or loaned to states ostensibly to mitigate the negative effects on citizens, have altered expectations. Instead of focusing on the exclusion of the Syrians from domestic public goods, citizens emphasize their right to be included in an expanded version of state services. "Lots of money is coming in because of the Syrians—where does that money go? Government pockets."[39] The prior acceptable level of services has become unacceptable. That others who are not nationals are receiving public goods, services that the states have not provided, has generated an awareness that the state can indeed provide these goods and services but is not doing so.

From Crisis Protests to Large-Scale Mobilizing

Initial mobilizing targeting the state consisted of crisis protests for goods perceived to have been affected by the demographic weight of the Syrians, particularly water, electricity, housing, trash, and jobs. These were fundamental problems, hindering the normal daily life of average people. The mobilizing that resulted from these felt threats followed expected patterns of protests against serious disruptions of daily life. The protests were not movements, but a series of collective actions that were little-planned, hastily organized, involved only the community immediately affected, and were sometimes violent. These crisis protests produced varying results, depending on the country. Jordan and Lebanon differ not only by the specific resources and fault lines that have been demographically strained by the Syrians, as would be expected between any two states, but also by the very different capacities, presence, and responsiveness of the states. In Jordan, demands from regime supporters in areas of high refugee concentration were quickly answered. The Jordanian monarchy cut through bureaucratic regulations and ministerial jurisdiction battles to effectively prioritize and channel international and national aid to these areas. When water was viewed as a problem, the regime gave absolute discretion in this field to one body, with unilateral decision-making power.[40] Many crisis grievances were eliminated. In Lebanon, crisis mobilizing continued as needs remained unmet and the government's main answer was to stall, ignore, and repress protesters. Lebanese ruling elites have been severely lacking in their ability and willingness to mount a coherent and effective solution to basic societal deficiencies.

Protests did not stop at demands over fundamental livelihood goods. Catalyzed by the Syrian demographic influx and its humanitarian response, crisis mobilizing launched thorough critiques of the regimes. In effect, the Syrians shined a spotlight on the underlying state failures generating these crises, opening opportunities to condemn the state. State elites, for their part, continued to deflect blame away from themselves and the state. Yet the populaces seemed to see through the attempts to scapegoat to proceed and indict the state itself. The example of aid to Syrians combined with the experience of daily scarcity for citizens resulted in increased senses of entitlement and expectations of their states. Citizens overtly compared the services and goods Syrians receive to those they historically have not received. The provision of services and benefits to the Syrians demonstrated the possibility of receiving public goods, contradicting long-standing state legacies of foisting the responsibility for services off onto society. By virtue of membership in the nation, citizens argued, they should have equal or better services than those foreigners receive. Governance was now denounced for failing to provide public goods not formerly within the purview of state services but that the citizens saw Syrian refugees receive. The historic lack of public services and concomitant legacy of low expectations in these states makes this outcome particularly surprising.

The varied demands and grievances, all implicating state incapacity, began to link together into movements. The grievances were tied plausibly, if not directly, to the presence of the refugees. Movements indicted the state for failing to protect citizens against the negative effects of the refugee crisis. Crisis grievances, combined with increased expectations and ideas of rights, coalesced into larger organized movements. In Lebanon, the trigger was primary goods and services that remained inadequate, even years into the Syrian crisis. The YouStink movement from the Lebanese trash crisis provided a physical manifestation of state failure, combining numerous demands around fundamental goods and services. This movement was a major development in nonsectarian mobilizing in Lebanon, as refuse piling up in public places escalated the felt need to act collectively and broadened societal participation. Protests continued to target the state as the relevant powerful actor, demanding improved governance, despite the lack of response in the Lebanese case. Through these protests and the particular grievances, we can see local ideals of good governance, concepts of economic and social rights, and how citizens want their state to be distinct from how that state has acted in the past.

The states then increased their extraction from the populace, in an effort to placate international actors and obtain loans for the purpose of coping with the Syrian crisis. The resulting increased taxation and decreased subsidies spurred broad popular opposition movements in both countries. Syrians would not pay income tax, and therefore citizens felt they were suffering for a crisis they did not create. They protested against the removal of subsidies, although the states attributed the inability to continue such financial support to the Syrians' high consumption of subsidized goods increasing state expenses. But instead of focusing exclusively on the Syrians, citizens blamed the poor management and corrupt practices of the states. Crisis mobilizing occurred both through larger movements and on an individual basis. Jordanians walked to the capital from the farthest reaches of the state for jobs.[41] Jobs were a key demand in both countries, and unemployment was perceived as being exacerbated by the Syrians. Lebanese continue to protest despite promises of aid, and their grievances about basic goods have yet to be solved.

The unity of demands in these movements, cutting across political divisions, demonstrates an important escalation of mobilizing against the states. After long accepting the monarchy as untouchable and the sectarian clientelist system as unchangeable, Jordanians and Lebanese, respectively, have begun directly implicating these systems in the deficiencies exacerbated by the Syrian refugees. Innovative as this demand making is, large movements are difficult to sustain in these countries, and they face an uphill battle. Jordan and Lebanon have lengthy histories of divisive identity politics. In Jordan, the historical divide between East Bankers and citizens of Palestinian descent has long hampered large-scale mobilization. Lebanon has numerous divisions, each one organized with political parties providing preferential goods and services to constituents. Both countries suffer from regional divides between the capital and rural areas, with the capital providing jobs and services superior to those available in the neglected rural areas. These geographical divisions overlap with those of political party and identity.

This research suggests that successful scapegoating is sometimes a dynamic of privilege and not of need. The attempts of state elites to blame a powerless group can backfire, as citizens reject this suggested blame and direct responsibility at the states themselves. The demographic weight of the refugees pushed enduring weaknesses into daily life threats. Syrians have ratcheted up the inability of citizens to live with existing problems, but the Syrians are incapable of solving these issues. As a result, instead of stopping at animosity toward the foreigner, Jordanians and Lebanese, particularly in the poorer, less-served areas most affected by the refugees, began demanding governance solutions to fix economic, resource, and infrastructure faults. Social movements and change, however, are not inevitable. The key insights of social movement theory remain: Grievances alone are not sufficient to generate protest. Other social, organizational, cultural, and political factors are important. Among other variables, sustained mobilization takes resources, organizational strength, focus, and leadership.

Understanding how the presence of refugees alters long-term politics in the host countries is central to analyzing the future of countries affected by mass migration. Few would argue that the Palestinian refugees in the Arab countries had no effect on their hosts. Most scholars concentrate on the military threat that the Palestinians generated. Only in detailed studies do we usually find accounts of changing opposition dynamics that include the hosts, or the secondary effects of the Palestinian presence, such as challenging local conceptions of governance. There is a reason why Palestinians are kept separate from locals in the Gulf States, and this fear has nothing to do with security concerns. Palestinians and foreigners in general have ideas that have been viewed by ruling regimes as threats to their culture, economy, and ways of life.[42] This is similar to the view of refugees in other regions.[43] Such influences can alter local dynamics, fostering ideas of citizenship and rights that the host regimes wish to avoid.

Method

This book generates theory through empirically delineating the results of hosting refugees on citizen grievances, demands, and mobilizing. I use an effects-of-causes method.[44] Presenting a big picture analysis provides insight into dynamics and cause-and-effect relationships more commonly viewed from a historical distance. By focusing on popular mobilizing and demands and their effects on political life, I challenge state-centric approaches that relegate the grassroots to a politically irrelevant afterthought. This analysis is all the more pressing as forced migration is forecasted to increase in the future. Identifying the ripple effects of refugees thus becomes imperative to understanding long-term changes in our world.

I utilize a multimethod approach, combining primary with specialized secondary works. The substantive data comes from fieldwork in Lebanon and Jordan, consisting of numerous yearly trips from 2015 to the present, and more than one hundred open-ended interviews with elites and citizens in refugee areas and less-affected areas, and with aid workers and scholars.[45] I particularly used local reports and interviews in areas where many researchers never set foot. I used snowball interviewing along several different connection networks per country, ensuring a more diverse array of interviewees. Interviews were mostly in local Arabic dialects, translated by myself. When necessary, I verified my interpretation of news reports or interviews with locals. I gave wide latitude for interviewees to talk, and, after asking a few basic questions about general changes over recent years, I let them speak about their concerns and perceptions. My long history of fieldwork in these countries (since 1998) and many local connections facilitated interviews, access, and trust.

Local interpretations and sources were key for understanding motivation, and I have erred on the side of caution in guarding the anonymity of interviewees to protect them. Doing research in countries where freedom of speech is not simple, or the realm of designated national security issues is broadly and politically drawn, is never straightforward.[46] The Syrian refugees have been deemed a national security topic, and writing on their effects is heavy with political implications. Data and access can be challenging. Media often do not report events and substantiating accounts of protest can be difficult. Jordan's media are subject to significant restrictions. Protests threatening to the government, such as those involving its key constituencies, are often not reported. Observations by elites and international humanitarian organizations that work in some of the locations where the impact of the refugees is felt most provided data in some cases, functioning as media reports do in other countries. From news reports or secondary data I have included only those protests that could be substantiated and that point to grievances popularly understood as being affected by the Syrians.

Map of the Book

This book focuses on the effects of the refugees on host countries, particularly the second-order or indirect effects.[47] The perceived demographic effect of the refugees has shone a spotlight on the endemic problems in these states, bringing these topics to the fore for debate as never before. The presumed and real effects of the Syrians have resulted in demands for solutions instead of citizens being satisfied with blaming the refugees. Animosity and near-universal blame of the Syrians did result, as a variety of negative social and economic situations has been attributed to the refugees. This animosity, however, has failed to deflect attention from the root causes of problems or from seeking solutions to livelihood issues. Such scapegoating has not succeeded because the issues at hand are critical to normal, daily life, and the Syrians have been incapable of fixing such problems.

Likewise, the aid complex accompanying the refugees removed the timeworn excuse that lack of funds accounts for states' infrastructural incapacity. The influx of massive international aid monies intended to offset the negative consequences of the refugees were highly publicized. When positive changes did not occur as a result of these monies, charges of state and elite corruption increased. The continuation of core citizen grievances amid large amounts of aid was now explained by corruption. Indeed, aid merely amplified the public's perception of elite corruption. Charges of injustice resulted when the Syrians received superior services to those received by citizens. Citizens contrasted the assumed generous services to refugees—including free health care in Lebanon's case—with the historic lack and recent decline of public services in their own states. The disparity between the services provided to foreigners and citizens violated the traditional concept that citizens should be prioritized within their own nation-states.

These causal variables generated mobilization among populaces to protest lack of services and grievances about injustice. Movements first organized along immediate crisis needs and then became increasingly formalized. As these causes multiplied, groups recognized similarities between their diverse grievances and placed them under an umbrella of state incapacity and unresponsiveness, and elite corruption. Movements then joined together smaller groups, encompassed their grievances, and began organizing under national catch-all concepts.

I begin in chapter 1 by providing important background information for nonspecialists on each country's lack of capacity. This chapter summarizes the history and context for refugees and the systemic state problems in both countries. I summarize their relevant histories of ruling through divisions, discuss how the Palestinian and Iraqi refugees affected them, and analyze the state of popular oppositions at the time of the Syrian refugee crisis. Chapter 2 presents each state's refugee policies at the start of the Syrian exodus and state legal obligations under international treaties. I analyze the effects of the refugees on the countries in the context of past incapacities. I begin by presenting conclusions from the refugee literature about the effects of forced migration, including the relevant variables. I then examine the numerous changes in rent, jobs, inflation, the public services of health care, education, and waste removal, and resource provisions of electricity and water, using available data. I discuss disputes about these data and detail the benefits that accrued to some citizens as a result of the presence of the Syrians and international organizations.

The immediate outcome of these effects was hostility toward the Syrians, which I discuss in chapter 3. Sentiment in both Jordan and Lebanon went from sympathy toward these victims of war to active resentment. Populaces felt threatened demographically, and they questioned why the Syrians received superior goods and services to themselves. They blamed their economic and resource problems on the Syrians in narratives that echo common refugee and migrant stereotypes globally. Yet popular demands were also focused on the states. In chapter 4 I demonstrate how, far from pacifying the populace by deflecting blame, grievances against the Syrians caused citizens to turn to their states for solutions. Citizens mobilized in protest for rent, water, and employment in Jordan, and for electricity, waste disposal, and wages in Lebanon, despite state actions that normally dampen activism. States both scapegoated the Syrians and promoted fear that protest would spread the chaos of the Syrian war. Still, expectations of the states changed or were activated into protest.

In response, Jordan and Lebanon changed their policies toward the Syrians, becoming more restrictive and increasing their overt scapegoating of the refugees. I look at these policy changes in chapter 5. Restrictive policies toward Syrians were interpreted by aid and international donors as signaling the need for more aid, in part to prevent Syrians from leaving these host countries and heading onward to Europe. As a result, the London Compacts traded massive aid, market access, and preferential loans from the international community in return for work permits to the refugees. To continue receiving these loans and aid, and to balance a budget presumably affected by the Syrians, the states made fiscal changes that generated more protests. Protests for basic goods continued in Lebanon, and in both countries the new austerity policies spurred mass protests over taxes, the removal of subsidies, and the numerous continuing grievances over basic goods and services. These protests turned into systemic indictments of the regimes. Protesters were not appeased by small political changes and remained skeptical of politicians' promises. These protests represented a wide swathe of the populations, joining political parties and politically separate groups into single movements.

The conclusion summarizes the argument and the practical implications of these findings for future movements toward good governance in these countries. I detail the types of protest that occurred in Jordan and Lebanon. I further examine the differential outcomes in aid effectiveness and movements in Jordan and Lebanon, and the dynamics of humanitarian aid on state sovereignty. The state has become more central in both counties, while specific services are subcontracted. Massive aid and loans, intended to alleviate pressure on refugee-hosting states and thereby help both refugees and citizens, appear to have triggered more protests while also not helping the refugees. Despite these immense resources, Syrians are still dying for want of a blanket and heat.

BEFORE THE SYRIAN CRISIS

As the Syrian refugees fled from their warring country, they entered neighboring countries that were already unable to provide adequate infrastructure and services to their existing populations. Populations in these countries regularly turned to the private sector to provide the social services the central state could not. Further, the Syrians were not the first refugees to arrive in Jordan and Lebanon; some earlier refugee groups had settled without negative political repercussions, while others caused large changes in national politics and disruptions in security. Citizens were well aware of their countries' deficiencies, and had sporadically mobilized for changes. Mobilization was ineffective, however, due to the regimes' use of political divisions and history of scapegoating to blame unpopular groups.

Prior to receiving the Syrians, the Lebanese had absorbed the Armenians, refused to incorporate most Palestinians, dealt with their own domestic population movements due to a civil war, and coped with some Iraqis. Jordan had incorporated most of the Palestinians, and complained repeatedly, first about the burden of hosting those Palestinians, then about the returning Palestinians from the first Gulf War, and finally about the Iraqis who fled in the 1990s and 2000s. The Armenians had come to Lebanon (and Syria) early in the 1900s, fleeing Turkey in large numbers. This different ethnic, religious, and linguistic group has coexisted peacefully since that time and remains in Lebanon. After independence, Jordan and Lebanon experienced two main groups of refugees prior to the Syrians: the Palestinians arrived in 1948 and 1967, and the Iraqis in the 1990s and beginning again around 2006. The result with the Palestinians was far from peaceful, and their presence affected the trajectories of both countries. Later, two waves of generally unarmed Iraqis went to both countries, more to Jordan than Lebanon. At the same time, Lebanon had been dealing with its own ongoing displacement crisis from the long civil war that ended in 1990. Lebanese were displaced throughout the country as they sought safety from active violence and threats from diverse sectarian militias. All this historical background informs the reception of the Syrians and locals' interpretations of their effects. In addition to hosting refugees, both states grapple with domestic opposition movements. Until recently those oppositions did not attract enough of the population to constitute regime threats. Even the era of the Arab Uprisings was tame in these states. These uprisings were small but secular in Lebanon, and short-lived and reformist in Jordan. In this chapter I review these countries' history with refugees and mobilizing prior to the arrival of the Syrians. I also review the status of the state as a referent for social demands, and its ability to respond to those demands in both countries.

The States and Infrastructure Problems

Jordan and Lebanon each host more Syrian refugees per citizen than any other countries. The two states have diverse capacities and regimes and differ in significant ways. Jordan is an electoral monarchy (monarchy with elections for parliament), while Lebanon is a consociational democracy (based on power-sharing among different religious groups). Jordan has centralized effective power, and some state institutions are capable, but the country lives by foreign aid. Lebanon's numerous and competing actors make centralized governance difficult. Its institutions are understaffed, underfinanced, cumbersome to negotiate, and generally dysfunctional. Its foreign alliances are split between the different domestic factions.

The similarities between the two countries are more striking for this book's purposes. Neither state has been able to fully employ its population or effectively provide basic services for citizens, and their economies merely hobble along. State corruption is a problem in both. Lebanon's rating on Transparency International's corruption index puts it near the bottom (143 out of 180).[1] Jordan's ranking on the same list is significantly better (59 out of 180), but the country has had some recent highly publicized scandals implicating members of the royal family. Public perception of corruption thus differs from that ranking. Corruption and the embezzlement of funds by political elites has been a hot topic for the last few years in both countries. Using identity and political divisions to rule and to distract the populace from effective regime criticism has been a way of life for political elites in Jordan and Lebanon. Divisions are political and sectarian in Lebanon, but based on ethnic or national origin in Jordan. Jordan's political use of the Jordanian-Palestinian distinction runs deep. The states have made a business of attributing systemic problems to other groups: Palestinians, Israelis, Iraqis, jihadis, Ba'athists, Communists, and now Syrians have all been blamed for domestic troubles.

Both states have used social groups as the basis for the provision of important welfare services to their populations. For both clientelism is instrumental in accessing a higher quantity or quality of welfare and social services, but the basis for clientelism varies between the two. In Jordan kinship and tribe are the operative calling cards for help, while in Lebanon sect or religious institutions and political party serve as the entrée to state services. Connections (*wasta*), or patronage, are used for state services and employment, particularly employment with the state, which is central to the economies of both countries. State employment provides access to privileged goods and health insurance. In Lebanon, services increase during elections and political campaigns.[2] Along with the prevalence of clientelism, in each country the same elite families and individuals tend to continually hold power. This has led to a popular confluence of the terms "state," "regime," and "government," since they are constituted by the same individuals and families. Furthering this confusion, Jordan's king has used the shifting or replacing of government figures to ameliorate popular anger.

The public sector in Jordan is about double the size that it is in Lebanon.[3] Jordanians' relationship to the state is more obvious than that of the Lebanese, since the state is higher in capacity and more united, being under a single ultimate ruler. Yet Lebanese are no less dependent on the state, particularly in the middle and lower classes. Lebanon's public sector is important socially for the benefits it provides, especially to public employees, notably in the security services and teaching professions.[4] The Lebanese state is an everyday inevitability, from the most visible security services (the military fighting extremists dominates the news) to the water and electric bills people must pay. This ordinary occurrence of the state has been missed by scholars, due to the power of nonstate actors and the incompetence of public services. In fact, numerous state institutions provide aid in Lebanon, albeit through the medium of sectarianism. Lebanon provides aid through the Council for the South (mainly for electricity), the Ministry of the Displaced (from the Lebanese civil war), the High Relief Committee (which coordinates NGOs and public aid agencies), the Ministry of Social Affairs, and the Ministry of Public Health, among others. The Ministry of Public Health subcontracts with NGOs in addition to providing its own services, aiding citizens with health bills. The Social Development Ministry and the Ministry of Public Health mainly operate through subcontracts with NGOs and state Development Service Centers. About 60 percent of the Ministry of Social Affairs' yearly budget of $60 million went to NGO contracts.[5] A new generation of scholars, not focused on the Lebanese civil war (1975–1990), when the state was neglected as barely an afterthought, have begun to examine Lebanese concepts of and relations to their state.[6] The omnipresence of sectarianism, on close examination, is shown to work partly through the state.[7] Everyday life is filled with state encounters: obtaining documents and permits, and dealing with security services (police, General Security, and for the numerous roadblocks, military). Maintaining food security is another expectation of the Lebanese state, some have argued.[8]

These countries have long-standing infrastructure problems that complicate the provision of basic goods: mainly water in Jordan and electricity in Lebanon. Electricity problems in Lebanon, in part a legacy of the civil war, are so bad that anyone able to afford it has a private generator, or more often a subscription to one.[9] At regular intervals the state electricity shuts off and generators take over, so smoothly that in richer areas the changeover is barely noticeable. Signs in hotel elevators state the precise times when electricity will shut down and inform riders to expect only a momentary delay in elevator service.[10] Still, the responsibility of electricity provision is clearly associated with the state. The coming and going of electricity is described as "the arrival of the state" and the "exit of the state," respectively.[11] Lebanon's unsafe tap water forces households to purchase their own water, imposing an added expense. Garbage collection is a problem, and landfills have turned into "mountains of trash" (*jibal al-zibaleh*) scattered throughout the country. Roads are not maintained, and potholes can be five feet wide.[12]

Strong regional disparities characterize both economies, with most economic activities and services concentrated in the capital cities. Life outside Amman and Beirut, where there are few services and jobs, differs significantly from life within the cities. Both countries' economies are dominated by services and remittances (and international aid in the case of Jordan), and both countries have few resources and more people than they can employ. A large percentage of workers are self-employed or in informal work.[13] The countries' economies have not fared well, according to macro indicators, either. Lebanon in 2010 had 27 percent poverty, using their own poverty line, in a population of five million.[14] In Jordan's population of more than six million people, 14.4 percent were poor in the same year.[15] Lebanon's unemployment rate before the Syrian war was 6.4 percent, while Jordan's in 2011 was 13 percent, conservatively.[16] Both governments are in debt. Jordan owed about 70 percent of its GDP, while Lebanon had to repay about 130 percent of its GDP when Syria's civil war began.[17] Jordan is dependent on aid and remittances, and Lebanon relies heavily on remittances.

Historical Experiences with Refugees

Jordan's and Lebanon's histories with refugees differ, and each country's policy varies by the specific refugee population.[18] The countries felt the impact of Palestinian refugees most heavily. Between 900,000 and 1 million Palestinians became refugees with the founding of Israel and settled primarily in Jordan and Lebanon, with fewer in Syria.[19] Around 70,000 went to the East Bank or present-day Jordan, while the bulk of the refugees went to the West Bank or Gaza. The 280,000 Palestinians displaced from the new Israeli state to the West Bank would later be under the administrative control of Jordan, as it absorbed this territory until its disengagement with the Palestinian territories in the late 1980s. Approximately 100,000 refugees went to Lebanon, 75,000 to Syria, and a few thousand to Iraq.[20] The Palestinians were armed militarily, which led to concern in both Jordan and Lebanon that their weapons would turn against their host states or that their actions would draw the states into a dangerous and doomed conflict with Israel. Their political ideas were also threatening to these regimes, as they leaned distinctly left economically and socially.

Palestinians found the best situation in Jordan for personal security, freedom of movement, activism, and employment, because most were granted citizenship. Syria was the second-most preferable, and Palestinians were worst off in Lebanon. The refugees and the host states were both, for the most part, adamant about repatriation, so Palestinians resisted permanent settlement. The effects of the Palestinians were distinct in each host country, although Palestinians were involved in violent conflicts in both. Demographics mattered. In Syria the impacts were not identifiable, since their numbers were relatively small. The Palestinians came to form a vibrant part of Jordanian society, while being rejected in Lebanon. In Jordan, after initial PLO organizing and violence against the Palestinians, most Palestinians settled into citizenship, albeit receiving lesser political status. Palestinians form a minority of elected representatives due to purposive, structural features of Jordan's electoral laws. Fears of Palestinian dominance by East Banker Jordanians continue, demonstrated in fights between soccer teams and current intense animosity against Queen Rania, who is of Palestinian descent.

The Palestinian situation reflects the larger history of refugees in these countries. From Armenians to Iraqis and now Syrians, the experiences of these states with refugees depended on the degree of impact each group made on the projects of state-building and national consolidation. Lebanon allowed the Armenians, of a different language, culture, and diverse religion from the arguable majority of Lebanese, to integrate,[21] but prohibited the three subsequent groups from doing so. Variables important for peaceful coexistence or the lack of it in these states have included the economic skills and investment the refugees bring to the state relative to existing needs of that state, and the presumed politicization of the refugees. In Jordan Palestinian refugees from 1948 and their descendants, believed to be more politically quiescent and less activist, have a different status than those who came in 1967. Already mobilized politically by 1967, these Palestinians and their descendants are treated differently than earlier refugees, and have been met with more suspicion during tense periods and sometimes legal administrative differences in rights and movement.[22]

Jordan and Past Refugee Waves

The Hashemite Kingdom of Jordan is a monarchical state of relatively recent origin. Until the early 1900s, it was not considered an entity in itself, but a passage to somewhere else—generally Damascus to the north or Mecca to the south. The Emir (Prince) Abdullah, son of the Sharif Hussein of Mecca, attempted to march to Damascus to avenge his brother who had been forced to abdicate his rule in Syria. The British, temporarily friendly with their French neighbors, convinced him to stay put midway on his journey from Mecca. What was then called Transjordan, the land on the other side of the Jordan River, became his home. His origins in the Arabian Peninsula have not been lost on the descendants of those living in what would eventually become Jordan, some of whom would later condemn his descendants as foreigners.

The new state was mostly desert. It contained mainly Sunni Muslims, with a few historical Christian villages in the west, as well as some Circassians who had been settled there recently by the Ottomans. Foreign aid propelled the new state and has remained crucial to Jordan's survival ever since. Those original inhabitants came to be known as East Bankers and inhabited mainly the peripheral, rural regions when the emir welcomed the Palestinians into his sparsely populated land in 1948.[23] Fleeing eastward from the conquering army that would become Israel, the Palestinians arrived in Jordan at a time when it needed labor and people. In the war that decided Palestine's fate, the emir ended up with administrative control over the West Bank (of the Jordan River), in addition to his original lands east of the river. These West Bank areas were important to the agricultural production of the Jordanian state.

To the emir's mind, the Palestinians were a welcome addition to the kingdom, and did not conflict with the native inhabitants at the time, as Palestinians did in Lebanon. Here the skill profile of the newcomers differed substantially from that of the natives, who were predominantly rural and less educated. The United Nations Relief and Works Agency (UNRWA) aided this different skill profile by training the Palestinians in occupations the state could use. Early relations were thus nowhere near as conflictual as they were in Lebanon. Later Palestinian political mobilization, however, proved uncomfortable for the monarchy.

In 1956–1957 a heavily Palestinian Arab nationalist political party won elections and gained the post of prime minister. Their success lay in the fact that the redistributive economic agenda of the party was attractive to many of the lower classes, while the Jordanian-Palestinian distinction was not sharp at this point. Society was highly mobilized in the 1950s.[24] Declaring the king a constitutional, not unlimited, monarch was perhaps the last straw for that democratic experiment. The monarchy defended its existence by encircling parliament with the army and instituting martial law. Elections would not return till the demonstrations of 1989, when price rises resulting from the International Monetary Fund's neoliberal economic reforms were met with riots.

The next wave of Palestinians entering Jordan in 1967 was viewed by the regime with suspicion, as they were already politicized and organized. The history of the Palestinians in Jordan since then has not been wholly peaceful and has indeed been punctuated by severe violence and animosity, particularly during periods of Palestinian political activity, both within the electoral framework of Jordan and among the Palestinians themselves. The battle between the PLO and the Jordanian state in 1970, called Black September, was a turning point for Palestinian political activity in Jordan. Although it did not spell the end of the Palestinian presence nor lessen their influence, the monarchy gained the clear upper hand in that conflict, expelled the fighters, and has since remained dominant.[25]

In the 1970s the public sector became the domain of the East Bankers and the private sector became more exclusively Palestinian through purposive regime policy.[26] Kicking many Palestinians out of the state sector was intended to solidify the East Bankers as a support base for the monarchy. As a state, Jordan provided little in the way of services to its population, whereas state employment provided benefits that were difficult for the working classes to obtain in the private sector. Ostensibly relying on a private sector, laissez-faire economic model, the state in fact employed a large percentage of the population, furnishing them with health care, the ability to take advances on their pay (effectively loans), and subsidized goods from government cooperatives. To take advantage of these goods, however, one had to have a family member in state or military employ. Over time, employment with the state in general and often in the military specifically (after economic neoliberalism began) were viewed as rights of East Bankers by virtue of their being "sons of the country," or *ibn al-balad*. Palestinians were thus pushed into the private sector, a division that persists to this day.

This new benefit for the East Bankers decreased in value during the oil boom of the 1970s. Jordan, by pushing Palestinians into the private economy, actually embedded them in the more profitable sector. Denied state employment in Jordan, Palestinians migrated to the Gulf states to work and, as an unintended consequence, earned significantly more than their Jordanian counterparts. The improved economic fortunes of the Palestinians in turn affected the economy of Jordan. They purchased real estate and came to dominate the middle strata of the private sector, while their remittances boosted inflation in Jordan. Inflation—increasing the price of living by three times—agitated even the Jordanian military. The regime responded with increased army salaries and subsidies and maximum prices for key food and nonfood items, including electricity and water, to support the domestic population.[27] Still worse off in general than the Palestinians, the rural East Bankers at least had a steady, dependable form of income. The private sector further developed after the Iraqi invasion of Kuwait. In 1990–1991, Palestinians "returned" to Jordan from Kuwait, bringing with them significant investment and creating whole new areas of the capital city.[28]

East Banker support for the Jordanian monarchy rested on a social contract that exchanged economic rights for political backing.[29] Economic goods and employment for this population, many of whom live in rural, underdeveloped areas with few economic opportunities, allow the regime to justify forestalling political reform. The state solidified this alliance with the East Bankers symbolically by emphasizing the place of the tribes in Jordan, enacting and reinforcing tribal rituals and methods of accessing power. The main economic good provided by the social contract was employment with the state, which accommodated a larger number of people than was needed, turning jobs into guaranteed pay checks without concomitant expectations of work. This contract was threatened by economic liberalization. In the 1990s, international lending organizations demanded a more balanced budget and cost-cutting from wasteful areas in return for continued international loans. Civil service was prime on their list of targets. Deprived of this avenue for generating political support, the regime turned to the military and security sectors as its base of support, and indeed did so with international approval in an age of insecurity.[30] This deal was not as solid as the prior one, particularly since aspects of the social contract other than employment were also being broken. Bread riots occurred in 1989 and 1996 with the partial removal of subsidies,[31] but bread and many other goods remained subsidized and served as a source of entitlement for East Bankers.

Those of Palestinian descent were not included in the bargain, and while they benefited from subsidized prices, they have been denied political representation in proportion to their numbers. Elections have continually given significantly more weight to East Bank and rural areas than Palestinian urban ones, both through different numbers of representatives elected by the various areas and through overt electoral manipulation. This division has been used as the major salient cleavage in political rhetoric and is conjured and stoked through false stories or rumors in the face of any threat to the regime. Palestinians are rhetorically coded as disloyal subjects and associated with urban life. East Bankers, meanwhile, are generally associated with tribalism and the rural areas.[32] In times of trouble, blame is routinely placed not only on Palestinians but on varied out-groups and foreigners. In 1989 with the bread riots, and even into the 1990s, the state tried out different groups for blame, moving from Ba'athists to Communists and later to Islamists.

Today Palestinians in Jordan occupy a wide range of social classes and run the spectrum from well-integrated and influential to completely marginalized. Locally, people know who is a Palestinian and who is not, although intermarriage has marred any strict lines. Jordan still has refugee camps for Palestinians, and their marginalization is clear, yet some Palestinians do well. Despite this partial social absorption, rhetorical and political integration has not proceeded apace. Statistics on Palestinian descent versus East Bank lineage demographics are kept secret. The issue is viewed as a national security threat, particularly as East Bank groups have mobilized previously against "foreigners," among whom they sometimes include the king (of Arabian peninsula origin).

After Palestinians, the next wave of refugees to arrive in Jordan consisted of Iraqis during the 1990s sanctions era, and even more arrived a few years after the second Iraqi war began in 2003, particularly in 2006–2007. While the Jordanian state maintained that up to a million Iraqi refugees were in the country, studies show fewer than 500,000, with only 49,000 registered with the United Nations High Commissioner for Refugees (UNHCR) in 2007.[33] Here as with the Palestinians before and the Syrians after, Jordan played with the numbers of refugees and exaggerated their effects to extract resources from the international community.[34] The reception of the Iraqis was similar to that given recent Syrian arrivals. Jordan restricted which refugees could enter the country and referred to them as "guests." After the 2005 terrorist bombings in Amman, committed by some Iraqis, Jordan severely limited the ability of Iraqis to enter the country.[35] The Iraqis were resented, blamed for skyrocketing rent prices, higher costs of living, and taking jobs from Jordanians by working for lower wages,[36] precisely the complaints levied against Syrian refugees today. These economic changes were caused by factors unrelated to the Iraqis, a fact that was publicized, but such facts failed to sway public opinion.[37] Other dynamics were similar to the later wave of Syrians. The Iraqis were viewed as a new invader, spurring fear of insecurity from the refugees and in particular the Iraqis who were Shi'a. The Iraqis were resented for not appreciating the benefits they received in Jordan. Jordanians complained about how the Iraqis acted, and how they received the worst of the Iraqis. One researcher referred to the Iraqis as a "handy punching bag" for Jordanian economic problems.[38] Jordanians today remember the Iraqi refugees and their reception of those refugees quite differently. Instead of recognizing their widespread resentment of this population, the common recollection is that Iraqis were richer than the Syrians, that they invested in the country, bought houses, and did not affect the rental market the ways Syrians do. The popular images are those of artists and people of means, more fitting for the Iraqis of the 1990s than the reality of the later Iraqi refugees. At a minimum, they are not currently viewed as having competed with domestic labor, in contrast to the Syrians.[39] The elderly Iraqi woman selling goods on the street did and still does exist, but Iraqi refugee numbers are now small enough to no longer generate negative opinions.[40] The dynamic in Lebanon toward the Iraqis taking refuge there was the same, as is the current discourse reinventing those older perceptions.

Mobilizing and Political Themes in Jordan

Jordan's pattern of large-scale mobilizing has been twofold. One set of themes focuses on international political problems, mainly around support for the Palestinians. This type of mobilizing is routine, and now a somewhat accepted part of Jordan's politics.[41] The other themes are interconnected and domestic. They are largely based on economic concerns, although governance and politics are ordinarily implicated in such criticisms. They are often episodic, less organized, and involve key regime-supporting regions. The lack of democracy and prevalence of corruption are recurring motifs, but these often spring from or are connected to economic problems. Until 2012 Jordan's king remained largely above criticism: It has been a fundamental political baseline that the monarchy should remain. To deflect criticism or problems, the king plays with parliament and the cabinet, shuffling them and dismissing them to placate popular discontent or buy time.[42] To contain protest, political freedoms have been narrowed and the legal and geographical ability to protest increasingly constrained. Added to these mechanisms, heavy repression and coercion have been used along with cultivated internal divisions to keep the opposition from becoming a threat to the regime.

Depicting Palestinians as the opposition, or at least with suspicion, has remained a political motif, and even Jordanians of Palestinian origin who are regime elites use this tactic, demonstrating the inherent ambiguity of the dichotomy.[43] Indeed, Jordanian Palestinians do not generally protest on their own terms but under broader causes or not at all. Palestinians are commonly associated with caring about the fate of Jerusalem and animosity toward Israel, but in fact these sentiments are widespread. The monarchy allows protest on these subjects, a way of blowing off steam in controlled, even scripted protests.[44] The main and largest opposition actor has been the Muslim Brotherhood, which has operated largely within regime-specified limits. This opposition overlays nicely with the regime-promoted rhetorical dichotomy of Palestinians as disloyal or suspect and East Bankers as stalwart nationalists and the regime's base.[45] The issue is more complicated, however, for while Islamism in its political guise in Jordan is currently associated with Palestinians, historically the Jordanian state has had warm relations with the Muslim Brotherhood. While such relations are not as cordial as during the formation of the state, Islamist leaders still have privileges.[46]

The few times the East Bankers have risen up, prior to 2011, were sporadic but important, and mainly focused on the group's entitlements. Jordan's bread riots, caused by the removal of subsidies and bread price rises, are an example of when the main issue began as an economic grievance but led neatly to a critique of those directing the economy, who were seen as unaccountable by the populace.[47] Bread has been viewed as fundamental to life, indeed as "life itself."[48] Such domestic grievances are interpreted as more threatening by the regime than the international political concerns associated with Palestinian protest. The threat perception is demonstrated in the speed of regime response, mobilization, and conciliation. This is unsurprising because, as we have seen, economic support has been key to the social contract forestalling political protest. Some organized economic mobilizing has increased over the past decade, with increasing strikes and labor actions.[49]

This dual-track pattern of protest origins was broken somewhat during the Arab Uprisings, as that movement combined overt political with economic grievances.[50] Jordan's protests in the uprisings were short, and were reformist rather than revolutionary.[51] The monarchy itself remained out of bounds, with a few exceptions.[52] The opposition demands during the Arab Uprising and after were centered on corruption and economic problems, intertwined with the royal family and their privilege (particularly Queen Rania), lack of democratic representation, and limits on royal power.[53] The Hirak al-Shababi (Youth Movement) was a major player in these protests, along with the March 24 Movement, the group of thirty-six tribal representatives, and the National Committee of the Military Veterans.[54] While the youth-based March 24 Movement went beyond the traditional Palestinian-Jordanian divide, the others did not.[55] The Hirak, the military veterans, and the tribes were all East Banker movements. March 24 was urban and young, based in a more cosmopolitan setting crossing traditional divisions. The East Bankers were motivated by economic policies, including privatization and neoliberal reforms, that threatened their historical, privileged social contract of receiving economic livelihood in return for loyalty to the regime. They were also motivated by the desire for increased democracy and by overt hostility to this king and surrounding elites, widely accused of corruption. The movements were brought down by internal divisions and traditional state actions that both placated protesters and repressed them. The regime lowered food prices, repressed and arrested demonstrators, and dismissed government ministers to quell the protests.[56] The fundamental grievances, however, remained.

Palestinian-Jordanian animosity curtailed the potential for opposition unity and demands, with East Bankers worried that equal representation would diminish their political power. Despite being heavily from the regime's core constituency,[57] the new protest movements of 2011 were charged with being disloyal, and stories circulated linking them with the Muslim Brotherhood, code for Palestinian.[58] This ethnic dichotomy was also brought to the fore when Queen Rania's Palestinian heritage and her family's presumed corruption earned her the express disapproval of Jordanian retired military leaders.[59] Many East Banker movements marginalize or are hostile to Palestinians. It is this division that has kept the monarchy as the only body able to rule the country and has prevented a mass uprising. Prior public relations campaigns by the state—"Jordan First" and "We are all Jordan"—have undertones of dismissing concern for any other state (including any future Palestinian one) and overtly uniting under the Jordanian national identity banner.[60] Protest became more difficult due to repression, and infrastructure and development projects altered urban geography, effectively preventing the physical location of large protest groups in central areas.[61] The popular hesitation to protest, due to fear of a repressive backlash from the regime and a desire to avoid the domestic spread of Syria's civil war, has combined with structural factors to subdue protest.[62] The regime strongly resisted moves to substantively democratize.[63] The year following the uprising brought demonstrations that pushed the margins still further, by beginning to criticize the king.[64] Still, these were far from revolutionary.[65]

Lebanon and Past Refugee Waves

Lebanon was formed out of a part of Greater Syria by French colonialism under the mandate system. France carved out a country that would be a bare majority Christian but also include the more heavily Shi'a grain-producing areas.[66] As a lush, rain-fed land, Lebanon was fully populated with a diverse array of people, many of whom had sought refuge centuries before in Lebanon's mountains. These mountain ranges served as a geographical barrier to conquest and assimilation. The state became a technical democracy with civil rights, run along consociational lines, with sectarian balancing in governmental positions and state policy. Founded by financiers and traders, the state was designed to be minimalist and dependent on the private sector.[67] The new state's political formula was built on the questionable census from 1932 and the National Pact of 1943, dividing power among the major communities. The state would be weak and dependent on France, as witnessed in the military's division into equal parts Christian and Muslim. Maronite Catholics held the main power among eighteen recognized sects in this consociational system. The National Pact solidified a deal between Maronite and Sunni Muslim elites for the presidency and prime minister, respectively, and entailed an agreement to disagree permanently over the country's identity: It would be neither pro-Arab nor pro-Western, an agreement that exists to this day. Lebanon had—and still has—a crucial political issue in the need to balance the sectarian demographics of its population and as a result is notoriously inactive as a government, making any policies difficult to pass or enact. Sectarianism even governs public expenditures and popular access to goods and services.[68] So fragmented is the state's identity that schoolbooks and even maps produced by different religious sects in Lebanon do not agree on the important national cities, highlighting different ones.

After a brief civil war in 1958, usually forgotten, when the Christian president wanted to expand his powers and renew his term illegally, the 1960s ushered in Lebanon's golden era, when it became known as "the Switzerland of the Middle East." Unfortunately, this growth was based on what would turn out to be the temporary ascendance of the Lebanese banks. Lebanon functioned as the intermediary for moving money from the Gulf, and this regionally strategic role would be bypassed with the advent of globalized banking. Class as an important variable, the urban-rural divide, the extreme contrast between the capital, Beirut, and the rural areas, and neglect of agriculture, industry, and state services were characteristic of this historical era, and remain relevant today.

When the Palestinians entered in 1948, the new state, run by Christians, granted the few Christian Palestinians citizenship but not the far more numerous Muslim ones. Apart from a few border villages that were naturalized over time, the Lebanese political elite was united against any *tawteen*, or naturalizing, of the Palestinians. Lebanon had no need for the added population, and the labor profile of the new refugees set them in competition with its own more educated population. Lebanon had never been able to employ all its people, demonstrated by the regular emigration of Lebanese to all parts of the globe from at least the latter part of the 1800s. Palestinians were popularly viewed as a threat to employment of Lebanese, not a complementary workforce. Lebanon was far more developed in industrial manufacturing and educational level than Jordan, indeed there were no Jordanians with a doctorate resident in the country, nor any institutions of advanced education till the 1960s and 1970s, respectively. The Lebanese solution to the economic pressure imposed by Palestinian refugees ultimately had political consequences. Muslim Palestinians were confined to camps near business enterprises, and, after being initially employed in factory work, these Palestinians were barred first from skilled work, then from almost all employment, and finally made dependent on UNRWA. Palestinians continued their attempts to return to their homeland through war, then took a side in the civil war that began in 1975. The camps thus became armed extrasovereign locations that were not policed by Lebanese security services or the military and have remained a security concern to this day.

The civil war lasted from 1975 to 1990, ending when Syria became an occupying force with the blessing of the United States and Saudi Arabia. The Ta'if Agreement ending the war changed some of the distribution of power among sects in the confessional system, but kept the basic system intact. Most notably, the Sunni prime minister now had significantly more power than the Christian president. The military reformed itself and eventually became the only trusted state institution.[69] The sometime prime minister Rafiq Hariri, along with continued corruption, dominated the postwar era, while the country sank deeper into debt because of loans for reconstruction. Hariri, a Saudi-allied billionaire, had construction companies and financial interests running through all these deals. His personal finances benefited greatly from this era of reconstruction while he was in public office.[70]

Lebanon attempted to recover its status as the Switzerland or Paris of the Middle East, building on the same formula that worked in the 1960s. But the world had changed and no longer needed Lebanese banks to process Gulf money. Hizbollah entered politics, stressing its domestic, Lebanese character. It did not forego its militia, however, and was the only one exempted from putting down its weapons when the Syrians, Hizbollah's ally, came to occupy Lebanon. The Shi'a organization continued its fight against Israel's occupation of the South until 2000, when the Israelis decided they had had enough and left Lebanon.[71] The reputation of Hizbollah soared with this Israeli departure not only in Lebanon but also in the wider Arab world, worrying Sunni states.

The Iraqi refugees came to Lebanon in the 1990s and after 2003, but they were comparatively small in number and mainly aided by fellow religious communities spread throughout Lebanon. Most Iraqi refugees in 2007 were Shi'a, followed in numbers by Christians. At that time, there were an estimated 40,000 Iraqis in the country.[72] The number might have been as high as 100,000, since they entered almost entirely through irregular border crossings and lived in the country illegally.[73] As such, their presence did not alter the basic lesson that Lebanon had learned about refugees—that they are a threat and should not be kept in camps where the state has no purview.

In February 2005 former prime minister Rafik Hariri was assassinated, and popular opinion accused Syria. Two demonstrations were held that foreshadowed the political climate of post-Syria Lebanon: On March 8 Hizbollah and its allies held a rally in support of Syria; on March 14 a counterdemonstration was held, including many Sunnis and Christians, insisting on Lebanon's freedom from Syrian occupation. These two divisions have held, with one change. Michel Aoun, who once fought a war against Syria and was a major player in the March 14 demonstration, changed sides. Aoun led the Christian Free Patriotic Movement. This movement later joined an alliance with Hizbollah and is now included in the March 8 group. Aoun, president of Lebanon from 2016, still cannot be accurately characterized as pro-Syrian despite this alliance with Syria's military ally Hizbollah.

The July 2006 war between Hizbollah and Israel demonstrated how far Hizbollah had come in obtaining domestic Lebanese recognition as a legitimate political force. Lebanese across the spectrum initially blamed Hizbollah, then defended the Shi'a and turned their condemnation on Israel. Yet this hard-won legitimacy was compromised, first by Hizbollah's use of its weapons domestically in a dispute with some March 14 militias,[74] and second, more gravely, by its entrance into the Syrian civil war on behalf of the Syrian regime. The UN's Special Tribunal for Lebanon, created to discover the perpetrators of the Hariri assassination, is another political element that overlay the pro- and anti-Syrian division in Lebanese politics.[75] First Syria and then Hizbollah were accused of killing the former prime minister. As a result, political life continued to be divided. Hizbollah protested its lack of a political role commensurate with its perceived demographic proportion, and the different sects could not agree on a president or a budget for years.[76]

This continued pro- and anti-Syrian division has an added religious layer. Hizbollah had been the main religious political actor, but now the *salafi* Sunnis have sided with the Syrian opposition, many mobilizing violently. A string of attacks and suicide bombings kept the army and police on alert and threatened Lebanese civilians and Syrian refugees alike. Hizbollah justified fighting on the side of the Syrian regime and domestically against Islamist actors as preventing the spread of Sunni jihadism. Whether it was a self-fulfilling prophecy or accurate forecasting, the threat of Sunni *salafism* did increase over time in Lebanon. Battles with the security services, attacks, and suicide bombings eventually changed much public opinion about Hizbollah's role in the Syrian war. While Lebanese, except for Hizbollah, have been against the Syrian regime, the increasing insecurity has swung Lebanese closer to Hizbollah's position.[77]

Lebanon and Syria before the Syrian Civil War

Lebanon's experience with the Syrians is complicated, distinct from Jordan's, and varies by individual political stances. Lebanon was historically part of Greater Syria, and Syria did not fully accept the separation of Lebanon into a state after the retreat of the Ottoman Empire and French colonialism. The countries have been called "rival siblings" due to their long history, mutual animosity, and intense interaction.[78] Syria was an occupier or savior, depending on political opinion. Syria occupied the country for fifteen years after the end of Lebanon's civil war, and had been involved in Lebanon during almost the entire war itself. Syria left Lebanon completely only in 2005, after demonstrations known locally as Lebanon's independence intifada and internationally as the Cedar Revolution. Lebanese attitudes toward Syria have often been characterized by a sense of superiority, even in a racial sense, and the conflict with Syrian refugees, together with the impact of the Syrian civil war, have given a degree of public acceptance to this facet of Lebanese opinion.[79]

For decades Syrians had been temporary or seasonal agricultural and construction workers in Lebanon, filling low-paid jobs and sending earnings back home to less-expensive Syria.[80] Even before the civil war, this history of work at menial and low-wage jobs meant that Syrians were viewed in Lebanon with hostility and from an attitude of superiority, being seen as lower-class, uneducated, and rural people.[81] Syrian workers departed after the end of the occupation in 2005, as they saw their security was not guaranteed and hostility was unleashed against them. Palestinians were then authorized, for the first time, to fill a number of low-paid occupations.[82] Eventually the Syrian workers returned and resumed work in Lebanon. Many have argued that Lebanon has a belief in its own superiority, but Jordan had no such superior ideas about Syrians at the start of the civil war. Indeed, Jordanian opinion could be characterized as one of admiration of the Syrian business and work ethic, Syrian food, and other facets of Syrian society.

Mobilizing and Political Themes in Lebanon

Lebanon's political and movement history has been heavily influenced by foreign powers and the Palestine-Israel conflict. Israel as a threat has been a dominant feature of Lebanese political thought, whether through invasions (in 1978 and 1982), direct wars or wars by proxy (using militias, especially the South Lebanon Army in the civil war and after), occupation of the southern strip of Lebanon, jets flying over Lebanese territory, brief but repeated incursions in the South, or uncovered spying attempts. Although standing up to Israel is commonly thought to be a trait limited to Muslims, Christians are no less proud of the Lebanese ability to stand up to Israel, even if it is through an organization they fear and dislike.[83] The first graduating military class before the civil wars, which was half Christian and half Muslim, demonstrated this unity of appraisal toward Israel. The students could agree on nothing other than the name for their class: Palestine.[84]

Foreign states and the role they play domestically in Lebanon are accepted by some, depending on the group or individual political stance, but decried in general. Foreigners are blamed for the ills of Lebanon and have been at least since the Palestinians first arrived. Numerous states funded militias in the civil war, and major regional actors are viewed as pulling the strings of domestic divisions (currently, the Sunnis by Saudi Arabia and the Shi'a by Iran). The omnipresence of foreign actors has earned Lebanon the moniker of a "penetrated" state.[85] Others have termed Lebanon a "weak state," or one that lacks sovereignty, if they deal theoretically with the Lebanese state at all.[86] More sophisticated analyses depict Lebanon's governance as "hybrid" or "plural."[87] The intertwining of state and society in Lebanon and an emphasis on the role of powerful elite individuals and political organizations can give the impression that no substantive state exists at all. Nonstate actors are indeed strong, but that does not mean the state is irrelevant. Lebanon's strong NGO sector is heavily intertwined with its political and sectarian structure.[88] Images of the state as an ideal coexist with low expectations of it in reality, given rampant, publicly acknowledged corruption.[89] The development and persistence of this ideal of a functioning state providing public goods is explained partly by domestic experiences of Hizbollah's current services and of militia states' services during the civil war.[90] As a result, the populace is hostile and suspicious of the existing state, fearful of political reform, and yet a significant portion of the population mobilizes for better state services.[91] Mobilization is, however, repressed, and demands that threaten the clientelist system are considered particularly dangerous.[92]

Lebanon's relatively free political climate, compared to its neighbors, led in part to its more vibrant and active civil, economic, and political society. Major longstanding organizations include organized labor, the teachers' union, and women's organizations.[93] Yet rarely have movements broken through the sectarian silos. Before the civil war, a large-scale popular movement did mobilize against the sectarian state, encompassing numerous social groups, including workers, students, and agricultural workers.[94] During the Syrian era, mobilizing was muted and highly regulated. After the independence intifada in 2005, insisting on Syria's departure, political freedoms increased somewhat. While that movement tried to be all-encompassing, it remained an amalgam of sectarian parties and groups.[95] The March 14 movement's base is Hariri's Future Movement, joined by a group of Christians (Qornet Shehwan) and the Druze. Ultimately, however, the independence intifada could not transition into an electoral party and had no program. It was a coalition of smaller groups, larger political parties, and individuals.[96]

Today's political elite sit atop an organized edifice of patronage along sectarian lines. Sectarian protests and movements conform to these existing lines of division in the state without threatening the patronage system and the accompanying corruption that underlies continuing elite privilege. Nonsectarian movements are more threatening to the state, as they attack the foundations of elite power. Between the end of the civil war and the Syrian refugee crisis, nonsectarian NGOs became more active as an alternative to confessional politics, demonstrating that there was a faction of the populace calling for political freedoms and a secular state.[97] Such movements include the fight against the reconstruction of Beirut's city center, victims' movements, sexual rights movements, some environmental organizations, and movements against privatizing the Beirut shore.[98] By and large, these are urban and located almost exclusively in Beirut. Most organizations remain small, attempting to transcend the sectarian system. They find this position difficult to maintain and are harassed by sects and sectarian parties, disrupted by them, pressured, bribed, or forbidden to act on another sect's "turf."[99] Even the self-proclaimed alternative organizations are often sectarian in some way. The Arab Uprisings did not signify a marked difference or break in mobilizing patterns in Lebanon.

The populace's dependence on patronage, sectarian divisions, and differing interests, as well as electoral vote buying, are factors keeping the existing system intact. While the confessional system is decried by most, many benefit from it and thus continue to use and sustain that system. Solutions to Lebanon's problems are also a matter of serious disagreement. Hizbollah wants an electoral system of proportional representation, since it would gain from that system due to its demographic numbers. Smaller groups fear the power of the majority and want some version of guaranteed power. Groups fight against having to share votes with different sects, wanting to elect "their own" representatives, despite what civil society theories have to say about integration leading to longer peace.

The Jordanian and Lebanese regimes have survived because political elites lay blame on others and divide their populations. Placing blame on the other party has worked. Citizens have survived periodic problems, jumps in inflation, scarce resources, infrastructure problems, and lack of services. At the same time, a number of movements have organized occasionally in both countries over disparate issues. Clientelism is rampant, and corruption is a problem. While they have differed in their openness to the Palestinian refugees in the past, both countries alike cannot now handle a larger population that further stresses employment. Nonetheless, into these countries with weak economies, broken infrastructures, and lack of public services have come the Syrian refugees. Their choice of residence outside of the camps has meant new challenges for host citizens. Instead of dealing militarily with camps, as they had at one time with the Palestinians, the states now confront large demographic competition for apartments, jobs, medical services, and education. Infrastructure problems have taken on new meaning, as electricity has declined in Lebanon and water has run low in Jordan. The numerous Syrians also draw on these resources. Prior national issues have thus been interpreted in light of the Syrians, who are perceived as adding an unsustainable burden, pushing barely acceptable infrastructural services over their limits.

2

ENTER THE SYRIANS

The Western world awoke to the Syrian refugee crisis four years into the Syrian civil war, when Syrians arrived on Greek shores as refugees fleeing. By then, the surrounding countries had been dealing with and suffering from the crisis for years, hosting millions of refugees. While previously the crisis was a side issue for the Western press, mainly focusing on the call for humanitarian aid, the reaction differed entirely once Syrians began landing on European shores. The Syrian refugee crisis filled the news, with initial sympathy and later a backlash against these foreigners. Europe's right wing began to use the issue for anti-immigrant appeals, often successfully. Yet no matter how swamped from refugees Europe felt, the European experience pales in comparison to the reality of Syria's neighbors, Jordan and Lebanon.

How did the Syrian refugees affect their host states? Specifically, do negative economic and demographic effects caused by the newcomers change popular attitudes and feed anger toward them? Analysts have repeatedly probed the relationship between racism, cultural discrimination, and scapegoating of immigrants, and their connection to adverse economic conditions caused by those minority groups. The search for an economically rational explanation has yielded no concrete conclusions. Currently, much research throws doubt on any actual links while pointing to status changes feared by the dominant group and the use of scapegoating language from political elites, particularly for elections.

This chapter investigates what basis Jordanians and Lebanese have for scapegoating Syrians. It finds that, despite macro benefits from the Syrians, there have indeed been adverse economic and demographic effects, felt mainly in poor regions outside the capital cities where refugees are concentrated. The essence of scapegoating as it is commonly used is not solely negative attitudes toward a vulnerable group but, crucially, distraction from state or other societal problems. Despite the real negative effects, Syrians did not decrease mobilizing against the state. The reason, documented below, is that some of these consequences pushed the needs of daily life beyond the tolerance of the populace. To re-establish normal life, populaces needed remedies. Not having enough water or electricity, a place to live, sufficient income to live on, or living with so much waste that children's health is felt to be at issue, are not superfluous problems. These situations upend whole patterns of life. Where fundamental elements of life are affected, people in these cases have not been content to spend their time and energy on what is arguably psychologically satisfying anger toward a group unable to fix their problems. It is the element of daily needs that distinguishes these cases from more developed countries where scapegoating does successfully distract from state problems. The specific goods and services affected by Syrians, together with INGO aid practices discussed in the next chapters, link hosting refugees with political changes among the citizenry and its ideas of rights and the duties of the state.

In this chapter I first analyze the entrance of the Syrian refugees to Jordan and Lebanon and those countries' initial policies toward the refugees. I then consider the effects of the Syrians, mainly on the economy and resources of the host countries, and the discord between local impressions and economic data. The rapid demographic increase pushed local infrastructure beyond its capacity, affecting nearby citizens, particularly at the outset of the influx. On a macro level and locally in some areas after the first few years, numerous benefits accrued to the hosting states and their citizens due to the presence of the refugees. Still, the general negative perception of Syrian effects has persisted. Perception—not data—has generated popular hostility (discussed in chapter 3) and pushed states to impose tougher policies toward the Syrians. These restrictive policies followed closely on the heels of criticism and protest directed at the states themselves for the effects purportedly caused by the refugees.

The Crisis Begins

The size of the Syrian refugee crisis strains comprehension: About one in five global refugees was Syrian in 2018,[1] and hardly any have been resettled to third countries. At the end of 2018, there were more than 5.5 million registered Syrian refugees, with many more displaced inside the country. Turkey received the most Syrian refugees numerically, about 3.6 million in 2018, but due to Turkey's size, state capacity, and economic strength, it was able to accommodate them far more

easily than Jordan and Lebanon. Lebanon has more than a million refugees registered, but many more never registered or were unable to do so after the Lebanese government told the UNHCR to stop registering them.[2] The number there
is probably closer to 1.6 million Syrians. Jordan has more than 600,000 registered,
but the state maintains that many more do not register, due to fear that information about them will be shared with the Syrian government.[3] The Jordanian government estimates that Syrians number 1.3 to 2.3 million, but the higher number is surely inflated.[4] Sizable numbers of Syrians have fled to Iraq, Egypt, and
other regional states as well.[5]

In line with documented patterns of refugee settlement for other cases, Syrian
destinations show a degree of choice alongside a predominantly proximity-based
determination of flight.[6] The destination of refugees is informed by ease of transport, finances, and historical links. Syrians in the North went to Turkey, those in
the West to Lebanon, and southern Syrians went to Jordan. Those with family in
any accessible country went to stay with them. If a family member was employed
in a neighboring country, the rest of the family joined him or her. In Lebanon,
many families left Syria to live with the male who was already in the country working in low-paid jobs. This dynamic fueled the Lebanese idea that these Syrians
were not refugees but economic migrants.[7] Residents of the agricultural villages
where Syrian workers have been a long-standing presence often deny that these
Syrians are refugees for that reason. The first to leave Syria were those with the
most to lose, those with significant contacts and resources. Syrian businesses established themselves in the surrounding countries early in the conflict, by 2012.
Most people, lacking the financial resources and networks to help them settle elsewhere, did not leave till later. These refugees who left later, as the war dragged
on, sought refuge abroad when they felt forced to, and usually had no resources
to establish themselves in another location.

The surrounding states and their citizens, except for Iraq, initially welcomed
the refugees. Even Lebanon, ladled with significant negative history with Syria,
welcomed the Syrian refugees as victims of an oppressive state. Many families in
both Lebanon and Jordan have close ties of kinship, work, trade, or social relations with Syrians and sympathized with the plight of the refugees. They maintained open-door policies for the first few years, as both refugees and citizens of
the hosting states expected the war to come to a quick end. As time went on, however, the war became more ferocious and engulfed more of Syria, creating increasing numbers of refugees. Turkey's relatively strong economy received the
highest number overall, but those high numbers amounted to only a small percentage of Turkey's population. Those who went to Lebanon or Jordan entered
weak economies and states lacking many capacities. Further, like the Iraqis before them, the Syrian refugees by and large rejected living in camps. Even where

camps were encouraged, an average of fewer than 10 percent of registered Syrians stayed in them.[8] The rest became urban or self-settled refugees, living among the population. This shift to self-settlement was one the UNHCR, with its existing model of the perfect refugee camp solution, would have to deal with, and it did so with a policy paper a few years into the conflict.[9] Aid agencies struggled with providing services for these self-settled refugees, often termed "urban refugees." Among the general population, the Syrian refugees used the same infrastructure and competed for housing and jobs with the domestic population in urban and rural areas.

The pattern of refugee effects on domestic populations varies by skill profiles and demographics, state capacities, and state and international policies toward the refugees. In general, those with assets or human capital benefit, while those without suffer relatively. Calculating the cost of refugees on host states is far from straightforward. Although much of the determination of effects is based on disputed and politicized data,[10] and significant benefits remain uncalculated, it is the perception of the effects that is most important for this study and for the ensuing protests.

The International Legal Framework for Refugees in Jordan and Lebanon

Jordan and Lebanon have different histories with refugees but similar legal frameworks: Neither country signed the UN Convention on Refugees.[11] Syrian refugees, like the waves of refugees before them in these countries, were not termed refugees nor given the rights of refugees. The main benefit of the UN Convention is non-refoulement, which prevents states from forcibly returning refugees to the country they fled. Despite having failed to sign this UN Convention, both countries signed other conventions and treaties that limit their ability to deal arbitrarily with the refugees and effectively provide this key protection of the convention. Customary international law in any case considers non-refoulement to be fundamental. The states indeed allow temporary refuge from war, another facet of customary law widely accepted as an international norm.[12]

The two countries have Memoranda of Understanding (MOU) with the UNHCR, allowing the UN's refugee agency to work there. Jordan's MOU in 1998 specifically outlines the state's policies regarding all non-Palestinian refugees and the provision of temporary refuge.[13] The MOU allows for the temporary protection of the UNHCR and stipulates that Jordan is not a country of permanent settlement for refugees. The understanding obligates the UNHCR to find other solutions for refugees within a short period of time, six months for Jordan and one year for Lebanon, a stipulation that has almost universally been breached.[14] Lebanon's MOU with the UNHCR is from 2003 and was written in the Iraqi refugee context. It entails the same understanding as the one with Jordan, that refugees are only to be in Lebanon temporarily till UNHCR resettlement.[15] The UNHCR was supposed to have a year to resettle any such refugees here.[16] Refugees in both countries were not given rights of housing, employment, freedom of movement, or public assistance. There is no legal basis under the MOU or refugee conventions to hold the host countries accountable for policies toward refugees. In essence, the MOUs depict a best-case scenario for those fleeing persecution and living in these host countries.

The Syrians are not the only refugees present in these countries. According to UNHCR, in 2017 Jordan still had about 65,000 Iraqis, 4,000 Sudanese, less than 1,000 Somalis, and almost 10,000 Yemeni refugees and asylum seekers. Lebanon had about 19,000 Iraqis, 1,400 Sudanese, and small numbers of refugees and asylum seekers from other countries. This is in addition to the 450,000 Palestinian refugees currently registered with UNRWA in Lebanon, and the 2 million Palestinian refugees in Jordan.[17]

Jordan: "Open" Welcome with Restrictions

Syrians entered Jordan first from the town that started the uprising, Der'aa. Many refugees went to live with relatives as soon as they crossed the border, flooding the northern Jordanian regions. Jordan allowed entry to all Syrians with official identification at this early point of the war—sometimes with the exception of single men.[18] Jordan did not give the Syrians the title of refugees but allowed the UNHCR to register them and for them to be classified with international organizations as refugees. Jordan received Syrian refugees within the framework of its Law of Residency and Foreigners' Affairs. Through this avenue Syrians were allowed to enter Jordan with their passports only, with visas and residency permits not required. Jordan gave the Syrians various titles other than refugee—brothers, guests,[19] and later gave them temporary protected status, a designation that lacks legal permanency and is dependent on the will of the country. Unlike refugee status, which can be revoked only for violations of national security, serious nonpolitical crimes, or involvement in combat, temporary protected status can be revoked collectively at will.[20] This temporary status provides the basic right of a refugee, that of non-refoulement, or the right not to be sent back to the home country as long as the status remains.

Jordan attempted to contain Syrians in camps, due in part to its fear of employment competition with its national population.[21] In July 2012, Jordan opened the now well-known Za'atari refugee camp. The locale is not an ideal one for the UN, but that choice was out of UNHCR's hands, being dependent on the government to provide a place where the Syrians could live. The running of the camp was given to a combination of UN administration and Jordanian security. Za'atari is Jordan's biggest refugee camp, with a population in 2018 of less than 80,000.[22] Later a number of other camps were set up, but they never rivaled the population of Za'atari, nor were the Syrians enthusiastic about living in them. Currently there are camps in Za'atari; Azraq; the Emirati-Jordanian Camp, or "Five-Star Camp"; King Hussein Park; and Cyber City. The Emirati-Jordanian Camp is a small camp (4,000 at the start) established in early 2013 in an isolated area of Zarqa. United Arab Emirates officials run the camp, with UNHCR in charge only of registration. Unlike Za'atari, refugees there are subject to strict controls for meals and other regulations and do not receive cash assistance. The camp purports to provide everything for families, but this is not as pleasant as it sounds.[23]

Despite aid and housing provision inside the camps, most Syrians live outside them and do not want to be bound to them. A little more than 80 percent of registered Syrians in Jordan are self-settled among the populace.[24] Jordan attempted to restrict Syrian movements out of the camps. In the beginning Jordan used the "bail-out" system, whereby a Jordanian relative of the Syrian could "bail out" someone in the camp, but it was abused as a paid service, often by prospective employers. Jordan later significantly curtailed the bail-out practice.[25]

The camps serve several purposes for Jordan. First, they are a photo opportunity to publicize the depth of the crisis that Jordan suffers. As one official stated, "If we hadn't built the camps, then the world would not understand that we were going through a crisis."[26] Since the bulk of refugees are scattered and living among the Jordanians, other than the camps there is no focal point to demonstrate the massive scale of the Syrian influx. Za'atari has become that photo op, almost universally used to show the Syrian crisis, demonstrated by a quick Internet search and the numerous photos of officials visiting Jordan. Second, camps remove Syrians from direct competition with local labor. Jordan received primarily rural Syrians without resources, skilled in trucking and agriculture, who compete with Jordanian labor from the regime's core constituency.

The Jordanian government quickly set up institutions to manage both regulations on refugees and the inflow of aid for their assistance. The Ministry of Planning and International Cooperation (MOPIC) handled the aid to refugees, authorizing INGOs and the UN to operate in the kingdom. MOPIC has almost complete discretion in approving projects for the refugees and even in creating policy. The Host Communities Support Platform, which would later turn into the National Resilience Plan, was set up in 2013 with an eye to aiding affected local Jordanian communities.[27] The Syrian Refugee Camp Directorate was set up early and changed in 2014 to the Syrian Refugee Affairs Directorate under and controlled by the MOI.[28]

At the border, the Jordanian military, the sole entity deciding entry for the Syrians, attempts to separate out and deny entrance to former military and current fighters.[29] UNHCR knows who is allowed to enter but has no idea how many Syrians are refused at the border. After entry, Syrians undergo an initial intake with UNHCR, then a second interview with government officials and a biometric scan. They receive a Ministry of Interior service card with which they can then get medical services, cash and food aid, and access education for children.[30] The entrance and registration of Syrians surged in 2012–2013, despite the closing of the official border between Ramtha and Der'aa in September 2012.[31] April 2013 is often cited as the peak of Syrian registration, reaching 90,000 refugees.[32] The UNHCR instructed employees to register Syrians however they could at that time, dropping all other work, and registering refugees night and day for months.[33] The resulting numbers would later be used by Jordan to demonstrate its generosity and suffering.

Early in the war, Jordan did not distinguish between Syrians and Palestinian refugees from Syria (PRS) for the purposes of entry into the country. This changed in April 2012, when Palestinians from Syria were prohibited from entering Jordan. To ensure that no Palestinians slipped in, anyone attempting to enter Jordan without identification, and men who had not completed military service in Syria, were denied entry.[34] For those who did manage to get in, their aid was handled by UNRWA as per its jurisdiction.[35]

Once inside the country, Syrians outside camps were allowed to enroll in Jordanian schools and use the public health care system but, with few exceptions, were forbidden to work. Few Syrians were given work permits, and professional Syrians were generally denied employment. Work was thus illegal and prosecuted, distinct from the situation in Turkey, where Syrians working illegally were benignly ignored. Living outside camps meant Syrians needed to work, however, and were therefore subject to poor working conditions, low pay, long hours, and the constant threat of imprisonment or being sent back to Syria. An estimated 160,000 Syrians work illegally at any given time.[36]

Public schools were technically open to Syrian children, and Jordan fared better than its neighbors in getting Syrian children to attend school. Nonetheless, many school-age refugee children could not attend due to other considerations, chiefly transportation, psychological issues, bullying, and work. Getting to school was itself a problem,[37] and schools quickly became overcrowded and hostile to Syrian children. Eventually the schools moved to a shift system, with Syrian children largely in the second, afternoon shift. This still affected the Jordanians' education, since teachers would work double shifts and presumably have less energy overall. The problems of transportation, war trauma, and hostility remained.

The UNHCR and World Food Programme provided vouchers and aid to urban or self-settled refugees, but again, as time went on, it was not enough to support them. Initial aid was generous, however, and resulted in skyrocketing rent prices as landlords took advantage of Syrians who would combine several families in one apartment. This presented problems for Jordanian renters but benefited landlords.[38] A lucky few refugees were supported by Gulf charities, but this was arbitrary, depended on connections, and subject to unknown rules.[39]

Lebanon: Fear of Camps

Unlike Jordan, Lebanon's initial approach toward the Syrian refugees was characterized by inaction and a lack of policy.[40] For the period of the initial refugee influx, Lebanon had no president, adding to difficulties agreeing on a policy. The earliest discussion and policy on the refugee crisis was the Baabda Declaration in 2012, in which political elites agreed to shun regional alliances in order to avoid a spillover of the Syrian crisis.[41] This would be quickly breached by Hizbollah, since the group entered the Syrian war on the side of the regime.

Ease and proximity made Lebanon a key destination, since major fighting was in the West and North, particularly Homs and the area of Syria up to Aleppo. The numbers of Syrians in Lebanon hit one million in 2014.[42] Due to the high number of unregistered Syrians, INGOs, the UNHCR, and analysts allege that the real number of Syrians far surpasses the official tally.[43] Many Syrians came in through informal border crossings, and many, including those with resources or those fearing the government, never registered. As in Jordan, Lebanon allowed UNHCR to register the refugees and classify them as refugees, but the Syrians were not termed or classified as refugees in Lebanese law. Lebanon called the Syrians *nazihoun*, or "displaced," signifying people moving within a single nation-state's territory.[44] No special law for refugees exists in Lebanon. Foreigners are governed by the 1962 Law Regulating the Entry and Stay of Foreigners in Lebanon and their Exit from the Country, which does, however, prohibit refoulement.[45] Lebanon's initial open border policy was informed by its 1993 bilateral agreement with Syria that allowed for the free flow of goods, people, and economic activity between the two countries. Additionally, Syrians could enter Lebanon and have legal residency for six months, renewable once, without charge. After one year, the fee for residency was USD 200 for each person over fifteen years old.[46] Despite this agreement, however, the Lebanese government has stated that the Council of Ministers, not existing domestic law, will decide policy for the refugees.[47] PRS were subjected to increasing restrictions in 2013 and denied entry altogether in 2014.[48]

By not making policies for the refugees, the central government, intentionally or not, offloaded policymaking onto local regions and the municipalities. Municipalities became the focal point for dealing with refugees and had a free hand to do so.

Most municipalities had few funds to spare for the newcomers and for the additional burden on public services. The result was diverse and arbitrary treatment depending on where a refugee happened to be. Generally, the Shi'a or Hizbollah areas treated the refugees the worst, while Sunni areas treated them the best.[49] The benefit for the central government of this arrangement was that the Ministry of Interior and Municipalities (MoIM) would be able to disclaim liability for what the municipalities did, since many their actions were bordering on or outright illegal. Among the policies of uncertain legality were unrestricted policing and security actions, as well as curfews forcing Syrians off the streets at night.[50] These municipal actions contributed to an international appearance of local conflict with the Syrians.

In early 2013, Lebanon began establishing dedicated institutions to deal with the refugees and the international humanitarian community. The General Security Office (GSO) in the MoIM is the agency primarily responsible for dealing with the refugees and it can issue policies on Syrian status, independent of law. By GSO decree, Syrians could renew their residency in mid-2013, without the condition of having to leave the country and re-enter.[51] Within the Ministry of Social Affairs (MOSA) a unit was charged with aid coordination and facilitating Syrian access to state-run social development centers. In May 2014, an Inter-Ministerial Crisis Cell was created, including the prime minister and representatives from the ministries of Foreign Affairs, the Interior, and Social Affairs.[52]

Lebanon has refused to authorize UN refugee camps, with broad agreement among all the major sectarian political parties in this decision. The consensus among the Lebanese that there would be no camps rested on fears of a repeat of their armed Palestinian experience.[53] The Palestinian camps were armed from the late 1960s to 1982, and remilitarized periodically after that. Thus the Lebanese debate focused on camps as potential bases for armed radicals, particularly amid the rise of Islamism.[54] In the absence of camps, Syrians with resources and connections lived with friends or relatives, or rented apartments till their savings were exhausted. Others lived with Syrians already in Lebanon. Poorer refugees stayed near the border and in less-expensive areas. Many, without alternatives, squatted on public land or rented private land, or lived in structures unfit for residences (warehouses, garages). Informal tented settlements (ITS) are encampments of tents or other handmade structures, and are popularly referred to as "camps." All of these are outside UN jurisdiction and lack basic waste, water, and electrical infrastructure. Without waste facilities, Syrians are unable to safely dispose of their human waste and garbage. Over half of refugees in the poor northern Akkar region live in either substandard buildings or informal settlements that have no water or other service infrastructure.[55] The environment is affected, sometimes including pollution of the groundwater. Knowledge of environmental dangers has not altered governmental policy against dedicated camps.[56] What would normally fall to the UN in camps is now left to the refugees themselves or thrust upon the already scarce public services, including not only infrastructure but also schools and health care. The cost of living in Lebanon is high and UN aid has never been adequate to fulfill the needs of the refugees, making work incumbent upon the Syrians. Funding decreased further as the crisis wore on and host countries tired of the Syrian presence, while Western countries suffered "donor fatigue."

The no-camp policy is consequential not only for Syrians but also for the Lebanese economy and infrastructure. Syrians inhabit areas home to the bulk of Lebanon's poor, including the northern areas of Wadi Khaled and Tripoli, the Beka'a, and Mount Lebanon. Almost four-fifths of poor Lebanese are in these areas, and now the vast majority (85%) of (registered) Syrians are there also.[57] Syrians with skills and money headed south and to Beirut.[58] In addition to further burdening the poorest areas, UN and aid organizations had difficulty even finding these Syrians to provide help, even though most large-scale INGO support is focused on this area.[59] So great is the focus on this region that little aid for structured support remains for refugees located elsewhere. The burden of hosting refugees in those other areas instead falls almost entirely on local communities.[60] In some places, including the majority Shi'a area of southern Lebanon, sectarian differences strain the presence of the overwhelmingly Sunni refugees.

At the outset, Syrian children were allowed to easily register in Lebanese schools. Public schools in Lebanon serve a minority of national students, generally those with fewer resources, and most Lebanese attend private schools. Despite this concession, there were many problems for Syrian children, many similar to those experienced in Jordan. Problems in just getting children to school included enrollment fees, transportation, lack of safe methods of getting to school, and checkpoints where parents feared to cross. School transportation problems included bus drivers deciding who they would and would not pick up, leading to accusations of a "bus mafia" that refused to bring Syrians.[61] Instruction was in English or French, not Arabic as students were used to in Syria, and exams were given in those foreign languages. When the numbers of Syrian children increased, a shift system was implemented, with Syrians given the afternoon shift. These second-shift teachers were reportedly tired from teaching the first shift, and thus there are strong accusations of low-quality teaching.[62]

The Effects of Syrian Refugees on Host Countries

Refugees had similar effects in some areas in Lebanon and Jordan, but the effects were experienced differently. Rent prices increased in both, and local resources such as water, electricity, and waste were strained. Overcrowding and traffic became a pressing issue and getting across Beirut during peak times now took longer than walking.[63] In Jordan, water was a key issue, and in Lebanon the main issues have been electricity and garbage. State budgets and institutions were stressed, as services had to cover a larger population. New state institutions to deal with the refugees also drew on limited state funds. Schools became extremely crowded, even though most Syrian children did not go to school, and medical lines long. Security turned into a pressing issue in Lebanon, but much less so in Jordan. Potential violent spillover of the Syrian war was used politically in both countries to quell dissent.

These neighboring countries suffered not only due to the refugees but from the economic effects of being near a war zone, a situation that entails costs all on its own. Many of the purported effects of hosting the Syrians were actually results of neighboring a warring country. War means a loss of trade, including trade decreased due to less production in manufacturing and agriculture in the warring country, and a decline in tourism from that country. Loss of trade can mean increasing prices domestically for staples like food, leading to inflation. Investors may also shun the host country due to a fear that the conflict will spread or due to real security concerns, and economic activity can be crowded out in the host country as it becomes increasingly dominated by the activities of international aid agencies.

International economic institutions have recently embraced the study of refugee economic effects with gusto. While Africa has been dealing with refugees for decades, the effects were often viewed as isolated, particularly since the early pattern was to establish camps far from urban areas. Aside from the side effect of locals buying humanitarian aid items from refugees,[64] the subject was not viewed as terribly consequential. With the advent of a clear turn to self-settled refugees, that assessment has changed. Further, as the new understandings of humanitarianism combine refugee assistance with development aid, economic data on host communities becomes essential.

Despite this new interest, reliable data are difficult to come by. Findings can differ by time period and method of data accumulation. Particularly in the Middle East, many studies are based on reporting from a few local people, and numbers vary widely. Other economic studies are aggregates of national income or trade, but obscure local effects. Employment may not decline by overall measures while escalating or declining in different subnational regions. Differential effects on employment in rural or marginal areas versus capital cities is a common scenario. Capital cities provide more employment and usually house the headquarters of international humanitarian organizations. The presence of INGOs offers employment benefits for the middle classes. Beirut and Amman serve as the bases of

organizations, some of whom only rarely frequent the locations with most refugees. Rural or marginalized areas, by contrast, can suffer and have fewer alternatives to fall back on when employment declines. The situation can be particularly
difficult when refugees settle in cheaper and less-advantaged areas, affecting what
little employment those areas have to offer. The effects vary across time, and can
be periodic: rents will spike at the outset, then tend to stabilize. Periods of drought
will additionally exacerbate the effects of a larger population. In the data that fol-
low, I gather some of the most reliable and representative statistics available to
present the effects of the refugees.

Total refugee population numbers are even more complicated than employment figures, and are only ever estimates. Numbers of Syrians are both politicized
and imprecise. States change them according to their goals. Jordan appears to desire increased aid money, and has inflated refugee numbers as they did with the
Iraqis,[65] while Lebanon appears to be less interested in using demographic statistics for aid than it is in diminishing the appearance of Syrian refugees to the Lebanese population. Indeed, Lebanon instructed the UNHCR to stop registering
refugees. Since then, INGO workers generally believe the number of Syrians in
Lebanon is much higher than the official registered numbers, probably by half a
million, while numbers of Syrians in Jordan are probably lower than official figures. There is general agreement on trends, however, and this should be the focus
over and above the precise data points.

Sheer demographics are not the sole determinant of refugee effects but interact with state policy, and this is especially the case with refugee employment.[66]
Where employment for refugees is allowed and legal, the effects do not appear to
be as adverse as when employment is prohibited to refugees who are also self-
settled. Needing to work, self-settled refugees illegally take jobs at lower wages
and with fewer restrictions, undercutting the existing labor arrangements and pay
rates. Refugee aid is also perceived as contributing to the ability to take lower
wages, effectively acting as a subsidy. Those who work illegally will also not pay
taxes, depriving the state of income while increasing the strain on services and
resources.

The effects of refugees are not all negative: Host countries benefit due to the
presence of the refugees. While lower wages hurt domestic workers, businesses
gain from the ability to pay less. Business profit, indeed, has been viewed as one
reason to prevent the establishment of camps.[67] Instead of competing with local
labor, refugees can be viewed as bringing new skills to a country. Marketplace demand also increases due to the population influx, and real estate owners profit
by charging higher rents or renting vacant properties. The international aid complex itself generates numerous possibilities in the host countries. Large amounts
of foreign money are spent as internationals move to host countries to work in

various agencies of INGOs and the UN. The advent of a large INGO and aid sector can boost the middle classes, or indeed anyone with a college education and foreign-language abilities. In addition to aid money given directly to the states, retail businesses profit as INGOs move from providing large-scale packages of goods to providing cash cards for the refugees to use locally.

Trade, Poverty, and Economic Indicators

The effects of refugees and the Syrian war itself on the economies of Jordan and Lebanon are exemplified by the impact on trade and tourism. The regional Syrian war complex closed borders, which cut trade. Syria had been a significant trade partner for Jordan and Lebanon, both in originating goods—manufactured and agricultural—and in being a transit country for goods.[68] After the war began, border towns' trading economies collapsed, just as they were simultaneously flooded with large numbers of Syrians. Food prices were affected,[69] although increases in the world price of food affected local prices at the same time,[70] making it difficult to disentangle the effect of the Syrians from changes merely coinciding with their arrival. The war decreased the availability of inexpensive goods in or through Syria. Before the war, a trip to Syria could outfit a family for a fraction of what it would cost at home in Lebanon. Tourism dropped off as the countries became too crowded or were deemed too insecure for anyone but expatriates to return, who still do in the summer months.[71] Insecurity caused investment likewise to decrease.[72] Security concerns were heightened by the fact that many Lebanese and Jordanians became involved in the Syrian war, traveling there to fight.

Early in the conflict, the World Bank issued an assessment of how the refugees could affect Lebanon. Their projections have been used politically, not as potential projections but as established data, which they were not. In particular, the estimate on poverty shows up time and again in analyses. Analysts repeat the World Bank's early estimation that 170,000 might be driven into poverty, predicted early in the Syrian conflict.[73] Recent data indicate poverty increased by 4 percent, amounting to around 240,000 persons, but this number now includes the refugees. Since most refugees are poor, one would expect the poverty figure to be much higher, over 700,000, since 70 percent of the refugees were poor in 2015.[74] The Lebanese government estimates 1.5 million vulnerable in Lebanon out of an estimated total population of 5.9 million, including Syrians.[75] In Jordan, the 2010 figure of 14.4 percent poverty is still in use.[76] Despite the lack of current figures, poverty and unemployment are assumed in international organization reports to have increased. Unemployment does not equal poverty here, given that individuals may receive direct compensation money from the government and other forms of income.

Public debt and the macro economies have also been affected. In 2013, the World Bank speculated that Lebanon would lose USD 7.5 billion in the 2012–2014 period due to lower economic growth, and the crisis would cost the government USD 1.1 billion in increased spending.[77] These projections included losses due to the war itself, not just the impact of refugees. Lebanon's official estimates were higher, claiming a cost of USD 16 billion in decreased economic activity and USD 1.5 billion in revenue lost to the government annually.[78] For Jordan, the direct fiscal effect on the Jordanian budget due to the refugees was put at more than USD 870 million annually for 2014, increasing public debt.[79] Other costs, such as increases in services, are indirect, but aid takes care of some of these, such as education. Around 9 percent of the government's budget goes to services for the refugees, a figure that includes security services.[80] This figure does not cover expenditures on subsidized goods, which the Syrians outside camps draw upon.

Overcrowding and Demography

Demographic effects are not only important in their gross numbers but also in their regional distribution. As mentioned, the geography of Syrian settlement has altered the countries, both increasing poverty as Syrians reside in the poorer, marginalized areas and potentially changing the regional political weight of those areas. In Jordan, refugees have effectively created a new city in the North, the refugee camp Za'atari, and much emphasis is now on this resource-poor area to the neglect of the South, another resource-poor region. Refugees are concentrated in Amman and in the northern governorates. Jordan maintains that more than 435,000 Syrians are in Amman, with 343,000 in Irbid, the next-largest city; then 208,000 in Mafraq; and 175,000 in Zarqa. That translates to more than 10 percent of the population of Amman, 20 percent of Irbid, 13 percent of Zarqa, and 38 percent of Mafraq. Yet at other times the government and observers have alleged higher numbers, arguing for a doubling or more of Mafraq's population due to Syrians.[81] Mafraq governorate, a northern and generally poor, marginalized area, is proportionally most affected by the Syrians. As a result, Jordanians migrated away from these refugee camp areas.[82]

In Lebanon, while refugees are spread across the country, the bulk (86%) are in 242 communities where two-thirds of the population is poor to lower class.[83] The poor area around Tripoli and Akkar in the North has the most refugees proportionally and is least able to manage this influx. Some villages have doubled in population due to refugees, and the average increase in this area is 30 percent.[84] Other figures say that the population of this area increased by 50 percent overall, hosting 280,000 registered refugees.[85] Due to the lack of registration of refugees these numbers may have changed over time. At least one village doubled due to the refugees, according to UNHCR officials' population counts, although many additional refugees remained unregistered there.[86] In one agricultural town in the Beka'a Valley, the previous Lebanese population of 400 people was joined by an estimated 10,000 Syrians in around 1,000 tents. They worked the nearby agricultural land for the landowner, purchasing all their goods from the local landlord-owned store.[87] On the border, Arsal was flooded with refugees and fighters from Syria, became a major security problem, and was cordoned off at one point.[88] Some areas with large numbers of Syrians have managed to cope better, some through extended kinship networks that both absorbed the Syrians and shared in the benefits of aid to the refugees.

Rent and Prices

Increases in rent are one of the main effects of the Syrian refugees on host countries, and housing is cited as a central reason for animosity toward the Syrians.[89] Syrians affect the housing market for low-to-middle-income families, decreasing its availability and increasing rental prices. Three-fourths of Syrians rented, raising housing demand by 2.5 times in the early period.[90] Eighty-three percent of Jordanians in these refugee-hosting areas stated that housing creates problems between refugees and citizens.[91] In addition to rising demand for housing, rent prices surged because the Syrians would simply pay more. Rent doubled and tripled in some places when Syrians moved in, partly due to an ill-considered policy on the part of humanitarian organizations. Many INGOs at the outset—including those based in the Gulf—merely handed Syrians money to pay for rent. This resulted in locals being evicted from their apartments so that landlords could rent at higher rates to Syrians. In 2013, Jordanians were evicted as landlords charged up to six times the current rent to Syrians.[92] In addition, the Syrians would pack two or three families in one apartment, allowing them to pay more collectively. Landlords took advantage of the fact that Syrians often cannot rent legally, demanding high rent for inferior housing spaces and inflating overall rental prices.[93]

While the presence of Syrians in the rental market has generally caused hostility, Ramtha has been held up by humanitarian organizations as an exception to the rule. Inhabitants of Ramtha are often kin to the Syrians, thus the refugees are believed to not generate as much hostility there. In fact, in addition to the existence of clear resentment against the Syrians during my visits, the case of Ramtha demonstrates the relationship between a different facet of culture and perception of effects. Ramtha does not have a "culture of the *shiqqa*," or a culture of "the apartment," for newlyweds, locals told me. To get married, people in Ramtha do not need to have a separate apartment, unlike the rest of Jordan, where that is a prerequisite. When the Syrians came, new couples in Ramtha crowded in with their families and rented other property to the Syrians to make money from them.[94] Still, some polls list housing as a source of tension even in Ramtha, again questioning the equation that kinship means lack of conflict.[95] In some areas of Lebanon rents doubled, and in others, like Beirut, they quadrupled.[96] As in Jordan, locals were being evicted as landlords sought to take advantage of the Syrians' absolute need and their consequent willingness to pay higher prices.[97]

Prices for other goods have increased, particularly staple foods.[98] In 2012, prices rose 15 percent and 6 percent in the Beka'a and the North, respectively.[99] Inflation caused additional expenditures for poor Lebanese of between 35 and 50 percent.[100] Prices in Jordan had already risen due to international food prices, as elsewhere, but rose 5 percent overall in the first year of the Syrian crisis.[101] Economic reports hold that inflation after the initial influx has been low, at a couple of percentage points,[102] although price rises are a popular complaint. While Syrians are also affected by high prices, those who receive food vouchers are more fiscally insulated than the domestic population, a fact that is not lost on citizens.[103]

Employment

Over the long term, refugees can have a positive impact on wage rates as locals move up the ladder into managerial and formal positions and refugees occupy the lower rungs. This is happening in Turkey but it has yet to be documented for Jordan or Lebanon, and certainly the populace does not perceive it to be occurring.[104] The data for job market effects are mixed, particularly for Jordan,[105] but fieldwork demonstrates both a united perception of the effect and evidence of politicized data. The common belief is that Syrians are taking Jordanian jobs. Sixty-nine percent of Jordanians felt that employment created problems between the two communities in one early study.[106] Jordan historically has had difficulty employing all its population, as has Lebanon, but, unlike Lebanon, the potentially affected population is integral to Jordan's regime support.

While many reports argue that the Syrians mainly had an impact on the low-skilled jobs that locals did not want in Jordan (agriculture, construction), some did affect other local jobs. Nationally, unemployment for Jordanians increased from over 14 percent before the Syrians arrived to over 22 percent in 2015.[107] One early study indicated that Syrians were pushing Jordanians out of jobs due to their low salaries and the lack of regulation for informal work.[108] Some studies concluded that vulnerable Syrian workers, working for less, have caused a decline in wages.[109] The International Labour Organization (ILO) placed the impact of the Syrians on the informal and lower end of the wage scale only, with not much effect on the macro level.[110] Some contend no effect on the domestic labor market at all.[111] The effects also depend on the region and profession. One study from 2015 found 40,000 Jordanian jobs lost to Syrians.[112] Government officials state that 160,000 Syrians worked illegally, replacing Jordanians in bakeries, auto mechanic shops, and restaurants, an often-repeated figure.[113] Various sources highlight Aqaba as employing a high concentration of Syrian labor.[114] Nevertheless, other studies found that 80 percent of Syrians are unemployed.[115]

The government and the ILO assert that Syrians compete with informal and migrant labor, mainly Egyptians, since Jordanians do not seek these jobs in construction and agriculture. Popular opinion, by contrast, held by both Jordanians and INGO employees, asserts that Syrians have indeed affected the labor markets beyond supplanting Egyptian workers. Syrians take different jobs, some state, because they differ from the Egyptians in skills and have their families with them. As single men, the Egyptians can stay in remote areas for long periods, while Syrians do not want to be separated from their families.[116] In contrast to Lebanon's view of the Syrians, Syrians are viewed as skilled and talented by Jordanians. Business in Jordan does indeed prefer Syrian labor, where these workers enjoy a reputation as more hard working and skilled, particularly in finer services and hospitality industries. Food preparation and serving were viewed as an area of Syrian competitive advantage. Jordanians declared Syrian food and waiters as more gracious, polite, and clean than Egyptian or Jordanian servers.[117] The Syrian work ethic is believed to be superior to the Jordanian one, with Syrians working harder and longer than Jordanians are willing to.[118] People told stories of relatives being hired and paid to stay at home, while the owner hired a Syrian to do the actual work.[119] On the books, the employer had a legal employee, in reality he employed a Syrian who worked longer hours for little money.

Syrians established businesses in Jordan, again in restaurants and food preparation, hiring other Syrians and not local business and labor.[120] As testament to the proliferation of Syrian food businesses, signs for the Syrian words for restaurants, bakeries, and nut shops, rather than the Jordanian ones, can be viewed throughout Amman. Jordanians frequent these establishments and often prefer them over the Jordanian ones. Stories of Syrians beginning their own informal but large-scale businesses in tiling, for example, abound. Other statistics dispute that Jordan is a more accommodating work environment for Syrians compared to Lebanon. UNHCR data put the poverty rate of Syrian refugees in Jordan at 93 percent, which is more than those in Lebanon, at 70 percent.[121]

In Lebanon, the data, think tanks, and popular opinion are all in agreement. Syrian employment and the effect on local wages are major grievances of the Lebanese population. While in Jordan migrant labor works in the informal sector and locals prefer formal work, in Lebanon a large part of the economy is informal. Lebanese work in this sector, including at the lower end of the wage scale, and thus Syrians compete with them.[122] As in Jordan, the overwhelming majority of Syrians work in low-wage jobs and live in poorer communities.[123] Syrians moved into areas of work that were previously Lebanese. Fifty percent more laborers are in the workforce, and wages have declined with the additional labor.[124] Whether competition is the cause, wages and working conditions have indeed declined. With Syrian child labor increasing,[125] employers find they can pay even less and get away with poorer working conditions. Some studies have documented agricultural wage rates declining by as much as 60 percent.[126] In other data, Syrians were willing to work for 40 percent lower wages and longer hours.[127]

Like Jordan, Lebanon had unemployment problems prior to the refugee crisis,[128] but unlike Jordan, does not have a significant state sector to employ people. Out-migration has been the typical Lebanese solution to unemployment, and that is even more in evidence now.[129] Youth want to emigrate, stating that they cannot find jobs and believe there is no future employment locally.[130] Unskilled youth are hit particularly hard. Syrians open unregistered businesses that sell inexpensively, competing with other retail outlets.[131] Unemployment is estimated at 20 percent, a doubling since the crisis, and youth unemployment has risen 50 percent.[132] Syrian manufacturers set up competing businesses, and Syrians drive taxis, competing in that sector as well.[133] Overall, Lebanese communities report decreased income due to several factors, including Syrian competition and insecurity.[134]

Education and Health Care

Schools are overcrowded, even though a significant portion of Syrian children in both countries do not attend school formally.[135] In Lebanon, about half of eligible refugees attended formal elementary schools in 2015. Of potential refugee secondary school students, almost none—3 percent—attended public schools in 2015.[136] In Jordan that year, 74 percent of elementary school-age registered refugees attended school. For children eleven years and older, the percentage dropped sharply.[137] Still, formal enrollment rates should be taken as guides only; dropout rates are not recorded and are estimated at up to 40 percent.[138] Many schools are double-shifted, as students who are citizens attend in the morning and Syrian children attend in the afternoon. In Jordan, more teachers have been hired for this second shift, which is run by the Ministry of Education, while in Lebanon the same teachers from the first shift teach the second also, paid by the UN. Teachers work a double day, and Lebanese parents complain that their children's education is suffering due to these newcomers. Already disadvantaged by being in the lower economic classes, they fear this will further compromise their children's future prospects.[139] Those able to afford the average private school fees of USD

4,000, compared to the USD 160 annual public school fee, have switched to the private sector. The result has been similar overcrowding of private schools.[140]

Jordanians likewise have complained about the shift system. Class times and the school day were shortened with double shifting, encompassing around two hundred schools.[141] The percentage of overcrowded schools in the regions with the most refugees, the northern rural areas and Amman, doubled after the arrival of the Syrians.[142] Jordan's long-standing plans to improve and renovate its education system were put on hold due to the Syrian crisis, adding to resentment against the refugees. Jordanian parents have been highly concerned about the quality of their children's education caused by the flood of children from another school system who speak a different dialect, and who have a background of witnessing the violence of war. Sixty-one percent of Jordanians and 44 percent of Syrians stated that education caused tensions due to uneven access, mixed classes (Jordanians and Syrians), overcrowding, and other reasons.[143]

The ability to provide public health care has been stretched to its limits. Jordan has witnessed an increase from three hundred Syrian refugees at government hospitals to more than ten thousand between January 2012 and March 2013.[144] Medications and staff are in short supply, and hospitals are overcrowded. The medical system in Lebanon has also been unable to cope with the influx of refugees, resulting in shortages and long wait times. The occurrence of serious diseases like tuberculosis has increased by 27 percent since the beginning of the refugee crisis.[145] Overcrowding has led the local population to resort to private health care amid a common perception that Syrians are taking the place of Lebanese in their own hospitals.[146]

Despite the popular opinion that Syrians are better off than citizens, the Syrians are in reality far worse off. Skin diseases and waterborne illnesses are on the rise in the most concentrated refugee communities, with the potential to spread to host communities.[147] Without access to clean water, refugees play in, bathe in, and drink contaminated water. Authorities fear cholera, while diseases such as scabies, hepatitis A, and leishmaniasis have already broken out.[148] One study found that, during the prior two weeks, 40 percent of Syrians in Lebanon had acquired dysentery due to water-based factors.[149]

Utilities, Resources, and Waste

The electricity sector has been overtaxed in both countries due to the increase in population, although the problem is felt more severely in Lebanon. Lebanon's old grid, the Électricité du Liban (EDL), was not able to handle its load before the refugee crisis, and the Syrians have taxed it further. Syrians use 486 megawatts daily, out of an EDL capacity of 1,800 megawatts.[150] The Ministry of Energy and

Water has estimated that Lebanese lose five hours of electricity daily per household due to the Syrians, and that Syrian electricity usage costs the government $333 million per year.[151] Most of this increased usage Syrians do not pay for. Informal tented settlements run off the grid illegally. Other electricity changes due to the Syrians are borne by public services, at the local or central state level. New streetlights have been added to increase safety in the newly settled areas, and the additional drain on water pumps, schools, and hospitals all contribute to this increased usage. Total demand is almost twice EDL's capacity, creating a gap that is filled by private generators.[152] Fixing one plant and renting two power barges increased capacity, but still left major shortages.[153] Transformers are operating at 150 percent capacity, reducing voltage and supply. Three hours daily of power outages are common in Beirut, while outside Beirut an average of half the day is spent without energy from the grid.[154] There is even an app to track when electricity is out.[155] In the absence of electricity from the grid, people who can afford it pay for private electricity through subscriptions costing far more than public power. Poorer people must subsist without electricity much of the time. Added to this, EDL operates at a loss, and, to keep it afloat, the Lebanese state gave the utility USD 2.4 billion. It is estimated that the generator business makes 70 percent of that amount in profit.[156] The middle classes complain that they have to pay two bills for everything: one the public service and the other for the private one. Lebanese blame the Syrians for these electricity problems, while admitting that the system was flawed previously. An official at the state electric company in the Beka'a Valley summarized the complaints, stating that Syrians steal the electricity. They often have no meter, and even when they do, the Syrians put too much pressure on the main generator. Lacking alternative facilities to heat water for example, they use electrical wires placed in the water, which requires more power.[157]

Refugees have increased water use in both countries, but in Jordan this has sparked vociferous protest against the state in those areas most affected by the refugees.[158] The countries had poor water systems to begin with, suffering both a lack of water infrastructure and polluted water. People feel no obligation to pay for such inferior water services, since water provisioning is unreliable and often contaminated or undrinkable when it does exist.[159] Jordan's tap water occasionally ran brown well before the Syrians arrived and would stop altogether for days.[160] One analysis determined that Jordanians in urban areas (generally receiving preferential water delivery) had twelve hours of piped fresh water per week. A water expert stated that the increase in population changed the entire water situation.[161] In 2009, before the refugee influx, Lebanon's public water network ranged between three and thirteen hours of water per day, depending on the season and with considerable regional variation.[162] A study by UN organizations found that 64 percent of Lebanese do not have regular access to safe water.[163] Many areas remain unconnected to the water grid at all.[164] Where clean water exists, theft and old infrastructure contribute to significant loss, and in both countries about 50 percent of water is unaccounted for. In Lebanon, estimates of water lost through old pipes reach 80 percent in some areas.[165] Refugees are concentrated in regions with poor water infrastructure, and water availability there has declined sharply, adding a burden to family budgets in the form of private water purchases.[166] An official at the Ministry of Energy and Water said that "because of the Syrians, a water balance that should have been negative in 2030 is negative now."[167]

Much of the public has avoided the polluted national water systems through illegal private wells in addition to massive private water purchases. In 2011, Jordan's water agency stated that there were 409 illegal wells in addition to almost 4,000 licensed private wells. In the year before the refugees' arrival, almost 900 new wells were licensed.[168] In 2014, Jordan had an estimated 1,500 illegal wells.[169] The actual numbers are almost certainly higher. Recently, Jordan's Ministry of Water and Irrigation announced that it cited 30,000 breaches of the water laws from 2013 to the present.[170] In Lebanon, wells pulling up to 100,000 liters per day of water have been exempt from regulation.[171] Even with this allowance, the World Bank estimated 20,000 illegal wells in the environs of Beirut. Private companies use these wells to deliver water by truck.[172] Three-quarters of the average household budget is spent buying water from private suppliers in Lebanon, which costs five times the amount of public water.[173] Overall, there are at least 50,000 private wells in Lebanon, possibly as many as 80,000, partly as a legacy of the civil war and the militias creating their own water supply. This is up from 3,000 in the early 1970s, while the state grid still works off of only 650 wells.[174]

Prior to the arrival of Syrian refugees in Jordan, the fresh water supplies in the kingdom were expected to run out around the year 2060.[175] With the rapid surge in population, in part due to the influx of refugees, the current expectation is that Jordanian water will not last far beyond 2030.[176] In 2017, Jordan announced its water could serve less than one-third of the population.[177] One pumping station in the North of Jordan was providing for 80,000 Jordanians before the refugee influx and is now attempting to serve over 200,000 people, and failing in that attempt.[178] Jordanians in northern poor rural communities, with higher percentages of refugees on average, have had water deliveries significantly curtailed as the supply is stretched to accommodate the newcomers.[179]

Refugee camps affect the surrounding water infrastructure. The largest of the camps, Za'atari, currently holds 80,000 refugees, down from a high of over 150,000.[180] Built somewhat hastily and located in the desert close to the Syrian border, the camp does not have direct access to Jordanian infrastructure. At the start, water was extracted from village wells in the nearby town of Mafraq, and this covered almost all of camp needs. This solution was unsustainable, however, and negatively impacted the resources of nearby villages. Later, internal wells were drilled within the camp, which still stressed overall groundwater levels.[181] The aquifer that Mafraq villages draw from had already been rapidly decreasing from overextraction prior to the refugee crisis.[182] Jordanians in Mafraq and across the northern parts of Jordan now receive water only once or twice a week, some less often.[183] Even after numerous efforts by international organizations to improve water systems, increasing demand means the water is still not sufficient.[184]

Waste increased in both countries, but in Lebanon the garbage crisis gave birth to a social movement, detailed in chapter 4. Waste, including solid trash and sewage, has moved to the top of municipalities' priorities since the refugees arrived. Some localities were able to cope with waste previously but are now overwhelmed.[185] Prior waste systems had been established without regard to future population increase, even increases in the resident Lebanese population.[186] Almost a third of Lebanon's two million tons of waste before the crisis was merely dumped in streets and vacant areas, and half was put in landfills that often accumulated to become a "trash mountain" (*jabel al-zibaleh*). In this situation, adding more waste from areas without infrastructure means increasing open waste disposal.[187] Lebanese and Syrians both report sewage-caused diseases. In 2014, the year of major influx, infectious waste increased in Lebanon by almost a fifth.[188] Population pressure on the garbage infrastructure contaminated water supplies as well.[189] Lebanese mention waste and groundwater pollution as key effects of the Syrian crisis.[190] By 2015, the health risks from sewage-infested water irrigating fruit and vegetables became a popular discussion topic and fear.[191]

While waste grew overall, around 16 percent in 2014 alone,[192] some areas were particularly affected by different types of waste. Trash doubled for some municipalities hosting numerous refugees or informal tented settlements.[193] One municipal official stated that the money municipalities receive from the state covers only a few months of waste collection now, due to the extra stress on services from the Syrians.[194] Syrians living in informal tented settlements aggravate the problem, as these lack infrastructure for waste disposal and the UN is hindered by the state from establishing sewage facilities. This waste thus becomes the responsibility of the municipalities, but without the funds allocated by the state to deal with it.[195] The poor northern area around Tripoli has seen its total waste double and the creation of "informal" sewage systems, which often means burying human waste or random disposal and burning of other trash.[196] Health hazards have resulted.[197] Waste increase was most felt where refugees were concentrated and the infrastructure was poor. In the Beka'a, solid waste increased by 38 percent, and in North Lebanon by 18 percent.[198] In Arsal, with a heavy concentration of Syrians, the existing sewage network, inadequate previously, was now overtaxed, resulting in sewage mixing with drinking water and affecting nearby towns.[199] Bar

Elias, a village near the Syrian border that doubled in population with the arrival of the refugees, has been unable to process its forty tons of daily garbage. The mountain of trash near an informal Syrian settlement is witness to this incapacity.[200]

In Jordan, 340 tons of daily waste were added to Jordan's system due to the refugees, and managing this was the highest priority for the bulk of northern governorates.[201] Increased waste was found to be a high priority in one survey from the refugee-populated North. Waste was mentioned as one of the biggest changes locally by a fifth of respondents to the survey, and almost 70 percent were upset by this rise in waste.[202] Municipalities already had problems collecting trash, and the new population influx just exacerbated that inability. Thirty-five percent of the people in areas hosting refugees do not have access to municipal sewage services. Those that do have seen drastic increases in infrastructure failures, often resulting in overflows of raw sewage. Complaints against local infrastructure administrators have doubled or tripled in many communities as a result of broken or clogged sewage systems.[203]

Groundwater can also be contaminated when infrastructure is lacking or breaks down.[204] Wastewater and sewage coming from Za'atari refugee camp can pose long-term damage. For the first few years after its establishment, the camp lacked both systems to bring water in and infrastructure to take sewage and waste out. Residents of the camp relied upon a network of ditches, lagoons, and cesspools that were periodically emptied to septic tanks away from Za'atari.[205] This opened up the possibility for serious groundwater contamination, since Za'atari refugee camp sits atop major aquifer systems. Essentially, because of a lack of infrastructure, the waste of around 80,000 refugees threatened to seep into the ground directly above two of the only sources of clean groundwater in the northern part of Jordan. While this was not a problem in a 2014 study,[206] reports projected that the aquifer under Za'atari would be polluted in the following few years.[207] Gradually, INGOs worked to establish permanent water and sewage facilities, in effect making the camp city permanent.

Security

Fear of spillover from the Syrian civil war was almost alarmist at the start of the refugee influx.[208] Lebanon has indeed been affected negatively by armed actors from the Syrian civil war, however the fear has been so overblown as to extend even to Syrian children and has been used politically. The major worry in Lebanon was that the war would inflame sectarian divisions among the population or alter the country's demographic balance as the refugees were mainly Sunni. Indeed, there have been clashes between Lebanese and refugees, particularly in northern towns with diverse populations. Political stances have mingled with religious identity and nationality; the Syrians were assumed by locals to be Sunni and pro-rebel. Numerous fights occurred on the streets of Tripoli between supporters of opposing sides in the war, or between Sunnis and Alawis.[209] Cells of jihadists and Islamists increased.[210] Hizbollah entered the Syrian civil war on the side of the government, causing tense relations with Sunnis and Christians, who were generally opposed to the Syrian regime. Major security problems occurred in the first couple of years, including car bombings and attacks.[211] Lebanese jihadis who joined the Syrian war took the name of a sheikh known for his opposition to the Shi'a organization.[212] Suicide bombs targeted mainly Christian villages along the border with Syria in 2016.[213] As the war progressed, the fear of extremist Islamism among the Syrian refugees would overcome the initial resentment against Hizbollah's support for the hated Syrian regime.[214] For Christians, the abduction of nuns in Syria was a turning point in assessing the relative dangers of Hizbollah or ISIS.[215] Every little child became suspected of being Daesh (the derogatory term for ISIS), and every Sunni a terrorist in locals' minds. In light of this presumed and partially real threat, Hizbollah's role was perceived as stabilizing.[216] Lebanese would assert that Hizbollah (and drug dealers) watching the borders would prevent Daesh in Lebanon.[217]

Through these and other dynamics, Hizbollah was militarily empowered. Cooperation increased between the Shi'a militia and the Lebanese Armed Forces (LAF) as the war went on and the LAF reached its jurisdictional limits. Being present on the Syrian side of the border, Hizbollah was in a position to aid LAF actions to expel or prevent the entrance of violent actors across the border.[218] The major example of this is that of Arsal, a northern border town that was flooded with refugees amounting to several times the number of locals.[219] The town became a hotbed of ISIS and its sympathizers, battling with Lebanese Internal Security Forces and LAF for years. The rise of ISIS created problems in Jordan as well. Jordan entered the fight against it while many of its citizens went to fight on the side of the jihadists.[220] Jordanians joked that the government should not worry about ISIS coming through the border from Syria, since they are already in the country.[221] Others feared "Daesh" thinking among the Syrian refugees.[222]

Not only military problems but also crimes were perceived as threats to the Lebanese.[223] Thefts and sexual crimes reportedly increased.[224] Lebanese complained that they did not feel safe, that they were afraid of street crime, that Lebanese women were harassed, and that they were subject to the annoying sound of motorcycles—all due to the Syrians. Motorcycles, being cheaper than cars, became associated with Syrians. These themes were repeated throughout Lebanon. To prevent Syrians from being on the street at night, municipalities began enacting curfews on foreigners, declared via prominent banners. "Foreigner" was code for lower-class Syrians, while those of other backgrounds, clearly not Lebanese, were not stopped. Legally, municipalities did not have the authority to impose curfews: only the military command or the Council of Ministers could do so. The central government took no action against the curfews, however. Curfews have been assessed as an attempt to prevent entry into richer areas, yet they were increasingly used in poor areas with heavy refugee concentrations as well.[225] Curfews were only one part of the municipal response. Municipalities also felt a need to increase local policing, another area of questionable legality.

Overall, the militaries of both countries benefited, as their realms of maneuver expanded and they received increased international support. According to Professor Bassel Salloukh, the Lebanese military is benefiting in numerous ways from the refugee crisis. They now can turn to their preferred job of focusing on security as opposed to being the country's peacekeeper, and are getting more training, weapons, and practice.[226] With a justified enemy, the military has returned to guarding the borders and identifying terrorists, boosting its professional role. The military is the most active and popular government institution in Lebanon, and it appears to be taking the lead in dealing with the refugees while also securitizing them. The Jordanian military's central role in the state and economy received a similar boost.[227]

Social Relations and Culture

Social effects on the host countries depend on point of view and country. Syrians are locally perceived as more liberal in behavior than Jordanians, but less socially liberal than Lebanese. The complaints in these countries align with these presumed variations. Jordanians claim Syrians are corrupting their women, showing them women can work (and ride motorcycles), while Lebanese women fear going out and having Syrian men stare at them.[228] "Girls can't go out on the balcony in Muslim areas with Syrians around," one man stated.[229] More concretely, in both countries there has been an increase in child marriage as Syrians choose the least bad among the untenable options. Marrying daughters has many advantages in a refugee situation. From the family's perspective there is one less mouth to feed and the family can gain economically from the new groom and accompanying dowry. While practiced in Syria prior to the war, the rate of child marriage has soared among the refugee population. It is not clear how widespread this trend is, although one study in 2015 put the rate at 23 percent. This is up from 13 percent of girls under age eighteen marrying while in Syria.[230] Young refugee marriages are sometimes brokered by agents from the Gulf and local imams with the promise of providing for the family. Almost half (44%) of all Syrian brides in 2015 were under seventeen years old.[231] "What choice is there for a girl, stay inside all day or get married? The girls want to go to school, but these are their choices," said one Lebanese researcher involved in refugee areas.[232]

Reportedly the presence of marriageable Syrian women has caused a lowering of the dowry, the amount prospective grooms give to the bride and her family, in line with increased supply lowering costs. Stories of men taking second wives abound. While the practice is legal in Jordan and Lebanon, previously early and second marriages were little practiced. Now, however, they are "affecting the morals" and "changing our culture," interviewees said. "Even in the educated areas," one (female) businessowner stated, "women have started to fear for their men."[233] A Jordanian man stated, "wives now get upset and fear the husband will take a Syrian wife if he comes home late."[234] One analyst stated that Syrian women are considered to be more deferential and beautiful, and accept lower dowries. This becomes a problem for single Lebanese women, an academic stated, since they face more competition for husbands.[235]

Benefits

All these negative effects must be put in perspective. While the states are indeed burdened in services, housing, and resources, they also benefit from the presence of the refugees, receiving billions in aid, infrastructure projects, and additional business. Some maintain that the economies are actually growing.[236] New Syrian firms create jobs,[237] and some argue that these Syrian businesses do not compete with local ones.[238] Cash assistance has fueled retail businesses and circulated through the economy. Grocery businesses saw their sales boom when they accepted the cash cards issued by the UN to the Syrian refugees.[239] Every dollar spent in aid has an estimated 1.6 multiplier effect in Lebanon, and thus humanitarian aid raises Lebanon's GDP by 1.3 percent.[240] Other data show that each aid dollar generates USD 2.13 in Lebanon's GDP.[241]

Many locals gain directly, through business contracts, real estate rentals, or employment in humanitarian organizations. The presence of the refugees has created new markets and services. The arrival of numerous INGOs created new business opportunities for anything catering to foreigners, including restaurants, services, and real estate. The majority of Syrians rent apartments or live on rented land. Even informal tented settlements are often charged rent. Some landlords force their refugee tenants to buy all services and goods from a central store, owned by the landlord.[242] Truckers are hired to bring water to the informal tented settlements, militaries get training and improved cooperation with their Western counterparts, and businesses hire Syrian child runners to deliver goods. The effect of increased demand is captured in one story from a UNHCR official who recalled that, soon after the establishment of Za'atari refugee camp, they started seeing produce weigh scales in the camp, the heavy weight-balancing type common to the Middle East. Surely the Syrians did not flee across the border carrying those scales. They had to have purchased them locally.[243] Grocery stores and restaurants hired four or five Syrian boys to deliver food, where before they could afford only one, increasing their business. Medium-sized industries like hair salons can afford Syrians to do the more menial labor, allowing Lebanese to move up the employment ladder. The result is a thriving of the informal sector.[244] Lebanese teachers strike for wage increases, but also teach a second shift with better pay from the UN. The number of local NGOs has proliferated, and INGOs hire the bulk of their employees locally.[245] College graduates have jobs with INGOs or local NGOs, staying to work in Lebanon when, before the refugee influx, they would have left the country to find employment, one recent graduate stated.[246] NGOs have seen their financing skyrocket and strategize how to maintain financing when donors shift to working within Syria instead of in the host countries.[247] Rural areas have seen social benefits as well. Mafraq is more vibrant, a Jordanian with long INGO experience told me. There are more restaurants and commerce, more space for young people to move and express themselves. "Before the crisis they had nothing to do. They went to work and came back home. Local NGOs are now more active with different programs [for youth], there are cafes, and you find women out in the streets and working with the NGOs."[248] Another person flatly stated, "If I don't find a job I will start an NGO."[249] Private education and educational NGOs have increased because, as locals perceive their public schools to be overrun by Syrians, they turn to the private sector instead.[250]

Governments benefit from aid money, a topic discussed in more depth in chapter 5, and ask for far more aid than the calculated impact of the Syrians. The Jordanian Ministry of Education estimated that it received more than USD 630 million per year due to Syrian students. This is a jump of 50 percent, but the number of students did not even rise 7 percent.[251] Most importantly, the infrastructure projects so desperately needed in both countries were going nowhere fast before the refugees arrived, forsaken in the name of state budgets. Now international organizations have stepped in to lay water pipes, fix electricity plants, and aid in problematic waste and sewage processing. Indeed, the estimate needed to fix Lebanon's infrastructure before the crisis was put at USD 20 billion, and it is not clear how Lebanon would have obtained that amount.[252]

Effects on the Syrians

The negative repercussions for the Syrians are more severe than those for the host populations, and too numerous to mention. Only a few will be mentioned here, those pertaining to the effects listed above. The increase in child marriage has gone hand in hand with the decline of childhood education and the increase in child work, legal and illegal. Female refugees face many changes, as they take on new roles in unfamiliar places. Women and children can rival men in contributing to support the family, and as male roles and earning potential often decline in tandem, repercussions for women can be violent. Women and children take on these new roles because of the greater obstacles men face in accessing resources for the family: in Lebanon, the danger of men crossing the numerous military checkpoints and risking arrest meant that women and children would travel instead for necessary goods, aid, and work.[253] For young women, this has resulted in predictable advances from some men and soldiers, putting them further at risk. Statelessness due to difficulty registering births or other reasons for lack of documents will remain a major problem for many Syrians.[254] Less clear are the effects on Syrians of the various charities that operate without transparency, such as those from the Gulf. Many are tied to religious organizations and practices, and how they choose recipients for their abundant aid is unclear.[255] Some care for martyrs' families. Others appear to enforce their view of morality on recipients.[256]

Refugee children are probably the most affected by their circumstances. Refugee child labor is rampant in both countries. Because the consequences for children caught working are less serious than those for adults, who can be deported or imprisoned, the family reasons it is less threatening to the family's survival if the children work.[257] One study in Jordan found that children's work contributed around half of all income, and 84 percent of employers had hired a child—as young as six years old—to work since the Syrian refugee crisis began.[258] Later Jordanian policy became harsher toward children caught working, who would be sent to camps, back to Syria, or to jail. If the child was sent to a camp, the family would have to agree to having the entire family remain in the camp in order to be reunited with the child.[259] Working children cannot attend school,[260] which many would like to avoid anyway, since school outside of camps is fraught with bullying for Syrian refugees. Even for richer Syrians, able to afford the best schools where the Jordanian royals send their children, students were exposed to bullying in addition to shouts of "go back to your country."[261] Humanitarian organizations have sometimes acted without thought to consequences, inadvertently making the refugees a target. Refugee children with brand-new backpacks from INGOs have been attacked for those very backpacks.[262]

The negative effects on Lebanon and Jordan's economies, resources, and services as well as the security threats were not predetermined but resulted from an interaction between state policies, state capacities, and the refugees. Numerous detrimental effects on the host countries were attributed to the refugees, and, at the very least, the Syrian refugees stressed existing problems in state and economic capacities. These effects were partly due to demographic stress on the existing in-adequate infrastructure and partly to the policies of the states toward the Syrians. Prohibiting legal work for Syrians meant undercutting the domestic labor market, generating the widespread perception of Syrians taking citizens' jobs. Lack of camps in Lebanon forced poor Syrians to live at the mercy of squatter settlement bosses (*shawish*) and work in agriculture while living in squalor. In urban areas, working Syrian children beg in the streets, interrupting the flow of traffic, or sift through trash for recycling payments. Jordan's main camp, in a water-scarce, poor, and traditionally neglected region, has generated stark comparisons between Syrian aid and local lack. The results have been partially predictable—hostility toward the Syrians, which is discussed in chapter 3—and partly surprising. In tandem with their animosity toward refugees, citizens have begun to demand that their own governments make substantive changes.

FROM BROTHERS IN NEED TO INVADERS

Sympathy waned after the initial honeymoon period of brotherhood when citizens of both Lebanon and Jordan aided the refugees. Even the Lebanese, with their history of conflict with Syria, mobilized to provide for the newcomers.[1] By 2012–2013, it became clear that the war would drag on. As Syrians continued to cross their neighbors' borders, the hosts became resentful. In relatively short order, host citizens' attitudes toward the Syrians went from welcoming brothers in need to considering Syrians to be invaders who should leave. This chapter examines popular opinion, media, and elite statements about refugees through interviews, press reports, and opinion polls. I use direct interviews and media sources; translations are my own, verified by a native speaker. Interviews were run more as discussions, where I let the individual or group talk about their concerns. I introduced myself as studying the countries after the Syrian war or in recent years, and the interviewees took over from there. Interviews in Lebanon were with Sunnis, Christians, and, to a lesser extent, Shi'a, while in Jordan they were with East Bankers and those of Palestinian background. Opinions of the Palestinian-Jordanians did not vary significantly from those of the East Bankers, with the exception that those of Palestinian descent were more likely to be geographically distant from areas of refugee concentration. They were sometimes, but not always, more subdued in their condemnation of Syrians, yet blame them they did. Palestinians in Jordan remember their history as refugees differently, believing they had been self-sufficient farmers who did not interfere with the local job market.[2] Camp residents were more resentful, according to UN officials, viewing Syrians as encroaching on their aid.[3]

While much writing about refugees and integration posits that common kinship and culture create stability, here the local populations began to view the Syrians as an "other." The view of Syrians as foreigners, competing for the country's resources, economic goods, and social relationships, preying on the resources and goodwill of the neighboring Arab countries, is a departure from historically close kin relationships between many areas of these countries. Aside from the fact that Syrians, Jordanians, and Lebanese speak the same language, share a religion for the most part, and have a similar culture, many residents of border areas have close family and cultural ties to the Syrians. Central to the change in viewpoint were the perceived and actual effects of the influx of Syrian refugees discussed in chapter 2, which have been felt disproportionately among poorer communities. While, as we have seen, there have actually been significant benefits from the Syrians' presence, perception is key.

These common views have been supported and propagated by the states and the media, which attributed to the refugees what have actually been long-standing problems. Apparently to justify requests for more aid, the states have continually emphasized the negative effects of Syrian refugees on the economy, as have humanitarian organizations. The media have joined in, repeating this emphasis and blaming the Syrians for whatever ails the countries. Indeed, this scapegoating, or identifying a powerless group as responsible for current problems in an attempt to divert populations away from blaming authorities, is a global trend. Yet some of the problems that have been highlighted are in fact consequential to daily life, whether caused by the Syrians or not. Water, electricity, rent, and waste affect the ability to live. Citizens have felt a sense of threat, both from the lack of services as well as from the Syrians. Shortages of goods and services deemed essential to livelihoods have caused citizens to turn to the state or other governance for solutions. The by-product of this process has been the generation of new or strengthened grievances and demands against the state and international organizations, which have, in fact, often yielded results. The idea that the state is responsible for public services grew, as the consequences for service failure became inescapable and populations compared the aid received by the Syrians to their own lack of goods. Some turned to municipalities or NGOs for short-term solutions, while still holding the state ultimately responsible.

Chapter 2 demonstrated that there has been no shortage of ammunition for elites' attempts to scapegoat the Syrians, and the data below show that animosity toward the Syrians has not been lacking either.[4] Both these elements usually lay the foundation for successful diversion of the populace from the state toward blame and hostility against another social group. State elites and the media have actively accused the Syrians of causing economic and state capacity problems, long-standing or not, such as issues of waste, water, and electricity. Chapter 4 demonstrates that, even with all these elements seemingly in favor of scapegoating success, the attempted blame backfired, and citizens still look to the state for redress of their basic life problems.

Demography and Identity

Animosity toward the Syrians began early. By 2012–2013, reports were coming in of hostility toward the refugees, even in border areas where researchers and INGO workers alike decreed there should be kin affinity.[5] Accusations against the Syrians were roughly the same in both Lebanon and Jordan, with some important variations. In both countries, demographic fears and the effects on services and goods were given as rationales for hostility. Similar stories were repeated, in areas with and without refugee concentrations, despite data arguing against these generalizations. Finally, citizens envied the goods and services Syrians supposedly enjoyed, and divisions deepened, tied to resentment about the privileges foreigners presumably received.

Interviewees categorically stated that Syrians have negatively affected their country, although criticisms were sometimes muted by overt concern for the refugees as Muslim brothers and sisters. The same problems were repeatedly blamed on the Syrians—with the economy, jobs, and resources—in both countries. The stories about Syrians were also remarkably similar. Jordanians were worried about cultural influences from Syrians, a culture close to but different from their own. Jordanians asserted that the Syrians have more liberal mores than Jordanians in prescribing women's realm of action, Lebanese on the other hand were more focused on Syrians as a threat to their security.

The simple fact of the influx of overwhelming numbers of Syrians was experienced as a demographic threat in both countries, by all sectors of society. "What does it mean to be Jordanian if 20 percent of the population is Syrian or Iraqi?" one former government official wondered, echoing the thoughts of his compatriots. The number of Syrians was felt to be a "ticking time bomb," outweighing other security problems.[6] Lebanese joked that Syrians were taking over the country. With various minor changes, the essence of the joke is that a group of Syrians walks by a Lebanese, and wonders, "What is he doing in *their* country?" Jordanians felt the presence of Syrians everywhere, pointing out the changing names of food and restaurants from Jordanian to Syrian ones. Offers of international aid were linked to demographic fears. UN aid was viewed as facilitating Syrian procreation, generating more babies that would become a burden on the country.[7] Many feared what the long-term outcome might be, whether the Syrians would become a permanent feature in their country, and how their presence would change social and marriage patterns, food, and employment. In the words of one observer, the fear rose to the level of "a syndrome."[8]

Many felt that their country and their resources are just too small for this number of people. Lack of space was a notable theme in Lebanon: the presence of the Syrians scattered throughout the country increased tensions.[9] One UN employee stated that, in some small towns in Jordan, Syrians numbered five times the population of Jordanian residents. Thirty-thousand people would crowd into a town that previously had five thousand.[10] "We have too many Syrians for the population. We have to be humanitarian toward them, the state and the UN do not help enough, so we have to do all the work. In other countries the state would help them more," one Lebanese (religious) sheikh and educator declared.[11] Lebanon is in the worst shape, but Jordanians too complain of the numbers. "There are too many Syrians for our population," a tribal sheikh in the Jordanian North stated. "We have to help them, but the result is crime and drugs because the Syrians cannot work and aid is not enough."[12] Syrian women have altered the demography of marriage, and the availability of Syrian women as second, third, or fourth wives was not received well by female nationals. Reports grew of men using the prospect of taking a Syrian wife to enjoin a spouse to accept behavior that had previously been unacceptable, including abuse.[13]

Hostility Linked to Perceived Effects

People immediately put the blame for all their problems on the refugees, one INGO employee stated. Because refugees in Lebanon live "in apartments and not in camps, citizens have to deal with these people who are supposedly ruining the country and dealing in weapons."[14] "We already had big problems, and the UNHCR and our ministries give Syrians free electricity and water. So they increased the use of them, we have less electricity and our [state] debt increased."[15] Early in the crisis, in 2013, almost 60 percent in Jordan felt that services were worse due to the Syrians.[16] In Lebanon, more than 70 percent felt the same, and, among municipalities, almost 80 percent stated that the Syrians negatively affected their ability to provide basic services. Half of Lebanese surveyed identified unemployment as their priority.[17] Real estate was perceived as affected by the Syrians to an overwhelming degree—by more than 90 percent of respondent Jordanians—although prices of common goods were the prime concern.[18] By 2013, almost three-quarters of Jordanians wanted to halt the influx of Syrians.[19] Even more wanted the existing Syrians to be restricted to the camps (80%). Fear of the effect on services was the chief concern about the Syrian influx.[20] Negative opinions pervaded all social groups and regions to differing degrees, particularly those without direct refugee contact.[21]

Jordanians quickly concluded that Syrians were taking more than their fair share of national resources and opportunities while also benefiting from international aid.[22] The large number of organizations focused on the Syrians gave the impression that they were receiving aid from numerous sources. "They are guests here and should make do as we do, live on limited amounts of water," one local NGO leader stated.[23] "All the *zakat* [Islamic tithing or charity] organizations switched their focus to the Syrians, and Gulf charities and merchants all gave money to the refugees," one elder in Ramtha stated.[24]

The immediate problem was lack of space and rent, and later lack of jobs and water. Housing was a major problem,[25] and reports of Syrians purchasing land only exacerbated the animosity.[26] Stories circulated of children forced to move in with their grandparents because their own families were evicted so that landlords could rent their homes to Syrians.[27] One UN employee recounted that he was in a governor's office in the North of Jordan while the governor was trying to reconcile two brothers. One brother wanted to kick the other out of his rental property in order to rent it to Syrians.[28] Jordanians complained about the negative effects on services and housing created by the Syrians, even in Ramtha with its tight social and kinship networks to Syrians across the border.[29] Problems in public education were blamed by the state on the Syrians, and parents mentioned their frustration with the lack of improvement to schooling. Long-discussed changes were put on hold, they claimed, of course due to the Syrians.[30] Individuals complained that Syrians ruined the infrastructure and health care, and stole electricity and water. In addition they felt that doctors had to work long hours and had no time for native Jordanians.[31]

In Lebanon, people believed that Syrians changed the supply and quality of water and energy either to a great extent (66%) or somewhat (27%).[32] Lebanese blamed the increasingly polluted water on the Syrians, and public opinion held that the water supply was also threatened by them.[33] Several polls found that degradations to the quality and quantity of available water were identified as a threat created by the Syrian refugees.[34] Lack of proper sanitation for the refugees, who lived in informal settlements instead of camps, meant that human waste was often buried, polluting the groundwater table. Seventy-nine percent of municipalities in Lebanon stated that providing services—water, electricity, and education for example—was their greatest challenge, and directly affected the Lebanese population.[35] Indeed, these fears about water ranked higher than concerns about the much-discussed sectarian balance.[36] Residents of Saadiya, near Zahle, Lebanon, blamed the polluted water on the Syrians and gave that as their reason for wanting the Syrians gone.[37]

As the Syrian presence in the country wore on and showed no signs of ending in the near future, sectarian concerns increased in importance. Most Lebanese in the early phases remained unconcerned about the local confessional demographics,[38] with the exception of the Shi'a-dominated South, where Syrians experienced more harassment.[39] Deeper analysis has demonstrated that sectarian conflict is compounded by other existing factors or becomes active once another conflict arises.[40] Years into the refugee crisis, the Syrian presence was understood to be dangerous, due to the realization that Syrian children were being born unregistered and the recognition of the sheer numbers of Syrians that were now residing in the country, according to interviewees.[41] People told me that the youth will be a problem when they grow up, since they do not go to school.[42] Syrians use resources but do not pay for them, many said, giving them an advantage and no reason to ration their use of resources. They asserted that Syrians use electricity and water but don't pay for it, that Syrians open the faucet and don't close it, wasting water.[43] I heard this same water story more than a dozen times, in both countries, despite UNHCR and economic reports that Syrians actually do not use much water at all.[44]

A prominent theme among interviewees was the idea that Syrians are ungrateful guests: this is not the Syrians' house (country) so why should they care about it? They should be grateful for what they are given, but instead they cause problems. We want to feel this nation is for the people (citizens) who live here, people told me.[45] The implication is that as guests, Syrians should behave better, since they live off the hospitality of the host country. And what bad guests they were! "They ruined infrastructure," another stated.[46] "We got the worst of the Syrians—they do drugs, have problems among each other, some just came for the money."[47] Jordanians felt less safe and that the entrance of Syrians to their neighborhoods created insecurity.[48] One elder in a border town with close kin links to Syrians stated that parents do not want their kids going out now because they do not want them to associate with people who their parents do not know, who do drugs coming from Syria. "Many of these Syrians have morally bad behavior," he said, including begging and not paying rent, despite having money stashed away.[49]

Syrians were believed to increase traffic, although tourists actually have more cars than Syrians. "Syrians took employment from our children, and are taking the place of Jordanians in universities," one businesswoman told me.[50] "The Syrians take everything—business, schools, water, electricity—and don't leave anything for the Lebanese. It is safe now, they should go back. They sent all the poor Syrians to Lebanon, this is a fact."[51] The numbers of beggars and street merchants increased, without it being clear whether they were Syrian or citizens. In Beirut's busy streets, beggars had their children with them, who would play in the streets. People became tired of them asking for money at the same place every day. And their numbers appeared to grow. Added to this, drivers had to dodge the children playing on the streets. Litter was blamed on the refugees, who were supposedly unable to put garbage in the trash can even "if it was in front of them."[52] At the same time, the Syrians in Lebanon worked for Lebanese as dumpster recyclers.

The overwhelming majority of Lebanese viewed Syrians as dangerous to their values and to the economy, and so they supported restrictions on Syrians' freedom of movement. In the northern Akkar region, a high percentage felt that Syrians were a security threat.[53] In one poll, half of Lebanese stated the presence of the refugees makes them feel unsafe.[54] The public assumed there was an increase in crime, and blamed the Syrians. In one typical instance, a Syrian employee was immediately accused when a young girl was killed on her way home from church. That crime was actually committed by a Lebanese man.[55]

People complained of their traditional recreation locations no longer being the same due to the presence of the Syrians, that the refugees have taken over the villages. One *mukhtar* (local administrative official) in Lebanon said, "The Lebanese has become a refugee in his own country."[56] Other host citizens said, "We have paid for this crisis. Syrians get benefits from the UN, rent, money for food, while the Lebanese goes without work."[57] The Syrians are criminals and dangerous, some declared.[58] An educator stated, "The Syrians here are the bad ones, from the rural areas. The city ones went to Beirut or abroad."[59] Others asserted, "The Syrians sit together at night, so we don't go out anymore. . . . They have different habits from us, a different culture. They are happy living in garages," since they are getting money from the UN.[60] Fears about going out at night due to supposed threats from the Syrians and their different, obnoxious habits, were expressed in both countries. Even those who had been sympathetic earlier later turned against the refugees, arguing that Lebanese society could no longer tolerate them. Hostility was voiced and supported by elites and academics, who claimed that Syrians have ruined Lebanon.[61]

Everywhere there was discussion of the presumed fact that Syrians were taking jobs and stressing services, complete with examples of friends and relatives out of work because Syrians worked harder, longer, and for lower pay.[62] In the North of both countries this is true to some extent. Certainly, the Syrians are pushing local public services beyond their current limits. The feeling, however, quickly spread to the national level, as those in the rest of the country repeated the same claims.[63] Small retail and service enterprises—like hair salons and small grocers—reportedly now hired four or five Syrian boys (eight to ten years old) to take the place of one Lebanese one, while paying the same amount overall. More people could get their groceries delivered this way, generating increased business.[64] The belief that Syrians have taken all the local jobs, and "every waiter" is Syrian, was expressed in both countries, but more so in Lebanon. Yet, when I asked about waiters in specific restaurants in Lebanon, few turned out to be Syrian.[65]

In Lebanon, feelings toward Syrians became worse after the Syrian presidential election in May 2014.[66] Most Lebanese outside Hizbollah supported the Syrian revolution, and believed that the Syrian refugees were victims of a cruel regime.[67] Refugee actions in the Syrian presidential elections, however, were experienced as a slap in the face to their hospitality. During the elections, masses of Syrians were photographed returning to Syria to vote, and Assad won by a landslide. Although this massive victory was not a surprising feat in an authoritarian regime, the Lebanese interpreted the vote for a dictator that the refugees were supposedly running away from to mean that these Syrians were not really refugees. Instead, the refugees were coldly using up Lebanese hospitality and resources. "If they like him so much, then they should go back and live there," Lebanese reasoned.[68] Researchers I spoke with told a different story: there were rumors that Syria would punish relatives of refugees who did not vote for Assad, or that they would not be allowed to ever return to Syria if they did not vote.[69]

The calls for Syrians to be sent back to safe or buffer zones (by Lebanese), or confined to camps (in both countries), increased over time. People stated that isolating Syrians would decrease the effect of the refugees on their resources, jobs, and daily lives. At a minimum, people wanted the Syrians to stop coming. By the fall of 2016, 85 percent of Jordanians supported either a full or partial closing of the borders to Syrian refugees.[70] By 2017, close to half of all Jordanians considered Syrians outside the camps to have a negative effect on their security, and the number of Jordanians who felt positively about Syrians had dropped by half since 2011. Positive opinions of Syrians went from over half of those surveyed before the war to about a quarter. Over three-quarters of the surveyed felt refugees negatively affected the economy and government services. Yet only a small number (7%) had actual conflicts with Syrians, and almost a third of those were over employment.[71]

One NGO head in Mafraq said, "They don't stay in the camps, which is wrong. They should be confined for security reasons. There is already pressure on our services—they are really bad. Now rent has doubled. They all work illegally. Everywhere you go you see Syrians working instead of Jordanians—restaurants, stores. Syrians take three or four Jordanian dinars per day instead of the ten Jordanians need." She continued that the government increased taxes and prices on fuel and fees because it can't fund its expanded budget. So it takes from the people, she said.[72]

Scapegoating Discourses by the State and the Media

State elites continually decried Syrians' effect on the national budget, the economy overall, services, and crucial resources. Such scapegoating discourses of blaming another group for state problems have long histories in these countries, and have been used to displace blame from the state's own faults. According to some analysts, scapegoating was a policy of the Lebanese state, intended to ward off threats to the core sectarian system.[73] Of course, state elites could believe the statements, yet their timing often came on the heels of critiques of the state in precisely those areas they blamed on the Syrians. After electricity failures, Lebanese state officials would state that if it were not for the Syrians, they could have fixed the electricity problem. Increases in the price of bread in Jordan have been blamed on the 2.5 million foreigners using the bread subsidies without contributing to the tax base, adding to budget difficulties.[74] In addition, the states used the effects of the Syrians to beg the international community for money.[75] Jordan's King Abdullah blamed diminishing resources on the Syrian refugees and in the next breath turned to the international aid community for help. Should they refuse to help Jordan "shoulder the burdens of the Syrian crisis," the king stated, Jordan would take whatever measures it needs to for its country.[76] The implicit threat was to refuse entry to Syrians and even kick out Syrian refugees who were living in Jordan, which could lead to more migration to Europe. The king and government elites reiterated their point that refugees and non-nationals were an unsustainable burden on the country.[77] According to the Jordanian government, Syrians cost the government $3,000 each per year through their use of subsidized goods and services, and the refugees accounted for half of the health budget.[78] Jordanian representatives continued to point out the potential cost to security in Jordan of Syrian terrorism and crime. The director of public finance stated that Syrians affected the Jordanian national budget through increased expenditures in public services and infrastructure.[79] "The official government discourse," one UNDP employee stated, "is that all would be well without the refugees, and we need support from the international community to pay for a problem we did not have a hand in creating."[80] The broad purpose of this discourse is to gain aid, which Jordan has, but the rhetoric remains influential among the general public.

Local media parroted government claims, popular opinions, and rumors blaming the Syrians, often without supporting data.[81] In one analysis early in the refugees' tenure, media were found to have politicized the refugee crisis by making it a political issue. Not only did the media link Syrians with crime, lack of jobs, and price rises, but they also questioned the use of aid money and government's ability to handle the situation.[82] The independent radio program "Eye on the Media," monitoring the coverage of Syrians, noted the prevalence of hate speech and blame on the Syrians for unemployment. They concluded that Syrians were an "easy target" for discontent.[83] Likewise, the media watch group Akeed, analyzing thousands of articles, observed that Jordan's media uses subtle, not overt, hate speech. In the bulk of media articles, Syrians were depicted as featureless masses and were dehumanized.[84] Social media have been even worse, rife with hostility toward the Syrians and encouraging the use of violence against their property.[85]

Early in the crisis, Lebanese officials declared the country would be unable to handle the Syrians, that their health system was so overwhelmed it could collapse, and new diseases would spread.[86] Lebanese elites have been creative in their blame, ignoring historical roots for current problems, and have been bolder than Jordanians in their animosity toward the refugees.[87] In one incident, the environmental minister stated his clear conclusion that the pollution of a town's river was caused by Syrians throwing trash into it, ignoring the nearby garbage bins. Yet that river was polluted by fertilizers and domestic sources as early as 1999. The minister's evidence amounted to repetition of rumors that Syrians littered, and the demographic reality that three hundred Lebanese lived there alongside four times as many Syrians.[88] Some politicians were worse than others, stating that the Syrians threaten Lebanon itself and the refugees caused Lebanon's economic problems.[89] President Michel Aoun's first speech in office requested repatriation of the refugees, whether war continued or not.[90] Aoun repeated often that the greatest challenge facing Lebanon was the Syrians.[91] He described the refugees as an "existential threat" that is "exhausting" Lebanon.[92] Even Sa'ad Hariri, viewed as more sympathetic to the refugees, declared at an international donor conference that Lebanon is now one big refugee camp.[93] Other elites joined in this trend. The head of the (Christian) Phalange Party declared the Syrians a national threat. "How can Lebanon's economic, social, political, and security capabilities take on such a burden?"[94] A leading religious figure declared that the economic problems of Lebanese were due to the refugees, who took locals' jobs and burdened the country.[95]

Media coverage in Lebanon went from sympathy at the outset to a split discourse, which treated Syrians as both a humanitarian issue and a threat. This split emerged partly as a reaction to international media and INGO critiques of Lebanon's treatment of the Syrians, to which Lebanese responded with stereotypes of the Syrians. In fact, some clearly detect a difference in how INGOs characterize Jordan's treatment of the refugees versus Lebanon's,[96] although these are surface impressions only.[97] Once the new discourse emerged, media routinely emphasized only the negative and not the positive economic effects of the demographic influx of refugees.[98] Further, media in Lebanon blamed current changes and problems on the Syrians, whose actions were "alien to the Lebanese way of life," despite those problems having pre-dated the arrival of the Syrian refugees.[99] Other complaints include loud motorcycles, associated with the Syrians, as well as Syrians taking over the traditional marketplaces and businesses. Fear and threat from the refugees dominated coverage. Media used extreme words including "massive," "overwhelmed," "torrential," "deluge," and "startling," among diverse other metaphors, to describe the refugee influx. Facts were joined to rumors and opinion, including expressions of animosity. Media used words and discourse that harkened back to the Lebanese civil war, triggering more popular anxiety. This "new" form of racism emphasized cultural differences and not racial ones. Negative news pieces on security were overwhelmingly focused on the refugees, mainly Syrian but also Palestinian, who were equated to the dangerous "stranger."[100]

Journalists mixed the terms "migrant" and "refugee," weakening and delegitimizing the claim of Syrians to refugee status. Prominent airtime was given to coverage of arrests due to drugs, assault, and theft, as well as security issues connected to the refugees, with journalists taking security services' reports verbatim. The image of Syrians that developed among the public closely paralleled these concerns and reports.[101] Articles were published claiming strangers (Syrians) were stealing Lebanese journalism jobs, echoing government ministers' language.[102] One television network "pranked" a refugee in an alarmingly humiliating way, including forcing him to remove his clothes.[103] In another incident, a journalist implied that an attack on an individual may have been warranted because the victim had a "non-Lebanese" (code for Syrian) accent.[104]

Resource scarcity was attributed to the refugees, as newspapers matter-of-factly stated that, due to the Syrians, there would be water and electricity shortages.[105] In Lebanon, a key current concern was the health effects of pollution and waste. There was ample coverage and numerous discussions about contaminated and cancer-causing air and water pollution, trash burning, and contaminated water used to fertilize vegetables and fruit. "Eating poison" was a theme. One Lebanese outlet reported that air pollution increased after the Syrians arrived, quoting an early World Bank study on the excessive cost of garbage and waste from the refugees.[106]

Violence by Host Citizens against the Refugees

This resentment and animosity resulted in conflict and "challenges to social cohesion," as the humanitarian organizations phrase it.[107] Almost three-quarters of Jordanians in the northern governorates with the majority of the refugee population said that competition or presumed competition (with the Syrians) over water, jobs, waste, and inflation generated tension in their community with the refugees.[108] Most was kept at a low level. Incidents in schools were reported in early incidents of violent hostility.[109] Among the early instigators of violence was the "Nashama al-Mafraq," discussed more in chapter 4, an organization that protested against the presence of the Syrian refugees with riots and tire burnings. They demanded that Syrians be deported.[110] In other early incidents in northern Jordan, Jordanians and refugees hurled stones at each other.[111]

In Lebanon, for various reasons, the violence against refugees was far worse. First, Lebanon's central government is not even minimally effective, and practical solutions were left to municipalities without adequate resources. This generated space for volunteers, or vigilantes, depending on the perspective, to fill in the gaps. These mobs often judge and punish according to community consensus, not rule of law. Second, Lebanon experienced more of Syria's conflict overflowing its borders and affecting its civilians. Third, the response in Jordan to early tensions was a mobilization of the humanitarian community to respond to Jordanian host community needs, with the express purpose of alleviating the hostility. INGOs focused on conflict prevention. Social cohesion measures and remedies were quickly enacted, channeling around half of overt aid to the Jordanian population. Their grievances were thus addressed. In Lebanon, by contrast, humanitarian organizations were uncoordinated and hampered in their work by the central government. Fourth, demographics are important. The refugees in Jordan settled in sparsely populated areas for the most part, while in Lebanon they caused overcrowding. Not only are the refugees in Lebanon double the number of the Syrians in Jordan, but they form a much larger percentage of the Lebanese population, making their presence almost unavoidable.

Violence against Syrians and limitations on their mobility were the main signs of conflict in Lebanon. Curfews on Syrians came early, established by the municipalities, and spread in later years to numerous locations. Municipalities were left on their own to make policies since the national government had abdicated that role.[112] Large banners announced the curfews, addressed either to "foreigners," which were limited to Syrians and excluded Westerners, or to "our brothers and sisters from Syria," instructing them to not leave their homes from dusk to dawn. These curfews were of questionable legality, if not being illegal outright. The curfew strategy was used in at least fifty-four localities, usually with the goal of increasing the perception of security. It would "calm down the residents." Some justified curfews on the basis that there were not enough police due to lack of funding.[113] Some municipalities relied on informal local policing, or militias.[114] In one case a man was beaten by one such local patrol or village watch group when he refused to give his identification card to them. They presumed (wrongly) that he was Syrian.[115]

The presence of Syrians was believed to increase crime and terrorism. While Syrians constitute a third of all prisoners in Lebanon,[116] people perceived that they got away with crimes and threatened Lebanon's security. "The police won't arrest the Syrians, no matter what they do. They can commit a crime right in front of the police," one municipal official in northern Lebanon stated.[117] Syrian military training, three years for each adult male, is used to justify numerous checkpoints throughout the country since they are perceived as well-trained.[118] Indeed, such fears combine with the reality that Syrians or associated jihadists have in fact attacked the security services and committed terrorist acts among the civilian population. Increases in the prevalence of drugs and drug-related crime were associated with the Syrians, partly due to the rise of drugs used in the Syrian civil war.[119]

Elites emphasized the security risk of Syrians.[120] Some violence against Syrians followed violence against Lebanese, such as when Lebanese soldiers were beheaded by jihadists.[121] Anger was directed against Syrians at large, with attacks on refugee camps and attacks on and kidnappings of Syrians.[122] Violence and discrimination against Syrians in Lebanon became bolder after such events.[123] In several cases, Syrians were told they would be kidnapped and hurt if they did not leave the town that day, either through posted flyers or WhatsApp.[124] Human Rights Watch recorded numerous incidents that the authorities did not stop and even watched. In one, citizens forced Syrian men in the road into traffic.[125]

When elites in Jordan and Lebanon blamed Syrians for economic and state capacity problems, they perhaps hoped to ride the wave of hostility against the Syrians and distract citizens from attention to state failures, in typical scapegoating fashion. Syrians were blamed for a mix of impacts, both real and perceived. Mixing concrete effects with rumors arguably made scapegoating discourses even more compelling. Aspects of reports that were already believed to be correct made other parts of the stories—true or not—more plausible. The extra population did affect supplies of scarce goods and services, and data substantiate locals' common-sense conclusions on this point. Water, electricity, space at schools, waste removal, and policing were all stretched to accommodate the rapid increase in population. Added to the animosity for stressing crucial services and goods was resentment against the refugees for being more "privileged" than nationals. In reality, a majority of Syrians in both countries were poor, in debt, and lacked sufficient food.[126]

In line with a common global anti-refugee narrative, a discourse of superiority and inferiority overlay feelings of hostility and resentment, of presumed innate privilege versus those without such.[127] Refugees were seen as unjustly receiving more than nationals, and, according to public opinion, foreigners should not receive better or more of anything than citizens. In Jordan, there was a deep sense of deprivation, inequality, and being left out. Previous entitlements were whittled down by increased taxation and the removal of subsidies. The state promised the Jordanian East Bankers a livelihood—at least, that was their perception. They see themselves as the "real" nation, sons of the soil, and thus partly this is a straight-forward nativist reaction. However, the similarity of Syrian and Jordanian cultures led humanitarian organizations to stress the brotherhood of these cultures. For the Lebanese, a sense of entitlement and right to services is new. They compare the paltry services they receive from the state or municipality with what they view as more extensive aid to the Syrians. They feel that if the Syrians, who are foreigners, can receive these goods and services, shouldn't they as well? Nationals began to demand what refugees received, directing themselves toward the state, and, as chapter 4 shows, their requests were often met by states and INGOs. The raised expectations on the state by the Lebanese, and the persistent expectations of the Jordanians, demonstrate that scapegoating attempts by these states have failed.

4

GRIEVANCES AGAINST GOVERNANCE

Clearly the citizens of Jordan and Lebanon had no problem blaming the Syrian refugees for their troubles, both those caused or perceived to be caused by the refugees and those that were pre-existing. The states likewise blamed the Syrians, perhaps attempting to distract attention from their own failings in typical scapegoating fashion. Identifying a minority or less powerful social group as culpable for society's ills has a long history, rallying majority groups around a common enemy. While citizens faulted the Syrians, they laid responsibility for remedying those problems at the feet of the state, a dynamic that the modern experience of scapegoating would not have predicted. Understanding the original meaning of scapegoating can help explain this unlikely outcome. Scapegoats were things, animals, or people that could not only be blamed for all of the community's ills, but who could transport those problems away from the community. Troubling issues would then be eliminated with the departure of the scapegoat, essentially fixing the pressing issues of a society.

While this use of scapegoating entailed a mythical belief system far different from our own, the ancient definition provides an answer to what we might call the dual blame witnessed in these cases. In societies with real daily problems, people can fault one group for causing the situation while at the same time holding another responsible for fixing it. Jordanians and Lebanese blamed Syrians in the causal sense, but directed blame at the state for failing to solve those issues.

The nature of the grievances is key to why a solution coming from the state was felt to be needed. Grievances identified in previous chapters affected the ability of Jordanians and Lebanese to live their daily lives. Early effects of the Syrian

79

refugee influx included stress on existing weaknesses in resource and service infrastructure tied to goods and services crucial to everyday life: water, electricity, housing, and waste. Early protests to secure these goods and services bore the hallmarks of crisis mobilizing or movements of daily-life disruption, as they were little-organized and often violent. Refugees' presumed privileges over nationals resulted in increased expectations of the state and demands for similar goods and services. Large amounts of aid flowing to the states, as economic conditions and livelihoods continued to decline, fed ideas that state elites were purposely taking the money for themselves at the expense of the citizenry (corruption) or that state policies were skewed toward the rich. While the protests were significant, they nonetheless were muted by a general societal fear of organizing, mixed with specific fears of an overflow of the Syrian chaos and of increased repression by security forces already tasked with imposing harsh security at the borders and internally toward the Syrians. Later protests combined the early grievances over fundamental goods and services under a general banner of state failure and corruption, demonstrating a higher level of organization than the early single-issue protests and a national, antisystemic discourse.

However unorganized or small some protests were, these conflicts were sufficient for humanitarian organizations and the Jordanian government to get the message. Humanitarian organizations altered their strategy and began catering to the locals in addition to the refugees.[1] For Jordan, the location of refugees among the state's traditional support base made these protests particularly dangerous, even as protests in other locations went unheeded. The Jordanian government appeased these protesters and quickly granted their requests. Lebanon's state elites, by contrast, have historically been able to mute societal discontent more effectively through partisan politics, reaffirming sectarianism and large-scale clientelism at the ballot box. Lebanon's electoral sectarianism and consociational system have been quite effective in shielding the state from social challenges, backed up by intense social sanctioning.[2] Thus, Lebanese had little faith in the ability of protest to enact real change while the state had tools to dismantle the effectiveness of protest, even if protesters succeeded in creating a large coalition. The Lebanese state's unwillingness to act and its incapacity also informed its failure to concede to the protesters.

In this chapter I take on the second part of the dual reaction to hosting refugees. In chapter 3 I showed how animosity and a sense of privilege fueled overt violence against and blame of the refugees for new and long-standing problems, as the theory of scapegoating would suggest. Yet, to the states' dismay, blame did not stop there. The second part of the reaction was to look to governance to fix the problems, a turn strengthened in Lebanon and affirmed in Jordan. Worse, from the states' perspectives, new expectations and demands arose for the same or better goods and services that refugees were perceived to receive. I here discuss the turn to the state and citizens' reasoning for why the state is responsible for problems in services, resources, and the economy. While they were still resentful and placed blame on the refugees, citizens wanted solutions, often responding to the state's attempts at scapegoating by blaming the state itself. This strong sense that the state needed to provide solutions did not always lead to protest and was mitigated by security fears and expectations of a response by authorities. Security was a top concern, more operative in Lebanon than Jordan. I also discuss the protests that occurred against the state over infrastructure grievances or effects directly due to the Syrians that states were called upon to solve.

Mobilizing and Threats

People do not immediately or easily mobilize over their grievances, and the protests described below should be viewed in light of the strong disincentives to activism present in both countries. Decades of research have shown that deprivation and grievances may be necessary, but are not close to sufficient conditions for mobilizing. Resources, methods and locations for mobilizing, and the perceived balance of threat and positive opportunity are some of the factors that must be present before grievance and deprivation turn into action.[3] Framing, a way of prioritizing particular events and understanding the issues to generate an overall conclusion, is central to mobilizing.[4] Frames can convince people that their own action can obtain change and that radical change outside the normal political channels is needed. The issue people ultimately protest about needs to be new: a change in something that is perceived to be important to daily life. Expectations are important.[5] If people were not used to having bread before, and still do not have bread, there is no change to rally around. Further, mass mobilization is easier when the lost good or service is irreplaceable. Locally relevant goods with no easy replacement (from the private sector, for example) are most likely to translate to activism, since their lack is felt more acutely.

Numerous factors inhibited mobilization in these countries. The existence of alternative private provisioning of goods in Lebanon, the lack of expectations of state services in both countries, and the security threats connected to the spillover of the Syrian civil war and ISIS all dampened the willingness of the population to protest over the scarcity of goods and services. Beyond all these factors, these states have historically used scapegoating to prevent societal protest. Governments use scapegoating and blame outgroups for their own failings, seemingly to distract from a focus on fundamental institutional and policy changes.[6] Lebanon and Jordan have indeed blamed refugees, as have citizens, as the previous chapters show. However, an outcome not predicted by scapegoating theory is that citizens also articulated a recognition that the states are ultimately at fault, as this chapter and the next attest. Jordanians and Lebanese mobilized, in spite of scapegoating and the obstacles discussed in this chapter, demonstrating both the failure of such attempted distraction and the raised expectations of the state due to the presence of the refugees.

Lebanon has private suppliers for many services the state fails to provide, in contrast to Jordan. Middle- and upper-class Lebanese purchase private water and electricity.[7] These classes are the ones with the most political weight and most likely to mobilize. The number of Lebanese able to afford private services is low and declining. In 2013, only about a quarter of Lebanese could easily pay their bills.[8] The others adapt or do without.[9] People outside Beirut suffer the most as their incomes and alternative service infrastructures are both lacking. "Business provides services, but it cannot cover everything or everyone," one man from Wadi Khaled stated. "For that, you need a state," he said.[10] Without such private-sector services, there would be more mobilization over electricity and water, one analyst of labor protest stated.[11] Some goods, however, are ill-suited to the private market as it is structured, like trash and sewage disposal. There is no parallel coping mechanism for trash in Lebanon as for electricity and water. One can pay to have one's own trash removed, but movement outside the home or village means one will still encounter trash piled in the streets.[12]

Further, expectations and ideas of rights apply not only to government in general but also to different levels of governance, and conceptions of these differ between the two countries. Lebanese do not expect much of their state for services, while East Banker Jordanians have clear expectations and senses of rights. Some services are, for historical and institutional reasons, believed to belong to either the local or national government's realm of responsibility.[13] In the absence of state provisioning in Lebanon, for example, some towns have organized trash collection.[14]

In addition to the system-maintenance dynamics discussed in chapter 1, for both countries incentives for organizing were muted by the threat of insecurity and repression, depressing demands for change in the system. The Syrian crisis generated a popular fear of violent spillover and an enhanced role for the domestic security services. In the colorful words of an older Jordanian near the Syrian border, "even if the government is eating the people [taking everything they have], they will be quiet if there is security."[15] Scholars of social movement theory have put it more prosaically, finding that the balance of threats is important to the question of mobilizing, and have included the variable of threats among the political opportunities prominent in social movement theory.[16] While populaces in both countries fear an overflow of the war,[17] Jordan has contained the majority of threats to its security. In Lebanon, insecurity is a lived reality, magnified by the fear of a return of the country's long civil war.[18] Dozens of terrorist attacks by Syrian-rebel-affiliated groups have occurred, not counting the hundreds of street battles and fights among unorganized Lebanese, reflecting the Syrian conflict's divisions.[19] Battles in Jordan have been few, mainly limited to the border and its environs (e.g., Irbid), with an occasional attack inside the country, notably, the 2016 attack in the Karak crusader castle.[20] Those involved and killed, apart from the militants themselves, were mainly members of the security services, with the exception of the Karak attack.

"People became aware of the need for strong security services with the refugee and Islamist crises," one academic explained.[21] Many discussions mentioned fear of Syria's chaos spreading, of radicals or extremists infiltrating demonstrations. Lebanese feared that protests would be taken advantage of by terrorists in the country. Jordan had emphasized the threat of violent Islamism to repress opposition groups as early as 2011.[22] It also changed the legal framework for protest, altering its terrorism law to allow punishment for broad crimes under its auspices, and charging individuals with terrorism for acts more akin to public disorder.[23] Commentators termed this "negative stability": Jordanians might be dissatisfied with many aspects of their state, but the lawlessness in neighboring Syria helped dissuade Jordanians from pursuing civil or violent actions that might destabilize their country.[24] Some have even labeled the Syrian war a "gift for the king," since Jordanians became more appreciative and less willing to criticize the monarchy after its outbreak.[25] "After all, at least we don't have the chaos they have in Syria," Jordanians would say.[26] People's gratitude for their stability showed in opinion polls, as prior negative evaluations of the Jordanian government moderated due purely to stability and security issues.[27] Not only did popular views of government change in the short term, due to the public's prioritization of security over goods and services, but the war next door offered a path for these states to increase repression. Jordan "doubled down" on its repressive and nondemocratic policies, regulating speech, the media, and public gatherings.[28]

Despite negative stability repressing mobilization, the lack of some goods crucial to livelihood pressed the issue. The absence of water demonstrates the extreme. If citizens don't have water, does it matter if the government represses protesters? Water is life, interviewees often stated, and it is their right.[29] Heat and lack of electricity threaten life as well as the lifestyles people are accustomed to, and waste piled up in the street can turn into a serious health risk, as mentioned to me in numerous conversations.[30] Observers and researchers pinpointed 2013 as a key turning point when grievances about lack of crucial resources outweighed fears about security. Indeed, although in that year the threat of ISIS became real, as it began governing in northern Syria, INGO officials stated that initial housing protests in Jordan demonstrated that the calculus surrounding protest participation had changed.[31] Later, expectations would change, as Syrians were perceived as receiving superior goods and services to those of citizens, leading to more protest.

Turning to the State for Solutions

Clearly there is no lack of evidence that there was popular hostility toward Syrians and that blame was directed at them for all sorts of presumed effects. Yet the closer I came to the refugee-hosting areas, the more the story began to change from one of pure hostility to one mixed with critiques of governance: "those Syrians do x, but the state is not helping us and is helping the Syrians." This discursive frame would grow from those particular areas to the national level. Citizens of both countries referred to governance responsibilities and the failure of their own governments, national and local, to protect them or compensate them.[32] The immediate problems were those generated by the demographic effect of the refugees as they stressed infrastructure that had long bordered on insufficient for citizens. This extreme pressure on the systems highlighted the existing problems and pushed citizen intolerance for such incapacity to the point of activism. While the government blamed problems such as lack of water and electricity on the refugees, Lebanese stopped believing it, and they blamed the state instead.[33] Researchers in Jordan stated the same. "People's first object of blame is the Syrians," one stated, "but, after a bit of thought, they say the government is ultimately responsible" for this allocation of benefits to refugees and not Jordanians.[34] As one Jordanian of Palestinian descent said, "Syrians caused our problems. But the government has to do something about it. We people have no influence, no power, we can't do anything. Who else can, besides the government?"[35]

Throughout interviews and discussions, there was a clear search for someone to be responsible for all these refugees, particularly among those living nearby and suffering from the lack of services. Someone or some institution should take control over the situation and mute the negative effects. In one poor northern region, a municipal assistant who is politically close to the Syrian refugees complained that the Syrians entered into and began to control everything, even "Lebanon's own house," because there was no state to regulate them.[36] Unfortunately, he stated, there "is no substitute for the state." In particular he complained about waste removal and insecurity. Another interviewee, the *mukhtar* of two small towns, asserted the same, that "the Syrian presence is unregulated here (*ashwa'iyya*), there are no laws. No one helps the Lebanese when the Syrians compete [successfully] against Lebanese businesses. The Syrians don't have to pay rent or for their water or electricity. . . . In every house here, you will hear them complain about and wish for the state to help," he stated. "Lebanese don't have a state or the UN to help them. We just want to be employed."[37] A sheikh in Tripoli summed up his discussion of Lebanon's problems: "There is no state—we have obligations to the state but no rights, no services from it." There is a clear relationship between services and state corruption, he said.[38] "Trash and sewage is a big problem the state does not help us with. The state is supposed to help us with sewage, trash, water and electricity—it is the state's responsibility,"[39] according to a local official. "People here want a state," a Lebanese military officer said. "There is corruption everywhere, at all levels. You can't get anything fixed without a connection. The simplest daily necessities are a hassle, taking about 20 percent of your day. . . . The waste problem has created cancer and health problems. The corruption is obvious now," he said.[40]

Some of the criticism of the state was a direct result of hostility toward the refugees, essentially asking the state to shield them from the negative effects of the refugees. This was particularly the case in regard to employment and business. Even though citizens' reactions to Syrian businesses and workers may have been xenophobic or based on a concern for their own profits and wages, they were still asking for the state to expand its reach. By demanding that states do more to regulate labor and business, the public's reaction demonstrates Polanyi's double movement in a different context. Neoliberal free movement of labor and competition was not welcome, and in response to the entrance of foreign business and workers, citizens have turned to the state. This is particularly interesting in the Lebanese context of a minimal state, where numerous regions of the country usually want nothing more than to be left alone.[41] In Jordan, the reaction is less of a break with the past, since the state has been active and supportive for a segment of the population—the East Bankers—who are engaged mainly in public-sector work. Still, observers in Jordan have noted the effect also, as the informal sector, which previously desired to remain unregulated, began using terms that opposed free market rhetoric, including calling for labor control and regulation or other state actions in support of citizen laborers.[42] Analysts make the same point, that it is government's responsibility to control foreign labor, and that lack of government control, combined with lower salaries for Syrians, is the reason Syrians are pushing locals out of jobs.[43]

Citizens said that it was the state's responsibility to either prevent the Syrians from affecting their status, lives, or access to basic necessities, or to fix the effects that resulted. One municipal authority stated, "we need harder laws here in Lebanon like they have in Jordan—the Jordanian government does not let the refugees take everything and not share," he explained.[44] In his opinion, the state is clearly responsible for the problems generated by the presence of the refugees. Lebanese employers are partly at fault, members of one focus group stated. Together with the government, they are responsible for the negative employment effects on Lebanese workers. "It is the fault of the state which has driven us to this degrading level."[45] "There are different levels and categories of blame," the head of one major INGO in Lebanon stated. "First there is corruption and corrupt politicians who are blamed. Then, the increasing number of refugees in communities. People split the blame," he explained.[46]

Interviewees felt that the government should support the refugees—they took them from the camps and let them work, in order to get money from Europe (part of the agreements with Europe discussed in chapter 5). "This is on the international community." Otherwise, they reasoned, "the refugees would steal, put pressure on our jobs, and decrease our pay. Prices rose because of the refugees [outside of camps]; even Beirut is cheaper than Jordan now," interviewees stated.[47] "Thirty-percent of all municipalities are in debt," a state official from Jordan stated. "The aid from the central government is not enough," he said.[48] Others have reported the same, criticizing the state's actions with that aid money. They contend that Jordan received so much money but still does not have enough medical care or jobs.[49] "It is the government's fault. They say government gets tons of money, but they don't give it to the people. It is the donors' fault also. They do not give enough. There is pressure on health and education, the environment is bad, schools and towns are crowded. People think this."[50] "We have two problems. First, funding, and second, the politicians," another said.[51] A high-level employee at the state electricity company said there was no reason not to install meters and charge Syrians for electricity. "So why don't they?"[52]

The belief that the situation is the responsibility of the state was bolstered by the amount of aid money coming in on behalf of the states hosting the Syrians. The public is well aware of these amounts and this helped to create expectations.[53] Money given to the central government is key to the resentment against the Syrians, one local official stated.[54] Aid given to the state because of the Syrians feeds anger against the state, one academic stated, "because it goes into corruption and then people are jealous of it."[55] "Lots of money is coming in because of the Syrians," one leader of a local NGO stated. "Where does that money go? Government pockets."[56] Numerous people reiterated this assertion, that aid is clearly coming in but they see no help, so it must be stolen.[57] Analysts noted the increasing expectations of the Jordanian government by citizens. In part the government has created this problem itself, from its continual announcements that new influxes of international aid, intended to compensate for hosting the Syrians, will improve the quality of life for Jordanians.

Interviewees explained that the politicians blamed the Syrians for infrastructure problems and that the politicians were then getting all this money for problems the Syrians supposedly caused. But the people turned against the politicians, saying the money that is coming in is not well spent. "You say you are getting all this money and nothing is happening (changing)—so now people blamed government corruption. The corruption is obvious now."[58] While I never brought up the topic of corruption, as it was outside the focus of my study, the sentiment of corruption as a central problem was mentioned in the majority of interviews and casual discussions with nationals in both countries. In some cases, similar phrases were repeated, that "the corruption has become obvious," and "everyone knows it now."[59] "Society is divided," an INGO worker stated. "In the back of their minds they realize it is their government that is failing. Sometimes they blame the Syrians, but more now they realize it [the Syrian issue] is used by politicians for their own benefit."[60] One Jordanian water expert, who headed operations to improve water in the refugee-concentrated areas, explained why citizens blame the state. "If I live in Mafraq [near the refugees where water is scarce] and see Syrians with water, able to buy it because they get UN vouchers for water, I start fights with him and with the government. The government is allowing this to happen, and the government could do something about it, that is how the average person feels."[61] Seeing that foreigners are prioritized, that they receive fundamental goods and services before citizens or that citizens do not receive at all, has fed the frame that corruption and state officials were responsible not just for current emergency problems like water and waste since the Syrians' arrival, but for pre-existing shortcomings of the state in other services and infrastructure as well.

The influx of aid highlights existing corruption because people are aware of the money coming in, but are very clearly not seeing it help them. Hence, aid is illuminating the source of existing grievances—elite corruption. At times resentment was directed at the international community for leaving nationals out of all this aid. At other times it was directed to the state for not helping nationals and channeling the aid to them, as the states said they would do. Indeed, the main argument for more international aid is to shield locals from the effects of the refugee crisis, and nationals hear of massive amounts of money being donated to their states, but they say none of it has gone to them. They feel that this money is going to the elites through corruption instead, intensifying an existing grievance. State actions violate their fundamental principles of fairness.[62] People recalled with resentment that local and international NGOs would provide clean water, for example, in this case to a rural northern area of Akkar, but only to Syrian refugees.[63] "Things were not perfect before the crisis. The situation was tense, the system was failing. The government could not keep providing rent to different groups for allegiance, and so discontent increased. Insert the Syrian refugees: services declined. Now there are not enough police for the amount of people, we need more municipal workers, garbage collection. Things started to fail even more than before."[64] Inflation increased, as did economic stress and competition for the same amount of goods and food.

Interview statements reveal resentment toward governments for not responding adequately to the immediate problems related to refugees, but people also connected these criticisms to deeper, longer-standing grievances over their own governments' lack of provision for its citizens. "The UN gives to Syrians because they have no state—maybe it thinks the Lebanese state gives to Lebanese, like the European states do, but it does not," a teacher explained.[65] "[Because] this area is deprived (*hirman*)," said another, "the state and its ministries do not treat people equally, like they do in other countries. The state does not take care of us, society does not either, because of this sectarianism (*ta'ifiyyeh*)."[66] The people need help because of all the pressure on them from employment and prices. "The Lebanese state is partly responsible for increasing employment opportunities," these Lebanese professionals stated. "After all, we have Syrian doctors employed here in Lebanon, about one hundred here in Akkar (a poor area in northern Lebanon)."[67]

While the state as a whole was viewed as responsible, the governance level most accessible and prominent in the refugee crisis was often the local municipality. Municipalities were the first to respond to the Syrian crisis, dealt directly with the Syrians, and many INGOs preferred to work with local governments.[68] Some municipalities looked to INGOs for help, lamenting the incompetence of the national government in Lebanon. A few municipal leaders in Lebanon stated they were fine without a state, and would prefer to run things themselves without state interference. These were in the richer areas, many funded by illegal goods and smuggling, particularly in the Beka'a Valley.[69] They were content to rely on INGOs, they told me. Most others do not have the finances or support to do without a state. Even when municipalities run on INGO aid, at the same time they acknowledge this solution is a stop-gap measure, to fix infrastructure and then pass along its maintenance to local authorities.[70] Domestic municipal funds were determined and constrained in both countries by the national government. Municipalities able to raise their own money through local taxes differed and had more economic independence than others. These were few in number, however, and located in the Beka'a, with its history of agriculture and drug cultivation. Increasingly, even in Lebanon, there was an awareness that national authorities would need to be involved, particularly for infrastructure, including waste disposal. People began to realize that local solutions would remain ineffective since trash from other regions could still adversely affect them. This was vividly apparent when trash would wash up on shore in the wealthier areas north of Beirut, completely overwhelming the entire beachfront.[71]

Protests Begin: 2013–2015

Although Syrians began arriving in 2011, it was not until 2013 that we can plausibly consider whether scapegoating was succeeding in deterring protest against the state. In 2013, the welcome wore out, and citizens realized the war—and Syrians' tenure in their country—would drag on. Previously, the "Arab Uprising" effect, or the diffusion of protest from what were then considered successful uprisings, could still possibly have influenced public protest. By early 2013, Arab Uprising optimism had been shattered by the reality of bloody battles in failed uprisings and the dubious nature of the outcome in Egypt's presumably successful uprising.

Scapegoating and continual state insistence that Syrians were to blame for current economic and infrastructure problems did not work as theorized to deter protests. Protests did occur, directed at the state rather than at the refugees themselves. I illustrate this dynamic using grievances that have a credible connection to Syrians and for which people popularly blamed the Syrians. The protests discussed below are meant to illustrate the dynamic of dual blame, not as a comprehensive survey of protests. This is partly due to endemic data problems. According to municipal and NGO officials in northern Lebanon and in Jordan, many protests were not reported. In Lebanon, protests would fail to meet the standard of news coverage compared to security issues and perceptions, particularly since protests are often dismissed, even by academics, as people just complaining.[72] In both countries, protests and institutional changes took place that were directly due to the presence of the Syrians, including protests demanding the same aid and benefits as the Syrians, demonstrations against Syrian economic competition, and the creation of new municipal security forces due to popular feelings of threat. Again, these protests and demands targeted different sources and levels of governance and service provision: the national states, INGOs, and municipalities, but usually not the refugees themselves.

Initial protests followed the pattern of emergency or crisis mobilizing, while later protests linked issues together, as grievances coalesced into a common refrain of the state not doing its job. Protests directed at the state were about two types of problems: those that were pre-existing and understood as problems of the state and those that were newly generated by the arrival of refugees. Protests varied by state, since expectations and capacities of the states differed. One type of protest resulted from demographic effects of the refugees on infrastructure (electricity), resources (water), goods (prices), and services (waste, medical care, education). In these cases, increases in demand altered supply or exceeded capacity, but the problems were pre-existing. Refugees merely pushed these national problems over the edge to scarcity, causing them to be felt in daily lives. The other type of protest was over issues arising solely from the refugees and would not have existed, despite population increases, without the influx of those refugees. These problems included housing, changes in security due to refugees and civil war spill-over, and demands for goods and services similar to those that citizens believed the refugees were getting. For Lebanon, this latter category of goods and services was broader than in Jordan, since the Lebanese state previously provided few services. Indeed, free education and medical care were the subjects of some Lebanese protests. Jordan provided these services, although not always well.

The most dramatic early reactions were in Jordan. In regime-supporting areas, protesters had faith that the government would respond and meet their requests, demonstrating the iterative relation between mobilization and state response—these cannot be analyzed separately or out of their historical context. As one opposition activist stated, citizens realized that the best way is a demonstration to force the government to provide services.[73] But the expected result was only obtained in those areas where refugees were concentrated. In the other areas of the regime's constituency, government did not in fact respond to demands. The Jordanian state directed aid money and exempted locals from some harsher rules in areas of heavy refugee settlement. In Lebanon, reactions were slower and cumulative. Instead of believing the state would respond to protest as in Jordan, Lebanese believed the state would either ignore the protests or respond to them with repression. Nonetheless, sporadic protests occurred in Lebanon till they culminated in a mass gathering that the Beiruti middle class could get behind: the trash protests.

Stressed Infrastructure, Services, and Employment

In the northern Jordanian areas of Mafraq and Ramtha, where the first concentration of Syrians was, protesters began in 2013 to press the government to redress the immediate problems caused by the Syrians, an example of crisis mobilizing about essential livelihood goods. Existing infrastructure for fundamental goods and services was stressed due to the demographic weight of the Syrians. To fix the situation, protesters directed their demands to the state. For housing problems, protesters asked the state to either cap rent prices or create housing projects specifically for Jordanians, since the influx of Syrians caused rent prices to rise and landlords to evict Jordanians in favor of Syrians.[74] Jordanians created their own "refugee camps" in the North, and many such protests went unreported in the press.[75] In Mafraq, at the end of March 2013, families calling themselves Hirak Nashama al-Mafraq, roughly translated as "the movement of the good people of Mafraq," set up twenty UNHCR tents and called themselves the "Jordanian Displaced People Camp Number 1" (Mukhayyam an-Naziheen al-Urduniyyin, Raqm

1). They were protesting their eviction by landlords in favor of renting to Syrian refugees. Even more Jordanians were evicted as the Syrians continued to arrive. "We are not against the Syrian people," one participant stated, "we just want our rights."[76] Others did blame the Syrians but still looked for redress to the government. The Mafraq group, Nashama al-Mafraq, had attacked a Jordanian charity (the Islamic Society) that worked with the refugees, along with other tire burnings and protests.[77] Likewise, fewer residents of Ramtha, also evicted, set up tents, with an explicit sign asking the king and chief of staff to solve their problem.[78] The Jordanians took their deprivation of housing and other goods, in favor of the refugees, as an attack on their very identity and its associated rights. This was demonstrated when one man in Mafraq threatened to give up his identity card, "since Jordanians have no rights," he said.[79] The protests worked: the government's response to the camp protest was to provide the people with housing and land.[80] The next year, a large protest against school overcrowding occurred, again in Mafraq. Local children were kept home to highlight class sizes of sixty or more students due to the influx of Syrians. The quality of education was being affected, and parents protested for a solution.[81] This was in addition to the more common pressure wielded by communities against the INGOs to force them to alter their educational policy toward locals.

Refugees increased water and electricity use in both countries. In Jordan, far more water-scarce than Lebanon, water shortages sparked vociferous protests against the state, particularly in those areas most affected by the refugees. Early in the crisis, one Jordanian town in the northern district, with the highest concentration of refugees, ran out of water. The villagers barricaded roads and burned tires. This was no ordinary protest: The king himself came to the scene, assuring the villagers he would get water to them in tankers. In a move uncharacteristic of Jordanian politics, the villagers refused. They wanted water piped directly into their houses instead. In the end, the king promised piped water.[82]

In other incidents, groups of armed Jordanians targeted the digging of new pipelines by international humanitarian organizations, based on the belief that such projects would divert water from local communities to refugees. Complaints to the Yarmouk Water Company over water increased fourfold during the initial period of refugee influx in 2011–2013. These complaints numbered more than 45,000.[83] International NGO water use fed the perception that Jordanians were overlooked while the state's resources were directed at the refugees.[84] Death threats against those working on the projects were common, as were hasty negotiations with officials from the water utility, who would regularly respond by promising priority water delivery to the assailant's village or neighborhood.[85] Water protests, involving burning tires and confronting water authorities with guns, shut down major roads and highways.[86] Participants insulted the government and accused it of failing in its duty to provide water, particularly during dry summers such as 2013.[87] Authorities were afraid to tell them to stop stealing the water. According to the water engineer in charge of INGO-led water infrastructure improvements, protests in the North were a regular occurrence. Residents would block work on the water lines with trucks, demanding water for their village. Work would stop, security officials and state representatives would arrive, and work would only start again after negotiations concluded.[88] Occasionally the protests turned deadly. In one case of these periodic water protests, a man was killed by a protester as he attempted to pass through the blockade.[89]

Water problems in the south showed the government's greater responsiveness to areas with high concentrations of refugees. Southern areas were likewise inhabited by East Bankers, members of the regime's constituency. Citizens aimed their protests at government symbols. Protestors blocked roads and burned tires here also, demanding water from the authorities.[90] The governor's office was the site of one protest in Karak over the lack of water.[91] In Karak governorate, one string of protests lasted more than a month, with protestors blocking streets and demanding access to water. However, the presence of the refugees in the South was not as demographically significant, and protests were not answered by the government as in the North.[92] The Water Authority merely stated that water was not in fact being disrupted for any long period.[93] Other water protests occurred for relatively minor disruptions in service, demonstrating the variation of protests based on expectations. Arjan, in Ajloun governorate (northern Jordan), protested when their supply of water was disrupted. As the origin of half of the governorate's water, Arjan was accustomed to regular weekly water deliveries, as opposed to biweekly deliveries for the neighboring areas, and thus protested when that changed.[94]

Lebanon's water is not as scarce as Jordan's and private sources still provide water, given the financial ability to afford it. Still, numerous demonstrations have occurred centered around water as a right.[95] Here too we see demands for state action. Protests for water have mingled with other issues, particularly electricity, which is needed to pump water.[96] In protests over electricity, participants attempted to attack the South Lebanon Water Authority in Sidon.[97] Beirutis questioned whether their country was still the "country of water and light" because of prolonged and serious electricity and water problems. Water became an item on the black market.[98] Extended periods of water scarcity in the southern town of Bint Jubayl prompted large-scale protests against the Water Authority, declaring it responsible for the crisis, with municipal officials echoing the grievances.[99] In a northern town (mainly Christian), the water problem was blamed on the refugees, but the populace's focus was on removing the local officials believed to be corrupt in their dealings with water provision.[100]

Electricity provision was stressed by the sudden increase in population, more so in Lebanon than in Jordan.[101] The Lebanese infrastructure for electricity was lacking even before the Syrian influx. Despite plausible and actual links to the Syrians increasing the draw on electricity (often without paying),[102] an assertion regularly reiterated by state officials, electricity protests still addressed the state or electricity officials. The electricity crisis, together with the critical waste situation, exposed the depth of government corruption, numerous interviewees said. Observing that Syrians steal electricity and do not pay for it, one interviewee concluded that the national government should fix the service infrastructure so the Syrians would pay like everyone else.[103] Baalbek, with the heaviest concentration of refugees, directed protests about energy blackouts in 2013 at the Energy Ministry.[104] In less peaceful protests, a Beirut suburb demonstrated against the lack of electricity by burning tires and blocking roads.[105] The military forcibly opened one highway in Beirut that had been blocked by protests against electricity cuts.[106] In Hizbollah areas of Beirut, electricity cuts generated protests that also included tire burning in the summer of 2015.[107] Another time, in September 2015, shortly after the largest waste demonstration of the #YouStink movement, Beirutis blocked a road in protest over the lack of electricity.[108]

The slogan "one bill, not two," was prominently used in electricity and water protests, referring to the fact that people must pay the state bill for these services, although they are insufficient, while also paying a private supplier.[109] Protesting against the national electric utility, EDL, in October 2015, one woman stated that now electricity was the top concern all over the country. Securing electricity needs ran an average of USD 1,300 a year, more than 10 percent of the average household income. The bulk of this money went to generator providers, who made up for state deficiencies in electricity, at least for those able to pay.[110]

Competition for jobs was an additional driver of protests, and again activists demanded state action and did not merely express hostility toward the Syrians. In Lebanon, the entrance of Syrians into the transportation sector compounded the existing grievances of union members. In addition to prior demands, unions added that they now suffered because of Syrians and "asked the concerned ministries to end what they described as 'illegal competition' eating away at their livelihood."[111] Protests about transportation jobs occurred mainly in the North and East and some on international roads used for trade with Syria. These protests increased in number and spawned new tactics over time. Other union labor demonstrations increased in the context of competition from Syrian refugees. Syrian workers competed particularly, but not solely, for informal work, which in Lebanon accounts for almost 20 percent of workers.[112] Lebanese civil sector workers' strikes and protests, representing ongoing concerns about cost of living versus pay discrepancies, ramped up during this time and persisted for years. In Jordan, residents of Mafraq, the center of refugee residence there, had better luck in their protests for jobs, at least temporarily. After they protested to be employed in the new refugee camp, Za'atari, instead of foreigners and refugees, they were hired, but later mostly pushed out.[113] People felt, according to one observer, that since it is their country, they should be the ones hired. After all, the refugees were already putting pressure on their national services and infrastructure.[114]

#YouStink: Beirut Mobilizes and the Rural Areas Join

Beirut's mass movement against the trash crisis, *tul'it rihetkun*, or "YouStink," generated much attention globally and was well-covered in the media.[115] Smaller protests against the increasing garbage problem turned into large-scale protest late in the summer of 2015. Pictures of garbage piled up to three stories high spread around the world in news coverage. One of the protests counted as many as ten thousand participants, the largest nonsectarian protest in decades. The unarmed demonstrations were met by violence from security services, imprisonment, and infiltration, and were the target of intense political pressure to disband. Internal divisions and diverse identities and goals affected movement cohesion.[116] The movement did succumb to these pressures and repression eventually; participation declined rapidly and protests largely stopped. The summer 2015 crisis itself was not related to the demographic pressure of the Syrian refugees; it was the closing of the Naameh landfill that caused trash to pile up in Beirut and its nearby regions.[117] Some indeed blamed Syrians for this waste crisis, as did government officials (when not busy blaming each other). But as interviewees stated, people did not buy it anymore: They no longer blamed the Syrians more than they blamed the government.[118] These demonstrations were organized mainly by the Beiruti, educated classes, and others reportedly felt unwelcome. Still, the participation of many newcomers was critical and has often been mentioned, although little analysis has focused on them or their demands.[119]

Trash and pollution have been major problems throughout Lebanon, particularly in areas with refugees. Complaints that refugees pollute the country with their overwhelming waste were common. Fifty percent of all waste is in the northern areas, and a further 20 percent in the Beka'a and Baalbek regions. Only 17 percent of total waste is in Beirut and North Lebanon.[120] In one village on the Lebanese border with Syria, garbage increased two and a half times its amount before the crisis, and the municipality could not handle it.[121] "Without the Syrians, we would have had time to improve our infrastructure. Now waste from the Syrians is dangerous to health," one municipality president in the Beka'a told me.[122] In some Beka'a towns, waste doubled due to the refugees. In others, it increased 30 percent. In still others, the Syrians and waste outnumbered residents by several times, particularly in the agricultural areas.[123] The refugees did not simply increase trash by the amount of their demographic presence—roughly 30 percent—which would have been significant enough. Rather, the refugees added to uncollected waste far above their numbers. By living in shelters not meant for residence, refugees were often unconnected to sewage or trash services. They were left to dispose of trash and human waste randomly. When it rained, plastic bags of trash floated along streams and sides of roads, and the stench was noticeable. Complaints about this effect were common, and the effect of the Syrians on trash and pollution in Lebanon was one of the most mentioned topics in interviews and general discussions in my fieldwork, along with corruption and the burden presented by the presence of the refugees.

Indeed, numerous protests occurred over garbage and related issues in areas outside Beirut, including women in Akkar protesting trash as well as the lack of electricity and social security. The two areas most affected by the Syrian refugee crisis, Akkar and the Beka'a, among others, also began mobilizing about garbage problems in their areas. Local campaigns blamed politicians for the resultant health problems.[124] Tripoli and the surrounding areas, highly affected by the refugee crisis, were relatively well represented in the trash protests in Beirut.[125] Tripoli and its suburbs mobilized locally about the trash crisis around the same time, organized by a new group called "Fed Up."[126] Akkar, Baalbek, and the Chouf all had significant movements. The garbage crisis there was compounded by feelings that the regions have historically been marginalized.[127] These protests involved heads of municipalities and local religious leaders, using their influence to meet with central government officials as an additional tactic to achieve change.[128] Regions outside Beirut made demands in other ways than the typical blocking of roads and burning of tires, particularly since they believed that if Beirut could not solve their own waste crisis with protests, then certainly the regions, with secondary political status, would have no chance.[129] Local authorities instead turned to other tactics, appealing directly to the international humanitarian community and its desire to avoid conflict while maintaining its access to aid the refugees. The EU stepped in early on in the refugee crisis in the areas most affected by the Syrian refugees.[130]

Trash was a tipping point, when infrastructure problems became popularly viewed as an unacceptable crisis, caused by the state, necessitating activism to fix the situation. Waste was a symbol for numerous societal grievances and gave an atmosphere of emergency to the various other infrastructure issues, including lack of public services, inadequate governance, and economic problems, which culminated in a sense of crisis. There was a sense that these other crises became too much to bear and resulted in widespread mobilization.[131] An opinion poll showed overwhelming support for al-Harak (the garbage mobilization movement) (79%), even after its repression by the security services and the halt of the protests. A large number of people (40%) wanted al-Harak to take up other issues, including water and electricity. Among those who did not support the movement, the main reasons were disillusionment with the possibility of change, particularly among the lower classes, or fear of insecurity and chaos.[132]

A significant problem in itself, the garbage crisis was framed in the protests and popularly as the result of political corruption, which was identified as the real problem. The trash crisis triggered the mobilization, although the deep grievances included lack of electricity and water.[133] Garbage was important because it mobilized a cohort of relatively privileged Beirutis who benefited from better services and higher income than the rest of the country. These educated, middle-class individuals were armed with superior resources and networks for mobilizing, in addition to being symbolic of the capital's respectability. While money could technically buy private trash cleanup services, activists repeatedly stated that trash, in their view, could not be solved by the private sector.[134] The YouStink base was joined by numerous other organizations, politically unaffiliated actors and political party members who now protested common grievances cutting across sect and party lines. Economic grievance actors, including the wage movement, took part. One analysis of 170 protesters demonstrated that their demands and grievances were mainly around infrastructure and service problems: public services, water, electricity, housing, education, health care, and other livelihood issues.[135] These protests increasingly demonstrated a changing expectation of receiving services from the state and a rejection of aid money. "We don't want donations; we have been living in the dark," one protester stated, "and it is our right to have electricity."[136]

As Professor Carmen Geha argues, the mobilization generated by the trash crisis may not have obtained its goals immediately, but it went on to affect elections and to field candidates at the municipal and, later, national level. Beirut Is My City (Beirut Madinati) and other local "my city" movements came out of this mobilization for the 2016 elections, along with the national-level so-called civil society political parties in the 2018 elections.[137] Municipalities gained importance and centrality in the national system also through the movements that arose out of these protests. In the 2016 municipal elections, Beirut Is My City received 32 percent of the vote, a significant accomplishment for a new nonsectarian organization in Lebanon, although they did not get any seats due to the structure of the elections.[138]

Price and Subsidy Protests: Jordan

Unlike Lebanon's protests, Jordan's continuing austerity protests during the early years of the crisis generated little interest apart from local news clips. Observers often interpreted them as "more of the same," demonstrating a clear lack of understanding of how movements are built and persist. Jordanians continued to protest against the government—and increasingly, the state or regime[139]—despite official blame of the Syrians for causing the budget crises in the first place.[140] Protest against the government in Jordan had been solved by the simple and time-tested method of sacking the offending minister. State- or regime-directed protest, however, goes to the heart of the Jordanian system as a whole, including the monarchy. It was thus understood by elites as more threatening than attacks on a particular government official. After the large 2012 protests, austerity demonstrations continued yearly, albeit on a lesser scale. This was due in part to the dampening effects of the Syrian war discussed above, along with more traditional Jordanian state techniques of cooptation and identity divisions.[141] Discussing the potential for removing the politically sensitive bread subsidy, the government blamed an increase in consumption of 35 percent, mainly in the North of the country where the refugees were located, taxing its budget.[142] The conclusion implicating the refugees was clear. Any doubt was removed by other official statements that the government still wanted nationals to benefit, but that non-Jordanians were consuming too much of the budget to be able to continue subsidies.[143]

In 2013, when anger and protests against the Syrian presence began in earnest yet fear of repression and the Islamic state was high, large numbers of people independently and diverse organized groups protested oil price increases.[144] Leftists, independents, and Islamists were some of those protesting against the rise in prices of basic goods. Like other price protests in Jordan's history, these were spurred by economic causes, but this time protest included political issues and grievances. The two were intertwined, as people believed their money was being stolen by corrupt politicians.[145] These demonstrations showed an increasing emphasis on the state system in its entirety, and not individual governments, however, potentially nullifying the key calming tactic of the regime, that of blaming and then removing a government figure to placate protesters. A key slogan in one heavily Islamist protest was "a crisis of rule [or regime], not governments."[146] Other protests, composed of al-Hirak (secular)[147] and Islamist groups, asked for a provisional, emergency government, denouncing contemporary reform policies as fake attempts to deceive the populace and distract them from their demands.[148]

Price rises continued to spur mobilizing by a diversity of new local groups alongside older ones, and protests combined economic grievances with demands for political change. Another demonstration, organized by the Islamist Youth movement and the Jordanian tribes coalition, addressed the king with more blatant language. Chants included some threatening the king with a similar fate to Tunisia's president, and accusing him of theft. In one protest, in addition to various religious slogans, people chanted: "Listen, listen, son of Hussein, the people's money, where did it go?"; "Either improve now ... or face the fate of Zayn al-Abideen [Ben Ali]"; and "Jordan above all else."[149] Other demonstrations around the country occurred at the same time, organized by local groups.[150] Protests took place in February, March, June, September, October, and November of 2013 about electricity and energy price rises, new taxes, and food prices.[151] Some of the protests were specific in their targets. The rise in the price of a carton of eggs spurred the "Egg Friday" protests.[152] The new tax on clothes generated a humorous trend on social media, as protesters made fun of the tax with suggestions to reject wearing clothing altogether.[153] At this point the various articles reporting these events were published in either small local news outlets, websites overtly belonging to the opposition, or in media based in regional countries. Journalists in the outlets presumed to be loyalist protested low salaries and increasing government control over their work, to no avail.

In early 2014, rising prices on food, water, electricity, and fuel generated protests in half of the twelve governorates.[154] This time, the disgruntled loyalist news outlets joined the trend, reporting on the protests and anti-regime chants.[155] The demonstrations identified the cause as the new state-imposed taxes and removal of subsidies. In northern Jordan, the "Sons of Jarash Coalition for Change and Reform" protested against price increases and asked the government to raise salaries in tandem. "Jordanian Youth for Change" and al-Hirak were involved in these protests also.[156] A group in Irbid that called itself Israr 12 (roughly, resolution, or decision, 12) protested prices.[157] Protesters repeated a prior theme, asking for a caretaker or emergency government to oversee a transition, presumably in regime.[158] Later that year, al-Hirak was involved in protests in Amman, Karak, and Tafileh. In the Karak demonstration, protesters rejected the policy of privatization and connected it to their falling livelihoods.[159]

Protests continued in 2015, mainly in the southern areas.[160] In December, these were joined by a social media protest tactic, a sarcastic Twitter hashtag soliciting suggestions for new price increases or taxes. Responses included taxing breathing and fees for watching Indian television programs.[161] The government was condemned as continually taking from the people. Protests that year also included the tactic of refusing to comply with the census in the southern area of Wadi Musa. In Jordan, the precise demographic numbers, consisting mainly of East Bankers (who include the residents of Wadi Musa) and those descendant from Palestinians, is political and not made public. Protesters held signs stating, "I don't want to be a number in a government that does not recognize us" and "Government does not recognize us or our rights. I don't want to be a number in its notebook."[162]

Security

Security was a chief concern in Lebanon, battling with employment for attention, and generally winning. The biggest demand of protests directly related to the influx of refugees in Lebanon was for security and for municipalities to play a larger role. Conflict mapping shows an emphasis on border events with the Syrians, fear of internal unrest, bombings, and the "threat" of Syrians. Syrians in Lebanon were spread throughout the country, increasing the perception of danger. Armed conflict was not limited to the border areas and was widely publicized in the media.[163] The result was protests against state authorities for more security, municipalities hiring their own police, and citizens' enacting security through vigilantism. This differs considerably from Jordan, where only in some areas were Syrians considered to be undesirable people or criminals, and even then, the matter was left to the police and military. Jordanian security services were popularly believed to be capable of handling the situation.

People protested on numerous occasions against insecurity in Baalbek. Incidents sparking protests included the use of rocket-propelled grenades, shootings, and robberies. Protests called for more security and for the Lebanese military to do more in the area.[164] Other protests were similarly directed either at the municipality or the national security services. Often the result was curfews against the Syrians and an increased role for the municipal police (MP).[165] Businessmen protested the increase in robberies, blocking highways and roads.[166] The state was called on to "assume its responsibilities on all levels" in order to take back land held by armed Syrian rebels.[167] Protests were held in support of the army when its members were captured, or in other cases to pressure the army to intervene and protect citizens.[168] Numerous protests were held over hostages taken by Islamists, accusing the military of ineffectiveness.[169]

Particularly in the initial years of the Syrian conflict, much of the responsibility in Lebanon for local security and Syrians in the community lay with the municipalities. The central government had declined to act, and even when it did later act, the national state still allowed wide latitude for local powers. In this way, the municipalities' jurisdiction de facto spread into new areas, despite the disputed legality of some of them. Municipalities increased their legal jurisdiction and enforcement having to do with the refugee influx, often creating their own regulations.[170] In addition to the omnipresent curfews against Syrians, municipalities began regulating labor practices, declaring professions banned to Syrians, and closing stores owned by Syrians, even when they had legitimate paperwork.[171] Their restrictions on Syrians varied. Syrians were evicted, forced to pay new fees, and treated with violence.[172] International organizations, including the World Bank, recognized this trend, and worked to bolster and educate about municipal governance, not only in Lebanon but also in Jordan.[173]

The establishment or expansion of municipal police was a key change for municipalities. The vast majority—78 percent—of municipalities hired more security forces after the refugee influx.[174] Municipal police forces increased significantly beginning in 2012, performing duties of questionable jurisdiction, such as arrest, imprisonment, surveillance (with cameras), and searching residences randomly. The initial spur toward the MP was associated with Hizbollah.[175] The MP would purportedly "strengthen stability and security over all Lebanese regions."[176] The legality and risks of the MP were debated. They were given scant (six weeks) training and recruited through unknown, arbitrary methods. Their jurisdiction was unclear, and their ability to arrest under dispute.[177] Concerns included their ability to contradict official national security services and the potential for the MP to act on their own and for their own interests.[178]

The main subject of MP actions was the Syrians, in a response to their increasing numbers—sometimes outnumbering town residents by several times—and a popular sense of decreased security.[179] The rationale ran that the thieves and terrorists have weapons and so should the municipalities.[180] Many doubled the number of police. Their methods against the refugees were clearly harsh.[181] The public debated the legitimacy of the MP, their insufficient training, and fear that such individuals holding guns could fire at anyone for even a routine traffic stop. The Lebanese gendarmerie had previously incited a popular uprising when they acted similarly to the MP.[182] But current circumstances differed, and the public believed the MP was a force to be used against the Syrians, not against host citizens. The head of one municipality stated clearly that MP activities, searches of buildings filled with Syrian residences in this case, were directed against the Syrians only.[183] His intent was to thwart a possible repeat of the civil war, when Palestinians were armed. The increase in violent crime, he contended, was due to sharing their town with ten thousand Syrians.[184] In one incident, several of the MPs were investigated, as a result of pictures of their actions being posted on social media and appearing in regular media, in response to claims that they arbitrarily arrested and humiliated Syrian refugees.[185] Another municipal head stated that arrests for annoyances such as noisy motorcycles (a key Lebanese complaint against the Syrians) or curfews were unnecessary; instead they took the motorcycle away for a few days, but only if the Syrian man was alone and not riding with his family.[186] In the latter case, they would issue a stern warning. By 2015, international organizations had begun training these MPs, hoping to increase the safety and human rights of Syrians in the process.[187]

Another side effect of felt insecurity was the rise of vigilantism. In a direct implication of the state for not doing its job, a vigilante page was created on Facebook called "Wainiyeh al-Dawle," or "Where Is the State?" Beginning in 2013, the page and activists posted information about crimes, including videos, asking people to identify perpetrators and, more often than not, act against them on their own. The page was heavily but not solely focused on Syrians and also included Lebanese acting in ways that users deemed immoral. The page had a quarter of a million likes when it was active.[188]

Aid and Raised Expectations

Protests were not the only result of the strain on resources caused by refugees; ideas of what rights citizens were entitled to changed also. Citizens compared their own services to those of the Syrian refugees, and their expectations shifted. In some cases, the services demanded were not historically provided by the government. The most dramatic example of this is for universal health care in Lebanon and for goods provided by NGOs exclusively to the Syrians in both countries. Some protested directly to NGOs to obtain the same goods, others targeted the municipality or the national state. When existing services were cut due to obligations to balance the budget (see chapter 5), indignation rose. No parallel reduction of services to the Syrians was perceived, and citizens now considered certain basic services as rights due to them as members of the state.

Initial refugee-associated shortages were the trigger for this larger dynamic. Concepts of citizen rights to services provided by the state began to change first in areas close to the refugees. As the flow of aid made its way to supposed beneficiaries, it also lined elite pockets, according to host nationals. This corrupt dynamic illuminated for citizens the causes of long-standing grievances, and greatly raised their expectations of the government by revealing to them the kinds of goods and services a state might provide. People reasoned that if the refugees, by definition not nationals, received a good, citizens should receive at least as much or more of that good. State provisions—or lack thereof—began to be criticized in this manner, even for goods that the state had not provided before. Health care and education in Lebanon are two examples. Lebanon is a notoriously privatized state, with goods and services allocated by political parties and religious groups, rather than the state directly, although the state does help to fund those services.

In Jordan, tensions with refugees were often expressed by concerns about the right to water and the anxiety that they would not have enough water.[189] Some expressed envy of the refugees' privileged access to water. As has occurred in other refugee situations, poor Jordanians wished to be refugees themselves, in this case in order to obtain water.[190] According to 71 percent of Jordanians, the issue of access to water created friction in their relationship with Syrians.[191] Close to 60 percent felt that newcomers (i.e., refugees) were responsible for lack of improvement in the water situation.[192] Similar stories about Syrians' culture of water use circulated around both Jordan and in Lebanon: that they let the sink faucet run and walk away, and they fill the bathtub for baths. The frequency of repetition probably indicates that these stories are rumors or urban legend. Still, the general statement that Syrian use of water differs from Jordanian use is valid, particularly given that Jordanians on average use less than the world minimum for water.[193] Syrians do not know how to make water last, people said. Some discussed how Syrians steal water and use more than their allotted amount, particularly since many Syrians live together, they stated.[194]

Some Jordanians said they wanted to attain the privileged access to water that they presumed the refugees have.[195] In the villages outside the Za'atari refugee camp, Jordanians watched tankers that once brought water to them pass through on their way to the refugee camp without stopping, not even selling to them. "Don't they realize that we need help too?" one resident of Za'atari village asked.[196] A member of one Jordanian NGO explained the broader sentiment: "Syrians are not working and are getting paid. Individuals from the Gulf come and hand out money for publicity. Why is he getting it and not me?"[197] Less-educated Syrian women are being employed over Jordanian women, they explained.

The fact that aid and goods are supplied exclusively to the Syrians has fueled universal resentment, even among those who are more financially secure. The hostility is aggravated when Syrians live side-by-side with needy citizens. In one example, Syrian school children received new book bags from UN agencies, causing friction with the Jordanian students, who received nothing. The Syrian children were then beaten up and their bags stolen.[198] Imagine poor children going to school alongside Syrian refugees, who have fresh fruit and nice school bags, one NGO employee described. Others articulated the implied second part of that resentment: that this is the citizens' country, not the refugees', and yet these foreigners are better off than we are. A resurgence in identity and nationalism was observed, although more studies need to be done to confirm its extent and character. In the midst of our discussion of the Syrian refugees, one man described telling his grandson, "Lift your head high, you are Jordanian!"[199]

Humanitarian organizations affirmed the sense of resentment and unfair treatment among nationals. In Jordan, nationals resented the large amounts of aid going to Syrians, including from traditional local charities, support that had previously aided nationals. Once the Syrian crisis started, this source of help was removed. A local charity near the Za'atari refugee camp had given aid and help to three hundred Jordanian families, but once the Syrians arrived, all its efforts turned to the refugees, in part due to donor requirements.[200] Needy Jordanians were passed over and, even when organizations claimed they helped Jordanians, Jordanians were turned away.[201] In 2014, 78 percent of Jordanians felt that aid was unfairly allocated between the communities and that identity and not need was the determining factor in receiving help.[202] International donors have in some cases lost legitimacy among nationals as many were required by funders to help only Syrians.[203]

One NGO employee who worked heavily in the North of Jordan explained

> "They [East Bank Jordanians] feel their privileges are decreasing. They
> had been privileged just by being loyal [to the regime]. When that sys-
> tem is not working or not able to provide for them, they get lost. There
> is a realization that I am losing my privilege, but I don't know how to
> transform my worth in this economy. My worth was just *being*. So we
> see envy of the Syrians. The Syrians came in and created their own im-
> portance in the community through productivity. Jordanians say these
> people are not privileged, not sons of the country, but they are making
> something—they have a variety of skills, better inter-personal skills,
> and entrepreneurialism of ordinary life, such as cooking food and sell-
> ing it out of their houses."[204]

Less-advantaged Lebanese and Jordanians, and those in the lower or unemployed middle classes, expressed envy at all the advantages the Syrians were receiving. One NGO distributed water filters in a northern Lebanese village only to
Syrian refugees, and the Lebanese protested. Lebanese were also drinking dirty
water and could have benefitted from filters.[205] The sight of humanitarian and
charitable organizations helping the refugees achieve advances above the lower
class of nationals created the desire for the states to intervene to prevent it, or aid
the nationals in the same or a better manner.

An attitude of "they are getting more than me" began to prevail, according to
numerous interviewees. "The Syrians have societies taking care of them, but the
Lebanese have no one to look out for us," one professional man stated in a group
discussion. "We are all in the same situation as the refugees," another stated.[206]
"Lebanon has many poor families the ministries do not cover." Gulf charities lavished Syrians with money, so goes the perception, while citizens questioned why
they were excluded.[207] "We were deprived (*hirman*) before the Syrians came, and
almost all of the Syrians here are lower class."[208] The image of Syrians selling their
cash aid cards or the goods they received further fueled these ideas, helping to create the idea that Syrians were doing very well economically. However, the goods
distributed to the refugees and even cash cards cannot be used for many of their
requirements, such as paying rent, so, far from being a sign of affluence, in fact
they exchanged their goods and debit cards for cash out of real need.

Numerous interviewees mentioned that Syrians were taken first for jobs and
services over Lebanese. They felt that Syrians received these benefits but did not
have to pay the expenses locals had to pay, since they received food aid, free health
care, and other goods.[209] Jordanians believed that their country gave more to Syrians than to them.[210] "The Syrians have it good here: they wait in line, get lots of

services, free hospital, food, and they still get money every month!" another stated.[211] "They have air conditioning in their tents," one municipal official claimed.[212] "The NGOs do everything for the refugees," another local official stated, "and we have no jobs."[213] An educator stated, "Of course the Lebanese feel that Syrians are getting more. In schools Lebanese get a medical exam once a year; Syrians get it twice. They bring a doctor in to check the kids." This educator also told of incidents of violence among the Syrians, such as a student bringing a knife to school.[214]

Free health care for refugees was a particular concern in Lebanon, where health care is privatized and quite expensive. That Lebanese had to pay, while Syrians received health care for free, was a stab to Lebanese patriotism, one article declared.[215] Another article discussed Lebanese pretending to be Syrian to obtain life-saving services they were denied when the hospital considered them Lebanese.[216] People stated that hospitals serve the Syrians immediately, without payment, before Lebanese (this complaint was heard mainly in Lebanon, which has predominantly private-sector health care). They asserted that Lebanese die because they don't have insurance, and "there should be balance (*tawazun*) between Syrians and Lebanese."[217] One woman reported seeing four Syrians get admitted into a hospital before one Lebanese. "All we are asking for is the same as the Syrians get," one woman in a group discussion said, and the others agreed.[218] Everywhere people gave examples of Syrians entering emergency services before Lebanese, and not needing to pay for it. As nationals, people believed themselves entitled to more privileges than the foreign refugees. If the Lebanese state wanted to, it could pay for health care for Lebanese, an INGO official offered.[219]

The influx of aid raised host citizens' expectations, and they began to have new demands. When Syrians in Za'atari camp were given heaters, Jordanians in nearby Mafraq demanded them also. Za'atari had streetlights, so Mafraq wanted road lighting too. In 2013–2014, Jordanians went to the municipality to demand lighting, and the municipality turned to UNHCR, arguing that it was unfair for the Syrians to get streetlights while their town remained dark. INGOs agreed to put in street lighting.[220] In Lebanon, technological and language training was provided to the refugees only. In response, Lebanese pretended to be Syrians to attend these free classes.[221] A number of Jordanians also pretended to be Syrian refugees and registered with the UNHCR, particularly during the initial two years of the conflict.[222]

In Mafraq, a health NGO for Syrian women was established right next to an existing local NGO. This new NGO gave care packages upon the birth of a new baby, and pregnant Syrian women would stop by to receive them. Jordanian women who frequented the nearby NGO began asking for the same, but the NGO stated it could not give anything to Jordanians since its aid was specifically mandated for the Syrians. The women protested in 2014, and the NGO changed its practices.[223] Also in Mafraq, Jordanians attacked domestic Islamic NGOs that provided aid to refugees, in an effort to stop the delivery of services. Warehouses owned by the Islamic Society were attacked in 2012 because the NGO's assistance was believed to be wholly for the Syrian refugees.[224] NGO workers were forcibly turned back to Amman by locals, since the NGOs at that time were restricted to giving aid only to the Syrians.[225]

Free education for Syrian refugees caused a conflict with Lebanese parents. Lebanese parents demanded the same, complained, and now do not pay school registration fees because the refugees do not.[226] "What will happen when the Syrians leave?" one INGO employee wondered. "Will they still expect their education fees to be paid?"[227] New book bags and books given to the Syrians by UNICEF caused a conflict in Lebanon, as in Jordan. The Lebanese nagged the agencies to get the same goods for their own children.[228] An official at Mercy Corps, Lebanon, stated that Lebanese repeatedly asked for the same services that Syrians received.[229] "Host citizens now demand that aid money be split fifty-fifty between them and the refugees," INGO officials said.[230] Some members of the public know that the agencies had begun helping Lebanese, but felt it was not enough. "In the last two years, aid from the UN has been 70 percent to the Syrians and 30 percent to Lebanese. We want equality between both—fifty-fifty."[231]

In Wadi Khaled, large crowds of people demonstrated in protest when the local health clinic, funded by Qatar, closed. Officials spoke in turn of the negative effects on the population and the refugees of closing the facility, which had served more than two dozen villages and towns. No other health clinics were available, and residents and refugees would now need to make the two-hour journey to Tripoli.[232] Options for Syrians later opened, and the UN paid all or 75 percent of Syrian medical bills. Yet this solution was only for the Syrians, contrary to the prior clinic that had served Lebanese, even if they did not have insurance. Many Lebanese no longer had health care after this change: about half of Lebanese are not covered by health insurance, and private-sector medical charges are steep.[233]

Analysts have been distracted by the scale of the refugee crisis from seeing the ways activism in Jordan and Lebanon was focused on the state despite elites blaming the Syrians. The refugee crisis was academically and journalistically all-consuming. Articles on the Jordanian and Lebanese protests (against the states) almost always mention that the context of Syrian refugees overwhelming infrastructure, increasing the state budget and straining the labor market, is crucial to interpreting the current waves of protests.[234] Despite the consensus that Syrians have exacerbated locals' problems, in the end, the presence of the Syrians did not deter targeting the state as responsible for solutions. Jordanians and Lebanese protested over housing, water, prices, security, electricity, jobs, waste, and to receive aid similar to the Syrians. Protests began to include various grievances and constituencies as the reasons for mobilizing multiplied.[235]

Initial threats to fundamental livelihood goods generated a turn to the local and national state for solutions. Municipal and national state elites focused on INGOs to solve their scarcity of goods and services problems, and to deliver more economic goods to their citizens. As discussed in chapter 5, the international humanitarian community took the animosity and conflict of these early years as a signal that they needed to help local communities in addition to the refugees, which they started doing. They began fixing services, water, and local trash, for example, alleviating some of the problems, and included locals in their training and employment programs. Much of the INGO work was centered on municipalities. Municipalities became rising actors, coinciding with the worldwide trend toward decentralization. This trend was supported by the national governments for reasons of their own, foisting responsibility for infrastructural outcomes onto local communities. In Lebanon, the municipalities allocated to themselves the power of policing and numerous other administrative powers over the refugees, often operating in legally ambiguous jurisdictions.

PUSHED TO THE EDGE

Early protests by citizens demanding services worked: they signaled that local populations needed help, and states and the international community altered their actions accordingly. Both switched to focus on host citizens rather than refugees exclusively. In essence, the humanitarian organizations joined public opinion, media, and government statements in blaming the refugees for the ills of their countries. The fear of conflict spinning out of control, encompassing society, drove many of these policies. As time went on, the humanitarian organizations and states proactively identified areas they believed would be subject to conflict due to the refugees and targeted aid to those regions over others. In Jordan's case, regions with regime supporters and a high refugee concentration were particularly sensitive and in need of preferential humanitarian treatment, according to the regime's logic. Humanitarian organizations in Lebanon developed a profile of the most deprived areas, assuming these would be vulnerable to conflict, and focused on those. Other areas were left out by both countries. Employment protests in Jordan continued unanswered in areas not hosting large numbers of refugees. Presumably less needy and more religiously homogenous areas of Lebanon were similarly left to their own devices. Because of these policies and aid provisioning, the problem of scarce resources was solved for some, especially in the northern areas of Jordan. Access to water improved, waste facilities were initiated, and medical clinics aided citizens. Jordanians and Lebanese were hired by local and international NGO programs geared toward the refugees, and a significant portion of aid went to the states and municipal areas for general budget support in addition to infrastructure.

Lack of infrastructure is a theme in countries that can't handle refugees.

Despite these improvements, state policies toward the refugees became increasingly restrictive in an attempt to curb the disruptive demographic influence of the refugees. The states successfully used claims of their own citizens' suffering to obtain large aid and loan packages. When Turkey opened the floodgates for refugees to cross the sea to Greece, Europe quickly began listening to Turkey's long-standing requests. At the same time, Lebanon and Jordan limited the entrance of Syrians, deported some, and put movement restrictions and harsh administrative requirements on the rest. This policy change would serve as a further signal to the humanitarian community and the EU to increase aid to the states in return for more lenient host country policies toward the refugees. As far-fetched as it might seem, Jordan successfully sold itself as Europe's "backyard," absorbing refugees instead of allowing them to proceed to Europe, albeit through two intervening states (Syria and Turkey) first.

Even before this new refugee policy was formalized in the "Compacts," the states and local societies had pressured the international community for more domestic aid for themselves. They had used both implicit and explicit threats of denying access to the refugees that the humanitarian and international communities had an intense desire to aid, for humane reasons and to keep them away from Europe. Jordan had demanded aid for Jordanians as a condition of providing for refugees for years, and Lebanese municipalities had leveraged conflict with the refugees and participation in refugee projects in return for allowing international humanitarian organizations to operate. Now these agreements were publicly promoted, and both states used the threat of refusing refugees as a source of leverage on a grand scale. International aid increased, and international lending institutions offered loans at preferential rates.

The new policy restrictions against Syrians started around 2015, the same year as mass migration to Europe made the news. Close on the heels of this mass migration, in early 2016, Jordan and then Lebanon negotiated the London Compacts. The Compacts, advertised internationally as a win-win policy within a work-oriented neoliberal framework, essentially formalized the exchange of state aid in return for concessions toward the refugees. The Compacts were an addition to existing deals, promoting employment for the refugees in the host countries as a solution to the refugee problem.[1]

These Compacts were not a straightforward win for the governments of Lebanon and Jordan, however. Commonly generalized as aid, the money was actually a mix of aid and loans. The requirements for receiving this new international money entailed changes in state fiscal policies. In return for concessionary financing, Jordan agreed to eliminate more subsidies, raise taxes, and crack down on water theft, despite the fact that these policies affected the regime's core constituency. Lebanon raised taxes, accommodating its budget to pay for civil servant salary raises in the process. These changes affected the core constituency in Jordan, and a main constituency in Lebanon. Imposing new taxes and withdrawing subsidies meant more expenditures for the lower and middle classes, which citizens protested. Governments continued to insist that the root of the problem was the expensive Syrians draining their budgets and infrastructures. A new round of protests ignored all of those factors, however, as citizens rejected the idea that their states were forced into these adverse policy moves. The massive money flowing in furthered the conviction that Syrians had little to do with government taxation or subsidy decisions.

In this chapter I show how international organizations responded to what they interpreted as a clear communication of civil discord. They began providing goods and services to locals, allaying many of the core grievances of early protests. In doing so, they displaced some citizen demands onto themselves, and indirectly increased expectations of the state due to the amount of aid the countries began to receive. The states responded to being blamed by pushing international organizations to provide public goods to their citizens and leveraging their policies toward the refugees to force the hands of donors and lenders. In turn, the international community wanted certain guarantees for its money, which would translate into painful economic policies for the citizens. Jordanians and Lebanese continued to protest against their states, demanding that the states halt the new austerity policies enacted to receive loans. While initial protests were focused on immediate crises and fundamental goods, this new round of protests united numerous grievances into the common refrain of the state not doing its job.

It's All about the Hosts

The donor community learned a lot from the tent protests, discussed in chapter 4, Mercy Corps officials in Amman said.[2] Those initial protests effectively signaled to the humanitarian community the serious negative implications of neglecting the host population.[3] They concluded that protests in the host population over the lack of goods and services were signs of the stress that refugees caused, which would naturally be reflected in hostility toward the Syrian refugees or their own governments. And so, they took up the task of expanding provision of those goods and services, in the belief that if the host community's suffering were alleviated, or if it possibly benefited from refugee-related aid, then societal conflict would be reduced. Mercy Corps wrote of needing a "paradigm shift," to start focusing on the countries affected and including these host populations in their response.[4] This was partly a result of the complete neglect and insensitivity by the humanitarian community to the host populations at the outset, when it turned

needy locals away.[5] It also reflected a prioritization of stability, with the repercussions of the Syrian influx now viewed as a "looming, historic threat" to that
stability.[6] From this perspective, it did not matter whether these problems were
indeed caused by the refugees, or instead were pre-existing.

Severe negative impacts affecting the livelihood of citizens were the heart of
the problem, INGOs reasoned, and these impacts either revitalized old conflicts
or generated new ones.[7] The imposition of curfews on Syrians in Lebanon was
one indicator of conflict, along with protests centered either on economic and
welfare issues or the Syrians themselves. Conflict was the focus, although some
noted different types of conflict. Mercy Corps accurately documented that tensions, often tied to the scarcity of resources and jobs, existed not only between
the Jordanian host community and the refugees but also between citizens and their
own government.[8] Tensions with the refugees or protests in general drew donor
aid and programs. In this sense, aid was conflict-driven.[9] Jobs and services would
lessen social conflict, the INGOs believed, since the countries' institutions could
not deal with the extra population. An early INGO report stated that the "crisis
exposed the fact that the needs of Jordanians were not adequately addressed by
local institutions, and that institutions' capacity to solve pressing issues is too
limited."[10] INGOs responded with integrated programs that included both hosts
and refugees and targeting the perceived negative effects of the refugees. Beginning in 2014, INGOs introduced a flurry of programs rhetorically framed around
social cohesion, refugee-host community relations, resilience, and social stability.[11] The international community targeted programs and aid to areas that would
alleviate the problems of citizens, including stocking pharmacies, offering paid
work, and supporting small businesses.[12]

The INGOs bought into the idea that Syrians negatively affected the host countries and, like the states themselves, begged for aid on the basis of how much
Syrians were hurting host citizens. In this way they put the negative implications
of the refugee presence center stage, lifting them from rumor to policy rationale.
Andrew Harper, the top UNHCR official in Jordan, echoed the need to aid the
average Jordanian, who was seen to be suffering the effects of the refugees. "They
[the Jordanians] just cannot be expected to be absorbing the consequences of
the international community's ineffectiveness in Syria by themselves," he said.[13]
World Bank reports repeated the same theme. As early as 2013, the World Bank
made an exception for Jordan because it was hosting the refugees, providing it
with a low interest loan. The World Bank stated that the bread subsidy enjoyed
by Syrians was a drain on the state's finances, yet, ironically, helped maintain this
subsidy against its prior strict neoliberal beliefs due to the desire to create stability between refugees and host citizens.[14] The World Bank later joined with other
international organizations to create the Global Concessional Financing Facility,

geared to helping host countries. The main focus was Jordan and Lebanon.[15] One prominent donor aid conference for Lebanon opened with the statement that more than 200,000 Lebanese have become poor due to the war and the influx of refugees.[16]

Both countries benefited from this aid, but the dynamics and effectiveness of the aid differed with each country's various capacities and institutional problems. While in Jordan the INGOs worked in coordination with the governments to fix infrastructure, in Lebanon citizens went directly to INGOs for help, bypassing the state. INGO officials responded variously to this call to stand in for the state without official permission. Some agreed, working with municipalities and avoiding the central government. Others attempted to work with the central government but then dropped the work altogether as it became cumbersome and fraught with difficulty and corruption. Still others insisted on educating the populace and encouraging them to turn to the state for their needs.[17] In Lebanon, counting on state help was not the norm, since the state was viewed by the populace and donors alike as unresponsive. Donors stated that they tried to circumvent the national state as much as possible, dealing with the municipalities instead.[18] The jurisdiction and policy realm of local authorities increased in tandem. Through these dynamics, the pre-existing belief by international funders and INGOs that the Lebanese state would remain incapable of responding to its people was inadvertently institutionalized as donors continued to avoid the state.[19]

The proliferation of local and international NGOs in Lebanon and Jordan since the Syrian influx has provided alternative solutions for receiving services outside the state. In many cases, society did not need to take to the streets in protest to achieve its goals, which were instead accomplished through direct and indirect pressure on the INGOs. In some cases, local communities understood their leverage and quickly began demanding aid from the international community directly. In others, humanitarian organizations shared community grievances and, seeking to decrease conflict, moved to address them. At other times, the pressure was overt but indirect, as municipalities received pressure from their residents for services and passed that on to the INGOs. In order to fulfill their mandates of aiding or registering refugees, these organizations would have to comply.[20] Thus, before operating in a town or in a particular building, serving Syrians and processing refugee applications, an aid organization would need to agree to upgrade facilities for host populations, including schools, garbage, electricity, and other goods and services. Demands would come from municipalities, local residents, and local NGOs. In this way, municipalities were at the forefront of communal pressure on humanitarian organizations to deliver more services and goods to citizens. With the Syrian crisis, the importance of municipalities increased, and their room to maneuver broadened, a change approved by the international community. In Lebanon, the absence of central state policymaking pushed this trend into overdrive, while in Jordan, policies promoting decentralization to local governments had previously been planned.

Conflict, Leverage, and Restrictions on Syrians

With international donors revealing their sensitivity to security concerns and the threat of instability posed by ongoing protests, Jordan and Lebanon recognized their strategic positions: they would be able to leverage their citizens' response to the refugees for increased international aid. (To be sure, Jordan had been playing this card for decades, first with the Palestinians, then the Iraqis, and now the Syrians.) Both countries emphasized how much they suffered, and how much funding they needed to continue without insecurity. This link between insecurity and hosting the refugees was the key to maintaining global attention and funding. As a UN humanitarian official in Lebanon stated, "This is not just a humanitarian crisis, it is also very much about maintaining stability in Lebanon."[21] To secure their humanitarian funding needs, the UN was competing for attention with other aid crises and threats of terrorism, not to mention donor fatigue. Yet earlier protests gave the states leverage that brought in increased aid, since instability in these countries would only spur further out-migration to Europe.

Not only the local state authorities but national ones also used their position as refugee hosts to extract aid money for locals. Part of this was allocating a percentage of money to go to citizens on the national level. States used the potential conflict between refugees and locals, threatening stability, to highlight their need for more programs and funding. To drive home the point that the national government could not be ignored, states implemented restrictions on refugees and denied them entry. The humanitarian community could only respond by attempting to sweeten the deal for the state, to convince it to allow the refugees in or just not deport them. After all, the humanitarian community could be shown the door at any point, and had no tools to force the domestic state.

The Jordanian state early on insisted on a large percentage of aid going to its own citizens, later formalizing this in the joint response plans to the Syrian crisis. The percentage usually mentioned is 30 percent of all aid channeled to host communities, but some INGOs have cited 40 percent or 50 percent.[22] This requirement was repeated in personal meetings with the Ministry of Planning and not publicized. As analyst Victoria Kelberer states, Jordan turned what was a humanitarian crisis into a developmental one, convincing the international community of such.[23] Aid moved directly to the state, much of it for budget support. Jordan used "migration diplomacy" to plead its case of suffering under the weight of the refugees, and received aid.[24] National response plans after 2014 thus turned from a focus on humanitarianism to one of national aid for development. The National Resilience Plan in 2014 called for USD 4 billion for Jordanian public services to alleviate the impact of the refugee crisis on Jordan itself.[25] "Resilience" here referred to the host country and its citizens, not the refugees.

Jordan established a special accounting system for aid money (the JORISS system), in order for the state to direct a portion to its priorities. These priorities were set in agreement with the aid community through the Jordan Response Plans.[26] Organizations would funnel their money through this new state accounting system, which would calculate percentages going to national projects and to refugees. Some aid providers complained that the system's accounting was not transparent, and that their own calculations did not coincide with the system's.[27] The state found creative ways to exclude certain aid from the "host aid" category, forcing a larger percentage to be spent on citizens.[28] Individual aid agencies, during private meetings with government officials, were told that higher percentages of aid needed to be directed toward citizens.[29] Jordan also played with refugee numbers for its own purposes. International humanitarian organizations did not openly confront the government on the differences in numbers, but they did not trust or use them either.[30] While Azraq camp was supposed to have more than twenty thousand residents, international aid officials told me they delivered bread for nine thousand people in 2015.[31] The state also directed money to citizens in other ways. Half of businesses in the new Azraq camp were required to be owned by Jordanians, per the agreement for the camp. It was the government's concern with optics, how it would look to Jordanians, that dictated this requirement, according to a UNHCR official.[32] Yet the result was funneling more aid money to hosts.

Although Jordan was more successful in this game, Lebanon also made aid for the refugees conditional on a portion being spent on the domestic population. The change in policy toward the refugees in 2014–2015 entailed utilizing the humanitarian sector to share costs and to aid Lebanese communities.[33] Lebanon would get help for the economic effects of refugees.[34] Again, reports vary of the precise percentages, with most agreeing 30 percent was allocated to nationals and other sources stating 40 percent. The ministries also differed on what they stipulated for aid.[35]

Indirect tactics were used to secure aid to the states, similar to actions used by municipalities, involving either restricting aid groups' access to refugees, or refugees' access to aid. In late 2014, Jordan stopped the provision of free medical care for Syrian refugees.[36] Syrians began paying the same as Jordanians, and those without Ministry of the Interior cards paid a higher rate, up to 60 percent higher.[37] This move was not announced beforehand to the NGOs or the international community.[38] It was later reversed. For educational payments, when UN organizations began paying Syrian school fees in Lebanon, the ministry pressed for the same benefits for Lebanese. Parents complained to the ministry, who passed along the grievances to the UN in return for continued access.[39] Apparently recognizing the power of this kind of leverage, two years into the crisis Lebanon stepped up its overt and indirect methods for keeping Syrians out. The Ministry of Education and Higher Education in 2014 halted the registration of Syrian children. Registration began again some five months later when the ministry received funding specifically for second shifts for Syrians.[40] With the Compacts in 2016, this trade of aid for access became overt.

Jordan's New Restrictions on Syrians

After various domestic effects of the refugees were felt in 2013–2014, Jordan enacted restrictions to entry for Syrians, put restrictions on their internal movement, and began deporting some Syrians. Jordan progressively decreased the number of border crossing points and moved them farther east.[41] Unofficial border crossings in the West, where the bulk of Syrians who came to Jordan lived, were closed in mid-2013.[42] Airport regulations against Syrian entrance increased in 2014.[43] Fewer Syrians were allowed in, they were subjected to more stringent criteria, and refugees were turned away before having the opportunity to register with the UNHCR.[44] Qualifications for entry became stricter. Even single girls under eighteen— traveling alone—were rejected if they lacked identification, even though these girls would be vulnerable crossing back through the desert and militia territories to any habitable land in Syria.[45] The only official entry point then was far east into the desert at Rukban. Jordan and Syria both constructed berms inside their borders, sand mounds to keep Syrians out of the legal entry point to Jordan but technically within the country's border. Syrians began to wait in these areas, stranded.[46] By 2016 there were some forty thousand people in the berms, without access to shelter or water or any regular aid from the international community.[47]

Regulations on the movement of Syrians within Jordan increased. Jordan attempted to push more Syrians into camps, and bailouts from the camps became more difficult, then halted altogether. In July 2014, Jordan told the UNHCR to no longer give Asylum Seeker Certificates to any Syrian who left a camp unless he or she had proof of bailout.[48] The bailout procedure itself was stopped in January 2015.[49] Jordan then set up an "urban verification program" forcing Syrians living outside of the camps to re-register with the Jordanian authorities.[50] Failure to meet the requirements would remove the individual Syrian's registration and thus decrease their benefits. To re-register under this program, they had to have certain items that made it almost impossible to do so, which turned out to be problematic for the government as well. For example, refugees needed a health certificate, and the medical backlog for these appointments with the Ministry of Health was years-long.[51] In addition, refugees needed a residence certificate or a stamped lease agreement with a copy of the landlord's identity card.[52]

There were increasing reports of deportations. In December 2014, nine Syrian refugee medical workers were sent back to Syria.[53] Fearing additional Palestinians in their country, Jordan deported Palestinian refugees from Syria or prohibited them from entering.[54] Jordan sent Syrians back to their warring country for various reasons, including sickness, employment, and sex work.[55] Jordan reportedly deported fifty-eight Syrians from 2014 to 2015, with eleven cases of children deported with families from Za'atari camp.[56] Working without a permit was a top reason for being deported, and in cases where children were caught, they were either deported or sent to a camp, where their parents would be obligated to live permanently in order to the retrieve the child.[57]

Lebanon Closes Its Doors

Lebanon's actions toward Syrians began to change in 2014. The Lebanese state started by changing guidelines for allowing entry to Syrians with the explicit goal of reducing their numbers. Because Syrians in Lebanon had voted in their home country's elections that year and re-elected their president, some Lebanese politicians argued they were not refugees. Sixteen-thousand Syrians had their refugee status removed by UNHCR as a result.[58] In June 2014, entry was restricted to Syrians from border areas engulfed in ongoing fighting. In the fall, the policy was formalized and became known as the October Policy, or Policy on Syrian Displacement. Borders were closed to Syrians for all but emergency cases, and refugee status was removed from Syrians who committed legal infractions, including entering through an unofficial border, or who returned to Syria, however briefly.[59] Internal military checkpoints increased through the country.

The open-door policy was over. Guidelines were issued and went into effect the following January in 2015 to both restrict legal entry and remove legal status from Syrians already in the country. To enter Lebanon legally, Syrians now had to fit into one of the specified categories, none of which was refugee. UNHCR registrations dropped dramatically. One way to enter was to claim to be a tourist, showing cash and a hotel booking at the border. A thriving business sector sprung up, specializing in providing fake hotel reservations and renting thousand-dollar bills to show the Lebanese officers. The money would be returned to the lender after crossing the border.[60] Syrians who were already in Lebanon had a choice to either renew their residency as a migrant worker, under the auspices of a Lebanese sponsor, or sign a pledge promising not to work and obtain residency based on UNHCR registration.[61] Residency would cost USD 200 annually for each

Syrian over fifteen years old.[62] Subsequently, the UNHCR recorded Syrians, but did not register them as Syrian refugees. In April, Lebanon asked the UNHCR to de-register more than a thousand refugees, due to their arrival after the January cut-off date.[63] If they had entered through an unofficial border, it would have cost more than USD 600 for them to obtain residency, and even then success was not assured.[64] In May 2015, the Lebanese government ordered the UNHCR to stop registering Syrians completely.[65]

Analysts referred to this as "manufacturing vulnerability," or pushing individuals into illegal status, since the new residency policies would all but guarantee most Syrians could not meet the requirements, and thus they would be staying in the country without legal permission. The residence of large numbers of Syrians became illegal with these new regulations, estimated conservatively at over half of the refugee population just in the first months.[66] Municipal measures against refugees increased, including curfews.[67] Syrians were kicked out of some municipal areas,[68] or their businesses shut down.[69] Richer Syrians could avoid these policies; the new rules were directed at those with few resources.[70] Lacking legal status and at the mercy of various difficult bureaucratic procedures, Syrians feared encountering the security services and obtaining sponsorship. Women were particularly vulnerable to abuse, and could be placed in a position of having to do what security personnel or a sponsor asked, or being jailed, tortured, or deported.[71] Children, who were presumed to be less vulnerable to arbitrary arrest, consequently took up the duties of adults by working to support their families. Among other jobs, Syrian children filled in for state incapacities by collecting trash for little money, cleaning up a trash crisis left unsolved by the state.[72] Their presence working on the streets was then another reason for the average Lebanese to resent hosting the Syrians.

The Compacts, or Bribery Humanitarianism

If restricting the access of aid organizations to refugees or playing on international fears of domestic instability proved useful leverage for the host countries, the 2015 avalanche of refugees hitting the shores of Europe gave them an even greater advantage. By 2016, international leverage had clearly switched to the host countries.[73] The international community was pressed by public opinion either to take care of the refugees in Lebanon, Jordan, and Turkey, or to accept more into Western countries. Intentionally or not, the harsh restrictions Jordan and Lebanon had imposed on the refugees sounded an alarm in the humanitarian community. In order for the humanitarian organizations to provide aid to the refugees, they would need to spend a significant amount of money on developmental projects within the host states, including infrastructure and employment activities aimed at citizens.

The Compacts were negotiated in London in early 2016, first with Jordan and then with Lebanon. The agreements appeared to be a win-win proposition that would justify keeping the refugees in the Middle East.[74] Aid and incentives to the host countries could be targeted to create jobs for refugees, resulting in economic gain for host citizens and refugees alike, somehow without competing with or angering domestic labor. The deal would exchange temporary work permits and enhanced education for refugees in return for generous loans, aid, and preferential trade agreements for the host countries. Ultimately, the deals would hopefully forestall northern migration and keep people where they were, both refugees and citizens of host countries,[75] pleasing a domestic European electorate swinging toward exclusionary nationalism. This new international refugee policy was supported not only by the EU but also by the International Monetary Fund (IMF) and World Bank.[76]

Jordan received outright aid for several years, loans at preferential rates, new investment, and access to the EU market for goods.[77] Initial benefits were USD 700 million in grants for each of the years from 2016 to 2018, several hundred million more from other donors, and possibly more than USD 1 billion in increased financing from international banks at concessionary rates.[78] For the 2016–2018 plan under the Compact agreement, Jordan requested UDS 8 billion over three years to compensate for the costs of hosting the refugees.[79] These benefits were contingent upon Jordan reaching benchmarks for Syrian employment, along with other benefits for the refugees.[80] The Jordanian government quibbled with the implementation of the Compacts, repeatedly stating that jobs for Syrians would depend on it receiving the promised money first, while the international community wanted proof of progress before transferring more money.[81] Despite the size of the developmental assistance provided to Jordan, little measurable progress was seen. Jordan was to provide 200,000 job opportunities for Syrians and increase access to education for Syrian refugee children. Syrian children would be allowed in schools without identification documents. After a year, almost half of refugee children remained out of school.[82] Aid benefits were tied to numbers of registered refugees, and, despite many repatriations or returns, both voluntary and involuntary, of Syrians from Jordan, the official number of registered refugees has remained stable for years. The government reportedly instructed UNHCR not to report these numbers, despite at one point having a shortage of buses to accommodate all the Syrians returning.[83]

Lebanon rode the coattails of Jordan's successful international negotiation and public relations, despite the fact that Lebanon is nowhere near as organized as a central government nor as unified, and donors fundamentally distrust the central government's ability to responsibly handle fiscal resources.[84] As a reflection of this skepticism and state incapacity, Lebanon benefited from the new compacts at a lower level per refugee.[85] Despite having double the number of refugees, if not more, Lebanon received only slightly more financing than Jordan. Still, the Lebanese state receives about 40 percent of all international financial aid from donors directly to its budget.[86] A total of USD 1.6 billion was pledged, almost all as grants.[87] The London Conference in February 2016 resulted in changes to Lebanon's policy in exchange for more support from the European countries. The Compact stipulated that Lebanon would facilitate access to education and employment for Syrians, in return for receiving funding for infrastructure projects, access to markets for Lebanese businesses, and loans, initially amounting to some USD 5.4 billion.[88] Residency restrictions for Syrians eased. The Lebanese government lifted some of the harsh restrictions on Syrians, now accepting a statement that a Syrian would honor Lebanese law instead of the previous promise that Syrians would not work in Lebanon. The burdensome residency fee was waived, but only for those who still had legal status. Those who had lost it previously remained vulnerable.[89] Fees continued to be imposed on Syrians, and their amounts varied by location.[90] As a result, the trend of Syrians living without legal residency continued.[91]

Aid Fixes Some Problems

The amount of money coming in to these countries because of the Syrian refugee crisis was already large; with the Compacts it was supersized. Donors began to focus developmental aid on problem areas of Jordan and Lebanon under the guise of offering humanitarian aid to help the refugees. The resulting aid did indeed fix many domestic infrastructure problems, particularly in Jordan, where the state is more capable than that of Lebanon. Aid poured in from numerous sources around the globe, individual countries and INGOs, to fix endemic domestic problems. In this way, donor countries now spun developmental aid as humanitarianism, while also justifying limiting the numbers of Syrians resettled in their own developed countries or rejecting resettlement altogether.

Loans and grants to Jordan concentrated on infrastructure and services, mainly water, waste, and electricity, but also roads, schools, and hospitals. Jordan's water sector demonstrates the domestic benefits of this approach. By 2018, contributions to water infrastructure had come from all over the globe, including Japan, the Netherlands, Germany, and Spain. State officials from these countries linked their aid to alleviating the problems caused by the Syrian refugees regarding sewage and water.[92] The European Bank for Reconstruction and Development and the UK provided USD 31 million to Jordan for dealing with solid waste.[93] The European Bank also provided USD 3.2 billion for infrastructure projects, more than USD 1 billion of which will come as a grant.[94] Loans by the World Bank and IMF in the hundreds of millions were either low- or no-interest. As of early 2017, USD 2.3 billion had been given to Jordan under the Compact agreements, $1.4 billion in grants and the rest in loans.[95] In 2018, Jordan listed its funding requirements at around USD 2.5 billion, dividing aid into budget support, refugee aid, and resilience, the latter going to domestic priorities delineated by the state, especially infrastructure, services, and livelihood.[96]

Lebanon has also received aid from the Compact, but not as much as Jordan by 2019, mainly due to governmental dysfunction. Inability to pass a budget or form a government after elections in 2018 delayed and then prevented the transfer of much aid.[97] Still, large amounts of aid were being spent in Lebanon on domestic projects due to the refugee crisis, in addition to that spent directly helping the refugees. In 2016, UN agencies spent an equivalent of 3 percent of Lebanon's GDP. While not all of this funding is exclusively related to refugees, the UN's overall budget has skyrocketed from the crisis. As one senior official with the UN Development Program put it: "Without refugees, our programming would be much smaller. To give you an idea, we spent $26 million [USD] in 2012, and in 2016 had reached almost three times that."[98] By 2018, Lebanon was seeking USD 17 billion in aid.[99] The UK itself provided 99 million pounds in 2015, increased from 2.5 million before the crisis.[100] A major part of aid went to waste, electricity, and water. USAID spent millions improving Lebanon's water networks.[101] Lebanon's CEDRE conference concluded that almost USD 11 billion would be needed to fix Lebanon's problems, and the numerous states and organizations attending would help to provide that amount.[102] Most of this would be in loans, and some of the grant money would even be used to subsidize the loans. Gulf donors spent more in aid, often given directly to the state. Saudi Arabia offered USD 1 billion,[103] and Kuwait opened its pledge with half a billion.[104]

INGO aid was important not only for states, but for individuals in the host communities as well. The UN and other INGOs provided not only infrastructure but garbage cans, blankets, heaters, and streetlights for local communities.[105] They incorporated citizens into their programs and employment as well. Numerous NGOs sprung up to capture some of the aid, employing a good portion of the middle and lower-middle strata, a fact illustrated through an anecdote: in Mafraq, in the space of two hours, I witnessed two men submitting their wives' resumes for jobs at two local NGOs. The NGO officials stated they receive many of these every day.[106] Other local NGOs feared the end of the Syrian war, predicting funds would be redirected inside Syria instead of remaining with the neighboring states. People are now less upset at the Syrians, Jordanians stated, because the international organizations are helping citizens.[107] This dynamic existed in Lebanon also. "We see how we can benefit from the NGOs," one *mukhtar* in Lebanon's

Beka'a Valley stated, "so the situation is better now. We just want people to be employed."[108] The Syrian crisis is an opportunity to earn money for many NGOs, and they employ a lot of local people, another INGO employee explained. Some local NGOs went so far as to rely only on international organizations, ignoring the state.[109]

Fiscal Changes to Receive Loans

Despite their strong ability to negotiate at a moment of European fear of refugee flows, Lebanon and Jordan did not receive assistance without conditions attached. To receive these loans and aid for infrastructure, development, and basic services for their populations, the states were instructed to alter their fiscal policies and decrease their debts. They followed guidelines set down by international lending institutions, including such tactics as removing subsidies and increasing taxes. For loans, these policies were necessary. For aid, they were not strictly necessary, but could signal the country's good faith attempt to improve the macro economy in ways international donors sought. Often, outright aid amounts surpassed loans, indicating these economic liberalization changes were not forced on the states. The specific policies and which domestic groups would suffer the economic costs of them were state decisions. The policies the states chose would increase costs to the middle and lower classes, generally exempting the elites, which in turn sparked protests. In some cases the policies weighed heavily on core regime constituencies.

Jordan entered into an agreement with the IMF for a USD 723 million loan through the Extended Fund Facility, with more to be decided.[110] The conditions for this loan were structural changes and reducing the debt-to-GDP ratio, which by this point was 93 percent.[111] In line with neoliberal dogma, Jordan chose to enact taxes and remove subsidies to lower its debt. These policies were highly unpopular. The state laid the groundwork for removing subsidies by emphasizing how much non-Jordanians (i.e., mainly Syrians) benefited from them, amounting to a waste of government spending.[112] Beginning in 2017, and ramping up from January 2018, taxes were increased incrementally but continually, several times in one month in 2018, and subsidies lowered.[113] Prices increased on fuel, electricity, taxes, a variety of consumer goods, and even bread. In one step, bread prices rose by between 60 percent and 100 percent.[114] Further, the new income tax law introduced in 2018 broadened the tax base, lowering the threshold for paying taxes.[115]

Various other existing policies were affected as well. To accommodate Syrian laborers according to the Compact agreement, Jordan altered its relationship with foreign migrant workers, particularly those from Egypt. Jordan made space in its domestic labor market for Syrians by attempting to reduce the number of Egyptian migrant workers. The relationship with Egypt, whose population relies on those remittances and labor, has been touchy on this topic ever since, with several high-level meetings devoted to discussing migrant labor.[116] In the water sector, Jordan demonstrated that it would be responsible with international money by cracking down on tolerated illegality among its base constituency, who had long been stealing public water. These attempts to stop theft were often met with violence against state officials.[117] The Jordanian government also capped the age for patients to be treated in the prestigious national cancer hospital, resulting in mass public anger through social media.[118]

Lebanon relied on fees and value-added taxes (VAT) as its main approach to decrease the deficit, which stood at 150 percent of GDP in 2018, and raise funds to cover the new public-sector salary scale.[119] Despite needing to reduce its expenditures, the Lebanese state had been pushed to increase salaries for public-sector employees, including teachers, public servants, and military retirees, through years of protest by these key electoral constituencies. In March 2017, the government passed twenty-two new taxes and fees, including the signature rise in the VAT by 1 percent, intended to finance the new salary scale. While exempting some basic goods, luxury goods were spared from tax, leading analysts to agree with popular opinion that the law was regressive.[120] Taxes rose on cigarettes, alcohol, Internet and phone services, among others. Energy subsidies were slated to decrease.[121] Despite these tax changes, to fund its large budget deficit Lebanon was actually counting on future, unproved oil resources yet to be developed.[122]

Grievances Multiply into Movements: 2016–2019

Despite the avalanche of aid and loans, many of the grievances of the populations were not resolved, and protests were not ultimately quelled. Specific livelihood problems continued to be important, and people still engaged in emergency or crisis protests. Increasingly, grievances combined, one spilling over into the next, and then broadened into overall systemic issues. The changes to state fiscal policy served to widen the range of communities with grievances, aiding this process. Protests included demands that were not only specific and concrete but also more abstract, with a special focus on demands against corruption. These grievances and claims were more programmatic and organized than the earlier round of protests, and increased in sophistication as time went on. Protests now encompassed more popular participation, expanding the included groups, and linking ethnically, geographically, and religiously diverse populations. Women, youth, and families were all involved.

The frame, or the central discursive meaning, of the protests changed, amplifying and affirming some existing beliefs and ideas. The rhetoric became focused on rights and entitlements on the basis of citizenship. This is particularly interesting in the Lebanese case, since the idea that these services were rights of citizenship was not common previously among the population. Lebanese had expected little of their state's health care system.[123] While Jordan provided public health care, the state was cutting those eligible for costly treatments. Decreasing the ages eligible for treatment at the national cancer hospital caused mass condemnation of the government on social media, lasting well after the state slightly relaxed its rules. The discourse was that health care was no longer a right, that health care was dead. A prominent Jordanian cartoonist depicted a memorial for health insurance,[124] echoed prominently in social media sites. Aid money coming in amplified a familiar frame, already resonant in these countries, of corrupt governments and officials stealing the money rightfully belonging to the people. Why should the people be taxed if the state was receiving so many resources in aid?

Jordan

Although local issues still generated demonstrations, taxes were the main trigger for protests after 2016. Protests over taxes were more encompassing and enduring than those over single-issue crises in infrastructure demonstrated in chapter 4.[125] Particularly offensive were the taxes introduced as a condition of receiving loans from international organizations. Sporadic protests in 2016 occurred over unemployment and other financial issues, particularly fees on cars, agricultural conditions, taxi competition, and student fees.[126] The most extreme were in Dhiban. Protesters there objected to the state of the economy and unemployment, and tried to kill themselves,[127] despite the fact that, in the Jordanian context, suicide is an extreme and generally unthinkable act. Overall, labor protests increased in 2016, with a number of protests over unemployment.[128]

In 2017, as prices of goods began increasing because of rising taxes and decreasing subsidies, protests against austerity policies ramped up all over Jordan. Protests began in January against prices, with youth picketing parliament.[129] These and later protesters argued that the government could find a way to raise money without affecting the less privileged. In February, towns in the South protested against taxes on fuel, food, and services. Major centers of protest included Karak, Tafileh, Salt, and Madaba, with several thousand people turning out in sparsely populated regions. Slogans attacked the economy and governance, highlighting corruption and privatization. People chanted and held signs that read "Shame on you, you have sold the country for a dollar," and "We cannot pay the bills for the corrupt."[130] Tactics included protesters riding on horseback, an attention-grabbing method of demonstrating their ability to reject rising fuel prices in favor of non-fuel alternatives.[131] Residents of Amman joined in the protests, with around 1,500 people calling for an end to the government. Slogans and signs equated the act of increasing taxes with danger for the government, stating "Raising prices is playing with fire," and "The government that impoverishes people must go."[132] A boycott of chicken began when its price rose during Ramadan.[133] Public opinion was further ignited when a video showing a citizen being physically kicked out of parliament because he was objecting to the budget went locally viral. An official was recorded in the video saying, "This is none of your business, citizen."[134] The overwhelming social media response was that because this man was a (tax-paying) citizen, it was definitely his business.

The largest demonstrations took place in June 2018, but numerous smaller protest actions had been held since the beginning of that year. In January, the government began increasing taxes, some incrementally, but many were raised numerous times in a short period. The price of electricity increased three times within a few months, for example.[135] Pharmacists warned that they would strike against the new medication tax.[136] Protests and "riots" occurred all over the kingdom over the price rises in February, demanding the government's resignation and a reversal of the new policies. These taxes hiked prices on more than 150 goods, foods, and services, including communications, fuel, and electricity. The price of bread also increased between 60 and 100 percent.[137] Bread prices had previously been considered untouchable, even by international institutions, yet to decrease the deficit, the government crossed this prior red line.[138] Farmers protested continuously to have the 10 percent tax on agriculture revoked, and threatened to step up their actions in what the journalist termed "relentless protests."[139] Later they prepared to sue the government for redress against this imposition.[140] Protests continued in March, as lawyers joined the fray, protesting the arrest of activists in price protests, including lawyers.[141] The northern city of Zarqa then protested tax increases along with the southern cities.[142]

Observers increasingly used terms indicating that popular frustration and grievances were growing: "resentment is building,"[143] "trust between the government and the people is at a new low."[144] Some feared "a revolt of the hungry," and many clearly attributed the economic crisis to the government, stating "The government and parliament are responsible"; "It is the political elite's fault that the country is on the edge of ruin."[145] Attribution of blame was now directed more at the system or regime, and less at individual governments or ministers.[146] "People no longer care who the prime minister is," one former politician stated, "because they know the king is really calling the shots. The monarchy is ruling directly."[147] While elites continued to blame external factors, the public did not believe the country's stance on Jerusalem translated into higher taxes and a poorer economy.[148] Media, activists, and the populace highlighted corruption as the key problem. Elites were seemingly getting rich through corrupt practices while the poor were paying steep taxes. In March, some of the poorest municipalities were allowed to buy luxury cars, paid for by the municipal budget. This decision, which would benefit municipal officials, sped through social media to mass disapproval.[149]

At the end of May, the largest demonstrations since 2011 began and lasted seven days. It was not only the taxes on goods, but now income taxes as well that were at issue. A proposed law would widen the tax base, requiring more Jordanians to file and pay income taxes. The June 2018 protests involved at least thirty-three associations and unions, including teachers, bankers, and doctors.[150] Reportedly, tens of thousands participated at the fourth circle in Amman, along with protesters in other cities around the country. Women and families were heavily involved. Youth and the professional middle class were at the front of the movement, which brought together numerous old and new groups.[151] Al-Hirak was involved, as was Taqaddam, the Civil Alliance, and the Ma'an youth organization, among others.[152] Diverse grievances were expressed in these protests, by people ranging from lower-income farmers and factory workers to middle-class engineers. Further, the established organizations were pushed by the populace to continue the demonstrations.[153] The protests appeared to be nonideological and to represent a cross-section of the country's population.[154] These demonstrations were supported by almost 70 percent of Jordanians, and few were overtly against them. Even fewer people believed the regime's typical rationalization, that external actors were responsible for the disruptive protests.[155]

The frames and rhetoric used in these protests demonstrated active rejection of government tactics of division, broad indictments against the regime, and the linking of multiple grievances into a single story against neoliberalism. Dividing tactics were recognized as diversions and rejected.[156] Slogans and signs included, "They are stealing our country before our very eyes,"[157] "corruption = hunger" written on loaves of bread,[158] "You have sold the land and the house," "They have sold Jordan for dollars," "We are not poor but were made poor, this is your policy, oh dollar."[159] One banner stated, "And popular will prevails,"[160] and another, "Do you hear us? We are broke."[161] The populace had reached a "tipping point," wrote one popular blogger. He stated that people now rejected government's historical tactic of scapegoating political organizations, foreigners, and refugees.[162]

Demonstrators disputed the state-promoted logic that these austerity policies were necessary. While the lending institutions put conditions on the states, the states chose the specific policies to enact. Societies felt that the states were taking from those who already did not have, instead of the corrupt and elites. The contradiction between massive aid coming in and making elites rich through corruption, and austerity measures being imposed on the lower and middle classes, was enlightening. Economic problems were now attributed to government policies and poor management of the economy and budget, not to the expense of hosting the Syrians that the government continually mentioned.[163] People asked where all this aid money went, while the majority of Jordanians were in debt.[164]

Hundreds of such events took place, according to security service press releases, and tens of thousands of Jordanians participated around the country. Some protests used the common tactics of burning tires and blocking roads. Protests were large, despite the fact that security forces prevented many potential activists from reaching the demonstration areas. Gatherings lasted well into the night. Slogans included "No to the income tax law," "We want the bread subsidy back," "We came to talk politics, to change the method of governance." In Karak in the South, they added, "Don't tell me 'security and stability' while you're protecting those thugs." In al-Salt, slogans included, "It's all a charade, the gang is still the same," and "We no longer say anything except that Abdullah is the only one responsible," in protests that had gone on since February.[165] In Mafraq, they rejected statements that these new measures were out of the government's control due to the demands of international organizations, saying, "You've impoverished Jordanian people and mortgaged them to the World Bank." At the University of Jordan, they declared their solidarity against this economic imposition, "We students are with workers against the gang of capitalists."[166] The social media hashtag #al-islah qabla al-driba (reform before tax) was used to spread the protest and express the desire for government to improve services before imposing additional taxes.[167] The word "reform" in this use did not mean neoliberal economic adjustments but instead substantive changes in the state bureaucracies and the regime, which would fix ongoing service and infrastructure problems. Other hashtags were #idrab_al-Urdun (Jordan protests) and #al-duwar al-rab'ia (fourth circle).

Protests started again after the revised income tax law was announced. At the end of November 2018, there were calls for protests, and they began in December. The new income tax law was officially published on December 2, to take effect the following January. These new demonstrations showed popular resolve: large numbers gathered in protest not only during the winter, when people in Jordan tend not to protest due to the weather, but also in the rain. Activists brought umbrellas, taking their children and families. The slogans included the hashtags #Maanash (we don't have any) and #MishSakteen (no longer silent) as well as "We know who the real corrupt are," "Your arrests will not intimidate us," "We know and citizens know that we are average people fed up with the lies."[168] Participating organizations included new local groups such as Hirak Dhiban (movement of Dhiban, southern Jordan) and Hirak al-Ramtha al-Shaabi (the movement of Ramtha youth, located on the northern border with Syria).[169] These protests continued for three weeks, and some persisted into the start of the New Year.[170]

Lebanon

The Lebanese persisted in demonstrations over the same basic grievances they had in previous years, but now added protests against prices and tax increases in 2017–2018. The idea that basic services were a right of the citizenry began to appear in media and protests. Lack of electricity and water continued to spur protests, particularly in the southern areas least served by international donors. Tyr protested when it was deprived of almost all state-provided electricity for two months due to government rationing. Demonstrations there included a broad consumer coalition led by youth, encompassing diverse political parties and groups, asking for the provision of electricity half of the time instead of the quarter they were receiving. Youth blocked entrances to the city, and after confronting the military, they agreed to end the protest.[171] Protests occurred in Tyr several times in 2018, over the lack of water and electricity, and over the expense of these goods if purchased on the private market.[172] Additionally, in southern Lebanon, Sidon residents demonstrated about the scarcity of water and electricity. Security forces blocked the path to the location of the demonstration, and citizens then protested for their right to protest, contending that preventing demonstrations was unconstitutional. During this period, electricity was out continuously for the majority of the day, and water absent for more than two weeks. Trash was an additional issue raised in this protest.[173] The next month in Sidon, when water service was disrupted for days, protesters again demonstrated by blocking roads and burning tires in front of the water headquarters.[174] Protests over electricity included demands for meters to be installed, allowing consumers to pay according to the amount used instead of a flat fee, a policy that generator operators strongly resisted, as it would decrease their profits. Generator bills could run USD 150 per month, even if little electricity was used, and this was on top of the household's bill for state electricity.[175] Generator operators staged their own protest against measures to limit their profits, stopping their provision during evening hours to resist the metering.[176]

In the northern city of Akkar, citizens cut electricity lines, demanding equal provision of electricity among the towns in the area.[177] Citizens, officials, political parties, and civil society groups protested pollution and lack of electricity in another town north of Beirut, and five were injured in confrontations with security forces.[178] In the eastern Beka'a Valley, residents blocked the town entrance by government offices, demanding an increase in electricity service.[179] In one of the highest refugee-concentrated areas, Bar Elias, residents blocked the Litani River to call attention to its pollution.[180] In Beirut, a month-long shortage of water generated protests, which were attended by a recently elected parliamentary member, elected on what was termed the "civil society" ticket, an affiliation outside the long-established political parties.[181]

In northern Tripoli, a region suffering from unemployment and poverty, protests over water, electricity, pollution, and health insurance produced a new movement. Almost 60 percent of residents in Tripoli were poor, and more than 50 percent of the potentially employed had no jobs.[182] In 2016, water shortages there had caused demonstrators to protest the municipality.[183] Local elites and officials had joined in protest on another occasion, targeting government officials and the Minister of Energy and Water, demanding that they allocate water justly.[184] Two years later, a movement calling itself "the revolution of the destitute" demanded water, health insurance, and electricity—at least to have these services for most of the day. Hospital stays, one protester stated, were too expensive for him to afford for his daughter.[185] Protesters demanded better health care and for hospitals to be open for all,[186] directly comparing the benefits Syrians receive with their own lack. People demonstrated online over the death of a Lebanese patient who did not receive treatment due to lack of means, condemning the Lebanese state for not providing free health care, even though it had not previously. A Twitter joke brought home the concept of health care as a right, not a dream, in an exchange between a Lebanese and a Brit. When the Brit inquired about the dreams of the Lebanese, the Lebanese responded: health care, water, and electricity. The Brit replied that he was asking about dreams, not rights.[187]

Unemployment and foreign competition from Syrians generated demands on the state to enforce regulations on non-Lebanese workers. Repeated demonstrations took place in the transport sector over these years. Although not all were related to competition from Syrians, foreign competition was specifically listed as a key grievance in many of these protests. Syrian competition undercutting Lebanese drivers mixed with other grievances against the state. In one such demonstration, workers in transport unions protested government policies and demanded that they focus on enacting regulations against foreign drivers.[188] Drivers directly acted against refugee competition in 2017 in Akkar, stopping Syrians driving pick-up trucks on the international highway.[189] Similarly, they demanded that the government do its job of regulating foreign workers, alleging that hundreds of citizens were unemployed due to these foreign drivers.[190] In another protest the next month that blocked roads, signs proclaimed that Lebanese livelihoods suffered due to the lack of regulation on foreign workers, again calling on specific ministries of the state to fulfill their supervisory and regulatory functions by enacting existing laws.[191] More protests in the same vein occurred in 2018. In July, the land transport union blocked roads, demanding, among other things, that the government track forged plates and foreign drivers, preventing them from undercutting legal local business.[192] The next month the transport union escalated their actions to organize a nationwide protest over fees and foreign competition involving taxi and truck drivers.[193] Grievances and demands continued into

2019, as another national protest of the land transport union occurred over the same medley of issues.[194]

Drivers were not the only ones protesting against Syrian competition, directing their demands for action at the state. In northern Akkar, people blocked roads, burned tires, and asked the labor minister and governor to stop Syrian workers and "protect the interests of Lebanese businesses and workers."[195] Business owners in Iqlim al-Kharoub asked the state to "assume its responsibilities" and close down businesses without licenses.[196] Protesters asked for Syrian businesses to be shut also in Zahle, in the Beka'a Valley, stating further that the Syrians get free medical care while Lebanese do not.[197] Leadership of the general labor union similarly asked the state to close down businesses that employ foreigners, calling on employees of hotels, where many Syrians work, to report to their union if a Syrian or other foreigner took their jobs.[198] Residents protested for three days against Syrian labor in the Zahle region. Protesters stated that Syrians can work for less, since the UN provides them food, health care, and other goods and services. Some decried the seeming lack of opportunity for Lebanese in their own country and asked the labor minister to enforce prohibitions on Syrian workers.[199] One media writer carried this further, expressing envy of the Syrians. "The UN is helping the Syrians, but who is helping me [a Lebanese]?"[200] The comparison of international organizations helping Syrians while no effective state existed to help Lebanese was mentioned in numerous interviews. Lebanese feelings of being deprived of these presumed benefits appeared to decrease host citizens' empathy for the Syrians.

Such sentiments came to a head when the government raised taxes. In March 2017, parliament announced an increase in the VAT by 1 percent to pay for the new salary scale for public-sector workers, including teachers, along with other taxes and fees on tobacco, alcohol, and travel. Public workers, particularly teachers, had been striking and demonstrating for years to raise their salaries, and demonstrated outside parliament in the rain for new pay rates.[201] Parliament agreed to a salary increase, but then funded it through added taxes, costs that affect those in the lower economic strata most. Locally, Lebanese said the two policies canceled each other. They would benefit through one policy but pay more through another. Lebanese took to the streets in Beirut, the South, and the North to denounce this sly move, shouting "We will not pay" (*ma rah nadf'a*) and "thief" at the prime minister and parliamentarians. Twitter hashtags such as "#Ways that an MP is a thief" trended, and users posted their rationales for participating under the hashtag "#Why I'm protesting." Protesters threw water bottles at the prime minister when he arrived at the protest. Thousands participated, holding signs that read "Take your hands out of my pockets," "Kiss my tax," "No food, no work," and "You steal, we pay!" One sign showed a picture of parliament, stating, "The bandits of Lebanon." Cartoons on Twitter showed government officials stealing from poor people's pockets, or wringing them dry. Protesters' gave their reasons for participating, which included the many economically needy people in Lebanon, high prices, the feeling that "it's not OK anymore," and no longer believing media and the government. There was a running theme of government not doing its job, not providing the most basic services of electricity and water, wasting people's money through corruption, betrayal of the people by officials, and the rich avoiding taxation while the poor pay. Overall, protesters felt that money for the higher salary scale could be funded by government in other ways, such as taxing business or ending corruption.[202] At the same time, generally secular groups with other grievances joined in the protests, voicing their own demands, including women's rights and environmental conservation.[203]

Labor Day of May 2017 was the next occasion for protests, which demonstrated that the various grievances had begun to coalesce under a frame of unjust and corrupt government, this time with significant Communist Party participation. Demands included improved working conditions and reduced competition from Syrians. The prime minister renewed his tactic of blaming the Syrians for affecting Lebanese jobs, services, and the economy in general, even as he promised to increase public-sector wages and decrease competition.[204]

Protests continued on Independence Day, November 2018. In relatively smaller protests, numbering in the hundreds, demonstrators railed against the lack of a government months after the elections. The main issues of these protests quickly combined the numerous outstanding demands from prior protests. Independence itself became a frame. Protestors decried that "We still lack housing and work and education. . . . We still lack independence"; "We still lack electricity and clean water. . . . We still lack independence"; and "True independence is when the state respects the worth of the people."[205] Independence came to mean rights for fundamental goods that Lebanese currently lacked. Signs listed grievances of war, no power, unemployment, pollution, lack of access to education and housing, and corruption.[206]

The next month, protesters gathered for more than ten days, motivated by the same issues throughout the country. At one point the demonstrators numbered in the thousands.[207] The wave of protests began with a demonstration in front of the Value-Added Tax building. Protesters erected signs that the building was closed.[208] The catalyst appears to have been the lack of a government, but the demands were centered on the economic situation. Demands included jobs, ending corruption, fixing water and electricity, and improved health care. Various groups were involved, including the new political party Sabaa, as well as the Communist Party, although the protesters emphasized the nonpartisan nature of the protest. Activist statements were directed at the government, insisting that officials declare their assets and take responsibility for the country's poor budget situation. The slogan "Return the stolen money" demonstrated the protesters' view that the budget problems were the result of politicians, not the Syrian burden as elites claimed.[209] Some violence was involved, including an attack by security forces on a journalist.[210] Slogans derived from classic literature described parliament, composed of 128 members, as "Ali Baba and the 128 thieves." Protesters accused the government of being traitors, stealing from the poor, and destroying the country. "Our air is polluted, our water is polluted, we lack rights, our garbage is eating us alive. We're here asking for the minimum. We're simply asking for our rights," one protester stated. Another participant focused on health care: "We demand respect for our rights. Where is the medicine? People are dying at the doors of hospitals." Free medical care, tax cuts, and lower food prices were some of the demands. Others simply chanted "revolution" and "We deserve a better living."[211]

The New Year (2019) did not halt the protests. Students demonstrated about economic issues, specifically rebuffing the argument that they were mobilizing due to the lack of a government.[212] In the South, an estimated five thousand people were involved in a protest, demanding again better health care, jobs, lower taxes, and an end to sectarianism.[213] The next day, protests involving several groups took place in numerous cities throughout Lebanon. One protester explained his reason for protesting: "I was not allowed in a hospital because I had to pay them before entering. We are dying at hospital doors and no one notices us. We are the [majority] that did not vote [in the parliamentary elections]." In one town they protested in front of the power plant, symbolic of the infamous failure of Lebanon's electricity. One slogan was, "We're all affected, so they're responsible," indicating the political elites. Another asserted that the state was just watching, standing on the sidelines, while Lebanese died of cancer, referring to the well-publicized relationship of pollution to cancer in the country.[214] Protests focused on corruption, particularly surrounding electricity and waste or pollution. "They are killing us—with cancer, hunger and cold," one protest leader stated. Another protester in the South was motivated by dignity, and not paying two bills for water and electricity. Nonparticipants in the protest affirmed their agreement with the issues, and lack of trust in the state.[215] A survey from the previous fall found that almost all Lebanese—95 percent—believed the "country is heading in the wrong direction." The concerns for most people were the economy, infrastructure, and corruption, in that order.[216]

Protests continued the next week, organized and led by a variety of older established organizations—the Popular Nasserite Organization, the Lebanese Communist Party, and workers' unions—and new, unaffiliated groups, popularly referred to as the "civil society" parties. The latter groups, including Sabaa and Beirut Madinati, were born out of the trash protests and were central participants in these demonstrations. Observers began noting the proliferation of groups joining forces around common concerns, uniting because of their economic grievances, denunciation of the state, and rejection of sectarianism. A sense of unity, separate from political elites, was developing. "We are saying we want national solutions to the problems in this country, not compromises and settlements," as the leader of the Nasserite organization summed up the mood. Another demonstrator declared that the people should not have to suffer for the political elites' failed policies. One growing concern motivating protesters was the rumor that the new government would increase taxes. Rejecting this solution, a protester said, "Their [politicians'] banks are flush with cash while the people are hungry."[217] A member of one of the new organizations, *Lihaqqi* (for my rights), also born from mobilizing around the waste crisis, reiterated the feeling that the little people were paying but the rich elites paid nothing: "There are no allies to this movement in the political class, because they all bear responsibility for what we're seeing today." Feelings toward further taxation and condemnation of the elites turned into rejection of the elites' system, sectarianism.[218]

The wave of demonstrations and anger at the government for a range of infrastructure and economic problems was kept alive by deaths popularly viewed as unjust and the fault of the political structure. In early February 2019, a father set himself on fire over his inability to pay his daughter's school tuition. The incident spurred protests and sit-ins, parents organizing in support and condemning the Ministry of Education, and expressions of support by party members and the church (the father was Christian). Protesters emphasized that this catastrophe was economic in origin, attributable to state policies in education and the broader economic situation, and many tied the economic framework to the system of "bosses" ruling the country through sectarianism and clientelism.[219] The almost weekly protests continued, some against the newly formed government repeated the same concerns. Using the slogan "No confidence in this government," demonstrators declared this government was no different than prior ones, and those had done nothing about fundamental electricity and waste problems.[220] Some protesters reported being motivated by the death of a toddler in December 2018. The child was turned away from several hospitals and, according to some, was denied medical treatment due to the family's inability to pay.[221] The death highlighted critical issues in the country's health care system, which was severely strained in part due to the refugees' demographic effect on health care and state services in general. This incident was also notable, as the child was Palestinian, and Palestinians are not generally considered to be part of the Lebanese nation. Despite the country holding much ill will toward the Palestinians, this incident spurred mass sympathy. Again, the newcomer Syrians could access free health care, but pre-existing Lebanese and Palestinians, in this case at least, could not.

State Responses to Protests

In both states, the authorities responded to the protests by doubling down on blaming the Syrians and repressing protesters. In Jordan, the government and king reiterated the stress the Syrians placed on the country and overtly linked painful economic measures to the burden of the refugees. Syrians were blamed for the inability of the government to support the bread subsidy, since "non-Jordanians" were heavily benefiting from it.[222] The numerical weight of the Syrians was also blamed for water problems and electricity price increases. The government had the added expense of providing for the Syrians, who drew on the subsidies.[223] "Too many new people are drawing on the supply, so we cannot subsidize it anymore," officials kept saying. This line was reiterated in news reports of meetings with foreign officials as Jordanians sought funding.[224] "The government is shouldering an economic burden that it did not have a hand in creating," went the official line.[225] Jordan continued repressing activists, often granting them amnesty later, presumably to demonstrate the magnanimity of the monarchy. Authorities accused protesters of incitement, a prosecutable offense.[226] Through official government-affiliated newspapers, the state reiterated that protest could generate insecurity and a situation similar to that in Syria, but this no longer stopped people from protesting.[227] The state used such typical diversionary tactics because economic protests were viewed as dangerous to the regime, in contrast to political demonstrations around Jerusalem's status and support for the Palestinians, which were permitted and even routine.[228]

Lebanon's rhetoric against the refugees was more extreme than Jordan's, particularly around the elections in 2016 and 2018.[229] State elites referred to refugees as "an unsustainable burden" and "a threat."[230] They stated that Syrians had pushed Lebanese out of jobs, stressed infrastructure and services, lowered growth, and pushed Lebanon farther into debt.[231] Economic studies were selectively used to back up their claims. Increased demand by Syrians created the electricity crisis, ministers stated, taking five hours of electricity a day from each Lebanese.[232] Lebanon loses USD 6 billion per year due to the refugees, one minister declared. Pollution, the cause for much popular anger, has become 20 percent worse since the Syrian crisis, and thus the crisis is due to the Syrians, another minister stated.[233] In a blunt attempt to divert attention from the government's culpability, elites blamed Syrians for the country's problems precisely when highly unpopular tax increases were announced. President Aoun stated that the country's real problem was the Syrians, and Prime Minister Hariri warned that economic disaster would result if the refugee crisis was not solved.[234] Scapegoating can be particularly effective when linked to security threats, and Lebanon emphasized the domestic criminal and terrorist threats coming from the Syrian refugees. President

Aoun reiterated that the Syrians were a security threat and that 40 percent of prisoners were Syrian. He threw in the demographic threat of Syrian children for good measure, warning that all these unregistered Syrian newborns would cause trouble for Lebanon in the future.[235] False reporting raced through the media, including one item alleging that 300,000 Syrian refugees were pregnant at the time.[236] As Jordan did, Lebanon repressed protesters, but even more fiercely, often without pardon, and tried some in military courts.[237]

As protests continued, authorities acknowledged the legitimacy of the grievances. Jordan's usual tactic of switching the prime minister to appease popular discontent had decreased in effectiveness, so Jordanian governments responded to protesters' demands directly in various ways. The government backed down on some taxes it attempted, taxes on medicine, for example, at least in the short term.[238] The king stopped the fuel price rise.[239] A tax on agricultural output was canceled after a prolonged protest by the farmers.[240] The government partially walked back a new rule banning those over age sixty from the state cancer center, allowing those already in treatment there to remain.[241] In a long unemployment protest in the South, the government used a combination of appeasement and repression by agreeing to get jobs for the protesters, but labeling them as troublemakers using violence.[242] The Ministry of Labor responded to complaints of Syrians working illegally and stepped up its implementation of the law.[243]

In addition, the Jordanian state seemingly attempted to generate support for itself and displace fault onto others by publicizing instances of Jordanians stealing water and electricity,[244] and emphasizing how much these crimes cost the government.[245] The state also highlighted local improvements funded by aid on a weekly basis.[246] State officials and the king promised to get tough and stop corruption, and promoted awareness of criminal corruption cases it had uncovered. Finally, the regime looked to aid from abroad to stop the protests. In reference to enacting the public works and employment aspects of the Compact for Jordanians, a government economist stated, "We should . . . start this program before we see protests."[247] Jordan begged for money from the Gulf, and the Gulf came through with promises after the 2018 protests, fearing more instability. Jordan was pledged USD 2.5 billion, mainly from Saudi Arabia, the UAE, and Kuwait.[248] Such aid had placated protesters in the past. Protesters acknowledged that this was a typical dynamic with aid money but denied that they could be so easily pacified. Activists used slogans saying that Gulf money could not stop Jordanian grievances.[249] After the large protests in June 2018, the prime minister admitted that there was a deep lack of trust in the state on the part of citizens and that traditional governance was not acceptable anymore.[250] Shortly thereafter, the king told parliament to pass a general pardon, as he did after the brief Arab Uprisings in 2011. The pardon would free almost half of all prisoners in Jordan, with the intent of "easing hardship and pressures faced by citizens," and generally de-escalating tensions from the recent protests.[251]

Lebanon's response was more muted. Lebanon did not roll back its few fiscal reform measures, but it did begin discussing the demands of protesters. Tackling the immense electricity problem was somewhat to be expected, but other demands stretching Lebanon's traditional state duties were also being considered.[252] The issue of health care was taken up by the government.[253] Lebanon's government promised to fight corruption while announcing future price rises,[254] arrested people for dumping garbage, and moved toward administrative decentralization for garbage, shifting responsibility to the municipalities.[255] In the midst of one protest over economic and service issues, the prime minister promised to fix the situation, while in the next breath highlighting the specific strains the Syrian refugees have caused to the Lebanese economy.[256]

Lebanon and Jordan were offered abundant loans and aid in return for hosting Syrian refugees, and loans were conditioned on diminishing their debts. In some cases, aid far surpassed the small amount of loans, particularly from the Gulf, but the loans directed state financial policy. Austerity, taxes, and the removal of subsidies were enacted in order to obtain these loans. The state blamed the necessity of the fiscal changes on the Syrians. Instead of accepting this, large-scale protests fiercely rejected the conditionality entailed in the new, low-interest loans, loans that were themselves only granted due to hosting Syrian refugees. The anti-austerity protests catalyzed long-brewing grievances rooted in the deep economic and infrastructure problems of Jordan and Lebanon.

The tax and subsidy protests in both Jordan and Lebanon concentrated on the states' decisions, not on the immediate cause of the debt, which the states continually reiterated was due to the burden of hosting the refugees. What was notable by its absence in these protests was popular blame of the Syrians for the economic situation. Protesters were not distracted from governance problems by the scapegoating of Syrians. Leaving the refugees out of the discourse, both Jordanians and Lebanese rejected the states' frame and maintained focus on deeper systemic factors. Protesters did not explicitly refute the state's framing, but rather ignored it and put forward their own assertions, slogans, stories, and grievances. Increasingly, activists explicitly accused the state of scapegoating the refugees to avoid responsibility itself.

REFUGEES AND CHANGING STATE-CITIZEN RELATIONS

How does the mass presence of displaced people alter politics writ large and the relationship between state and citizen? The sheer size of the Syrian refugee crisis has overwhelmed scholars and analysts. As a consequence, they have unwittingly ignored important secondary effects of the presence of Syrian refugees in host countries. Single-minded focus on the plight of the refugees and negative reactions to them, important topics in themselves, obscures effects on the host society. Analyzing refugees only through lenses of xenophobia, militarization, and humanitarianism conceals refugees' and forced migrants' wider roles in catalyzing changes in state-society relations. Hosting refugees changes a society in various indirect ways, including the society's discourses, understandings of rights, and grievances, all of which will last well after the refugees have left.

Around the globe, elites have historically used migrant and minority populations as scapegoats, objects of blame and anger to generate votes and support, and to distract from the faults of governance. Jordan and Lebanon have long histories of displacing blame from their states onto unpopular groups, including refugees, other migrants, Islamists, and communists, to name a few. Yet here this common elite tool failed. While the Syrian refugees may well be hated, xenophobia has not turned into scapegoating: demands have not been redirected from the state to hatred for an outsider group. The reason is the type of grievance. The goods and services affected—or perceived to be affected—by the Syrians are central to survival and to citizens' daily lives. Not only do such problems call out for solutions, but the Syrians clearly cannot help solve them. Societies can prioritize solutions and survival over blame against a group that cannot plausibly fix their livelihood grievances. Because animosity toward the Syrians was irrelevant to solving daily problems, it did not serve to divert scrutiny from the state. The Syrians might have been at fault for creating problems, people believed, but citizens mobilized to assert the responsibility of the state for fixing those problems. The more elites blamed Syrians for these grievances, the more society focused on elite corruption and the squandering of international aid money. When fundamental livelihood goods are threatened, blame to distract from governance faults can backfire.

That the tactic of scapegoating failed was not the only surprise. While immigrants often generate societal demands that the realm of state public goods redistribution be narrowed,[1] particularly to exclude the newcomers, the opposite dynamic has occurred here. Jordanians and Lebanese protested for an expansion of state services and inclusion into the goods and services believed to be provided to the Syrian refugees. As opposed to pushing migrants out of shrinking public goods, Jordanians and Lebanese rejected neoliberal governance models in favor of the UN's example. Crossing internal divisions, citizens argued together for an expansion of the pie. The Syrians have a better state than we do, they told me; the UN provides more to the refugees than our state does to us. When state elites responded to protest by asserting the fiscal difficulties of the state, citizens countered, pointing to elite corruption and to the massive aid given directly to the states ostensibly to offset the effects of hosting refugees. Citizens saw no benefit from the aid, only economic pain through increased taxes and austerity.

Large-scale demographic changes in these cases did not so much create new problems as aggravate existing ones, deepening the fault lines within states, exacerbating current state problems, and revealing long-term unstable defects in the system. Problems of water, electricity, and waste pre-existed the Syrian crisis. It was the demographic stress of the Syrian influx on infrastructure and resources that pushed these issues to the front of the public imagination. By exacerbating and putting a spotlight on state faults, the Syrian refugees inadvertently turned attention to state failures in ways that generated activism. People had recognized state faults before; now they demanded solutions.

The long-term implications of the refugee crisis will outlast the Syrians, through new institutions, spheres of jurisdiction, changes in power relations, and straightforward economic winners and losers. The story is complex, necessitating nuance, a knowledge of history, and the interaction of variables. Simple models will not capture it. Yet, we know from historical studies using a demographic lens that population growth has had stark consequences for states through changing resources and demands.[2] In this case, the demographic change was abrupt and large. Rapid population pressure both stresses infrastructure and creates sudden grievances, and such abrupt grievances produce activism more often than steady, existing hardships.[3] Indeed, loss-based grievances spur mobilization more readily than the prospect of potential benefits.[4]

This book demonstrates that, in agreement with other recent writing, the nature of the particular grievance must be considered in the potential for mobilization.[5] I add to the growing body of work in social movement studies emphasizing the role of pivotal goods in spurring protest. Particular grievances hold a privileged place in mobilization, whether they are objective needs, such as water, housing, and food, or goods and services locally understood as crucial to everyday existence. They involve two powerful motivators: real crises and strong senses of injustice. From bread and austerity protests to disruptions of livelihood, research confirms that some grievances generate quick mobilization and involve a strong sense of injustice, particularly when the international community is involved in removal of central goods.[6]

Economics and public goods are central to grievances that generate mobilization. Anti-austerity protests are spreading throughout the world, protesting the neoliberal model.[7] Despite the neoliberal drive for a minimalist state and rampant privatization of public goods, many around the world fiercely disagree with shunting what were previously considered to be public goods onto the private sector. Ideological assertions in favor of an abstract market for all goods conflict with enduring ideas of the commons or the collective. In Lebanon, often lauded for its well-developed private sector, much of the populace is comparing the free health care provided for the Syrians with their own, poor excuse for a private system, and as a result demanding universal public health care.[8] Political parties here have furnished access to, and funding for, such private services as their basis for clientelism and remaining in power. The presence of refugees has served as an opportunity for host citizens to demand better governance and services from their own states, particularly when the refugees are perceived as receiving goods and services superior to those of the citizenry. Instead of being an unqualified burden, refugees can spur improved accountability and the establishment of new institutions.

Why and when do people turn to the state? In these cases, citizens attributed responsibility for the economy and infrastructure to the state. Some had given up on the state and turned to INGOs or local municipalities instead, but most exerted pressure on local and national governments, who then passed along their demands to INGOs. The state, variously conceived, was held ultimately responsible for the negative effects experienced by nationals, and, the refrain went, it should take care of its citizens first and foremost, before foreigners. In many cases, there was no reasonable alternative to the financial and organizational ability of the state. In others, the demonstration effect of the Syrians being provided with public services and the often-explicit comparison to the European state drove ideas of what their own states should do. Even in rural areas, people would discuss in detail the duties that states should perform, drawing on news or experience abroad. That the Syrians were given health care while Lebanese were left to die violated a fundamental sense of justice for nationals.[9] Despite the long history of these states relying on the private sector, kin groups, and political parties for health care, the example of free medical care for Syrians was a powerful motivator for demands. Public services are political, not just in the banal sense that politicians (mis)manage them, but that public goods reflect the heart of politics even beyond who gets what. Who is included in the public community, and how does society provide what individually the average person cannot? What are considered fundamental rights? The analytical lens of mobilizing against austerity provides evidence of the populace's idea of the common good and how that should be organized.

The data in this book affirm the idea that the everyday lives of people matter, and that they can affect the long-term trajectory of state-level politics. No story of politics can be complete without considering livelihoods. Instead of essentializing economics or imputing our own ideas of what a presumed rational individual would do, we need to discover the priorities, needs, and opportunities of real people. What they choose to do often conflicts with our preconceived ideas. Observers would have predicted that criticism of the king in Jordan was off-limits, and that the various sects in Lebanon could not unite for a national good, both of which occurred. The decisions of people in the context of securing their daily livelihoods together contribute to what are typically viewed as more important political outcomes. State- and international-level political decisions affect how people live their lives, but the people take these changes and make what they will of them, resulting sometimes in backlashes against the states themselves.

The Argument

Syrian refugees in Jordan and Lebanon make up a higher proportion of the total population than refugees do in any other country. As such, these countries are extreme examples of what can occur when hosting refugees. The demographic effect of the Syrians in these host countries exacerbated the existing infrastructure, service, and state-capacity problems. By doing so, the entrance of the refugees has highlighted underlying weaknesses. Previously, the states muddled through. While daily life issues may not have been problematic enough to cause societal unrest previously, the effect of the refugees has been to turn such issues into strong grievances. These crises were caused by the sudden arrival of a large number of people dependent on public infrastructure; this population increase need not have been caused by the Syrians, or even by refugees. The presence of refugees has generated massive flows of aid for infrastructure and development, fixing some endemic problems and providing employment for many. Water and electricity, the source of much popular discontent, are two areas on which the international community has focused its efforts.

No matter the facts, the pervasive discourse in both countries was that their economic predicament was at least partly due to the Syrians. Culturally similar and at first welcomed with admirable hospitality and empathy,[10] this population quickly became considered an opposing and sometimes threatening identity group. Public opinion surveys, fieldwork discussions and interviews, and the media all repeated this rhetoric. Elites, the media, and the Jordanian and Lebanese populaces agreed that the problems in resources, services, jobs, and prices were due to the Syrians, often despite data to the contrary and the long-standing nature of many of these issues.[11] Lebanese and Jordanians do believe their salaries have been lowered due to the Syrians, that unemployment and prices increased because of the refugees. Authorities quickly jumped to reap the potential of these beliefs, whether they believed them or in order to absolve themselves of responsibility for the economy. They lavished blame on the Syrians within their states and on the international community outside it, accusing the latter of failing in its duty to the refugees and host states. This tactic usually works against a migrant group: framing from elites and leaders can lead the public to perceive threat.[12] Blaming others for negative situations can alleviate one's own sense of guilt or increase one's sense of control over an uncontrollable reality.[13] Elites have incentives to use this tactic, not only to avoid blame but to secure election.[14] So powerful is this psychological tactic that the size of the group need not matter for the ability to scapegoat.[15]

Even with all these factors seemingly boding well for scapegoating, Jordanians and Lebanese have largely directed their demands and protest elsewhere. Why is blaming Syrians failing to distract citizens from the deficiencies of the states, even when those problems are perceived to be caused by the Syrians? The key lies in the type of grievance and the specific deficiencies of the states stressed by the entrance of the Syrians. Jordanians and Lebanese have practical problems that beg for solutions in order for everyday life to continue as usual. These are not well-to-do economies with the majority of people secure in their livelihoods. Grievances here were not over luxury goods, but over fundamental, basic goods, some necessary for survival. Their lack was experienced as threat. The psychological satisfaction of blaming another group is insufficient to quell this discontent, just as it cannot provide water or electricity. The original meaning of scapegoating entailed both culpability and responsibility for fixing the situation. Problems were not merely attributed to the fault of the scapegoat, but, in that belief system, the scapegoat then left with the problems, effectively ridding the community of them. Today, groups are often indicted as blameworthy, but some problems are so severe as to call for a remedy in order for normal life to continue. Scapegoated groups rarely have such power. Nationals separated blame into immediate cause and ultimate responsibility, and laid the latter at the state's door, in both Jordan and Lebanon.

The grievances were exacerbated by the Syrians, but the presence of these refugees also directed attention to problematic areas of state provisioning and infrastructure. Particularly after money began flowing into these states, expectations of the states were raised both by the aid, which removed the illusion that lack of funds was to blame for state ineffectiveness, and by the demonstration effects of the Syrians receiving goods and services. We saw a comparison dynamic, where citizens decried superior (they believed) access by Syrians to goods and services. This belief, and in some cases reality, revealed the hollowness of the idea that citizens were prioritized by their national government. Instead locals felt their power was devalued relative to foreigners. These goods and services began to be understood as rights of citizenship, elevating state duties to provide them. The inability to provide fundamental goods and services with all this apparent aid money, while Syrians were perceived and viewed obtaining them, in turn opened a window to critiquing the state and rejecting long-standing problems as acceptable.[16] Recognition of failure to provide basic, fundamental livelihood goods and services broadened to recognition of overall state failure, as historical memory joined the understanding of present crises. Long-standing grievances of corruption, lack of accountability, and lack of voice would continue and resurge as the states enacted price rises to accommodate their failing budgets, and deficits were continually blamed on the cost of the refugees. Still, populaces' attention would remain fixed on the state, while simultaneously having no love lost on the refugees: populaces were resentful and even violent, wanting the refugees to leave.

The result of these cumulative processes was movements against the states that were increasingly organized and antisystemic compared to earlier single-issue protests. Movements in both countries progressed to central critiques of the regimes themselves. The new movements and their protests encompassed numerous grievances, framing them all under the umbrella of elite corruption and the failure of the state to perform its rightful role. Mobilization broadened in terms of participants, demands, and persistence. The austerity protests demonstrate a progression, a building and allying of movements, from single practical issues to linked, more abstract ones, and political demands. Protests came to encompass various grievances and peoples. The cost of living for the average family was a central grievance driving middle classes to protest in Jordan, while health care and the inability of ordinary people to afford hospital stays motivated much protest in

Lebanon. Trash and power plants became symbols of government dysfunction in Lebanon. In Jordan, the default solution of blaming a prime minister, then dismissing him, wore thin as the populace saw through the traditional placating measures of the regime. They even questioned the scapegoating of refugees, and while refugees were the backdrop for all these grievances, most protests left them out of the picture to focus directly on root causes. The individuals and groups involved expanded. Women and families began to participate. Young girls stayed at the protests late into the night. New names of groups arose, suggesting increased organization and formality, and alliances among groups formed. Contributing to the large scale of these protests were newcomers and individuals from outside the capitals, areas where Syrians are concentrated and where new municipal movements were demanding better services. Protests listed grievances covering diverse groups, and simultaneous, coordinated protests occurred in different parts of the countries. Activists experimented with innovative ways of making demands, not only the locally typical burning tires and cutting off roads. Humor and social media were heavily involved in networking to mobilize people, with relatable stories and rationales for why people were participating. Groups arising from these protests began to organize in formal politics and run for elections in Lebanon, making some small but significant strides at the municipal (2016) and, later, national (2018) levels.

Jordan and Lebanon are now confronted with increasingly severe indictments of their governance. What will occur next is not clear. Movements' demands are targeting the heart of the regimes, under the banners of ending corruption (and getting rid of those who are corrupt) and removing austerity policies. In addition to the difficulty of making state institutions competent, satisfying new citizen demands will require altering the fundamental political arrangements that have kept these regimes in power. Corruption is ingrained, and solving it will not be an easy task. Shortages in these countries are linked to the absence of privilege, and access is skewed by wealth and connections. Elites impose monopoly terms in Jordan and regularly skim off public monies in Lebanon. In Jordan, the regime's core support base is active in protests, representing a long-term threat to the regime as it currently stands. Lebanon has been able to use clientelism and sectarianism to sustain the present regime thus far, but the joining of grievances among urban and rural, the entrance of youth and middle classes increasingly into activism, could be a force for uniting opposed political forces.

Reasoning from past experiences, analysts may tend to dismiss such possibilities as doomed to fail. While this may well occur, the academic failure to identify potential opposition mobilizing leading up to the Arab Uprisings should give analysts pause in such conclusions. Social movement studies demonstrate that mobilization and the failure to achieve reform can mean simply that activists are learning, practicing, refining tactics and discourses, and making crucial alliances. Movements do not usually arrive on the scene fully formed. Alliances and the spread of grievances throughout the countries made the Arab Uprisings in Tunisia and Egypt large scale, uniting diverse but similar demands. The recognition of their similarity facilitated a systemic and regime-centered discourse of ultimate fault, turning economic demands into political ones.[17]

The Protest Types

Five types of protest occurred in Jordan and Lebanon with the arrival of the Syrian refugees, because of grievances that are perceived as relating to the Syrians. In all of these protests, except for one, activists directed their demands at the government (local and national) and asked for changed policies, intervention, or state action. This is true even in Lebanon, where observers often claim citizens rely on the private sector and do not look to the state for solutions.[18] The specific goods and services spurring protest vary between the two states since expectations and capacities of the states differ. First were protests and demands for specific improvements in the availability of services and goods, for those items whose scarcity the Syrians were perceived to have worsened. Many such issues were preexisting structural deficiencies of the state, aggravated and highlighted by the demographic effects of the refugees. Strain on infrastructure (electricity), resources (water), and services (waste, medical care, education) demonstrates this dynamic. In these cases, increases in demand altered supply or exceeded capacity. Refugees merely pushed these national problems over the edge to scarcity and effects on daily lives. Some issues were newly generated due to the refugees and would not have existed separately from this large demographic influx, despite steady indigenous population increase. These include housing and changes in security due to refugees and civil war spillover.

Soon after, the second type of protest emerged, which involved complaints about and demands to receive the same aid as the Syrians that nationals had not received previously. These grievances may have existed among the population but were elevated to widespread condemnations of the state with the Syrian presence. Demands for the same quality and quantity of water, streetlighting, health care, and free enrollment at schools are examples of this dynamic. The growing severity of the demand for public health care, particularly in Lebanon but also in Jordan, is another example of the demonstration effect. Citizens' statements that they were denied health care or paid exorbitant rates for it were repeatedly juxtaposed to declarations that foreigners receive free health care or are treated before nationals. These demands were later spun as rights of citizenship. For Jordan, most of these services were not new. However, when the state attempted to limit access to the prestigious Jordanian cancer hospital, prohibiting many from accessing medical care there, social media erupted with condemnations of the government as sentencing nationals to die. Syrians' free medical care, often presumed to be superior to national health care since it is provided by international organizations, was compared to the declining availability of health care for nationals. The state pushed back on the limits, but the image of the state withdrawing coverage amid an influx of aid, and the provision of health care to the Syrians, remained as a serious stimulant to critique of the state.

Together these newer grievances coalesced and gave strength to pre-existing grievances in the third type of protest. Protests and demonstrations over austerity policies and corruption, amplified by the economic crisis popularly attributed to the Syrians, represented a continuity of grievances from the past. Outrage at these policies was exacerbated by the plentiful aid available due to the Syrian crisis, negating in some people's minds the need for austerity. Austerity policies were presented as conditions to which the countries had agreed in order to receive loans that were intended to make up for the effect of the Syrians on the countries. This led many citizens to question why their own livelihoods should suffer for a crisis not of their own making. Responses to the austerity policies joined together many of the different types of grievances, particularly those for services. Demands for public goods and services similar to those the Syrians received were now discussed as a right, and long-standing anticorruption issues (and antisectarian ones in Lebanon) were a focus. Protests turned increasingly far away from things the Syrians had actually affected as they grew more overtly political, but those grievances remained at the base, having spurred initial mobilization, and they continued to be core grievances for many involved in the protests. Explanations of individual motivation remained focused on the economy, jobs, water, electricity, and trash.

The last two types of protests and demonstrations dealt directly with the Syrians, either reflecting xenophobia and the desire to expel the refugees, or asking the state to enforce its laws against the Syrians. Hostile protests asking for the Syrians to leave occurred, as did violence against them. More often, citizens demonstrated to demand that the state stop labor or business competition and protect the economic status of its own citizens. The object of demands was the Syrians only in the former case, while the state was still the target for the other protests. Overall, despite Syrians being popularly accused of causing most of the issues, demands targeted the state and not the refugees, except in a minority of protests.

Differences in Outcomes in Jordan and Lebanon

Jordanians and Lebanese were united in their negative opinions of Syrians, yet Lebanese had strong pre-existing hostility toward Syrians while Jordanian feelings have been more subdued. Some humanitarian organizations believe that whether people benefit from refugee aid makes the difference in their feelings toward those refugees, a dynamic that remains to be tested. The cause for this variation could simply be demographic: the Syrians are a much higher percentage of the population in Lebanon than in Jordan. Further, they are spread throughout the country—in a few towns they far outnumber citizens. Jordan's effects are concentrated in the North, and its society has been able to benefit from refugee aid and the mass influx of INGOs. The labor setting differs between the two countries also, and Syrians affected diverse domestic labor sectors in Jordan and Lebanon. Lebanon's long and hostile relationship with Syria is a factor in these different outcomes. In infrastructure, Lebanon is by far the worse off, riddled with corruption preventing any effective state capacity. In addition, the Lebanese state has not been as responsive to popular demands as Jordan's has. Mobilization depends on popular beliefs about the capacity of the object of protest to fix the situation; grievances for which people cannot imagine a solution do not generate protest. Interviewees in the Beka'a Valley, where municipalities prefer to deal exclusively with INGOs and not the state for their needs, viewed the crisis of waste in Beirut as proof that the Lebanese state is incompetent. If Beirut cannot deal with a crisis, they certainly do not care enough about the rural areas, perceived as second class, to help them.[19]

In Jordan, mobilizing was quickly answered by state appeasement of demands in the areas with refugees. Humanitarian organizations did likewise. INGOs viewed all protest similarly—protests against the state were interpreted akin to conflict between locals and refugees. Both signaled a need to help citizens, and the humanitarian community altered its practices to cater to locals. Protests worked in refugee areas, but in others, the Jordanian state did little to alleviate difficulties. In Lebanon, protests and conflict signaled to the international humanitarian community but not the state. The Lebanese state is notoriously unresponsive, and real security fears of armed Syrian and allied actors tempered activism against the state. Even with these mitigating factors, there is ample evidence of protest against state institutions to fix problems people believed were created or exacerbated by the Syrians.

Another difference between the two countries is the security situation. Security is an important priority for all countries, and Lebanon suffered severe insecurity as a result of the Syrian civil war. Fear of terrorism and instability were realistic. Insecurity can deflect criticisms of the state, and elites can label such protest as unpatriotic under the circumstances.[20] Civilians have been bombed and killed in Lebanon in a spillover of the war,[21] and in violent crimes committed by Syrians. One particularly heinous crime in Lebanon spurred evictions and strict regulations on Syrians.[22] Jordan also had violent crimes committed by Syrians, but the long-term reaction differed.[23]

State policies toward the refugees played a role in these outcomes. The Lebanese state, through purposeful nonaction, and later incompetence and corruption, sidelined itself and was marginalized by international donors. Jordan, on the other hand, actively intervened, placing itself as mediator for all international agencies and monies. The Jordanian state competently forced money to filter through its institutions toward its listed national developmental priorities, and played this card particularly well. The Lebanese state attempted to capture the new resource stream as time went on, following Jordan's example, but was never able to monopolize the money coming into the country as Jordan did. Being a divided state, to put it mildly, aid money in Lebanon does not have the same effect due to rampant corruption and political divisions. Instead, the aid community has bypassed the national state whenever possible, dealing with municipal leaders in its place. Those municipalities have been at the forefront of policy toward the Syrians in Lebanon, and local leaders there and in Jordan made demands of the aid community. Another difference is historical political fissures in movements. Sectarianism and the power of clientelism are powerful divisive factors in any cross-sectarian movement against the current Lebanese regime.[24]

State Sovereignty for Refugee Hosts

What are the repercussions for state legitimacy, capacity, and sovereignty of hosting refugees? Part of this question has to do specifically with hosting refugees and the range of potential militarization they can bring. State legitimacy and sovereignty can also be changed by the immense aid complex and its intervention in what were previously considered state duties.

The question of potential military or traditional security threats coming from refugees is more straightforward than effects on state legitimacy or administrative capacity, and has been the subject of much study. Among the important variables here are state military and policing capability, the location of camps, the prior organization of the refugees and their goals with respect to the ongoing war, the use of refugees by neighboring states, and the ability of the aid community to deliver aid directly or through armed groups. While refugees have attacked the states, more so in Lebanon than Jordan, the attacks have generally not risen to the level of sovereignty threats. Sovereignty, however, can be punctuated, and the case of Arsal, Lebanon, demonstrates an area that became removed from military purview for a time. Overall, regarding military duties, the quintessential preserve of state sovereignty even in neoliberal accounts, the state has been bolstered.[25] Military sovereignty and reach appear to have extended and not contracted. Numerous new funds, trainings, and equipment have been given to the Jordanian and Lebanese militaries. Their role in dealing with potential spill-over from armed parties in the Syrian war and in deterring the passage of Syrians onward to Europe has assured them aid. From a prior role of often handling internal security, the militaries now are solidly engaged in border management and active battles, more in line with professional military roles than policing domestic squabbles. Security's role in society has also been enhanced. Fear of terrorism and the spread of ISIS chaos (during 2014–2016, especially) caused society to support security over opposition to the state. Indeed, humanitarian aid has been securitized,[26] and security concerns have been privileged by the international community. After all, Europe has bought the idea that Jordan is its "backyard," or a buffer state, and allocated billions of aid dollars to stabilize it.[27]

The growing aid complex, provided first to the refugees and now to nationals, could potentially affect state sovereignty. The new humanitarian model overtly links aid with peace building and development.[28] Humanitarianism has broadened its reach to include development and services to citizens normally considered receivers of state services. New humanitarianism legitimates the mix of aid to citizens with help for the refugees, and incorporates the sensitivity to conflict with nationals that can later be used as leverage for aid. The London Compacts were the concrete result of this optimistic mix of humanitarian aid, development, and work incentives. Theoretically, the new model results in a win-win for the international community, the refugees, and the states, as refugees work, the states develop, and their economies presumably boom from the development aid.[29] The win-win, of course, includes a justification for refugees staying where they are and not traveling to the West.[30] Some have doubted the projections in the Compacts, and clearly Jordan, the test case for this refugee developmentalism, has not lived up to expectations.[31]

Such growth of NGOs into humanitarian and developmental duties is not limited to refugee situations but is a trend spreading from disaster situations to less-capable states. Fixing infrastructure and paying for development has become increasingly removed from state institutions. While the turn away from government as service providers has been encouraged by neoliberalism, an ideology endorsed by most international funders, the potential effects of this turn to NGOs worry analysts and funders alike.[32] There are two main concerns about this relationship. First, that the provision of services by nonstate entities could erode the legitimacy of the state, and second, that a parallel service sector could further decrease what are usually weak state capacities to begin with.[33] Service delivery has been viewed as instrumentally related to legitimacy: citizens identify with and respect their state because that state provides for them. Thus, the fear is that service delivery could grant these organizations not only purview over what used to be considered public (state) services but also that along with these services would go legitimacy. Outside the Middle East, Haiti and Liberia are examples of this dynamic. Local elites blame INGOs for attacking the state and its sovereignty in Liberia. In Haiti, the overwhelming presence of INGOs has further decreased the ability of state institutions.[34]

Comparative research has shown that the link between legitimacy, capacity, and NGO service provision is neither straightforward nor does it run in only one direction.[35] Dominant ideas can enter into local judgments about state legitimacy.[36] State elites can successfully co-opt INGO projects, presenting themselves as the ultimate patron bringing such projects to the region.[37] States can control the direction of investment, while using INGOs for the actual work, as Jordan did. The distinction between the state and these humanitarian organizations often becomes unclear.[38] Some see the example of the humanitarian community as helping generate democratization.[39] Technical proficiency and bureaucratic design standards have rubbed off on the national institutions and persons. Jennifer Brass has shown that accountability and administrative capacity can be strengthened.[40] Citizens can learn new concepts of expectations and rights, based on a model of the state embraced by humanitarian workers and corresponding to the ideal European state. Interviews in Jordan and Lebanon revealed a commonplace comparison of the goods provided to citizens with those in European states or the goods and services furnished by the UN to the Syrian refugees.

The Jordanian and Lebanese states have been reinforced as the center of demands for improved governance and services. Despite ongoing austerity, the states have not hollowed out but deepened as the referent for demands. The numerous and ongoing protests in Jordan and Lebanon highlight the popular focus on the state to solve national problems. With each protest or elite response, the dynamic is strengthened. Society perceives the state as controlling the levers for solving grievances. States can become more significant in people's lives even when INGOs are perceived as subcontractors.

At least some state capacities toward INGOs remained strong in these cases. This book details numerous examples of successful state negotiation with the humanitarian aid complex, from Jordan diverting funds to its own priorities to local and national officials insisting on goods for citizens along with refugees. Lebanon offers its own stark demonstration of state sovereignty, when state officials rejected UNHCR policy on voluntary repatriation for Syrians. The dispute saw Lebanon sanction humanitarian staff by canceling their residency permits.[41] When it decided to act, the Lebanese state could enforce core aspects of state sovereignty, deciding the terms of residency for foreign staff.

Continued Plight of the Syrians

Ironically, attention to Syrians has been sidelined amid all this focus on the domestic communities. Aid to host countries is treated as equivalent to helping the refugees, yet a large portion goes to infrastructure, national development projects, and state budgets. In Jordan, the beneficiary of much aid, refugees stuck at the border lack food and basic necessities, and are barred from entering Jordan. Confined to a no-man's-land between berms, one starving mother in this border area attempted to kill herself and her children, a rare and desperate act in this region.[42] Refugees in Lebanon struggle to survive, as snow and rain from winter storms encompass their tents and settlements. Syrians die for lack of heat, electricity, basic food, and medicine, while large amounts of money flow into these countries. Syrian refugees sell their organs to survive,[43] or risk death to escape.[44] Refugee babies freeze to death.[45] Children forego their youth to work in vulnerable occupations on the streets, female refugees marry as children, and few receive education.[46]

Jordanian and Lebanese policies have been successful in one aspect: to make life so miserable for Syrians that they want to return home despite continuing dangers. Returns to Syria, especially from Lebanon, began in earnest in 2018, despite continued fighting and regime repression toward those it labeled as opposition. The fact that potentially returning refugees currently live under conditions of deprivation and continued hostility in the host countries brings into question the voluntary nature of such repatriation. Some of the returns are overtly forced, as Jordan and Lebanon deport and evict Syrians from their homes.[47] The ostensible focus of humanitarian aid has been to help those without a state, without the means of protecting themselves legally or supporting themselves economically. In these goals current humanitarian aid falls far short, and the everyday misery of forced displacement continues for the Syrian refugees.

Notes

INTRODUCTION

1. Faris al-Rifa'i, "Mukhayyem lil-naziheen al-Urdunieen fil-Mafraq ihtijajaan 'ala al-luju' al-Souri" [Tents for Jordanians displaced in Mafraq protesting the Syrian refugees], *Zaman Alwasl*, April 2, 2013, https://www.zamanalwsl.net/news/article/37297; and "75 d'awa ikhla' manazil bi-haq muwatineen bil-Mafraq li-ghayat taskeen al-laji'een al-Sourieen" [75 legal eviction cases in Mafraq because of Syrian refugee housing demands], *Saraya*, March 25, 2013, https://www.sarayanews.com/index.php?page=article&id=192342.

2. Areej Abuqudairi, "A Tale of Two Za'ataris."

3. UNHCR, Operations Portal Refugee Situations, Syria Regional Refugee Response, https://data2.unhcr.org/en/situations/syria.

4. Interview, former government minister and diplomat, Amman, September 19, 2015. This figure on the Syrian population is certainly inflated.

5. A scapegoat can be defined as "a person [or group] standing-in for others in order to accept blame and responsibility for some occurrence." Douglas, *Scapegoats*, 6.

6. Rhys Dubin, "Refugee crisis strains Lebanon's deficient electricity network," *The Daily Star*, February 22, 2017, http://www.dailystar.com.lb/News/Lebanon-News/2017/Feb -22/394578-refugee-crisis-strains-lebanons-deficient-electricity-network.ashx and "Syria conflict: Jordanians 'at boiling point' over refugees," BBC News, February 2, 2016, http:// www.bbc.com/news/world-middle-east-35462698.

7. Mercy Corps, "Mapping of Host Community-Refugee Tensions in Mafraq and Ramtha."

8. "Baalbek Residents Stage Protest over Blackouts," *Daily Star*, December 21, 2013, http://www.dailystar.com.lb/News/Lebanon-News/2013/Dec-21/241886-baalbek -residents-stage-protest-over-blackouts.ashx.

9. Mercy Corps, "Tapped Out," 33.

10. Discussion, Amman, September 11, 2017.

11. Interview, American University of Beirut graduate from the northern border with Syria, Beirut, May 16, 2018.

12. Interview, sheikh and teacher at a private school, Tripoli, Lebanon, May 16, 2018.

13. Interview, businesswoman and elected municipal council member, Irbid, Jordan, September 21, 2017.

14. Interview with Lebanese UNICEF employee, Beirut, March 16, 2017. In line with the populaces here, I use the terms "Syrian" and "Syrian refugee" interchangeably, since this book deals with Syrians only residing in neighboring countries. They are either refugees who arrived after the war started, or refugees *sur place*, Syrians who were in other countries before the war, but now cannot return. I use the term "governance" because the level and institution of the state or international NGO can vary. I use "the state" as locals do, as *dawla*, which refers generally to the broad regime structure and institutions. When "government" is referred to, I use that term instead.

15. I recognize that the distinction between host and refugee communities is blurred and that these are not distinct communities. Many are related through intermarriages, long-standing relationships, or extended families. However, I use the terms because both researchers and detailed data continually refer to "hosts" versus "refugees," and this presumed clear divide has been consequential for public attitudes.

16. Focus group interviews with professional men, Halba, northern Lebanon, May 16, 2018.

17. Interview, senior protection coordinator, UNHCR, Beirut, March 14, 2017; Ozaras, Balkan, and Yemisen, "Prejudice and Reality about Infection Risk among Syrian Refugees."

18. Conversations, Beirut, March 14, 2017.

19. Chit and Nayel, "Understanding Racism against Syrian Refugees in Lebanon."

20. Haider-Markel and Joslyn, "Gun Policy, Opinion, Tragedy, and Blame Attribution"; Hameleers, Bos, and Vreese, "'They Did It'"; Polletta, "Contending Stories."

21. Javeline, *Protest and the Politics of Blame.*

22. Rothschild et al., "A Dual-Motive Model of Scapegoating."

23. Thompson, "Moral Economy of the English Crowd"; Walton and Seddon, *Free Markets & Food Riots.*

24. Goldstone and Tilly, "Threat (and Opportunity)"; Van Dyke, "Threat." This is referred to as "loss aversion."

25. Snow et al., "Disrupting the 'Quotidian'"; Borland, "Quotidian Disruption."

26. Simmons, "Grievances Do Matter in Mobilization."

27. Kerbo, "Movements of 'Crisis' and Movements of 'Affluence.'"

28. Porta, *Social Movements in Times of Austerity*; Beinin, "A Workers' Social Movement on the Margin of the Global Neoliberal Order."

29. Porta, "Late Neoliberalism and Its Discontents," 4; Mansbridge, "Making of Oppositional Consciousness."

30. Jasper, *Art of Moral Protest,* 118–19.

31. Tilly, "Blame Game," 386–88. The clergy abuse scandal demonstrates this dynamic. Catholic (and other) clergy's sexual abuse of children spurred mass condemnation of church authorities as the number of cases increased, and the public held these authorities ultimately to blame for covering up crimes and allowing the malevolent behavior to continue.

32. Baylouny, *Privatizing Welfare in the Middle East*; Cammett, *Compassionate Communalism.*

33. Mouawad and Baumann, "Wayn Al-Dawla?"

34. Hermez, "When the State Is (n)Ever Present," 509; Obeid, "Searching for the 'Ideal Face of the State.'" This concept of a state is not unified, but some criticisms converge on public services the state should provide.

35. On electricity, see Nucho, *Everyday Sectarianism in Urban Lebanon.*

36. Landau, *The Humanitarian Hangover.*

37. For example, Mercy Corps, "Mapping of Host Community-Refugee Tensions in Mafraq and Ramtha," and Jones and Ksaifi, "Struggling to Survive."

38. Focus group interview, Akkar, northern Lebanon, May 16, 2018.

39. Interview with NGO official, Mafraq, Jordan, September 18, 2017.

40. Interview with INGO engineer who implemented new water infrastructure for Mercy Corps in the north, Amman, September 20, 2017.

41. Osama Al Sharif, "Hundreds of Jordanians march toward capital demanding jobs," Al Monitor, March 6, 2019, https://www.al-monitor.com/pulse/originals/2019/03/jordan-youth-march-sit-in-royal-palace-unemployment.html.

42. Jamal, "The 'Other Arab' and Gulf Citizens"; Jamal, "The 'Tiering' of Citizenship and Residency."

43. Hovil, "Self-Settled Refugees in Uganda," 604.

44. Goertz and Mahoney, *A Tale of Two Cultures,* 41.

45. This research was approved by my university's Institutional Review Board. In the majority of cases, I identify interviewees by their professions, the date, and location, omitting their names due to the politicization of refugees and research in the Middle East.

46. Clark, "Field Research Methods in the Middle East"; Suleiman and Anderson, "'Conducting Fieldwork in the Middle East.'"

47. I therefore do not deal as much with the refugees themselves, although their fate is inevitably part of the story. Many scholars are contributing to this area, including understanding the precise humanitarian conditions of the refugees, their livelihoods, mental health issues, problems, and poverty.

1. BEFORE THE SYRIAN CRISIS

1. Transparency International, Corruption Perceptions Index, 2017, https://www.transparency.org/country/LBN and https://www.transparency.org/country/JOR. Accessed January 27, 2019.

2. Cammett, *Compassionate Communalism*.

3. See the World Bank dataset for government wage bills for the two countries. World Bank, "Size of the Public Sector: Government Wage Bill and Employment," http://www.worldbank.org/en/topic/governance/brief/size-of-the-public-sector-government-wage-bill-and-employment. Accessed September 21, 2018.

Another source puts public-sector salaries at 35 percent of government expenditures in 2005. See Osama Habib, "World Bank Urges Lebanon to Reduce Size of Public Sector," *Daily Star*, October 3, 2005, http://www.dailystar.com.lb//Business/Lebanon/2005/Oct-03/6392-world-bank-urges-lebanon-to-reduce-size-of-public-sector.ashx.

4. Numerous interviewees repeated this point, including female military officers in Lebanon. Some felt it was their obligation to help the family by taking a public-sector job. Every family has someone in civil service, one Lebanese told me, explaining why the teachers' strikes for higher pay resonate with the country.

5. Jawad, "A Profile of Social Welfare in Lebanon," 323; UNDP. "A Profile of Sustainable Human Development in Lebanon."

6. Mouawad and Baumann, "Wayn Al-Dawla?"

7. Nucho, *Everyday Sectarianism in Urban Lebanon*; Salti and Chaaban, "Role of Sectarianism in the Allocation of Public Expenditure."

8. Saghieh, "Right to Food Safety."

9. "Do-It-Yourself: Public Services in the Arab World."

10. Author experience in Ras Beirut, May 2018.

11. Nucho, *Everyday Sectarianism in Urban Lebanon*, p. 2.

12. A Twitter user posted pictures of one pothole filled with water and people using it to fish. This was in Zahle, a richer town with full independent electricity. See Yasa for Road Safety, @yasalebanon, for other examples of road and traffic dysfunction.

13. Gaspard, *Political Economy of Lebanon*, 69; World Bank, *Unlocking the Employment Potential in the Middle East and North Africa*, 103.

14. World Bank, Country Profile: Lebanon, http://databank.worldbank.org/data/views/reports/reportwidget.aspx?Report_Name=CountryProfile&Id=b450fd57&tbar=y&dd=y&inf=n&zm=n&country=LBN. Accessed January 27, 2019.

15. Dawass, "Poverty in Jordan," 6.

16. World Bank Group, "Unemployment, Total (% of Total Labor Force) (Modeled ILO Estimate), Data—Lebanon," September 2018, https://data.worldbank.org/indicator/SL.UEM.TOTL.ZS?locations=LB; and for Jordan, calculated from International Monetary Fund, Report for Selected Countries and Subjects, https://www.imf.org/external/pubs/ft/weo/2018/01/weodata/index.aspx. Local think tanks believe the number is higher. Both accessed January 27, 2019.

17. Calculated from International Monetary Fund, Report for Selected Countries and Subjects, https://www.imf.org/external/pubs/ft/weo/2018/01/weodata/index.aspx. Accessed January 27, 2019.

18. Davis et al., "Hosting Guests, Creating Citizens."

19. Abu Sitta, *Palestinian Nakba 1948*.

20. Husseini, "Jordan and the Palestinians"; Brand, *Palestinians in the Arab World*, 9.

21. Dionigi, "Statehood and Refugees."

22. Descendants of 1967 Palestinians have been denied exit from the country during periods of internal turmoil. Author experience and discussions, Amman, 1999–2000.

23. Tell, *Social and Economic Origins of Monarchy in Jordan*; Gaspard, *Political Economy of Lebanon*, 69; World Bank, *Unlocking the Employment Potential in the Middle East and North Africa*, 103. This distinction is artificial, as many intermarriages occurred and lineages cross current state borders. The more apt division, rural versus urban, often overlaps with the Palestinian versus the Transjordanian one. For more on these identities, see Brand, "Palestinians and Jordanians: A Crisis of Identity."

24. Anderson, *Nationalist Voices in Jordan*.

25. Adnan Abu-Odeh, *Jordanians, Palestinians, & the Hashemite Kingdom in the Middle East Peace Process*, United States Institute of Peace Press, 1999, chapter 9.

26. Again, this is a generalization, not a precise dividing line, but is widely used by the citizens themselves. Abu-Odeh, *Jordanians, Palestinians, & the Hashemite Kingdom in the Middle East Peace Process*.

27. Mazur, *Economic Growth and Development in Jordan*.

28. On the returnees, see Le Troquer and al-Oudat, "From Kuwait to Jordan: The Palestinians' Third Exodus."

29. See Schwedler, *Protesting Jordan*.

30. Baylouny, "Militarizing Welfare."

31. Andoni and Schwedler, "Bread Riots in Jordan."

32. Yom, "Tribal Politics in Contemporary Jordan," 246.

33. O'Donnell and Newland, "Iraqi Refugee Crisis," 165.

34. Seeley, "Politics of Aid to Iraqi Refugees in Jordan"; Arar, "Leveraging Sovereignty," 14.

35. Sassoon, *Iraqi Refugees*, 53.

36. O'Donnell and Newland, "Iraqi Refugee Crisis," 165. Crisp et al., "Surviving in the City," 13.

37. Nanes, "Jordan's Unwelcome 'Guests.'"

38. Ibid.

39. Asfour, "Jordan: Local Perceptions on Syrian Refugees (Part 2/2)"; discussions with Jordanians, September 2015 and September 2017.

40. On the political use and derivation of numbers of Iraqi refugees, see Stevens, "Legal Status, Labelling, and Protection: The Case of Iraqi Refugees in Jordan."

41. Schwedler, "Routines and Ruptures in Protests and Policing in Jordan."

42. International Crisis Group, "Popular Protest in North Africa and the Middle East (IX)."

43. Bustani, "Jordan's New Opposition and the Traps of Identity and Ambiguity."

44. Schwedler, "Routines and Ruptures in Protests and Policing in Jordan."

45. See the tactics of organizers to discount the numbers of Jordanians of Palestinian descent, Karmel, "How Revolutionary Was Jordan's Hirak?"

46. When Islamist leader Laith Shubailat was released from prison after a short stay, the king himself drove him home. Reuters, "King Hussein Gives His Foe Ride from Jail," *New York Times*, November 10, 1996, https://www.nytimes.com/1996/11/10/world/king-hussein-gives-his-foe-ride-from-jail.html.

47. Andoni and Schwedler, "Bread Riots in Jordan."

48. Martinez, "Bread Is Life."

49. Adely, "Emergence of a New Labor Movement in Jordan." See also the reports from the Phenix Center for Economic and Informatics Studies, Amman, http://www.phenixcenter.net/en/home.

50. For a full account of the Arab Uprising in Jordan, see Ryan, *Jordan and the Arab Uprisings.*

51. Ryan, "Identity Politics, Reform, and Protest in Jordan"; Bustani, "Jordan's New Opposition and the Traps of Identity and Ambiguity."

52. Karmel, "How Revolutionary Was Jordan's Hirak?"

53. Al Shalabi, "Jordan: Revolutionaries without a Revolution."

54. Yom, "Tribal Politics in Contemporary Jordan"; Tell, "Early Spring in Jordan." On the Jordanian identity and anti-Palestinian nature of the military veterans, see El-Sharif, "'Restoring Pride in Jordanian National Identity.'"

55. Blanco-Palencia, "Jordanian Youth in Collective Action."

56. International Crisis Group, "Popular Protest in North Africa and the Middle East (IX)."

57. However, as Jillian Schwedler shows, this presumed loyal constituency has a long history of protesting the Jordanian regime, and views its relation to that regime in transactional terms. Schwedler, *Protesting Jordan.*

58. Interviews, Amman and northern regions, September 2017.

59. Al Shalabi, "Jordan," 98.

60. Shihab-Eldin, "Jordan First"; Ryan, "'We Are All Jordan' . . . But Who Is We?"

61. Schwedler, "Political Geography of Protest in Neoliberal Jordan."

62. See chapter 3 of this volume for interview data on this. Staton, "Young Reformers Want Debate, Not Protest, to Drive Change in Jordan."

63. Abu-Rish, "Doubling Down." For a nuanced analysis of regime survival, see Ryan, *Jordan and the Arab Uprisings.*

64. Bustani, "Jordan—A Failed Uprising."

65. Beck and Hüser, "Jordan and the 'Arab Spring.'"

66. The 1932 census establishing Christians as the majority included overseas Christians, thus their status as a domestic majority at the time is debatable.

67. Gates, *Merchant Republic of Lebanon.*

68. Salti and Chaaban, "Role of Sectarianism in the Allocation of Public Expenditure"; Nucho, *Everyday Sectarianism in Urban Lebanon*; Cammett and Issar, "Bricks and Mortar Clientelism."

69. Baylouny, "Building an Integrated Military"; Mourad and Piron, "Municipal Service Delivery, Stability, Social Cohesion and Legitimacy," 15.

70. Leenders, *Spoils of Truce*; Ciezadlo, "Sect Symbols."

71. Norton, "Hizbullah and the Israeli Withdrawal from Southern Lebanon."

72. Mokbel, "Refugees in Limbo."

73. Sassoon, *Iraqi Refugees*, 92.

74. Nicholas Blanford, "Hezbollah Phone Network Spat Sparks Beirut Street War," *Christian Science Monitor*, May 9, 2008, https://www.csmonitor.com/World/Middle-East /2008/0509/p05s01-wome.html.

75. Wimmen, "Long, Steep Fall of the Lebanon Tribunal."

76. Yacoubian, "Facing the Abyss"; "Why Lebanon Has Not Passed a Budget for 12 Years."

77. Interviews in Lebanon; Corbeil, "Hezbollah Re-Ascendant in Lebanon."

78. Wieland, "Syrian-Lebanese Relations."

79. Chit and Nayel, "Understanding Racism against Syrian Refugees in Lebanon."

80. Chalcraft, *The Invisible Cage.*

81. Chit and Nayel, "Understanding Racism against Syrian Refugees in Lebanon."

82. Rym Ghazal, "Lebanon to let Palestinians Obtain Work Permits," *Daily Star*, June 28, 2005, http://www.dailystar.com.lb/News/Lebanon-News/2005/Jun-28/7668-lebanon-to-let -palestinians-obtain-work-permits.ashx.

83. Saad-Ghorayeb, "People Say No."

84. Barak, "Commemorating Malikiyya," 64.

85. Najem, *Lebanon: The Politics of a Penetrated Society.*

86. Stel, "Review Essay: Lebanon"; Mouawad and Baumann, "Wayn Al-Dawla?"

87. Hourani, "Lebanon: Hybrid Sovereignties"; Hazbun, "Assembling Security in a 'Weak State.'"

88. Clark and Salloukh, "Elite Strategies, Civil Society, and Sectarian Identities in Postwar Lebanon."

89. Obeid, "Searching for the 'Ideal Face of the State'"; International Crisis Group, "Lebanon's Self-Defeating Survival Strategies," Report. Leenders, *Spoils of Truce*; Beck, "Contextualizing the Current Social Protest Movement in Lebanon."

90. Baylouny, "Born Violent"; Flanigan and Abdel-Samad, "Hezbollah's Social Jihad." The role of the demonstration effect and the influence of an international model of governance on Lebanese ideas of a state have yet to be investigated.

91. Paler, Marshall, and Atallah, "Fear of Supporting Political Reform"; "Chopping up the Tree of State"; Mourad and Piron, "Municipal Service Delivery, Stability, Social Cohesion and Legitimacy."

92. Baumann, "Social Protest and the Political Economy of Sectarianism in Lebanon."

93. Salloukh et al., *The Politics of Sectarianism in Postwar Lebanon*, chap. 5. Clark and Salloukh, "Elite Strategies, Civil Society, and Sectarian Identities in Postwar Lebanon."

94. Traboulsi, *A History of Modern Lebanon*, chap. 10.

95. Knio, "Lebanon: Cedar Revolution or Neo-Sectarian Partition?"

96. For an excellent account of the independence intifada as a nonviolent social movement, see Jaafar and Stephan, "Lebanon's Independence Intifada."

97. Geha, *Civil Society and Political Reform in Lebanon and Libya.*

98. Nagle, "Between Entrenchment, Reform and Transformation"; Nagle, "Ghosts, Memory, and the Right to the Divided City"; Kingston, "Patrons, Clients and Civil Society."

99. Clark and Salloukh, "Elite Strategies, Civil Society, and Sectarian Identities in Postwar Lebanon."

2. ENTER THE SYRIANS

1. UNHCR, "Refugee Facts: Statistics," https://www.unrefugees.org/refugee-facts/statistics/.

2. UNHCR, "Syria Emergency," http://www.unhcr.org/en-us/syria-emergency.html.

3. Communication with UNHCR protection officers, Amman and Los Gatos, California, October–November 2018.

4. Mohammad Ghazal, "Population Stands at around 9.5 Million, Including 2.9 Million Guests," *Jordan Times*, January 30, 2016, http://www.jordantimes.com/news/local/population-stands-around-95-million-including-29-million-guests. For disputes about this number, certainly inflated, see Wasfi Khushman, "Number of Refugees in Jordan . . . Different Sources Cause Confusion in Results," Akeed (Jordan Media Credibility Monitor), https://akeed.jo/en/post/1397/Number_of_Refugees_in_Jordan_Different_Sources_Cause_Confusion_in_Results, and Lenner, "Blasts from the Past."

5. UNHCR, Operations Portal Refugee Situations, Syria Regional Refugee Response, https://data2.unhcr.org/en/situations/syria; Ministry of Environment, Government of Lebanon and UNDP, "Lebanon Environmental Assessment of the Syrian Conflict," 41.

6. Moore and Shellman, "Whither Will They Go?"; Fafchamps and Shilpi, "Determinants of the Choice of Migration Destination"; Bohra-Mishra and Massey, "Individual Decisions to Migrate During Civil Conflict."

7. Mourad, "From Conflict-Insensitive to Conflict-Driven Aid."

8. Calculated from country figures other than Lebanon, where camps are not allowed. UNHCR, Operations Portal Refugee Situations, Syria Regional Refuge Response, https://data2.unhcr.org/en/situations/syria.

9. UNHCR, "UNHCR Policy on Alternatives to Camps," July 22, 2014, http://www .unhcr.org/en-us/protection/statelessness/5422b8f09/unhcr-policy-alternatives-camps .html.

10. As an example, see the excellent analysis of competing institutional incentives for inflating numbers in Lenner, "Blasts from the Past."

11. See the UNHCR, "The 1051 Convention Relating to the Status of Refugees and Its 1967 Protocol," September 2011, http://www.unhcr.org/en-us/about-us/background /4ec262df9/1951-convention-relating-status-refugees-its-1967-protocol.html.

12. Lambert, "Temporary Refuge from War."

13. Memorandum of Understanding between the Government of the H.K. of Jordan and the UNHCR, April 5, 1998, http://carim-south.eu/database/legal-module/memorandum -of-understanding-between-the-government-of-the-h-k-of-jordan-and-the-unhcr/; Achilli, Yassin, and Erdogan, "Neighbouring Host-Countries' Policies for Syrian Refugees," 17.

14. Achilli, "Syrian Refugees in Jordan," 3; Ward, "Refugee Cities," 83.

15. Akram et al., "Protecting Syrian Refugees," 29.

16. Janmyr, "Precarity in Exile," 63.

17. Data from UNHCR, Population Statistics for 2017, http://popstats.unhcr.org/en /persons_of_concern and from UNRWA, "Where We Work," https://www.unrwa.org /where-we-work.

18. Orhan, "Situation of Syrian Refugees in the Neighboring Countries," 23.

19. El-Abed, "The Discourse of Guesthood."

20. Numerous countries, including the United States, use this status to avoid providing permanent refugee rights to a population, but it allows them to stay for a certain time.

21. Turner, "Explaining the (Non-) Encampment of Syrian Refugees."

22. UNHCR Factsheet—Zaatari Refugee Camp, October 2018, https://data2.unhcr.org /en/documents/download/66598.

23. Orhan, "Situation of Syrian Refugees in the Neighboring Countries," 26–27. Refugees are reportedly unhappy there and attempt to leave. Providing meals also deprives women of their traditional importance in the family and according to UN officials has had adverse consequences for women and children. Interview with UNICEF official, Amman, September 14, 2015.

24. UNHCR, Operational Portal, Syria Regional Refugee Response: Jordan, https:// data2.unhcr.org/en/situations/syria/location/36. Figures from September 2018.

25. Interviews with Norwegian Rescue Committee and UNHCR officials, Amman, September 16 and 19, 2015, respectively.

26. Quoted in Betts, Ali, and Memisoglu, "Local Politics and the Syrian Refugee Crisis," 9.

27. Achilli, Yassin, and Erdogan, "Neighbouring Host-Countries' Policies for Syrian Refugees," 17, and interviews with INGO employees.

28. UNHCR, "Jordan Refugee Response: Inter-Agency Coordination Briefing Kit," May 2016, https://reliefweb.int/report/jordan/jordan-refugee-response-inter-agency -coordination-briefing-kit-may-2016.

29. Documented by the United Nations Office for the Coordination of Humanitarian Affairs (OCHA) and affirmed through author interviews. At one point, Jordan toyed with the idea of sponsoring rebel fighters among the Syrian refugees and had an all-male camp for that purpose among others. It later abandoned that idea and further refused entry to Syrians who had served in the military, even if they were defecting. Interview with senior UNHCR official, Amman, September 19, 2017.

30. Akram et al., "Protecting Syrian Refugees," 63.

31. Amnesty International, "Growing Restrictions, Tough Conditions."

32. Achilli, "Syrian Refugees in Jordan," 10.

33. Orhan, "Situation of Syrian Refugees in the Neighboring Countries," 21; interviews with former senior protection assistant, UNHCR—Jordan, Los Gatos, California, June 2018.

34. Interviews with UN officials, Amman, September 2015; Achilli, "Syrian Refugees in Jordan," 4; Human Rights Watch, "Not Welcome"; Zetter et al., "Syrian Displacement Crisis and a Regional Development and Protection Programme."

35. UNHCR handles only refugees not already covered, at the time of its establishment, by other UN agencies. In other words, it exempts the Palestinians who were under UNRWA already. UNRWA's mandate for solutions to the situation of refugees differs from that of the UNHCR, and essentially concentrates on Palestinians staying where they are and training them for the local job market. UNHCR prioritizes repatriation.

36. Taylor Luck, "In Jordan, Tensions Rise between Syrian Refugees and Host Community," *Washington Post*, 21 April 2013, https://www.washingtonpost.com/world/middle _east/in-jordan-tensions-rise-between-syrian-refugees-and-host-community/2013/04 /21/d4f5fa24-a762-11e2-a8e2-5b98cb59187f_story.html?utm_term=.29f3432f7f3b.

37. Christophersen, "Educating Syrian Youth in Jordan."

38. Stated in numerous interviews with Mercy Corps, Action Aid NGO in Mafraq, residents of Ramtha and Irbid, various dates, September 2015 and 2017.

39. Dickinson, "Shadow Aid to Syrian Refugees"; discussions with Jordanians, September 2015 and September 2017.

40. Mourad, "'Standoffish' Policy-Making"; El Mufti, "Official Response to the Syrian Refugee Crisis in Lebanon, the Disastrous Policy of No-Policy."

41. This was called the policy of disassociation. "Baabda Declaration Needed Now, For Future: Sleiman," *Daily Star*, November 16, 2013, http://www.dailystar.com.lb/News /Lebanon-News/2013/Nov-16/238054-baabda-declaration-needed-now-for-future-sleiman .ashx; Hamdan and Bou Khater, "Strategies of Response to the Syrian Refugee Crisis in Lebanon," 31.

42. Naufal, "Syrian Refugees in Lebanon," 1.

43. Orhan, "Situation of Syrian Refugees in the Neighboring Countries," 33.

44. The label is ironic on its face, given Lebanon's adamant denial of being part of Greater Syria, and Syria's long insistence that Lebanon is a part of it. However the intention is to reinforce that the Syrians are not refugees and thus do not have the accompanying rights of refugees.

45. Amnesty International, "Pushed to the Edge," 11.

46. Janmyr, "Legal Status of Syrian Refugees in Lebanon," 11.

47. Akram et al., "Protecting Syrian Refugees," 293; Hamdan and Bou Khater, "Strategies of Response to the Syrian Refugee Crisis in Lebanon"; Oxfam, "Lebanon Looking Ahead in Times of Crisis."

48. Amnesty International, "Denied Refuge."

49. Betts, Ali, and Memisoglu, "Local Politics and the Syrian Refugee Crisis."

50. El Helou, "Refugees under Curfew." Mourad counts at least 142 municipalities with curfews. Mourad, "Inaction as Policy-Making."

51. Hamdan and Bou Khater, "Strategies of Response to the Syrian Refugee Crisis in Lebanon," 25.

52. Ibid., 24.

53. Yassin and et al., "No Place to Stay?," 46. Lebanon does have some privately run settlements commonly referred to as camps, not administered by the UNHCR. See Union of Relief & Development Associations (URDA) website, http://urda.org.lb/en/Programs .aspx?PID=9.

54. Interview with Bassel Salloukh, professor, Lebanese American University, Beirut, March 17, 2017.

55. REACH and UNHCR, "Livelihoods Assessment of Syrian Refugees in Akkar Governorate," 11.

56. Ruth Michaelson, "Refugees Pay the High Price of Lebanese Cost-Cutting," *Al Jazeera*, April 30, 2015, https://www.aljazeera.com/news/2015/04/refugees-pay-high-price-lebanese-cost-cutting-150412095256439.html.

57. REACH, "Livelihoods, Employment and Tensions in Jordanian Communities Hosting Syrian Refugees," 11.

58. Van Vliet and Hourani, "Regional Differences in the Conditions of Syrian Refugees in Lebanon."

59. Ghanem, "Local Governance under Pressure," 20.

60. IRIN News (now The New Humanitarian), "Syrian refugees head to Lebanon's Shi'a south," January 29, 2013, http://www.thenewhumanitarian.org/news/2013/01/29/syrian-refugees-head-lebanon-s-shia-south. Accessed December 10, 2019.

61. Interview with education specialist, Beirut, January 20, 2016.

62. Khawaja, "Growing Up without an Education."

63. Interview with professor of urban planning and member of the party Beirut Madinati, Beirut, March 16, 2017.

64. Reed and Habicht, "Sales of Food Aid as Sign of Distress, Not Excess."

65. As another example, International Organization for Migration (IOM) delivered bread to feed 9,000 people in 2015 in the Azraq refugee camp. Official numbers were more than double that at the time. Interviews with IOM officials, Amman, September 17, 2015.

66. World Bank Group, *Forcibly Displaced*, 68; Clemens and Hunt, "Labor Market Effects of Refugee Waves."

67. Turner, "Explaining the (Non-) Encampment of Syrian Refugees."

68. Atrache, "Lebanon's Resilience under the Weight of Syria's War."

69. Abdih and Geginat, "Economic Impact of the Syrian Conflict on Jordan"; World Bank Group, *Forcibly Displaced*, 68.

70. Abdih, Gamba, and Selim, "Jordan: Selected Issues," 5.

71. Seeberg, "Jordan's Migration Diplomacy and the Syrian Refugees," 2; Oxfam, "Lebanon Looking Ahead in Times of Crisis," 14.

72. World Bank, "Lebanon," 45.

73. Ibid.

74. Errighi and Griesse, "Syrian Refugee Crisis Labour Market Implications in Jordan and Lebanon," 19–20.

75. Government of Lebanon and the United Nations, "Lebanon Crisis Response Plan 2015–2016," 3.

76. Ajluni and Kawar, "Impact of the Syrian Refugee Crisis on the Labour Market in Jordan," 7. See the World Bank data page on Jordan, https://data.worldbank.org/country/jordan; The Hashemite Kingdom of Jordan, "Jordan's Way to Sustainable Development," 40.

77. World Bank, "Lebanon," 2, 43.

78. Oxfam, "Lebanon Looking Ahead in Times of Crisis," 14.

79. MOPIC, "Jordan Response Plan for the Syria Crisis 2016–2018," 2015, http://www.jrpsc.org/, 150; Achilli, Yassin, and Erdogan, "Neighbouring Host-Countries' Policies for Syrian Refugees," 13; Nasser and Symansky, "Fiscal Impact of the Syrian Refugee Crisis on Jordan," xi.

80. Nowrasteh, "Economics of the Syrian Refugee Crisis."

81. Mohammad Ghazal, "Population Stands at around 9.5 Million, Including 2.9 Million Guests," *Jordan Times*, January 30, 2016, http://www.jordantimes.com/news/local/population-stands-around-95-million-including-29-million-guests; Khetam Malkawi,

"Mafraq, Ramtha Population Doubled since Start of Syrian Crisis," *Jordan Times*, November 27, 2015, http://www.jordantimes.com/news/local/mafraq-ramtha-population-doubled-start-syrian-crisis%E2%80%99; Qasim Muheidat, "Syrians Make Up 88% of Jordan's Mafraq Population," *Al Bawaba*, March 1, 2015, https://www.albawaba.com/news/syrians-make-88-jordan%E2%80%99s-mafraq-population-663034.

82. El-Mallakh and Wahba, "Syrian Refugees and the Migration Dynamics of Jordanians."

83. Defined here as living on less than USD 4 per person per day. This group in the population represents 37 percent of Lebanese. Oxfam, "Lebanon Looking Ahead in Times of Crisis," 5, 24.

84. Ghanem, "Local Governance under Pressure," 42, 46.

85. UNHCR, Operations Portal Refugee Situations, Syria Regional Refugee Response, https://data2.unhcr.org/en/situations/syria.

86. Interviews with UN officials, Beirut, March 2017.

87. Interview with owner of agricultural land in Delhamiyyeh, Beka'a Valley, Lebanon, May 21, 2018.

88. Jacobsen, "Cities of Refuge in the Middle East," 13–14.

89. Taylor Luck, "In Jordan, Tensions Rise between Syrian Refugees and Host Community," *Washington Post*, 21 April 21, 2013, https://www.washingtonpost.com/world/middle_east/in-jordan-tensions-rise-between-syrian-refugees-and-host-community/2013/04/21/d4f5fa24-a762-11e2-a8e2-5b98cb59187f_story.html?utm_term=.29f3432f7f3b.

90. Hüser, "Syrian Refugee Crisis and Its Impact on Jordan," 87.

91. Ibid., 88.

92. Mercy Corps, "Mapping of Host Community-Refugee Tensions."

93. Ali et al., "A Town's Sudden Growth."

94. Interviews in Ramtha, Jordan, September 21, 2017.

95. REACH, "Evaluating the Effect of the Syrian Refugee Crisis," 10.

96. Masri and Srour, "Assessment of the Impact of Syrian Refugees in Lebanon," 38–39.

97. Thibos, "One Million Syrians in Lebanon," 4; Masri and Srour, "Assessment of the Impact of Syrian Refugees in Lebanon," 39.

98. World Bank, "Lebanon," 47.

99. Masri and Srour, "Assessment of the Impact of Syrian Refugees in Lebanon," 39.

100. Oxfam, "Lebanon Looking Ahead in Times of Crisis," 26.

101. Lozi, "The Effect of Refugees on Host Country Economy."

102. Errighi and Griesse, "Syrian Refugee Crisis Labour Market Implications," 8.

103. Kukrety and Al Jamal, "Poverty, Inequality and Social Protection in Lebanon," 12.

104. International Rescue Committee (IRC), "Policy Brief," 3.

105. Abdih, Gamba, and Selim, "Jordan: Selected Issues."

106. REACH, "Livelihoods, Employment and Tensions," 8.

107. Stave and Hillesund, "Impact of Syrian Refugees on the Jordanian Labour Market," 6.

108. "Jordanians Losing Jobs to Syrian Refugees," Phenix Center for Economic and Informatics Studies, October 7, 2013, http://www.phenixcenter.net/en/read-news/80.

109. Ajluni and Kawar, "Impact of the Syrian Refugee Crisis on the Labour Market in Jordan," 6.

110. ILO, "The Jordanian Labour Market."

111. Fakih and Ibrahim, "Impact of Syrian Refugees on the Labor Market in Neighboring Countries."

112. Carrion, "Syrian Refugees in Jordan."

113. Luck, "In Jordan, Tensions Rise."

114. About 100,000 Syrians are said to be employed in the Aqaba Economic Zone. Interviews with IOM officials, Amman, September 17, 2015.

115. Asfour, "Jordan: Local Perceptions on Syrian Refugees (Part 2/2)."

116. Interview with Jordanian professor, University of Jordan, Amman, September 12, 2017.

117. Discussions and outings with Jordanians, September 2015 and September 2017.

118. These supposed characteristics of Syrian labor were repeated universally by all interviewees in Jordan, including academics, business owners, and INGO officials. They said that Syrians take pride in their work, are cleaner, more gracious, that they trust Syrian waiters, Syrians do not have an attitude of entitlement, and so on. They also felt that Syrians are suited for the finer points of construction—tiling and painting—better than the Egyptians, who are believed to have a body type suited well for gross physical labor requirements.

119. Interview with Jordanian professor, University of Jordan, Amman, September 12, 2017.

120. While Lebanese prefer their own food over Syrian food, Jordanians like Syrian food. As one business owner responded to the question as to how have the Syrians affected Jordan, "Now we have good food." Interview with businesspeople, Young Entrepreneurs Association meeting, Amman, September 20, 2017.

121. USA for UNHCR, "Refugee Facts: Statistics," https://www.unrefugees.org/refugee-facts/statistics/.

122. Farhat, "Repercussions of the Syrian Refugee Crisis on Lebanon," 13.

123. Yassin and et al., "No Place to Stay?," 44.

124. IRC, "Economic Impacts of Syrian Refugees," 2.

125. Cochrane, Halabi, and Ross, "Child Labor in Agriculture on the Rise in Lebanon."

126. Food and Agriculture Organization of the United Nations (FAO), "Agricultural Livelihoods and Food Security Impact Assessment," 36.

127. Jarmuzek, Nakhle, and Parodi, "Lebanon"; Masri and Srour, "Assessment of the Impact of Syrian Refugees in Lebanon."

128. Ajluni et al., *Towards Decent Work in Lebanon.*

129. Dibeh, Fakih, and Marrouch, "Youth in Lebanon."

130. Ghanem, "Local Governance Under Pressure," 58.

131. Masri and Srour, "Assessment of the Impact of Syrian Refugees in Lebanon and Their Employment Profile, 2013," 38.

132. Government of Lebanon and The United Nations, "Lebanon Crisis Response Plan 2015–2016," 9.

133. Farhat, "Repercussions of the Syrian Refugee Crisis on Lebanon," 12.

134. AEMS, "Impact of the Syrian Crisis on the Lebanese Power Sector and Priority Recommendations," February 2017; Ajluni, Salem, and Mary Kawar, "Impact of the Syrian Refugee Crisis on the Labour Market in Jordan" 2014.

135. Families' economic need for children to work is one reason they do not attend school. Another reason is that children coming from war zones suffer from mental health problems. Unaddressed, fears and issues from the war have actually led children to stay away from school, even if they have transport and do not work.

136. Khawaja, "Growing Up without an Education."

137. Valenza and AlFayez, "Running on Empty," 24–26.

138. Interview with UNICEF employee, Beirut, March 16, 2017.

139. Group discussion with parents of children in public schools, January 20, 2016, Beirut.

140. Less than a third of Lebanese students attend public school. Khawaja, "Growing Up without an Education"; Josephine Deeb, "In Lebanon, Even Private Schools Caught in Education Crisis," January 12, 2017, Al-Monitor. https://www.al-monitor.com/pulse/originals/2017/01/lebanon-syrian-displaced-students-public-private-education.html.

141. Mahmoud Al Abed, "Jordan Allows Syrian children with No Documents to Join Schools—Officials," *Jordan Times*, September 25, 2017, http://jordantimes.com/news/local/jordan-allows-syrian-children-no-documents-join-schools-%E2%80%94-officials.

142. Hüser, "Syrian Refugee Crisis and Its Impact on Jordan," 86.

143. REACH, "Education and Tensions in Communities Hosting Syrian Refugees," 1.

144. Achilli, Yassin, and Erdogan, "Neighbouring Host-Countries' Policies for Syrian Refugees," 14.

145. Cherri, González, and Delgado, "Lebanese-Syrian Crisis," 169.

146. Numerous interviewees mentioned that Syrians are taken first over Lebanese, and Syrians do not pay, whereas Lebanese do. Masri and Srour, "Assessment of the Impact of Syrian Refugees in Lebanon," 40.

147. Nour Malas, "Refugee Crises in Mideast Spawn Health Threats," *Wall Street Journal*, June 27, 2016, http://www.wsj.com/articles/refugeecrisesinmideastspawnhealththrea ts1467064144.

148. Elsa Buchanan, "Lebanon: Doctors Warn of Spread of Cholera in Refugee Camps as Rubbish Crisis Intensifies," *International Business Times*, January 28, 2016, http://www .ibtimes.co.uk/lebanon-doctors-warn-spread-cholera-refugee-camps-rubbish-crisis -intensifies-1519262; Saroufim et al., "Ongoing Epidemic of Cutaneous Leishmaniasis among Syrian Refugees, Lebanon."

149. Information on this study from interview with Roland Riachi, postdoctoral fellow at the Issam Fares Institute for Public Policy and International Affairs and lecturer at the Faculty of Agricultural and Food Sciences, American University of Beirut, Beirut, March 20, 2017. Verified in interview with UNICEF water coordinator, Beirut, March 20, 2017.

150. AEMS, "Impact of the Syrian Crisis on the Lebanese Power Sector," 10.

151. Rhys Dubin, "Refugee Crisis Strains Lebanon's Deficient Electricity Network," *Daily Star*, February 22, 2017, http://www.dailystar.com.lb/News/Lebanon-News/2017/Feb -22/394578-refugee-crisis-strains-lebanons-deficient-electricity-network.ashx; "Refugee Crisis Hits Lebanon's Electricity Network," UN Lebanon, February 2017, http://www.un .org.lb/english/stories/the-ongoing-syrian-refugee-crisis-is-damaging-lebanons-already -poor-electricity-infrastructure. Accessed October 30, 2018.

152. "Lebanon's Electricity: The Need for Market Solutions," *Daily Star*, September 22, 2016, http://www.dailystar.com.lb/Business/Local/2016/Sep-22/373108-lebanons-electricity -the-need-for-market-solutions.ashx.

153. Dubin, "Refugee Crisis Strains Lebanon's Deficient Electricity Network."

154. AEMS, "Impact of the Syrian Crisis on the Lebanese Power Sector," 10.

155. Sylvia Westall, "No Light at End of Tunnel for Lebanon's Power Crisis," Reuters, October 26, 2015, https://www.reuters.com/article/us-lebanon-electricity/no-light-at-end -of-tunnel-for-lebanons-power-crisis-idUSKCN0SK1LH20151026.

156. Berthier, "Abracada . . . Broke."

157. Interview with official from EDL, Beka'a, May 21, 2018.

158. For more on water and the refugees in Jordan and Lebanon, see Baylouny and Klingseis. "Water Thieves or Political Catalysts?"

159. Darwish et al., "Salinity Evolution and Crop Response to Secondary Soil Salinity," 152; International Committee of the Red Cross, "Bled Dry—How War in the Middle East Is Bringing the Region to the Brink of a Water Catastrophe," 21. Accessed September 30, 2018.

160. Interviews and participant observation, Jordan, 1998–present.

161. Interview with senior research fellow, Sustainable Development Pillar, WANA Institute, Amman, September 10, 2017.

162. Riachi, "Private Modes of Water Capture in Lebanon," 40.

163. Study referenced in interview with coordinator of Water Projects, UNICEF-Lebanon, Beirut, March 20, 2017.

164. El Amine, "Lebanon Water Forum," 10.

165. Riachi, "Beyond Rehashed Policies"; "Bled Dry"; Oxfam International, "Syrian Refugee Influx Adding to Jordan's Water Worries."

166. Drinking water alone (not bathing or cooking) can cost several dollars per day per person, amounting to more than USD 300 per month for a five-to-six-person family.

167. Quoted in Peter Schwartzstein, "Syrian Refugees in Lebanon Camp Reliant on 'Hell Water' That Reduces Metal to Rust," *The Guardian*, May 26, 2015, https://www.theguardian.com/global-development/2015/may/26/syrian-refugees-lebanon-shatila-camp-hell-water.

168. Barham, "Is Good Water Governance Possible in a Rentier State?," 4.

169. Hana Namrouqa, "Illegal Wells in Al Lubban Sealed under Agreement with Tribal Leaders," *Jordan Times*, August 16, 2014, http://www.jordantimes.com/news/local/illegal-wells-al-lubban-sealed-under-agreement-tribal-leaders%E2%80%99.

170. Hana Namrouqa, "Authorities Tackle 30,000 Violations on Water Resources since 2013," *Jordan Times*, May 6, 2017, http://www.jordantimes.com/news/local/authorities-tackle-30000-violations-water-resources-2013.

171. Riachi, "Beyond Rehashed Policies."

172. "Preserving Lebanon's Water before the Wells Run Dry."

173. Riachi, "Private Modes of Water Capture in Lebanon"; El Amine, "Lebanon Water Forum," 12.

174. Riachi, "Private Modes of Water Capture in Lebanon," 41.

175. Embassy of the Hashemite Kingdom of Jordan, "Quick Facts," http://www.jordanembassyus.org/page/quick-facts. Accessed October 30, 2018.; Mercy Corps, "Tapped Out," 13.

176. Mercy Corps, "Tapped Out," 15.

177. "Water Restrictions Imposed as Heat Rises," *Jordan Times*, July 2, 2017, http://www.jordantimes.com/news/local/water-restrictions-imposed-heat-rises.

178. Mercy Corps, "Tapped Out," 19.

179. Rania Abouzeid, "Jordan's Rural Chafe under the Burden of Hosting Syrian Refugees," *Al Jazeera*, October 21, 2013, http://america.aljazeera.com/articles/2013/10/21/jordana-s-rural-poorchafeundertheburdenofhostingsyrianrefugees.html.

180. Joi Lee, "Syria's War: Inside Jordan's Zaatari Refugee Camp," *Al Jazeera*, April 1, 2018, https://www.aljazeera.com/indepth/inpictures/syria-war-jordan-zaatari-refugee-camp-180326115809170.html.

181. Interview with UNICEF official, Amman, September 14, 2015.

182. Global Risk Insights, "Water Scarcity in Jordan Increases with Refugee Flows," May 31, 2013, http://globalriskinsights.com/2013/05/water-scarcity-in-jordan-increases-with-refugee-flows/. Accessed October 30, 2018.

183. UNHCR, "Syria Regional Refugee Response: Jordan," http://data.unhcr.org/syrianrefugees/regional.php. Accessed September 26, 2018; Francis, "Jordan's Refugee Crisis," 1.

184. Hana Namrouqa, "Water Deficit Drops by 8 Per Cent Thanks to 'More Efficient Supply,'" *Jordan Times*, May 31, 2018, http://www.jordantimes.com/news/local/water-deficit-drops-8-cent-thanks-more-efficient-supply.

185. UNDP, "The Syrian Crisis"; Ghanem, "Local Governance under Pressure," 51.

186. Interview with INGO employee working on host-refugee relations, formerly working on Mercy Corp's waste management projects, Qalamoun, Tripoli, Lebanon, May 16, 2018.

187. Ministry of Environment, Government of Lebanon and UNDP, "Lebanon Environmental Assessment of the Syrian Conflict," 39.

188. Ibid., 3.

189. Ghanem, "Local Governance under Pressure," 49.

190. Interviews and discussions in Beirut, January 2016 and March 2017.

191. Conversations in Beirut, early 2016, reflected this popular concern. By May 2018 the majority of conversations mentioned this fear of being poisoned by food irrigated with sewage, and the hazards of eating fruit and vegetables.

192. Ministry of Environment, Government of Lebanon and UNDP, "Lebanon Environmental Assessment of the Syrian Conflict," 41.

193. World Bank, "Lebanon: Economic and Social Impact Assessment of the Syrian Conflict," 4.

194. Interview with municipal official, al-Bire, Akkar region, northern Lebanon, May 16, 2018.

195. Saadallaoui, "Competing for Scarce Resources."

196. Ghanem, "Local Governance under Pressure," 9.

197. Human Rights Watch, "'As If You're Inhaling Your Death.'"

198. Ministry of Environment, Government of Lebanon and UNDP, "Lebanon Environmental Assessment of the Syrian Conflict," 41.

199. Interview with UNICEF employee, Beirut, March 16, 2017.

200. Ellen Francis, "In Lebanese Town, Mounting Trash Shows Strain of Refugees," Reuters, March 31, 2017, https://www.reuters.com/article/us-mideast-crisis-syria-refugees /in-lebanese-town-mounting-trash-shows-strain-of-refugees-idUSKBN1721Q7.

201. Ministry of Planning and International Cooperation, "Needs Assessment Review," 11.

202. REACH, "Social Cohesion in Host Communities in Northern Jordan," 4.

203. Mercy Corps, "Tapped Out," 29.

204. Ibid., 20.

205. Al-Harahsheh, Al-Adamat, and Abdullah, "Impact of Za'atari Refugee Camp on the Water Quality in Amman-Zarqa Basin," 17.

206. Ibid., 23.

207. Hana Namrouqa, "Authorities Seek to Identify Pollution Sources at Zaatari," Jordan Times, September 26, 2013, http://vista.sahafi.jo/art.php?id=3b7fd87451736dcde91f 76905c60d10afd5d81a1.

208. "Widespread Middle East Fears That Syrian Violence Will Spread."

209. "Sectarian Tension Keeps Tripoli on Knife-Edge," Daily Star, June 6, 2012, http:// www.dailystar.com.lb/News/Lebanon-News/2012/Jun-06/175862-sectarian-tension -keeps-tripoli-on-knife-edge.ashx.

210. Abou Zeid, "A Time Bomb in Lebanon"; Alami, "Impact of the Syria Crisis on Salafis and Jihadis in Lebanon."

211. Atrache, "Beirut Bombing Widens Lebanon's Shiite-Sunni Divide"; Thibos, "One Million Syrians in Lebanon," 7.

212. International Crisis Group, "Too Close For Comfort: Syrians in Lebanon," 21.

213. "Second Wave of Bombings Hits Lebanese Border Village," New Arab, June 27, 2016, https://www.alaraby.co.uk/english/news/2016/6/27/second-wave-of-bombings-hits -lebanese-border-village.

214. International Crisis Group, "Lebanon's Hizbollah Turns Eastward to Syria."

215. "Syria Rebels Free Kidnapped Nuns." BBC News, March 10, 2014, https://www .bbc.com/news/world-middle-east-26510202.

216. Interviews with Sahar Atrache, (then) senior analyst, International Crisis Group, and several other academics, Beirut, March 2017.

217. Interviews with various Lebanese, January 2016–May 2018.

218. Interview with Karam Karam, ESCWA and Common Space Initiative, March 20, 2017, Beirut; various other interviews, Beirut, May 2018.

219. International Crisis Group, "Arsal in the Crosshairs."

220. Alice Su, "Fade to Black: Jordanian City Ma'an Copes with Islamic State Threat," *Al Jazeera*, September 2, 2014, http://america.aljazeera.com/articles/2014/9/2/jordan-maan -daashthreat.html; "Five Jordanians Jailed for ISIL Membership," *Al Jazeera*, November 17, 2014, http://www.aljazeera.com/news/middleeast/2014/11/five-jordanians-jailed-isil -membership-20141117155225707489.html; Mercy Corps, "From Jordan to Jihad"; Bondokji and Harper, "Journey Mapping of Selected Jordanian Foreign Fighters."

221. Discussions with Jordanians, Amman, September 2017.

222. Interviews in Irbid, Jordan, September 21, 2017, and various others throughout Jordan.

223. Interview with Karam Karam.

224. Ghanem, "Local Governance under Pressure," 8–9; Molnar, "Discretion to Deport," 24–25.

225. Al-Saadi, "Examining Curfews against Syrians in Lebanon."

226. Interview with Bassel Salloukh, professor, Lebanese American University, Beirut, March 17, 2017, and with INGO official, Beirut, March 20, 2017. See also Salloukh, "The Syrian War."

227. Baylouny, "Militarizing Welfare"; Moore, "Jordan's Long War Economy."

228. Discussions in both countries, and see the BBC's "Viewpoints: Impact of Syrian Refugees," BBC News, August 24, 2013, http://www.bbc.com/news/world-23813975

229. Interview with local leader, al-Uwaynat village near the Syrian border, Lebanon, March 16, 2018.

230. UNICEF, "A Study on Early Marriage in Jordan 2014."

231. Reportedly, the Gulf countries cracked down on this out of fear that they would lose control over citizenship and need to include refugee children. Interviews with researchers and INGOs, Amman, September 2017; Karin Laub, "Spike in Number of Syrian Teens Marrying as Child Brides in Jordan," *The Independent*, August 7, 2017, https://www .independent.co.uk/news/world/middle-east/child-brides-jordan-syrian-teenage -refugees-a7880831.html; Save the Children, "Too Young to Wed"; United Nations Population Fund, "New Study Finds Child Marriage Rising among Most Vulnerable Syrian Refugees."

232. Interview with Lebanese academic and researcher, Beirut, March 14, 2017.

233. Interview with businesswoman and member of municipal council, Irbid, Jordan, September 21, 2015.

234. Interview in Ramtha, Jordan, September 21, 2017.

235. Interviews with Atrache and with Lebanese academic, Beirut, March 14, 2017.

236. Nowrasteh, "Economics of the Syrian Refugee Crisis"; Cali and Sekkarie, "Much Ado about Nothing?"

237. Karen Leigh and Suha Ma'ayeh, "Syrian Firms Take Refuge Abroad—and Create Jobs," *Wall Street Journal*, March 12, 2016, https://www.wsj.com/articles/syrian-firms -fleeand-create-jobs-amid-the-refugee-crisis-1457712969.

238. Harb, Kassem, and Najdi, "Entrepreneurial Refugees and the City." Businesspeople had been hoping for a cross-fertilization of Jordanian and Syrian labor to improve Jordanians' skill set, but government policy in Jordan prevented this, at least legally. Interviews with businesspeople and industrialists, and interview with owner of Jordanian chocolate factory, Amman, September 20, 2017.

239. Nora Schweitzer, Agence France Presse, "Refugee Cash Card Scheme Boosts Lebanese Grocers," *Daily Star*, June 29, 2017, http://www.dailystar.com.lb/News/Lebanon -News/2017/Jun-29/411126-refugee-cash-card-scheme-boosts-grocers.ashx.

240. IRC, "Economic Impacts of Syrian Refugees," 5.

241. IRC, "Emergency Economies," 6.

242. Interview with head of local NGO, Beka'a Valley, and visit to informal settlement and accompanying store, May 21, 2018.

243. Interview with senior UNHCR official, Amman, September 19, 2015.

244. Interviews with political scientists, Beirut, March 14 and 17, 2017.

245. Interviews with analyst and with Norwegian Refugee Council, Amman, September 16, 2015.

246. Interviews with Mercy Corps employee and with American University of Beirut graduate, Beirut, both May 24, 2018.

247. Focus group interviews with local NGO employees, Amman, September 17, 2017.

248. NGOs are popularly viewed as acceptable employment for women in Jordan, where women's employment is viewed more conservatively than in Lebanon. Interview with UNDP employee specializing in the North of Jordan, Webdeh, Amman, September 20, 2017.

249. Conversation in Amman, September 2017.

250. I randomly met three people in two days starting businesses in private education, Amman, September 2017.

251. Yusuf Mansur, "Refugee Arithmetic," *Jordan Times*, February 17, 2014, http://www.jordantimes.com/opinion/yusuf-mansur/refugee-arithmetic. JD amounts were converted to USD amounts.

252. Yara Bayoumy, "Lebanon Needs $20 Billion for Infrastructure," Reuters, October 20, 2010, https://www.reuters.com/article/us-mideast-summit-lebanon-infrastructure/lebanon-needs-20-billion-for-infrastructure-idUSTRE69J3MB20101020.

253. Norwegian Refugee Council, "Consequences of Limited Legal Status for Syrian Refugees in Lebanon," 21–22.

254. IHRC and Norwegian Refugee Council, "Registering Rights"; Howard, "Analyzing the Causes of Statelessness in Syrian Refugee Children."

255. Ababsa, "Gulf Donors and NGOs Assistance to Syrian Refugees in Jordan"; Dickinson, "Shadow Aid to Syrian Refugees."

256. Ali et al., "A Town's Sudden Growth."

257. Interview with UNICEF official, Amman, September 14, 2015.

258. Achilli, "Syrian Refugees in Jordan," 8; Save the Children and UNICEF, "Small Hands Heavy Burden," 11.

259. Interview with UNICEF official, Amman, September 14, 2015. Because families knew these children would be cared for by international organizations and that living in a camp would be undesirable for the family and their other children, some families chose to leave the detained child in the camp. This, again, is one of the difficult choices that refugee families must weigh for their survival.

260. Aranki and Kalis, "Limited Legal Status for Refugees from Syria in Lebanon."

261. Interview with NGO founder and UN consultant, Amman, September 19, 2017.

262. Interviews with Mercy Corps officials, Amman, September 14, 2017.

3. FROM BROTHERS IN NEED TO INVADERS

1. Interviews throughout Jordan, September 2015 and September 2017; Mitri, "Challenges of Aid Coordination," 5; Carpi, "Against Ontologies of Hospitality"; Carpi, "Everyday Experience of Humanitarianism in Akkar Villages"; Naufal, "Syrian Refugees in Lebanon," 15; Mackreath, "Cosmopolitanism in Akkar?"; Madoré, "Peaceful Settlement of Syrian Refugees."

2. Asfour, "Jordan: Local Perceptions on Syrian Refugees (Part 2/2)"; discussions with Jordanians of Palestinian descent.

3. These differences are not the main focus of the study, but are interesting as a topic in itself.

4. This chapter focuses on hostility through 2016. This is not to suggest that the hostility ended there, only that this period of time is the focus of this chapter. In fact, animosity toward the Syrians continues to increase, particularly in Lebanon, resulting in attacks and evictions.

5. Gomez and Christensen, "Impacts of Refugees on Neighboring Countries," 11.

6. Interview with Jordanian academic and former diplomat, Amman, September 19, 2015.

7. "Sharl 'Ata lil-Umam al-Mutahidda: li-iyqaf al-musa'adat 'an al-lajieen al-Sourieen fi Lubnan," [Charl Ata to the United Nations: Stop the assistance to the Syrian refugees in Lebanon], *El-Nashra*, November 8, 2017, https://www.elnashra.com/.

8. Interview with Sahar Atrache, (then) senior analyst, Lebanon, International Crisis Group, Beirut, March 14, 2017.

9. Ibid.

10. Interview with UNDP researcher specializing in northern Jordan, Amman, September 20, 2017.

11. This statement also speaks to the concept of "the state" and a comparison of the Lebanese state with the "ideal" or "European" one. Interview with sheikh in Tripoli, Lebanon, May 16, 2018.

12. Interviews in the northern border areas with Syria, Akkar region, May 16, 2018.

13. Similar stories circulated in Syria and Lebanon. Constanze Letsch, "Syria's Refugees: Fears of Abuse Grow as Turkish Men Snap up Wives," *The Guardian*, September 8, 2014, https://www.theguardian.com/world/2014/sep/08/syrian-refugee-brides-turkish-husbands-marriage.

14. Interview with former Mercy Corps researcher in charge of waste projects, Qalamoun, Tripoli, Lebanon, May 16, 2018.

15. Focus group interview with professional men, al-Azm Charitable Association, Halba, Akkar, Lebanon, May 16, 2018.

16. Khaled Neimat, "Majority of Jordanians Call for End to Syrian Refugee Influx," *Jordan Times*, April 15, 2013, http://vista.sahafi.jo/art.php?id=dd4935045944a00a7a5feaa87b2811c8f7009652.

17. Mercy Corps, "Engaging Municipalities in the Response to the Syria Refugee Crisis in Lebanon," 3.

18. International Republican Institute, "Survey of Jordan Public Opinion, November 30–December 6, 2013," 16.

19. Center for Strategic Studies, "Istitlaa' lil-rai al-'am hawla ba'dh al-qadaya al-rahina fil-Urdun," 25.

20. Nicholas Seeley, "Most Jordanians Say No to More Syrian Refugees," *Christian Science Monitor*, October 1, 2012, https://www.csmonitor.com/World/Middle-East/2012/1001/Most-Jordanians-say-no-to-more-Syrian-refugees, citing a poll from the Center for Strategic Studies, Amman.

21. Some studies show that interaction decreases hostility to the refugees. See Mercy Corps, "Seeking Stability."

22. Hüser, "Syrian Refugee Crisis and Its Impact on Jordan," 91.

23. Interview with head of an NGO, Mafraq, Jordan, September 18, 2017.

24. Interviews with a tribal sheikh and his relative, Ramtha, Jordan, September 21, 2017.

25. Taylor Luck, "In Jordan, Tensions Rise between Syrian Refugees and Host Community," *Washington Post*, April 21, 2013, https://www.washingtonpost.com/world/middle_east/in-jordan-tensions-rise-between-syrian-refugees-and-host-community/2013/04/21/d4f5fa24-a762-11e2-a8e2-5b98cb59187f_story.html?utm_term=.29f3432f7f3b.

26. Khaldoun Bani Khalid, "Al-Mafraq: Suriyoun yashtaroun aradi wa manazil fi balda al-Za'atari bi-asma' Urduniyeen" [Mafraq: Syrians buy land and houses in the town of Za'atari in the name of Jordanians], *al-Ghad*, August 30, 2016, https://alghad.com/.

27. John Reed, "Jordanian Border Town Feels the Strain of Refugee Influx," *Financial Times*, May 17, 2013, https://www.ft.com/content/0f571098-be3a-11e2-bb35-00144feab7de.

28. Interview with UNDP researcher specializing in northern Jordan, Amman, September 20, 2017.

29. Rana F. Sweis, "Resentment Grows Against Syrian Refugees in Jordan," *New York Times*, May 9, 2013, http://www.nytimes.com/2013/05/09/world/middleeast/09iht-m09-jordan-syria.html?pagewanted=all&_r=0.

30. Interviews with elites and parents, Amman, September 2017.

31. Interview with businesswoman and member of municipal council, Irbid, Jordan, September 21, 2017, and interview with head of an NGO, Mafraq, Jordan, September 18, 2017.

32. Christophersen et al., "Lebanese Attitudes towards Syrian Refugees," 57.

33. Interviews, Beirut, January 2016 and March 2017.

34. Beirut Research and Innovation Center, Lebanese Center for Studies and Research, "Citizens' Perceptions of Security Threats."

35. Mercy Corps, "Engaging Municipalities," 1.

36. A little more than half the respondents felt Syrians threatened the sectarian balance. Beirut Research and Innovation Center, Lebanese Center for Studies and Research, "Citizens' Perceptions of Security Threats," 4.

37. Interview with academic head of research unit at American University of Beirut, Beirut, March 14, 2017.

38. Mourad and Piron, "Municipal Service Delivery," 33.

39. Al-Masri, "Social Stability Context in the Nabatieh & Bint Jbeil Qazas."

40. Ghanem, "Dialogue and Local Response Mechanisms," 22; Mourad and Piron, "Municipal Service Delivery, ," 33.

41. Interview with political analyst and writer, Beirut, March 14, 2017.

42. Conversations with Lebanese military officers, March 14, 2017.

43. Interviews in Lebanon and Jordan, from January 2016 to May 2018.

44. Interviews with David Adams, coordinator of Water Projects, UNICEF, Beirut, March 20, 2017; Roland Riachi, postdoctoral fellow at the Issam Fares Institute for Public Policy and International Affairs and lecturer at the Faculty of Agricultural and Food Sciences, American University of Beirut, Beirut, March 20, 2017.

45. Interview with Orthodox priest in a Lebanese border town with Syria, May 16, 2018.

46. Interview with businesswoman and member of municipal council, Irbid, Jordan, September 21, 2017.

47. Interview with tribal sheikh and businessman from Ramtha, Amman, Jordan, September 17, 2017.

48. Center for Strategic Studies, "Jordanians Feel Less Safe."

49. Interviews with a tribal sheikh and his relative, Ramtha, Jordan, September 21, 2017.

50. Interview with businesswoman and member of municipal council, Irbid, Jordan, September 21, 2017.

51. Interview with head of a municipality, Beka'a, May 21, 2018.

52. Interview with local governing leader, al-Bire, northern Lebanon, May 16, 2018.

53. Harb and Saab, "Social Cohesion and Intergroup Relations," 5.

54. Alsharabati, "Survey on Perceptions of Syrian Refugees in Lebanon."

55. Interview with head of an international think tank, Beirut, March 17, 2017.

56. Interview with *mukhtar* of two villages in Beka'a, Lebanon, May 21, 2018.

57. Interviews in Lebanon and Jordan, from January 2016 to May 2018.

58. Madoré, "Peaceful Settlement of Syrian Refugees."

59. Interview with teacher and administrator at a public school, Beka'a, Lebanon, May 21, 2018.

60. Focus group interview with teachers and women from Aidamoun, Akkar, northern Lebanon, May 16, 2018.

61. Abu-Fadil, "Lebanon: Mixed Messages."

62. REACH, "Livelihoods, Employment and Tensions in Jordanian Communities," 1.

63. Connable, *From Negative to Positive Stability*, 25.

64. Interviews in Beirut, March 2017 and May 2018, and author experience.

65. Interviews and discussions, Beirut, May 2018.

66. AP, "Syrians in Lebanon Battle Crowds to Vote for Bashar al-Assad," *The Guardian*, May 28, 2014, https://www.theguardian.com/world/2014/may/28/syrians-lebaanon -vote-assad-embassies-refugees-boycott.

67. See also "Widespread Middle East Fears That Syrian Violence Will Spread."

68. Interview with Sahar Atrache; Yazan al-Saadi, "The Diversion Strategy: Lebanese Racism, Classism, and the Refugees," *Al Jazeera* (English), June 10, 2014, https://english .al-akhbar.com/print/20121.

69. Interviews with various analysts in Beirut, Lebanon, March 2017.

70. Center for Insights in Survey Research, "Survey of Jordan Public Opinion: National Poll #14."

71. Center for Strategic Studies, "Jordanians Feel Less Safe."

72. Interview with head of an NGO, Mafraq, Jordan, September 18, 2017.

73. Chit and Nayel, "Understanding Racism against Syrian Refugees in Lebanon."

74. The government proposed limiting bread subsidies to nationals. Martínez, "Leavened Apprehensions."

75. Tsourapas, "Syrian Refugee Crisis and Foreign Policy Decision-Making."

76. Agence France Presse, "King Says Syria Refugee Influx Depleting Jordan," *Daily Star*, November 3, 2013, http://www.dailystar.com.lb/News/Middle-East/2013/Nov-03/236648 -king-says-syria-refugee-influx-depleting-jordan.ashx.

77. For example, "Syria Conflict: Jordanians 'at Boiling Point' over Refugees," BBC News, February 2, 2016, http://www.bbc.com/news/world-middle-east-35462698; "Safadi Meets with US Officials over Syria," *Jordan Times*, September 4, 2018, http://www .jordantimes.com/news/local/safadi-meets-us-officials-over-syria.

78. Natasha Tynes, "Recent Visit to Amman Reveals: When in Doubt, Blame the Syrians," *Huffington Post*, May 24, 2013, updated July 24, 2013. https://www.huffingtonpost .com/natasha-tynes/syria-refugees-jordan_b_3331360.html.

79. "Al-Hazaymeh: al-azmeh al-Sourıyyeh atharat ʿala al-muwazına" [Al-Hazaymeh: The Syrian crisis has affected the budget], *Jordan Zad*, February 24, 2014, http://www .jordanzad.com/index.php?page=article&id=150586.

80. Interview with UNDP researcher specializing in northern Jordan, Amman, September 20, 2017.

81. I do not examine the international media and think tanks, which were just as alarmist, if not more. According to their reports, destabilization of states and chaos would surely result from this refugee crisis. See, for example, Ridge and Smith, "Confronting the Global Forced Migration Crisis."

82. Mercy Corps, "Mapping of Host Community-Refugee Tensions," 18.

83. Lenner, "Alternative Voices on the Syrian Refugee Crisis in Jordan," 11.

84. See Salamah, "Violations of Professional Principles."

85. Interview with head of an NGO, Mafraq, Jordan, September 18, 2017.

86. "Miqati: li-musa'da Lubnan fi ʿaba' lil-lajieen al-Sourieen" [Miqati: Help Lebanon to Handle the Burden of the Syrian Refugees], *Al-Anba'*, June 18, 2013, https://anbaaonline .com/?p=123299.

87. Yazan al-Saadi, "Attacks on Syrians in Lebanon: Scapegoating, Par Excellence," *Al Akhbar* (English), September 16, 2014, https://english.al-akhbar.com/node/21557.

88. Gasia Trtrian, "Syrian Refugees Responsible for River Waste Pollution: Environment Minister," *Daily Star*, January 8, 2018, http://www.dailystar.com.lb/News/Lebanon-News/2018/Jan-08/432886-syrian-refugees-responsible-for-river-waste-pollution-environment-minister.ashx.

89. "Bassil: The Syrian Refugee Crisis Poses an Existential Threat," MTV, November 2014, https://www.mtv.com.lb/en/news/articles/418239/bassil_the_syrian_refugee_crisis_poses_an_existential_threat; "Lebanon's Foreign Minister Blames Downtrodden Economy on Syrian Refugees"; *New Arab*, July 10, 2018, https://www.alaraby.co.uk/english/news/2018/7/10/lebanons-foreign-minister-blames-downtrodden-economy-on-syrian-refugees.

90. "Refugees in Lebanon, Turkey and Jordan Losing Hope," *Ammon News*, 16 January 2017, http://en.ammonnews.net/print.aspx?articleno=33839.

91. "Our Burden Today Is Displaced Syrians: President Aoun," *Daily Star*, May 17, 2017, http://www.dailystar.com.lb/News/Lebanon-News/2017/Mar-17/397930-our-burden-today-is-displaced-syrians-president-aoun.ashx.

92. "Aoun: Syrian Refugee Crisis Is 'Existential Threat' to Lebanon," *Daily Star*, October 30, 2017, http://www.dailystar.com.lb/News/Lebanon-News/2017/Oct-30/424451-lebanon-and-cyprus-strengthen-diplomatic-ties.ashx; "Aoun: Syrian Refugee Burden Is Exhausting Lebanon," *Asharq Al-Awsat*, February 18, 2018, https://aawsat.com/english/home/article/1178986/aoun-syrian-refugee-burden-exhausting-lebanon.

93. George Azar, "Hariri Says 'Lebanon One Big Refugee Camp,'" *An-Nahar*, April 25, 2018, https://en.annahar.com/article/795887-hariri-voices-concern-over-perpetual-syrian-refugee-crisis.

94. "Gemayel: Syrian Refugees Have Become Threat to Lebanon," *Naharnet*, April 15, 2013, http://www.naharnet.com/stories/en/79584.

95. "Al-Lubnanioun yatathahiroun lil-mutaaliba bi-mughadira al-lajieen al-Sourieen . . . fa-ma alathi yudafa'hum lithalik?" [Lebanese protesters demanding repatriation of Syrian refugees . . . what motivates them to do so?], *AlSouria*, October 14, 2017, https://www.alsouria.net/.

96. Hourani, "Media and the Syrian Refugees in Lebanon."

97. Jordan is just better at hiding its human rights violations, but they are clearly present vis-à-vis the Syrians. UN interviews affirmed what Human Rights Watch has documented.

98. Hourani, "Media and the Syrian Refugees in Lebanon."

99. Chit and Nayel, "Understanding Racism against Syrian Refugees in Lebanon."

100. Sadaka, Nader, and Mikhael, "Monitoring Racism in the Lebanese Media."

101. "The Fear and Loathing of Syrian Refugees in Lebanon," *Listening Post, Al Jazeera*, October 28, 2017, https://www.aljazeera.com/programmes/listeningpost/2017/10/fear-loathing-syrian-refugees-lebanon-171028121205744.html.

102. Abu-Fadil, "Lebanon: Mixed Messages," 93.

103. Ibid., 92.

104. Abou-Zahr, "Refugees and the Media in Lebanon."

105. "Lebanese to Deal with Further Electricity, Water Shortages during Summer," *Naharnet*, July 3, 2014, http://www.naharnet.com/stories/en/137267-lebanese-to-deal-with-further-electricity-water-shortages-during-summer.

106. Abu-Fadil, "Lebanon: Mixed Messages," 91.

107. To keep within the topic of citizens' reactions to the refugees, I do not examine here the important topic of torture and imprisonment of Syrians by the states and the formal security forces.

108. REACH, "Social Cohesion in Host Communities in Northern Jordan," 3.

109. REACH, "Understanding Social Cohesion and Resilience," 12.

110. "Ihtijajat wa shaghab wa qata' lil-taruqat min qibl al-shabab al-Urduni 'ala al-tawajid al-Souri fil-Mafraq" [Protests and vandalism and blocking roads by Jordanian youth against the presence of Syrians in Mafraq], *Al-Kawn News*, September 21, 2014, http://www.alkawnnews.com/article/29111/.

111. Hani Hazaimeh, "Syrian Refugees, Ramtha Residents Clash outside Bashabsheh Complex," *Jordan Vista*, July 23, 2012, http://vista.sahafi.jo/art.php?id=ebf6b9ce017ee05 3eaf2541a70a2ea9adaf993a1; Mercy Corps, "Mapping of Host Community-Refugee Tensions," 15–16.

112. See Mourad, "'Standoffish' Policy-Making."

113. Al-Saadi, "The Diversion Strategy"; El Helou, "Refugees under Curfew."

114. El Helou, "Refugees under Curfew."

115. Interview with Sahar Atrache.

116. "Syrian Refugees Make up One Third of Lebanon's Prison Population," *An-Nahar*, August 8, 2018, https://en.annahar.com/article/842279-syrian-refugees-make-one-third-of -lebanons-prison-population.

117. Interview with Orthodox priest on the border with Syria, May 16, 2018.

118. Conversations with Lebanese military officers, March 14, 2017.

119. Brent Bambury, "Meet Captagon, the Nightmare Drug Fueling Syria's Civil War," CBC Radio, June 3, 2017, https://www.cbc.ca/radio/day6/episode-340-amphetamines-in -syria-stanley-cup-bassist-noriega-s-pen-pal-subversive-board-games-and-more-1 .4139584/meet-captagon-the-nightmare-drug-fuelling-syria-s-civil-war-1.4139601; Chavala Madlena and Radwan Mortada, "Syria's Speed Freaks, Jihad Junkies, and Captagon Cartels," *Foreign Policy*, November 19, 2015, https://foreignpolicy.com/2015/11/19/syria -isis-captagon-lebanon-assad/. In Jordan, see "5,000 Narcotic Pills Seized in Northern Badia," *Jordan Times*, May 26, 2018, http://www.jordantimes.com/news/local/5000-narcotic -pills-seized-northern-badia.

120. Laila Bassam and Tom Perry, "Exclusive: Lebanon Army Chief Sees Growing Risk from Syrian Camps," Reuters, November 26, 2015, https://www.reuters.com/article/us -lebanon-security-idUSKBN0TF1PG20151126; Human Rights Watch, "Lebanon: Rising Violence Targets Syrian Refugees," September 30, 2014, https://www.hrw.org/news/2014 /09/30/lebanon-rising-violence-targets-syrian-refugees; Kareen Shaheen, "Near Batroun, fear of Syrians prompts patrols," September 19, 2014, *The Daily Star*, http://www.dailystar .com.lb/News/Lebanon-News/2014/Sep-19/271186-near-batroun-fear-of-syrians -prompts-patrols.ashx.

121. "Syrians Come under Attack in Lebanon after Jihadists Behead Two Captured Lebanese Soldiers," Associated Press, September 13, 2014, http://www.foxnews.com/world /2014/09/13/syrians-come-under-attack-in-lebanon-after-jihadists-behead-2-captured -lebanese.html.

122. Mona Alami, "Averting a Crisis: Syrian Refugees in Lebanon," May 28, 2013, Carnegie Middle East Center, http://carnegie-mec.org/2013/05/28/averting-crisis-syrian -refugees-in-lebanon-pub-51905; Kathryn Maureen Ryan, "Syrian Refugees Attacked in Lebanon," Impunity Watch, September 16, 2014, http://impunitywatch.com/syrian -refugees-attacked-in-lebanon/.

123. Al-Saadi, "Attacks on Syrians in Lebanon."

124. "Civilians Threaten Syrian Refugees, Demand They Leave," *Now*, updated September 9, 2014, https://now.mmedia.me/lb/en/lebanonnews/562988-civilians-threaten -syrian-refugees-demand-they-leave.

125. Human Rights Watch, "Lebanon: Rising Violence Targets Syrian Refugees."

126. "UNHCR: 85% of Syria Families in Jordan Live below Poverty Line," *Middle East Monitor*, May 29, 2018, https://www.middleeastmonitor.com/20180529-unhcr-85-of-syria

-families-in-jordan-live-below-poverty-line/; UNHCR and UNICEF, "Vulnerability Assessment of Syrian Refugees in Lebanon."

127. Interview with Sahar Atrache.

4. GRIEVANCES AGAINST GOVERNANCE

1. Given the scarce amounts of funding relative to the numbers of refugees, the reallocation of aid to locals would come at the expense of helping many refugees.

2. See Geha, *Civil Society and Political Reform in Lebanon and Libya*; Kingston, *Reproducing Sectarianism*. On social sanctioning despite desires for reform, see Paler, Marshall, and Atallah, "Fear of Supporting Political Reform"; Paler, Marshall, and Atallah, "Social Costs of Public Political Participation."

3. McAdam et al., *Comparative Perspectives on Social Movements*.

4. Johnston and Noakes, *Frames of Protest*, 3.

5. Snow et al., "Disrupting the 'Quotidian.'"

6. I did not interview state elites about their rationale for blame of the Syrians, and they would probably not have admitted to it. However, there is a historical pattern in these states, and analysts maintain that these states attempt to deflect blame onto others.

7. These private-sector service providers are well integrated, and people can barely notice the switch from state to private electricity. Elevators and hotels post announcements of precise times the electricity will cut out momentarily and then restart.

8. Mona Naggar, "Lebanon's Middle Class Steadily Shrinking," DW, January 7, 2013, https://www.dw.com/en/lebanons-middle-class-steadily-shrinking/a-16503404.

9. There is even an app for electricity blackouts. Alexandra Talty, "Power Outages and Military Roadblocks? In Lebanon, There's an App for That," Techonomy, July 1, 2013, https://techonomy.com/2013/07/electricity-cuts-and-military-roadblocks-in-lebanon-theres-an-app-for-that/.

10. Interview with resident of Wadi Khaled, Akkar, May 21, 2018.

11. Interview with labor specialist, American University of Beirut, Beirut, May 25, 2018.

12. Bekdache, "Lebanon's Garbage Crisis."

13. Mourad and Piron, "Municipal Service Delivery," 23.

14. Only Zahle has 24-7 electricity, and that was hard fought.

15. "Hatta iza houmeh 'am biyakalouhoum, hinneh biyaskoutu." Interview with senior in Jordanian border town with Syria, September 21, 2017.

16. For example, Goldstone and Tilly, "Threat (and Opportunity)"; Van Dyke and Soule, "Structural Social Change and the Mobilizing Effect of Threat."

17. See also "Widespread Middle East Fears That Syrian Violence Will Spread."

18. For a balanced assessment of such risks that does not stereotype refugees as radicals, see Hourani, "State Security and Refugees."

19. Information on numbers of attacks is available from the Global Terrorism Database, University of Maryland, "Lebanon, 2011–2017," www.start.umd.edu/gtd/. For more, see Zelin, "Jihadism in Lebanon after the Syrian Uprising."

20. Rana F. Sweis, "ISIS Is Said to Claim Responsibility for Deadly Attack in Jordan," *New York Times*, December 20, 2016, https://www.nytimes.com/2016/12/20/world/middleeast/jordan-attack-isis-karak.html. More recently, police and militants were killed in a raid in Amman in 2018. See Suleiman Al-Khalidi, "Four Security Personnel, at Least Three Militants, Killed in Jordan Shoot-out," Reuters, August 12, 2018, https://www.reuters.com/article/us-jordan-security-militants/four-security-personnel-at-least-three-militants-killed-in-jordan-shoot-out-idUSKBN1KX07I.

21. Interview with professor from Lebanese American University, Beirut, March 17, 2017.

22. Yom, "New Landscape of Jordanian Politics," 293.

23. Kamal Taha, Agence France Presse, "Jordan Amends Anti-Terror Law to Face Syria Fallout," *Daily Star*, April 24, 2014, http://www.dailystar.com.lb/News/Middle-East/2014/Apr-24/254217-jordan-amends-anti-terror-law-to-face-syria-fallout.ashx and AFP; "Jordanians Charged with 'Terrorism' over Campus Clash," *Daily Star*, November 20, 2013, http://www.dailystar.com.lb/News/Middle-East/2013/Nov-20/238441-jordanians-charged-with-terrorism-over-campus-clash.ashx.

24. Connable, *From Negative to Positive Stability*; Barnes-Dacey, "Syria."

25. Deborah Amos, "In a Rough Neighborhood, Jordan Clings to Its Stability," All Things Considered, National Public Radio, July 1, 2013, https://www.npr.org/sections/parallels/2013/07/01/196656296/stability-or-democracy-in-jordan-its-a-fragile-balance; Grigg, "One Year after Jordan's Fuel Protests."

26. Interviews. This worked less well as time went on, particularly after the downfall of ISIS.

27. International Republican Institute, "IRI Poll: Jordanians Encouraged by Stability."

28. Abu-Rish, "Doubling Down"; Nermeen Murad, "Here Is How Jordan Escaped the Arab Spring," *Al Jazeera*, February 9, 2014, https://www.aljazeera.com/indepth/opinion/2014/02/here-how-jordan-escaped-arab-spr-20142510106257977.html; Staton, "Young Reformers Want Debate."

29. Interview with businesswoman and municipal council official, Irbid, Jordan, September 21, 2017.

30. The awareness of health risks in Lebanon increased through the years of research, but already in 2016 it was a major concern of those employed in the rural areas. Conversations in Beirut, January 2016.

31. Interview with officials at Mercy Corps, Amman, September 14, 2017; Amos, "In a Rough Neighborhood, Jordan Clings to Its Stability."

32. Compare to Polanyi's double movement of demanding protection against the free market. Polanyi, *The Great Transformation*.

33. Interviews, Beirut, March 2017.

34. Interview with lead researcher, WANA institute, Amman, September 10, 2017.

35. Street discussions in Amman, September 11, 2017.

36. Interview with assistant to municipal head, al-Bire, Lebanon, May 16, 2018.

37. Interview with *mukhtar* of two towns in Beka'a, Lebanon, May 21, 2018.

38. Interview with sheikh at Madrasa Imam [Imam School], Tripoli, Lebanon, May 16, 2018.

39. Interview with *mukhtar* of two towns in Beka'a, Lebanon, May 21, 2018.

40. Interview with military officer, Hamra, Beirut, May 19, 2018.

41. The Beka'a and other border regions engage in smuggling and trade in illegal or unregulated goods.

42. See the interviews with laborers quoted in Harris, "Transforming Refugees into 'Illegal Migrants,'" 77.

43. "Jordanians Losing Jobs to Syrian Refugees," Phenix Center for Economic and Informatics Studies, October 7, 2013, http://phenixcenter.net/en/jordanians-losing-jobs-to-syrian-refugees-3/.

44. Interview with president of a municipality, Beka'a, Lebanon, May 21, 2018.

45. Masri and Srour, "Assessment of the Impact of Syrian Refugees in Lebanon," 38.

46. Interview with country director of Mercy Corps, Ashrafieh, Beirut, May 17, 2018.

47. Interview with municipal official, Zarqa, Jordan, September 14, 2017.

48. Discussion with Jordanian government official, Washington, DC, June 2, 2017.

49. Areej Abuqudairi, "Syria's War Haunts Jordanian Border Town," *Al Jazeera*, May 11, 2015. https://www.aljazeera.com/news/2015/05/150510083150067.html.

50. Interview with municipality official, Zarqa, Jordan, September 14, 2017.

51. Focus group interview with professional men, al-Azm Charitable Association, Halba, Akkar, Lebanon, May 16, 2018.

52. Interview with EDL official, Beka'a, May 21, 2018.

53. Connable, *From Negative to Positive Stability*, 27.

54. Interview with municipality assistant in largest village in central Beka'a, May 21, 2018.

55. Interview with professor at the Lebanese University Political Science Department, Beirut, May 24, 2018.

56. Interview with head of NGO in Mafraq, Jordan, September 18, 2017.

57. Interviews with UNDP researcher specializing in northern Jordan, Amman, September 20, 2017; German NGO country director, Amman, September 25, 2017; and with television political talk show host and former MP, Amman, September 24, 2017.

58. Interview with graduate research assistant at American University of Beirut, from Aid'amoun, Akkar, May 16, 2018.

59. Interview with military officer, Hamra, Beirut, May 19, 2018.

60. Interview with UNICEF employee, Beirut, March 16, 2017.

61. Interview with engineer, formerly in charge of water projects throughout the North, Amman, September 20, 2017.

62. Interviews in Jordan and Lebanon, 2015 to 2018; Achilli, Yassin, and Erdogan, "Neighbouring Host-Countries' Policies for Syrian Refugees," 29; Mercy Corps, "Mapping of Host Community-Refugee Tensions," 17–18; Seeley, "Jordanian Hosts and Syrian Refugees," 49–51; Carrion, "Syrian Refugees in Jordan."

63. Interview with Mercy Corps official, Ashrafieh, Lebanon, May 17, 2018.

64. Interview with UNDP researcher specializing in northern Jordan, Amman, September 20, 2017.

65. Focus group interview with teachers and women from Aidamoun, Akkar, northern Lebanon, May 16, 2018.

66. Focus group interview with professional men, al-Azm Charitable Association, Halba, Akkar, Lebanon, May 16, 2018.

67. Ibid.

68. Conversations with INGO and funding officials, Beirut, January 2016.

69. Interviews with the head of municipality of a Syrian border town and an official of the largest village in the central Beka'a, Beka'a Valley, Lebanon, May 21, 2018.

70. Interviews with Mercy Corps officials, Beirut, May 17 and 25, 2018.

71. Joe McCarthy, "Stunning Photos Show Scale of Lebanon's Garbage Crisis," Global Citizen, January 24, 2018, https://www.globalcitizen.org/en/content/lebanon-trash-overflowing-beach-crisis/; Nada Homsi, "A Sea of Trash on Lebanon's Beaches," *New York Times*, January 23, 2018, https://www.nytimes.com/2018/01/23/world/middleeast/trash-lebanon-beach.html.

72. Interviews in Beirut with academics, May 2018, and local NGOs in Mafraq, Jordan, September 2017.

73. Interview with municipal official, Zarqa, Jordan, September 14, 2017.

74. "Urdunioun yadtaridoun lil-a'ish fil-khiyyam ba'd irtifa' iyjar al-shuqaq bi-sabab al-laji'een al-Sourieen" [Jordanians forced to live in tents after apartment rent prices rose due to the Syrian refugees], CCTV Arabic, April 17, 2013, http://arabic.cctv.com/; Hüser, "Syrian Refugee Crisis," 92.

75. Interview with municipal official and business owner, Irbid, Jordan, September 21, 2017.

76. "75 d'awa ikhla' manazil bi-haq muwatineen bil-Mafraq li-ghayat taskeen al-laji'een al-Sourieen" [75 legal eviction cases in Mafraq because of Syrian refugee housing demands],

Saraya, March 25, 2013, https://www.sarayanews.com/index.php?page=article&id=192342; Mercy Corps, "Mapping of Host Community-Refugee Tensions," 9.

77. Mercy Corps, "Mapping of Host Community-Refugee Tensions," 16.

78. Ibid., 10.

79. Ibid., 14.

80. John Reed, "Jordanian Border Town Feels the Strain of Refugee Influx," *Financial Times*, May 17, 2013, https://www.ft.com/content/0f571098-be3a-11e2-bb35-00144feab7de.

81. Laila Azzeh, "Sama Sarhan Schools Empty in Protest against Overcrowding," *Jordan Times*, October 26, 2014, http://www.jordantimes.com/news/local/sama-sarhan-schools-empty-protest-against-overcrowding.

82. Proctor, "Refugee Crisis Draining Jordan's Water Resources."

83. Proctor, "High and Dry with the Hashemites."

84. Mercy Corps, "Tapped Out," 24.

85. Ibid., 33.

86. Such protests against water shortages occurred in Karak and Arjan. "Protests Erupt in Karak Village Following Water Cuts," Roya News, July 2, 2017, http:// en.royanews.tv /news/10585/Protests_erupt_in_Karak_villag, and Hana Namrouqa, "Arjan residents protest disruption to water supply," *Jordan Times*, October 4, 2016, http://www.jordantimes .com/news/local/arjan-residents-protest-disruption-water-supply.

87. Proctor, "Refugee Crisis Draining Jordan's Water Resources."

88. Interview with engineer in charge of Jordanian water projects in the north, Amman, September 20, 2017.

89. Petra News Agency, "Man Killed during Demonstrations over Water in Beit Ras," *Jordan Times*, July 13, 2014, http://www.jordantimes.com/news/local/man-killed-during -demonstrations-over-water-beit-ras.

90. "Residents of South Jordan Town Block Street, Sunday, in Protest over Water Disruption," July 3, 2017, MENAFN—Alghad newspaper, http://www.menafn.com/1095595141 /Residents-of-South-Jordan-Town-Block-Street-Sunday-in-Protest-over-Water-Disruption.

91. Petra News Service, "Karak Residents Protest over Water Supply Disruptions," *Jordan Times*, July 6, 2014, http://www.jordantimes.com/news/local/karak-residents-protest -over-water-supply-disruptions.

92. Interview with Basim Tweissi, dean of Jordan Media Institute, Amman, September 24, 2017.

93. "Residents of South Jordan Town Block Street." See also "Protests Erupt in Karak Village Following Water Cuts," Roya News, July 2, 2017, http://en.royanews.tv/news/10585 /Protests_erupt_in_Karak_villag.

94. Hana Namrouqa, "Arjan Residents Protest Disruption to Water Supply," *Jordan Times*, October 4, 2016, http://www.jordantimes.com/news/local/arjan-residents-protest -disruption-water-supply.

95. Riachi, "Private Modes of Water Capture in Lebanon," 41; interview with Roland Riachi, American University of Beirut, Beirut, March 20, 2017. In addition to those listed below, protests included those described in these articles: "Palestinians Protest Water Cuts in South Lebanon Camp," *Daily Star*, October 20, 2016, https://www.dailystar.com .lb/News/Lebanon-News/2016/Oct-20/377324-palestinians-protest-water-cuts-in-south -lebanon-camp.ashx; "Lebanese University Students Protest Electricity and Water Cuts," *Daily Star*, April 4, 2017, http://www.dailystar.com.lb/News/Lebanon-News/2017/Apr- 04/400514-lebanese-university-students-protest-electricity-and-water-cuts.ashx.

96. "Anti-Establishment Protests in Lebanon Escalate," *World Weekly*, August 27, 2015, http://www.theworldweekly.com/reader/view/magazine/2015-08-27/anti-establishment -protests-in-lebanon-escalate/4573.

97. "Lebanon Residents in Sidon Protest Prolonged Electricity Cuts," *Albawaba*, August 4, 2015, http://www.albawaba.com/business/lebanon-residents-sidon-protest -prolonged-electricity-cuts-726932.

98. Ilyas al-Helou, "Shah al-miyah ila al-mwajiha mujaddaan . . . ahali Beirut ghadi-boun!" [Scarcity of water again at the forefront . . . The people of Beirut are angry!], *An-Nahar*, March 5, 2014, https://newspaper.annahar.com/.

99. Fayez Diab, "Intifada ahali Bint Jubayl: 'aasimat al-intisar al-ilahii 'atsha" [People of Bint Jubayl revolt: The capital of the gods' triumph is thirsty], Janoubia, June 23, 2014, http://janoubia.com/.

100. "Claims of Corruption Add to Al-Qaa Water Woes," *Daily Star*, April 17, 2014, http://www.dailystar.com.lb/News/Lebanon-News/2014/Apr-17/253587-claims-of -corruption-add-to-al-qaa-water-woes.ashx.

101. I am not including protests over lack of electricity when it was due to striking electricity workers, since these are not plausibly connected to the Syrians.

102. Because Syrians often lived informally in tented settlements or other housing not meant for residence, they tapped into the electricity grid without paying electricity fees or any monitoring. Electricity officials stated they could put a monitor in these places; it was a simple thing to do. Interview with EDL official, Beka'a, Lebanon, May 21, 2018.

103. Interview with local NGO director, Beka'a Valley, Lebanon, May 21, 2018.

104. "Baalbek Residents Stage Protest over Blackouts," *Daily Star*, December 21, 2013, http://www.dailystar.com.lb/News/Lebanon-News/2013/Dec-21/241886-baalbek -residents-stage-protest-over-blackouts.ashx.

105. "Sportive City Way Reopened after Locals Protested Power Outage," National News Agency, July 1, 2014, http://www.nna-leb.gov.lb/en/show-news/29183/Sportive-City-way -reopened-after-locals-protested-power-outage.

106. "Protesters Briefly Block Highway over Electricity Cuts," *Daily Star*, July 7, 2015, http://www.dailystar.com.lb/News/Lebanon-News/2015/Jul-07/305593-protesters -briefly-block-highway-over-electricity-cuts.ashx.

107. AP Archive, "Hezbollah Supporters Burn Tyres in Protest over Electricity Cuts," Youtube.com, July 21, 2015, https://www.youtube.com/watch?v=kTca-2n-1C4.

108. "Locals Block Aisha Bakkar Road to Protest Electricity Outage," National News Agency (accessed through Open Source Enterprise), September 9, 2015, http://nna-leb.gov.lb.

109. AFP, "Lebanon Activists Block Ministry in Electricity Protest," Youtube.com, September 29, 2015, https://www.youtube.com/watch?v=shjkDd-VPig; Breaking Gulf News, "Lebanon Activists Block Ministry in Electricity Protest," Youtube.com, September 29, 2015, https://www.youtube.com/watch?v=-ZebULXTzu4.

110. Syvlia Westall, "No Light at End of Tunnel for Lebanon's Power Crisis," Reuters, October 26, 2015, https://www.reuters.com/article/us-lebanon-electricity-idUSK CN0SK1LH20151026.

111. "Lebanese Bus Drivers Protest 'Illegal Competition'," *Daily Star*, May 3, 2014, http://www.dailystar.com.lb/News/Lebanon-News/2014/May-03/255235-lebanese-bus -drivers-protest-illegal-competition.ashx; "Lebanese Bus Drivers Protest Foreign Competition," *Daily Star*, December 5, 2015, http://www.dailystar.com.lb/News/Lebanon-News /2015/Dec-05/326065-lebanese-bus-drivers-rally-en-masse-on-main-highway.ashx.

112. Bou Khater, "Public Sector Mobilisation despite a Dormant Workers' Movement," 129.

113. Interview with former MP and political talk show host Dr. Rula al-Farra al-Hroub, Amman, September 24, 2017; Abuqudairi, "A Tale of Two Za'ataris."

114. Interview with Dr. Rula al-Farra al-Hroub.

115. For specifics of the crisis and mobilization, see Lebanon Support's timeline, https:// civilsociety-centre.org/timeliness/4923#1; and list of players, https://civilsociety-centre .org/party/social-movement-responding-lebanese-garbage-crisis.

116. AbiYaghi, Catusse, and Younes, "From *Isqat an-Nizam at-Ta'ifi* to the Garbage Crisis Movement."

117. The organizers were adamant in maintaining separation from the effects of the Syrians. This distinction would keep the focus and blame on the state, in line with their underlying premise that it is state corruption that causes all the infrastructure problems. As one activist stated, "the state is taking all this money because of the refugees, but still blaming them." Interview, Beirut, March 16, 2017.

118. Interview with Roland Riachi, American University of Beirut, Beirut, March 20, 2017; Abu-Rish, "Garbage Politics." Indeed, facts have rarely stood in the way of official scapegoating.

119. For an exception, see Kerbage, "Politics of Coincidence," 6.

120. Yassmine Alieh, "Cabinet Approves Plan to Rehabilitate Dumpsites," Business News by Lebanon Opportunities, February 19, 2018, http://www.businessnews.com.lb/cms/Story/StoryDetails/6411/Cabinet-approves-plan-to-rehabilitate-dumpsites.

121. Interview with official in Majd al-Anjar, Lebanon, May 21, 2018.

122. Interview with official in Sa'adnaya, Lebanon, May 21, 2018.

123. Interviews in Delhamiyyah, Lebanon, May 2018.

124. AbiYaghi, Catusse, and Younes, "From *Isqat an-Nizam at-Ta'ifi* to the Garbage Crisis Movement," 78; Geha, "Politics of a Garbage Crisis," 6. See also articles in the *Daily Star* on Akkar and Tripoli from 2015.

125. Interviews with former Mercy Corps employee specializing in waste, Qalamoun, Tripoli, May 16, 2018; Mercy Corps official, Ashrafieh, Beirut, May 25, 2018; and Lebanese University professor from the North, Beirut, May 24, 2018.

126. Rania Hamza, "'Tafh al-kayl' fi Trablous ma' karitha al-nifayyat" ['Fed up' in Tripoli with the trash crisis], *al-Mufakira al-qanouniyya* [The legal agenda], August 19, 2015, http://74.220.207.224/article.php?id=1215&lang=ar.

127. AbiYaghi, Catusse, and Younes, "From *Isqat an-Nizam at-Ta'ifi* to the Garbage Crisis Movement," 79.

128. "Al-harak yatanaqqal bayna Beirut wa al-Jiyya wa 'Akkar wa al-Beqaa': rafdan khuttat al-nifayyat wa mutaliba bi-istirdad al-amlak al-bahriyya wa mu'alija azmat al-kahraba' wa al-fasad" [Al-harak moves between Beirut, Jiyya, Akkar, and Bekaa: refusing the trash and asking to recover the ocean's resources and fixing the electricity crisis and corruption], *Al-Binaa*, October 5, 2015, http://www.al-binaa.com/archives/article/71681.

129. Interview with head of a municipality on the border with Syria, May 21, 2018.

130. Elise Knutsen, "EU Pitches in on Bekaa Valley's Trash Problem," *Daily Star*, January 31, 2014, http://www.dailystar.com.lb/News/Lebanon-News/2014/Jan-31/245897-eu-pitches-in-on-bekaa-valleys-mounting-trash-problem.ashx.

131. Atrache, "Lebanon's Un-Collected Problems"; Geha, "Politics of a Garbage Crisis"; AbiYaghi, Catusse, and Younes, "From *Isqat an-Nizam at-Ta'ifi* to the Garbage Crisis Movement"; Bekdache, "Lebanon's Garbage Crisis"; interview with Carmen Geha, professor, American University of Beirut, March 16, 2017.

132. "Istitlaa' 'ara'": 79% min al-Lubnanieen yuayidoun al-hirak" [Survey of "opinions": 79% of Lebanese support al-hirak], Almodon, November 11, 2015, https://www.almodon.com/portal.

133. Geha, "Politics of a Garbage Crisis," 6.

134. Interviews with activists in Beirut, Tripoli, and Akkar, March 2017 and May 2018.

135. Kerbage, "Politics of Coincidence," 5.

136. "Al-harak yatanaqqal bayna Beirut wa al-Jiyya wa 'Akkar wa al-Beqaa': rafdan khuttat al-nifayyat wa mutaliba bi-istirdad al-amlak al-bahriyya wa mu'alija azmat al-kahraba' wa al-fasad" [Al-harak moves between Beirut, Jiyya, Akkar, and Bekaa: refusing the trash and asking to recover the ocean's resources and fixing the electricity crisis and corruption], Al-Binaa, October 5, 2015, https://www.al-binaa.com/archives/article/71681.

137. Interview with Beirut Madinati member, Beirut, March 16, 2017; Geha, "Politics of a Garbage Crisis"; Harb, "Cities and Political Change." On Beirut Madinati, see Lebanon Support, "Beirut Madinati," https://civilsociety-centre.org/party/beirut-madinati. These parties are locally referred to as the "civil society" candidates or parties, since they come from outside the usual parties and were active in many civil society organizations.

138. Abu-Rish, "Municipal Politics in Lebanon."

139. Numerous demonstrations began attacking the regime itself, rejecting the notion of government change achieving anything, which had served as one of Jordan's main methods of appeasing protesters. They began discussing how all governments are the same and asking for an emergency or provisional caretaker government.

140. See chapter 3. See also, for example, "Al-Hazaymeh: al-azmeh al-Souriyyeh atharat ʿala al-muwazina" [Al-Hazaymeh: The Syrian crisis has affected the budget], Jordan Zad, February 24, 2014, http://www.jordanzad.com/index.php?page=article&id=150586.

141. Grigg, "One Year after Jordan's Fuel Protests"; Tell, "Early Spring in Jordan."

142. Omar Obeidat, "Consumption of Subsidised Bread Surges as Refugee Crisis Continues," Jordan Times, June 4, 2014, http://www.jordantimes.com/news/local/consumption-subsidised-bread-surges-refugee-crisis-continues.

143. "No Decision Taken Yet on Bread Subsidy—Minister," Jordan Times, April 7, 2014, http://www.jordantimes.com/news/local/no-decision-taken-yet-bread-subsidy-%E2%80%94-minister.

144. "Al-Urdun: masirat hashida ihtijajan ʿala rafaʿ asaʿr al-wuqud" [Jordan: Large marches protesting against raising price of gas], Al-Serat al-mustaqeem [religious newspaper], March 2, 2013, http://www.nsr313.com/home/archives/51081.

145. For the major corruption scandals, see Khorma, "Myth of the Jordanian Monarchy's Resilience to the Arab Spring."

146. "Amman tashhad tathahura ihtijaj did al-hukuma" [Amman witnesses protest demonstration against the government], Qanaʿa al-'alam, March 16, 2013, https://www.alalamtv.net/.

147. Hirak in Jordan and Harak in Lebanon come from the same root—movement (HRK). The difference is local use, pronunciation, and writing conventions.

148. Muhammad al-Damah, "Muthaharat fil-Urdun ʿanawinaha tashkil al-hukuma wa hal majlis al-nuwab wa taʿdeel asʿar mushtaqat al-naft" [Demonstrations in Jordan over reforming the government, dissolving parliament and fixing oil prices], Asharq al-Awsat [international mainstream daily], March 16, 2013, https://aawsat.com/. The article distinguishes between secular movements and Islamist ones.

149. "Bi-suwar muthaharat fil-Urdun tuhadid al-malik "Ya taslih al-heen . . . ya talhaq Zayn al-Abideen" [In pictures: the Jordanian demonstrations, threatening the king: either improve now . . . or face the fate of Zayn al-Abideen], Al-Watan [Egypt], June 14, 2013, https://www.elwatannews.com/.

150. "Masira lil-alaf fil-Urdun lil-mutaliba bil-islah wa mukafaha al-fasad" [Thousands demonstrate in Jordan asking for change and to fight corruption], O News Agency, June 14, 2013, http://onaeg.com/.

151. See "Al-Urdun: muthaharat fil-aʿsima ʿAmman wa al-Karak wa al-Tafileh lil-mutaliba bi-raheel al-hukumeh" [Jordan: demonstrations in the capital Amman, Karak and Tafileh asking for the government to quit], Al-Alam al-yawm, October 26, 2013, http://www.worldakhbar.com/middle-east/jordan/6441.html; "Muthahara fil-Urdun lil-mutaliba li-istiqala al-hukumeh" [Demonstration in Jordan asking for the resignation of the government], BBC Arabic, September 28, 2013, http://www.bbc.com/arabic/multimedia/2013/09/130928_jordan_protests; Raid Abu Abeed, "Al-mutaliba bi-islah wa muhariba al-fasad wa waqf al-asʿar . . . abraz mutalib muthaharat al-Urdun" [Demanding reform and to fight corruption and stop prices . . . the top demands of Jordan's demonstrations], Al-Ahali, November 23,

2013, https://www.hashd-ahali.org/main/ahali/?p=18026; "Muthahara did al-as'ar wal-nuwab wal-fasad—Irbid tugheeb wal-Zarqa tadkhal 'ala al-khat" [Demonstration against prices, representatives, and corruption—Irbid absent and Zarqa joins the line], *Ahrar al-Tafileh* [blog], March 8, 2013, http://ahraraltafilah.blogspot.com/2013/03/blog-post_1414.html, among others.

152. Muhammad al-Najjar, "Hirak al-Urdun ya'oud bi-rasa'il al-rafadh" [Jordanian Hirak returns with a message of rejection], *Al-Jazeera*, February 22, 2013, https://www.aljazeera.net/.

153. "Masira lil-'oura wa ta'liqat sakhira 'ala qarar rafa' asa'r lil-malabis" [Demonstration to nakedness and sarcastic commentary on the decision to raise the price of clothes], JBC News, September 18, 2013, http://www.jbcnews.net/.

154. "Fa'aliyyat ihtijajiyyeh fi sitt muhafithat tutalib bi-waqf raf'a al-as'ar" [Protest events took place in six governorates asking to stop raising prices], Saraya News, January 10, 2014, https://www.sarayanews.com/index.php?page=article&id=234368.

155. "Sahafiyou al-Urdun ya'lanoun al-'isiyan did hukumeh al-Nsour" [Jordanian journalists announce rebellion against the Nsour government], *Al-Arab* [UK], November 7, 2013, https://alarab.co.uk/. For example, "Masirat wa waqafat ihtijajiyya did raf'a as'ar al-mahruqat wa al-kahraba'" [Demonstrations and marches protesting against raising prices of fuel and electricity], *al-Dustour*, January 4, 2014, https://www.addustour.com and "Masirat wa waqafat ihtijajiya tutalib bil-islah wa 'adam rafa' al-as'ar" [Marches and demonstrations protesting asking for reform and to not raise prices], *al-Rai*, January 10, 2014, http://alrai.com.

156. "Masirat wa waqafat ihtijajiyya did raf'a as'ar al-mahruqat wa al-kahraba'" [Demonstrations and marches protesting against raising prices of fuel and electricity], *al-Dustour*, January 4, 2014, https://www.addustour.com/.

157. "Masirat wa waqafat ihtijajiya tutalib bil-islah wa 'adam rafa' al-as'ar" [Marches and demonstrations protesting asking for reform and to not raise prices], *al-Rai*, January 10, 2014, http://alrai.com/.

158. Jamal Ibrahim, "Masirat fil-Urdun tutalib bi-hukumeh "inqath watani" [Demonstrations in Jordan asking for a provisional government], *al-Ittihad* [Emirati], January 11, 2014, https://www.alittihad.ae/.

159. "Masirat wa waqafat ihtijajiyya fil-Urdun tutalib bi "al-islah" wa "muhariba al-fasad" [Protest marches and demonstrations in Jordan asking for "reform" and "fighting corruption"], al-Rai Media [Kuwait], June 1, 2014, http://www.alraimedia.com/Home/Details?Id=253adcae-10b4-4873-9ca5-28e614e585d7.

160. "Muthaharat li-isqat hukumeh al-Nsour" [Demonstrations for the fall of the al-Nsour government], All of Jordan, December 6, 2015, http://www.allofjo.net/index.php?page=article&id=108847.

161. Muhammad al-I'rsan, "Awda al-ihtijajat al-mutaliba bi-isqat al-hukumeh fil-Urdun" [Return of demonstrations demanding the fall of the government in Jordan], Arabi21, December 5, 2015, https://www.arabi21.com/.

162. "Bil-suwar . . . muwatanoun yaqata'oun al-ihsa'at bi-yawmi-ha al-awal fi Wadi Mousa" [In pictures: Citizens boycott census on the first day from Wadi Mousa], Saraya News, November 20, 2015, http://www.sarayanews.com/index.php?page=article&id=337741.

163. Conflictivity Index, Civil Society Centre, https://civilsociety-centre.org/cap/ci/armed_conflict.

164. Nidal Solh, "Angry Baalbek Residents Hold Protest after Clashes," *Daily Star*, October 8, 2015, http://www.dailystar.com.lb/News/Lebanon-News/2015/Oct-08/318095-angry-baalbek-residents-hold-protest-after-clashes.ashx.

165. "Residents Protest in Bourj Hammoud," Civil Society Knowledge Centre, Collective Action, May 22, 2014, https://civilsociety-centre.org/collective/residents-protest-bourj-hammoud.

166. "Baalbeck Highway Blocked," Civil Society Knowledge Centre, Conflict Incident Report, September 8, 2015, https://civilsociety-centre.org/sir/baalbeck-highway-blocked; Nidal Solh, "Baalbek Traders Block Roads over Robberies," *Daily Star*, October 12, 2015, http://www.dailystar.com.lb/News/Lebanon-News/2015/Oct-12/318586-baalbek-traders -block-roads-over-robberies.ashx.

167. "Ras Baalbek Asks Army to Free Land," *Daily Star*, August 3, 2015, http://www .dailystar.com.lb/News/Lebanon-News/2015/Aug-03/309406-ras-baalbek-asks-army-to -free-land.ashx.

168. "Families of Kidnapped Soldiers Stage a Sitin [*sic*] in Dourges," National News Agency, August 9, 2014, http://www.nna-leb.gov.lb/en/show-news/31323/Families-of -kidnapped-soldiers-stage-sitin-in-Doures; "Arsal People Block Road in Beirut, Call for Army to Enter Arsal," National News Agency, August 6, 2014, http://www.nna-leb.gov.lb /en/show-news/31114/Arsal-people-block-road-in-Beirut-call-for-army-to-enter-Arsal.

169. "Several Road Blocks in Beirut's Southern Suburbs, Central Bekaa and the North," Civil Society Knowledge Centre, Conflict Incident Report, September 6, 2014, https:// civilsociety-centre.org/sir/several-road-blocks-beiruts-southern-suburbs-central-bekaa -and-north.

170. Barjas, "Municipal Regulation of Syrian Refugees in Lebanon."

171. Laure Ayoub, "Lebanese Municipalities: Regulating Refugee Presence Is 'Our Ju- risdiction,'" Legal Agenda, May 29, 2017, http://legal-agenda.com/en/article.php?id=3689.

172. Ilham Barjas, "La marja'iyyeh lil-baladiyyat fi 'tantheem' iqama al-lajieen" [No legal basis for the municipalities to "organize" refugees' affairs], Legal Agenda, Septem- ber 6, 2016, http://www.legal-agenda.com/article.php?id=1729.

173. World Bank, "Municipalities at the Forefront of the Syrian Refugee Crisis."

174. Mercy Corps, "Engaging Municipalities in the Response to the Syria Refugee Cri- sis in Lebanon," 1.

175. Muhammad Nimr, "Shurta al-baladiyyat al-musallaha aw akhtar al-amn al-thati- al-dakhiliyya tughatti-ha wa ittihad al-dhahiyya yu'azizha" [Armed municipal police or local security risks? Interior Ministry supports it and the suburbs support it], *An-Nahar*, September 10, 2013, https://www.annahar.com/.

176. "Charbel: To Activate Municipal Police Role," National News Agency, October 24, 2013, http://nna-leb.gov.lb/en/show-news/15694/.

177. Personal communication with Lebanese human rights organization official, Au- gust 8, 2018. In one instance the municipal police put up kiosks in Beirut, but the ISF (In- ternal Security Forces) told them to take the kiosks down.

178. Nimr, "Shurta al-baladiyyat al-musallaha."

179. 'Abd al-Rahman 'Uraabi, "Lubnan: Al-shurta al-baladiyya dayf jadid 'ala al-amn al-thati" (Lebanon: Municipal Police a New Force for Local Security), *Al-Arabi al-Jadeed*, October 13, 2014, https://www.alaraby.co.uk/portal.

180. Nimr, "Shurta al-baladiyyat al-musallaha."

181. The abuse was critiqued by the minister of interior. AFP, "Lebanon Warns Police to Stop Syria Refugee Abuse," Al-Monitor, July 14, 2016, https://www.al-monitor.com /pulse/contents/afp/2016/07/lebanon-syria-conflict-refugees-police.print.html.

182. Amal Khalil, "Al-shurta al-baladiyya: 'bidaa' kullou'" [Municipal Police: It does everything], al-Akhbar, October 19, 2013, https://al-akhbar.com/Community/59105.

183. The head or president (*ra'is*) of the municipality differs from the *mukhtar*. The latter is a representative of the central state, often with administrative duties. The head of the municipality has duties more akin to that of a mayor. See Stel, "Mukhtars in the Middle."

184. "Ra'is baladiyya al-Dekwaneh: Nunafith 'amaliyyyat dahm li-masakin al-Sourieen li'alla tatakarar al 75" [President of the Dekwaneh municipality: We are conducting searches

of Syrian residences in order to avoid repeating the 75 war], El Nashra, September 13, 2014, https://www.elnashra.com/.

185. Yousef Diab, "Lubnan: tawatur fi balda 'Amsheet ithr tawqif 'anasir min al-shurta al-baladiyya i'taqalou naziheen sourieen ta'sfaan" [Lebanon: Tension in Amsheet as municipal police arbitrarily arrest displaced Syrians], *Asharq al-Awsat*, July 15, 2016, https://aawsat.com/.

186. Interview with president of the municipality in one of the main areas of refugee concentration, Beka'a, Lebanon, May 21, 2018.

187. Personal e-mail communication with NGO head involved in municipal police training, August 8, 2018. See the discussion of NGOs attempting to improve practices of municipalities in Lebanese Center for Policy Studies, "Supporting Municipalities in Responding to the Refugee Crisis."

188. Victoria Yan, "When Civilians Are Police, Jury, Judge," *Daily Star*, October 24, 2017, http://www.dailystar.com.lb/News/Lebanon-News/2017/Oct-24/423729-when-civilians-are-police-jury-judge.ashx; "Online Vigilantism: A Threat to Justice in Lebanon," SMEX, September 26, 2017, https://smex.org/online-vigilantism-a-threat-to-justice-in-lebanon/; Waddell, "Facebook Vigilantism Is a Scary Thing."

189. "Syrian Refugee Crisis Strains Water Supply," Al Jazeera Report, August 26, 2015, http://www.aljazeera.com/news/2015/08/syrian-refugee-crisis-strains-jordan-water-supply-150827011123701.html

190. Agence France-Presse, "Jordanian Thirst for Water Grows," *Daily Star*, 1 October 2012, http://www.dailystar.com.lb/Article.aspx?id=189741.

191. REACH, "Access to Water and Tensions in Jordanian Communities," 2.

192. Ibid., 12.

193. See World Health Organization, "What Is the Minimum Quantity of Water Needed?" https://www.who.int/water_sanitation_health/emergencies/qa/emergencies_qa5/en/.

194. Observations and interviews throughout Jordan, September 2017.

195. Agence France-Presse, "Jordanian Thirst for Water Grows," *Daily Star*, October 1, 2012, http://www.dailystar.com.lb/Article.aspx?id=189741.

196. Ali et al., "A Town's Sudden Growth."

197. Group interview at the Hikaya NGO, Amman, September 17, 2017.

198. Interviews with officials at Mercy Corps, September 14, 2017.

199. Interview in Ramtha, northern Jordan, September 21, 2017.

200. Tom Blackwell, "'They Have Harmed the Country': Jordanians Growing Resentful as Jobs, Resources Go to Syrian Refugees," *National Post*, May 22, 2013, http://nationalpost.com/news/jordanians-growing-resentful-as-jobs-resources-go-to-syrian-refugees.

201. Participant observation in Amman, September 2015.

202. REACH, "Understanding Social Cohesion and Resilience," 26.

203. Interview with lead researcher, WANA institute, Amman, September 10, 2017.

204. Interview with UNDP researcher specializing in northern Jordan, Amman, September 20, 2017. Indeed, some observers began to notice Jordanians picking up these business models from the Syrians. Interviews with UNICEF workers, women's small business fair, Amman, September 23, 2017; researcher, Amman, September 16, 2017.

205. Interview with country director and regional program advisor, Mercy Corps, Beirut, Ashrafieh, May 17, 2018.

206. Focus group interview with professional men, al-Azm Charitable Association, Halba, Akkar, Lebanon, May 16, 2018.

207. Ali et al., "A Town's Sudden Growth."

208. Focus group interview with female teachers and young women from Aidamoun, Akkar, northern Lebanon, May 16, 2018.

209. Interviews, Akkar and the northern region, Beirut, and the Beka'a valley, Lebanon, May 2018.

210. Ruisi and Shteiwi, "Economic and Social Integration of Migrants and Refugees in Jordan and Lebanon," 45.

211. Interview with teacher and administrator at a public school, Beka'a, Lebanon, May 21, 2018.

212. Interview with municipal official, central Beka'a, Lebanon, May 21, 2018.

213. Interview with local governing leader, al-Bire, Lebanon, May 16, 2018.

214. Interview with the director of a public school, Beka'a, Lebanon, May 21, 2018. This apparent violence among children is part of the mental health issues stemming from exposure to war.

215. Bascal Abu Nadir, "Musa'adat istithna'iyya lil-naziheen al-Sourieen fa-matha 'an al-Lubanieen?" [Emergency assistance to displaced Syrians but what about Lebanese?], Saidacity.net, July 17, 2014.

216. Nadeen al-Ali, "Fuqara' Lubnanioun yantahiloun sifa "lajieen Sourieen" [Poor Lebanese pretend to be Syrian refugees], Now, February 18, 2013, https://now.mmedia.me /lb/ar.

217. Interview with Orthodox priest on the border with Syria, May 16, 2018.

218. Interviews in the northern border areas with Syria, Akkar region, May 16, 2018.

219. Interview with Mercy Corps official, Ashrafieh, Lebanon, May 17, 2018.

220. Personal communication with former UNHCR protection officer who worked in Za'atari and Mafraq at that time, Los Gatos, CA, December 2018.

221. al-Ali, "Fuqara' Lubnanioun yantahiloun sifa "lajieen Sourieen."

222. Interviews with Aysar Hammoudeh, senior protection assistant, UNHCR, Jordan, 2012–2014, Los Gatos, CA, November 2017. UNHCR sees this in many refugee crises, and it has been documented in various African cases as well.

223. Group interviews with employees at the Hikaya Center for Civil Society Development, September 17, 2017. Several employees were from Mafraq and worked with NGOs there.

224. Mercy Corps, "Analysis of Host Community-Refugee Tensions in Mafraq, Jordan," 6.

225. Interview with researcher at WANA, Amman, September 10, 2017.

226. Interview with the director of a public school, Beka'a, Lebanon, May 21, 2018.

227. Interview with former Mercy Corps employee, Beirut, May 24, 2018.

228. Several such incidents among children were reported. Interview with employee, Mercy Corps, Ashrafieh, Beirut, May 25, 2018. These incidents were one factor in convincing humanitarian organizations to rethink their practices.

229. Interview with employee, Mercy Corps, Ashrafieh, Beirut, May 25, 2018.

230. Interviews with officials at Mercy Corps, Amman, September 14, 2017.

231. Focus group interview with professional men, al-Azm Charitable Association, Halba, Akkar, Lebanon, May 16, 2018.

232. Amer Uthman, "I'tisam fi Wadi Khalid rafadan li-aqfal mustawsaf sihi yuqadam khaddamat sahiyya la-hum" [Strike in Wadi Khalid rejecting closure of a health clinic providing them health services], Tripoli Scope, July 31, 2015, http://tripoliscope.com/.

233. Kukrety and Al Jamal, "Poverty, Inequality and Social Protection in Lebanon," 13.

234. Rossi, Kumar, and Han, "Factbox."

235. Interview with Bassel el Hassan, political science professor, Lebanese University, Beirut, May 24, 2018.

5. PUSHED TO THE EDGE

1. Taylor Luck. "Syrian Refugees: Can Europe Help Jordan Turn a Burden into a Boon?" *Christian Science Monitor*, May 19, 2016, https://www.csmonitor.com/World/Middle-East /2016/0519/Syrian-refugees-Can-Europe-help-Jordan-turn-a-burden-into-a-boon and "Peace, Bread, and Work," *The Economist*, May 5, 2016, https://www.economist.com/news /middle-east-and-africa/21698260-jobs-syrian-refugees-help-them-and-their-hosts-and -slow-their-exodus-peace.

2. Mercy Corps has the most documentation of these protests and early tensions over primary goods. Interviews with Mercy Corps officials, Amman, September 14, 2017; UNDP researcher specializing in northern Jordan, Amman, September 20, 2017.

3. Interviews with Mercy Corps officials, Amman, September 14, 2017; Mourad, "From Conflict-Insensitive to Conflict-Driven Aid."

4. Mercy Corps, "Charting a New Course," 2.

5. Interviews with NGO and UN officials, September 2015, Amman.

6. Mercy Corps, "Charting a New Course," 2.

7. Norwegian Refugee Council and IRC, "No Escape: Civilians in Syria Struggle to Find Safety Across Borders," 12; Human Rights Watch, "Jordan: Syrians Blocked, Stranded in Desert."

8. Mercy Corps, "Seeking Stability," iv. Later, differentiations among refugees would come into play as aid programs helped some but not all.

9. The extent to which these programs incentivized conflict is not yet clear. Mourad, "From Conflict-Insensitive to Conflict-Driven Aid."

10. REACH, "Evaluating the Effect of the Syrian Refugee Crisis," 8.

11. Van Vliet, "Syrian Refugees in Lebanon," 89.

12. IRIN "To Avoid Tensions with Refugees, Lebanese Hosts Need Support."

13. Rana F. Sweis, "Resentment Grows against Syrian Refugees in Jordan," *New York Times*, May 9, 2013, https://nyti.ms/13AAB0W.

14. Martinez, "Bread Is Life."

15. World Bank Group, Global Concessional Financing Facility, https://globalcff.org/.

16. "Joint Statement," CEDRE (Conférence économique pour le développement, par les réformes et avec les entreprises) [Economic conference for development through reforms with the private sector], Paris, April 6, 2018, https://www.diplomatie.gouv.fr/IMG /pdf/cedre_statement-en-_final_ang_cle8179fb.pdf.

17. Interview with Mercy Corps officials, Ashrafieh, Beirut, May 25, 2018.

18. Discussions with donors, Beirut, January 2016.

19. Lebanon is not the only state where donors and INGOs take over what are considered public services. The conclusion discusses comparative cases.

20. The dynamic is similar to the conditions for access to warring areas but both more subtle and less overtly threatening than access to militia-controlled areas.

21. Elise Knutsen, "Refugees, Host Communities Hope Kuwait III Will Bring Funds," *Daily Star*, March 31, 2015, http://www.dailystar.com.lb/News/Lebanon-News/2015/Mar -31/292737-refugees-host-communities-hope-kuwait-iii-will-bring-funds.ashx.

22. Interviews with INGO officials, Amman, September 2015 and 2017. See Asfour, "Jordan: Local Perceptions on Syrian Refugees (Part 2/2)."

23. Kelberer, "Negotiating Crisis," 154.

24. Seeberg, "Jordan's Migration Diplomacy and the Syrian Refugees."

25. Achilli, Yassin, and Erdogan, "Neighbouring Host-Countries' Policies for Syrian Refugees," 17.

26. Interviews with INGOs and funders, Amman, September 2015; Salemi, Bowman, and Compton, "Services for Syrian Refugee Children and Youth in Jordan," 9.

27. Interview with large international donor, Amman, September 13, 2015.

28. Interview with major funder of Jordanian projects and budget support, September 13, 2015.

29. Interview with employee, Mercy Corps, Ashrafieh, Beirut, May 25, 2018.

30. Lenner, "Blasts from the Past," 15.

31. Interviews, International Organization for Migration, Amman, September 17, 2015.

32. Interview with UNHCR protection officer, Amman, September 19, 2015.

33. Hourani, "Media and the Syrian Refugees in Lebanon," 3.

34. Amnesty International, "Pushed to the Edge," 9; Janmyr, "Legal Status of Syrian Refugees in Lebanon," 13.

35. Interview with Mercy Corps, Ashrafieh, Beirut, May 25, 2018; Thair Ghandour, "Abraz 'ashara mafahiim Lubnaniyya khati'a 'an al-lajieen al-Sourieen" [The 10 most significant Lebanese misconceptions about Syrian refugees], Rasseef22.com, May 19, 2017, https://raseef22.com/.

36. Ruth Sherlock, "Jordan Repeals Free Medical Aid for Syrian Refugees," *The Telegraph*, November 28, 2014, http://www.telegraph.co.uk/news/worldnews/middleeast/syria/11261468/Jordan-repeals-free-medical-aid-for-Syrian-refugees.html.

37. Amnesty International, "Living on the Margins," 18.

38. Ibid., 31.

39. Interview with Mercy Corps, Ashrafieh, Beirut, May 25, 2018.

40. Hamdan and Bou Khater, "Strategies of Response to the Syrian Refugee Crisis in Lebanon," 26.

41. Tamer al-Samadi, "Jordan Shuts Down Border Crossings from Syria," Al-Monitor, June 13, 2013, https://www.al-monitor.com/pulse/security/2013/06/jordan-closes-border-crossings-syria.html.

42. Amnesty International, "Growing Restrictions, Tough Conditions."

43. Human Rights Watch, "Jordan: Syrians Blocked, Stranded in Desert."

44. Estimates vary, but between one-third and 80 percent were denied entry or refouled. Norwegian Refugee Council and IRC, "No Escape," 12; Human Rights Watch, "Jordan: Syrians Blocked, Stranded in Desert."

45. In one case, a girl had a relative that the UNHCR found, living in Za'atari. UNHCR officials pleaded with the authorities in these situations, and offered to help find relatives, but could not insist on any particular course of action. They were bound to national dictates and laws; their only powers were persuasion. Obtaining such identification in wartime, however, was not an easy task, particularly when one's house has been bombed, as in this case cited. Interview with senior UNHCR protection officer, Amman, September 19, 2015.

46. Rana F. Sweis, "No Syrians Are Allowed into Jordan, Agencies Say," *New York Times*, October 8, 2014, https://www.nytimes.com/2014/10/09/world/middleeast/syrian-refugees-jordan-border-united-nations.html.

47. Amnesty International, "Living on the Margins," 22.

48. Achilli, "Syrian Refugees in Jordan: A Reality Check," 20. Achilli, Yassin, and Erdogan, "Neighbouring Host-Countries' Policies for Syrian Refugees," 18.

49. Amnesty International, "Living on the Margins," 14.

50. See discussions of documentation and urban verification problems in Norwegian Refugee Council and IHRC, "Securing Status"; IHRC and Norwegian Refugee Council, "Registering Rights."

51. Interview with senior UNHCR protection officer, September 19, 2015.

52. Ibid.; Amnesty International, "Living on the Margins," 13.

53. Human Rights Watch, "Jordan: Syrian Medical Workers Deported."

54. IRIN, "The Case That Exposes Jordan's Deportation Double Standards."

55. Molnar, "Discretion to Deport."

56. Ibid., 22.

57. Interview with UNICEF official, Amman, September 14, 2015.

58. Mourad, "Inaction as Policy-Making."

59. Hamdan and Bou Khater, "Strategies of Response to the Syrian Refugee Crisis in Lebanon," 23–24.

60. Janmyr, "Precarity in Exile," 67.

61. Oxfam, "Lebanon Looking ahead in Times of Crisis," 17.

62. Rami Ruhayem, "Syrian Refugees Living in Fear as Lebanon Tightens Its Laws," BBC News, September 12, 2016, https://www.bbc.com/news/world-middle-east-37260994, Human Rights Watch, "'I Just Wanted to Be Treated like a Person.'"

63. Amnesty International, "Pushed to the Edge," 12.

64. LHIF, "Background Paper on Unregistered Syrian Refugees in Lebanon," 9.

65. One consequence of this policy was a lack of means for the security forces to distinguish among the Syrian population or know their whereabouts. As one official was quoted by the Crisis Group, "We don't know where most refugees are, don't have means to monitor their movements. We simply have lost control." International Crisis Group, "Too Close For Comfort: Syrians in Lebanon," 8.

66. Janmyr, "Precarity in Exile," 71.

67. Amnesty International, "Pushed to the Edge," 8.

68. Barjas, "Municipal Regulation of Syrian Refugees in Lebanon."

69. Dana Halawi, "Lebanon to Survey Unlicensed Syrian Businesses," Daily Star, November 25, 2013, http://www.dailystar.com.lb/Business/Lebanon/2013/Nov-25/238763 -lebanon-to-survey-unlicensed-syrian-businesses.ashx.

70. Saghieh, "Manufacturing Vulnerability in Lebanon."

71. Kareem Shaheen, "Life Goes from Bad to Worse for Syrians after Lebanon Tightens Border Controls," The Guardian, March 12, 2015, https://www.theguardian.com/world /2015/mar/12/syrians-lebanon-border-controls-un-refugee; Human Rights Watch, "Lebanon: Syrian Women at Risk of Sex Trafficking."

72. Kareen Chehayeb, "As Beirut's Trash Crisis Drags on, Children Recycle to Survive," CityLab, November 1, 2018, https://www.citylab.com/environment/2018/11/beirut-trash -refugee-children-recycle/574312/.

73. On the origins of this agreement, see Howden, Patchett, and Alfred, "The Compact Experiment." See also Arar, "The New Grand Compromise."

74. The notable scholars Alexander Betts and Paul Collier were at the forefront suggesting these ideas before the Compacts were negotiated. See Collier and Betts, Refuge: Rethinking Refugee Policy in a Changing World.

75. Taylor Luck, "Syrian Refugees: Can Europe Help Jordan Turn a Burden into a Boon?" Christian Science Monitor, May 19, 2016, https://www.csmonitor.com/World/Middle-East /2016/0519/Syrian-refugees-Can-Europe-help-Jordan-turn-a-burden-into-a-boon.

76. World Bank, "Economic Opportunities for Jordanians and Syrian Refugees."

77. Arar, "The New Grand Compromise," 310.

78. Kelberer, "Negotiating Crisis," 149.

79. Achilli, Yassin, and Erdogan, "Neighbouring Host-Countries' Policies for Syrian Refugees," 18. See also Hashemite Kingdom of Jordan, "Jordan Response Platform for the Syria Crisis," http://www.jrpsc.org/.

80. Arar, "The New Grand Compromise," 310.

81. Government of Jordan, "The Jordan Compact"; Pop, "Jordan Prince Pours Cold Water on EU Initiative for Syrian Refugees."

82. "Jordan Allows Syrian Children with No Documents to Join Schools," Jordan Times, September 24, 2017, http://jordantimes.com/news/local/jordan-allows-syrian-children-no -documents-join-schools-%E2%80%94-officials.

83. Interview with Aysar Hammoudeh, former senior protection assistant, UNHCR, Jordan, Los Gatos, CA, March 2018. One official put the number of Syrians returned at 150,000. Arar, "The New Grand Compromise," 308.

84. Interviews with EU representatives and UN organization representatives, Beirut, January 2016.

85. See Kelberer, "Negotiating Crisis"; "Supporting Syria and the Region: Post-London Conference Financial Tracking."

86. Ali Al-Amin, "Syrian Refugees in Lebanon and the Policy of Escapism," Al Arabiya, June 24, 2018, https://english.alarabiya.net/en/views/news/middle-east/2018/06/24/Syrian-refugees-in-Lebanon-and-the-policy-of-escapism.html.

87. "Supporting Syria and the Region," 13.

88. Republic of Lebanon, "London Conference."

89. Khawaja, "Gaps in Lebanon's New Refugee Policy."

90. Federica Marsi, "Hurdles Impede Implementation of Residency Waivers," *Daily Star*, April 1, 2017, https://www.dailystar.com.lb/News/Lebanon-News/2017/Apr-01/400101-hurdles-impede-implementation-of-residency-fee-waivers.ashx.

91. Finbar Anderson, "Number of Syrians without Residency up 26 Pct," *Daily Star*, December 16, 2017, http://www.dailystar.com.lb/News/Lebanon-News/2017/Dec-16/430428-number-of-syrians-without-residency-up-26-pct.ashx.

92. "German Loans Worth 97 Million Euros for Water Sector," Roya News, December 17, 2018, https://en.royanews.tv/news/16260/2018-12-17; "Germany Grants Jordan More Than €460 Million in Aid," Roya News, October 24, 2018, https://en.royanews.tv/news/15603/Germany_gives_Jordan_more_than.

93. Nibal Zgheib, "EBRD and UK Provide JOD 22 Million to Upgrade Amman's Solid Waste Operations," European Bank for Reconstruction and Development, May 9, 2018, https://www.ebrd.com/cs/Satellite?c=Content&cid=1395273967628&d=Mobile&pagename=EBRD%2FContent%2FContentLayout.

94. Mohammad Ghazal, "EBRD Offers $1 Billion to Finance Infrastructure Projects in Jordan," *Jordan Times*, May 10, 2018, http://www.jordantimes.com/news/local/ebrd-offers-1-billion-finance-infrastructure-projects-jordan.

95. "Supporting Syria and the Region," 12.

96. Jordan Response Platform for the Syria Crisis, JRP 2018 Financial Update, http://jrpsc.org.jo/test/newadmin/JRP2018FinancialUpdate.aspx.

97. Reuters, "Lebanon Cannot Ask for Donor Funding without Passing 2018 Budget," *US News & World Report*, February 19, 2018, https://www.usnews.com/news/world/articles/2018-02-19/lebanon-cannot-ask-for-donor-funding-without-passing-2018-budget-minister.

98. Quoted in Rosalie Berthier, "Monetising Syrian Refugees," Lebanese Economy Watchdog, December 11, 2017, http://www.synaps.network/lebanese-economy-watchdog#chapter-3177383.

99. George Azar, "Lebanon Seeks $17 Billion at Paris IV Conference," *An-Nahar*, February 20, 2018, https://en.annahar.com/article/759181-paris-4-investment-program-valued-at-17-billion.

100. Berthier, "Monetising Syrian Refugees."

101. "USAID Supports the North Lebanon Water Establishment with $2.8 Million Infrastructure Works to Improve Services in Koura," U.S. Embassy Beirut, January 31, 2018, https://lb.usembassy.gov/usaid-supports-north-lebanon-water-establishment-2-8-million-infrastructure-works-improve-water-services-koura/.

102. "Joint Statement," CEDRE.

103. "Saudi Arabia Offers $1bn to Lebanon in Apparent End to Protests over Hezbollah," Middle East Eye, April 7, 2018, https://www.middleeasteye.net/news/saudi-offers-1bn-lebanon-apparent-end-protests-over-hezbollah-917599595.

104. "Lebanon Seeks $1B to Cope with Syria Crisis," *Daily Star*, March 31, 2015, http://www.dailystar.com.lb/ArticleRelated.aspx?id=292789.

105. Interviews with Aysar Hammoudeh, former senior protection assistant, UNHCR, Jordan, Los Gatos, CA, November 2017.

106. Interviews with officials and author experience at two NGOs, Mafraq, Jordan, September 18, 2017.

107. Interview with former member of parliament and host of political talk show, Amman, September 24, 2018.

108. Interview with *mukhtar* of two towns in Beka'a, Lebanon, May 21, 2018

109. Interview with Mercy Corps officials, Ashrafieh, Beirut, May 25, 2018.

110. "IMF Reaches Staff-Level Agreement with Jordan on a Three-Year Extended Fund Facility," Press Release 16/294, IMF, June 20, 2016, https://www.imf.org/en/News/Articles/2015/09/14/01/49/pr16294.

111. Mohammad Ghazal, "Jordan Signs Letter Accepting Terms of $700m Deal with IMF," *Jordan Times*, July 27, 2016, http://www.jordantimes.com/news/local/jordan-signs-letter-accepting-terms-700m-deal-imf.

112. Suleiman Al-Khalidi, "Jordan Ends Bread Subsidy, Doubling Some Prices, to Help State Finances," Reuters, January 26, 2018, https://www.reuters.com/article/us-jordan-economy-subsidies-bread/jordan-ends-bread-subsidy-doubling-some-prices-to-help-state-finances-idUSKBN1FF2CP.

113. Areej Abuqudairi, "Jordanians 'at Breaking Point' over Austerity Measures," *Al Jazeera*, February 21, 2017, https://www.aljazeera.com/indepth/features/2017/02/jordan-worsening-economy-sparks-wave-protest-170221055031620.html.

114. Al-Khalidi, "Jordan Ends Bread Subsidy."

115. Suleiman Al-Khalidi, "Jordan's Parliament Passes IMF-backed Tax Law to Reduce Public Debt," Reuters, November 18, 2018, https://www.reuters.com/article/us-jordan-economy-tax/jordans-parliament-passes-imf-backed-tax-law-to-reduce-public-debt-idUSKCN1NN0IK.

116. "Jordan, Egypt Reach Compromises on Outstanding Issues," *Jordan Times*, August 9, 2016, http://www.jordantimes.com/news/local/jordan-egypt-reach-compromises-outstanding-issues.

117. Baylouny and Klingseis, "Water Thieves or Political Catalysts?"

118. "Jordan's King Approves Cabinet Reshuffle to Absorb Discontent over Economy," New Arab, February 26, 2018, https://www.alaraby.co.uk/english/news/2018/2/26/jordan-approves-cabinet-reshuffle-to-absorb-discontent-over-economy; "Jordan Makes Amendments to Decision Banning over-60s from Treatment at Prestigious Cancer Centre," New Arab, February 20, 2018, https://www.alaraby.co.uk/english/news/2018/2/20/jordan-amends-decision-banning-over-60s-from-cancer-centre.

119. Dana Khraiche, "Lebanon Debt on 'Unsustainable Path' as World Bank Cuts Forecast," Bloomberg News, October 4, 2018, https://www.bloomberg.com/news/articles/2018-10-04/lebanon-debt-on-unsustainable-path-as-world-bank-cuts-forecast.

120. Hussein Dakroub, "Parliament Passes Tax Hikes, Attention Shifts to Budget," *Daily Star*, October 10, 2017, http://www.dailystar.com.lb/News/Lebanon-News/2017/Oct-10/422129-parliament-passes-tax-hikes-attention-shifts-to-budget.ashx; "Lebanon's Taxation Smokescreen," SYNAPS, November 4, 2017, http://www.synaps.network/lebanese-economy-watchdog#chapter-3018675. The law was successfully challenged in court but later passed in similar form. "Executive Summary of the Major Taxes' Increases and Changes," ALDIC, http://www.synaps.network/lebanese-economy-watchdog#chapter-3018675.

121. Farah-Silvana Kanaan, "Hariri: Govt to Slash Energy Subsidies in 2019," *Daily Star*, December 22, 2018, http://www.dailystar.com.lb/Business/Local/2018/Dec-22/472437-hariri-govt-to-slash-energy-subsidies-in-2019.ashx.

122. "Approval of Petroleum Tax Law Draws Praise," *Daily Star*, October 25, 2017, http://www.dailystar.com.lb/Business/Local/2017/Oct-25/423820-approval-of-petroleum-tax-law-draws-praise.ashx.

123. Interview with Sahar Atrache, (then) senior analyst, Lebanon, International Crisis Group, Beirut, March 14, 2017.

124. Facebook page for *haqna na'arif* (we know our rights), run by Emad Hajjaj, January 31, 2019.

125. Some protests over water and electricity continued in this time period in Jordan, although they were fewer, as INGOs were indeed fixing the infrastructure problems leading to the fundamental grievances. INGOs were concentrating first on the areas with heavy refugee concentrations, and the protesting towns were outside these areas. A town in Ajloun protested when its water was disrupted, and protests in southern areas like Karak included blocking roads and burning tires. Some lasted longer than a month. Hana Namrouqa, "Arjan Residents Protest Disruption to Water Supply," *Jordan Times*, October 4, 2016, http://www.jordantimes.com/news/local/arjan-residents-protest-disruption-water-supply; "Residents of South Jordan Town Block Street, Sunday, in Protest over Water Disruption," MENAFN—Alghad newspaper, July 3, 2017, http://www.menafn.com/1095595141/Residents-of-South-Jordan-Town-Block-Street-Sunday-in-Protest-over-Water-Disruption. See also "Protests Erupt in Karak Village Following Water Cuts," Roya News, July 2, 2017, http://en.royanews.tv/news/10585/Protests_erupt_in_Karak_villag.

126. Umar Faris, "11 yawman 'ala i'tisam al-Urduniyya: al-talba yandamoun wa matlab al-taraju' 'an rafa' al-rusoum baqin" [The protest at the University of Jordan enters day 11: more students to join and they are determined to demand no increase in fees], 7iber.com, April 9, 2016, https://www.7iber.com/society/11th-days-of-jordan-university-protests/; "Istimrar i'tsam tujjar al-sayyarat bil-Urdun lil-yawm al-thalith 'ala al-tawali" [Car dealers' protest in Jordan has been going for 3 days], El Dorar, August 17, 2016, https://eldorar.com/node/101854; "I'tisam li-sa'iqi al-takasi fi Amman/suwwar" [A protest by taxi drivers in Amman/Photos], Sawaleif, October 9, 2016, www.sawaleif.com; "I'tisam maftouh li-muzari'i Wadi al-Urdun" [Open-ended protest by farmers in the Jordan Valley], al-Maqar, March 22, 2016, www.maqar.com; and "Tullab al-Urdun yantifidouna didda al-rusoum al-jami'iyyah" [The students of the University of Jordan revolt against study fee], *Al-Jazeera*, February 29, 2016, www.aljazeera.net.

127. "Collective Suicide Attempt Raises Concerns about Employment in Jordan," Al Bawaba, May 12, 2016, https://www.albawaba.com/news/collective-suicide-attempt-raises-concerns-about-unemployment-jordan-839588.

128. Hana Namrouqa, "Labour Protests Rise by 22% in 2016—Report," *Jordan Times*, April 9, 2017, http://www.jordantimes.com/news/local/labour-protests-rise-22-2016-%E2%80%94-report.

129. "Protesters Picket Parliament over Rising Prices, Taxes," *Jordan Times*, January 15, 2017, http://jordantimes.com/news/local/protesters-picket-parliament-over-rising-prices-taxes.

130. Abuqudairi, "Jordanians 'at Breaking Point' over Austerity Measures."

131. Susanna Goussous, "Karak Residents Stage Horseback Protest to Say 'Neigh' to Price Hikes," *Jordan Times*, February 12, 2017, http://www.jordantimes.com/news/local/karak-residents-stage-horseback-protest-say-neigh%E2%80%99-price-hikes.

132. "Jordanians Protest over Price Increases," *Al Jazeera*, February 24, 2017, http://www.aljazeera.com/news/2017/02/jordanians-protest-price-increases-170224163930537.html.

133. Laila Azzeh, "Consumer Society Starts Chicken Boycott Campaign," *Jordan Times*, May 31, 2017, http://www.jordantimes.com/news/local/consumer-society-starts-chicken-boycott-campaign.

134. Mohammad Ghazal, "Video of Expelling Citizen out of Parliament Sparks Outrage," *Jordan Times*, November 27, 2017, http://www.jordantimes.com/news/local/video-expelling-citizen-out-parliament-sparks-outrage.

135. "Jordan Raises Electricity Prices for Third Time since December," Middle East Monitor, March 1, 2018, https://www.middleeastmonitor.com/20180301-jordan-raises-electricity-prices-for-third-time-since-december/.

136. Ana V. Ibáñez Prieto, "Pharmacists Denounce Tax Hike on Medicines, Threaten Work Stoppage," *Jordan Times*, January 21, 2018, http://jordantimes.com/news/local/pharmacists-denounce-tax-hike-medicines-threaten-work-stoppage.

137. Muath Freij, "Protesters Call for Parliament Dissolution over Bread Price Hike," *Jordan Times*, February 2, 2018, http://www.jordantimes.com/news/local/protesters-call-parliament-dissolution-over-bread-price-hike; "Riots Break out in Jordan over Bread Price Hikes," New Arab, February 5, 2018, https://www.alaraby.co.uk/english/news/2018/2/5/riots-break-out-in-jordan-over-bread-price-hikes.

138. Osama Al Sharif, "Jordanians Protest Price Hikes but in Surprisingly Small Numbers," Al-Monitor, February 20, 2018, https://www.al-monitor.com/pulse/originals/2018/02/jordan-tax-price-hikes-pubilc-protests-no-confidence.html.

139. Hana Namrouqa, "Farmers Union, Lawmakers Hopeful for More Tax Exemptions," *Jordan Times*, February 27, 2018, http://www.jordantimes.com/news/local/farmers-union-lawmakers-hopeful-more-tax-exemptions.

140. "Jordan Farmers to Sue Government over New Tax," Middle East Monitor, March 12, 2018, https://www.middleeastmonitor.com/20180312-jordan-farmers-to-sue-government-over-new-tax/.

141. Hannah Patchett, "Jordan Protests Escalate as Lawyers Boycott Court," Al-Monitor, March 23, 2018, https://www.al-monitor.com/pulse/originals/2018/03/jordan-lawyers-boycott-state-security-court-arrest-protester.html.

142. "Protests in Dhiban, Karak and Zarqa Call for Revoking Tax-Hike Decision," *Jordan Times*, March 3, 2018, http://www.jordantimes.com/news/local/protests-dhiban-karak-and-zarqa-call-revoking-tax-hike-decision.

143. Suha Ma'ayeh, "Jordan Protests against Price Rises Signal Growing Resentment," *The National*, February 5, 2018, https://www.thenational.ae/world/mena/jordan-protests-against-price-rises-signal-growing-resentment-1.702036.

144. Al Sharif, "Jordanians Protest Price Hikes but in Surprisingly Small Numbers."

145. Ali Younes, "Jordan's Economic Crisis Threatens Political Stability," *Al Jazeera*, February 14, 2018, http://www.aljazeera.com/news/2018/02/jordan-economic-crisis-threatens-political-stability-180214112245542.html.

146. Al Sharif, "Jordanians Protest Price Hikes but in Surprisingly Small Numbers."

147. Interview with former minister, Amman, September 25, 2017.

148. Al Sharif, "Jordanians Protest Price Hikes but in Surprisingly Small Numbers,"

149. Mohammad Ghazal, "Approval for Purchase of 'Luxurious' Cars for Mayors Stirs Public Outrage," *Jordan Times*, March 11, 2018, http://www.jordantimes.com/news/local/approval-purchase-luxurious-cars-mayors-stirs-public-outrage.

150. Mohammad Ghazal, "33 Associations, Unions Strike against Income Tax Law," *Jordan Times*, May 30, 2018, http://www.jordantimes.com/news/local/33-associations-unions-strike-against-income-tax-law.

151. Schwedler, "Jordan's Austerity Protests in Context."

152. Laith Al Ajlouni, "The Recent Protests in Jordan and the Way Forward."

153. Mohammad Ghazal, "Unionists Pressured by Crowd to Resume Protests," *Jordan Times*, June 7, 2018, http://www.jordantimes.com/news/local/unionists-pressured-crowd-resume-protests.

154. Taylor Luck, "Jordan's Young Protesters Say They Learned from Arab Spring Mistakes," *Christian Science Monitor*, June 5, 2018, https://www.csmonitor.com/World /Middle-East/2018/0605/Jordan-s-young-protesters-say-they-learned-from-Arab-Spring -mistakes.

155. Rana Husseini, "68% of Jordanians Supported June's Protests—Poll," *Jordan Times*, July 4, 2018, http://jordantimes.com/news/local/68-jordanians-supported-june %E2%80%99s-protests-%E2%80%94-poll.

156. Mustafa Abu Sneineh, "In Struggling Jordan, Grassroots Movements are Demanding Political Change," *Middle East Eye*, July 6, 2018, https://www.middleeasteye.net/news /Jordan-protest-king-Abdullah-political-change-Dhiban-Arab-Spring; Ababneh, "Do You Know Who Governs Us?"

157. Luck, "Jordan's Young Protesters."

158. "Jordan Withdraws Tax Bill after a Week of Protests," *Middle East Eye*, June 7, 2018, https://www.middleeasteye.net/news/jordan-withdraws-tax-bill-after-week-protests -775683696.

159. Ababneh, "Do You Know Who Governs Us?"

160. Twitter, @7iber, June 7, 2018.

161. Rana F. Sweis, "Jordan's Prime Minister Quits as Protesters Demand an End to Austerity," *New York Times*, June 4, 2018, https://www.nytimes.com/2018/06/04/world /middleeast/jordan-strike-protest.html.

162. "Jordan's Gabba3at Moment."

163. Ibid.

164. Interview with former member of parliament and host of political talk show, Amman, September 24, 2018.

165. Dalal Salalmeh and Dina Gibreel, "Day Five Roundup: Al-Mulki's Government Resigns and Protests Continue," 7iber, June 5, 2018, https://www.7iber.com/politics -economics/day-five-roundup-al-mulkis-government-resigns-and-protests-continue/.

166. Dina Gibreel, "Roundup of Day Four of Protests in Jordan," 7iber, June 4, 2018, https://www.7iber.com/politics-economics/roundup-of-day-four-of-protests-in-jordan/.

167. Aaron Magid, "Jordanians Fed up with More of the Same," Sada—Carnegie Endowment for International Peace, October 3, 2018, https://carnegieendowment.org/sada /77401.

168. Taylor Luck, "Jordanians Brave Downpour to Protest at [*sic*] Corruption in Amman," *The National*, December 20, 2018, https://www.thenational.ae/world/mena /jordanians-brave-downpour-to-protest-at-corruption-in-amman-1.804884; Jassar Al Tahat, "'Demonstrations Will Not Stop until We See Serious Changes'," *Jordan Times*, December 12, 2018, http://www.jordantimes.com/news/local/%E2%80%98demonstrations -will-not-stop-until-we-see-serious-changes%E2%80%99.

169. Jassar Al Tahat, "Opposition Figures, Activists Join Rally at Fourth Circle," *Jordan Times*, December 7, 2018, http://www.jordantimes.com/news/local/opposition-figures -activists-join-rally-fourth-circle.

170. Laith al-Juneidi, "Protests Continue in Jordan Capital for 3rd Week in Row," Andalou Agency, December 20, 2018, https://www.aa.com.tr/en/middle-east/protests -continue-in-jordan-capital-for-3rd-week-in-row/1344502#; "Protesters Hold New Rally at 4th Circle," *Jordan Times*, January 3, 2019, https://jordantimes.com/news/local /protesters-hold-new-rally-4th-circle.

171. "Qatta' madkhal madinat Sour bi-itijahayn li-sa'atayn ihtijajaan 'ala tsqneen al -kahraba" [Sour entrance blocked from two directions for two hours protesting rationing of electricity], *Elnashra*, July 17, 2018, https://www.elnashra.com/; Suha Jaffal, "Al-taqneen al-kahraba'i fi Sour yufajr ihtijajat sh'abiyya" [Electricity rationing in Tyre caused popular protests to break out], Janoubia, July 16, 2018, http://janoubia.com/.

172. "Ahali Sour da'ou ila muthahira haashida al-ahad ihtijajaan 'ala inquitaa' al -kahraba" [People of Tyre invited to a huge demonstration Sunday protesting cutting off of electricity], *An-Nahar*, January 6, 2018, https://en.annahar.com/; "Tyre Residents Protest Electricity Outages," *Daily Star*, July 2, 2018, http://www.dailystar.com.lb/News/Lebanon-News/2018/Jul-02/455017-tyre-residents-protest-electricity-outages.ashx.

173. Samir Za'etr, "Sa'ad sharik bi-i'stisam ihtijaji li-muwajiha azma al-kahraba" [Sa'ad participated in the protests against electricity crisis], Aliwaa, July 28, 2018, http://aliwaa .com.lb /; Mohammed Zaatari, "Sidon Residents Protest Power Cuts, Surging Generator Prices," *Daily Star*, July 28, 2018, http://www.dailystar.com.lb/News/Lebanon-News/2018 /Jul-28/458206-sidon-residents-protest-power-cuts-surging-generator-prices.ashx.

174. "Sidon Residents Protest as Water Shortage Bites," *Daily Star*, August 27, 2018, http://www.dailystar.com.lb/News/Lebanon-News/2018/Aug-28/461419-sidon-residents -protest-as-water-shortage-bites.ashx.

175. Richard Hall, "Lebanon's Power Struggle Looms between Government and 'Generator Mafia'," *The National*, August 8, 2018, https://www.thenational.ae/world/mena /lebanon-s-power-struggle-looms-between-government-and-generator-mafia-1.758182.

176. "Generator Owners Cut Services in 2-hour Protest," *Daily Star*, November 6, 2018, http://www.dailystar.com.lb/News/Lebanon-News/2018/Nov-06/468496-generator -owners-to-cut-services-for-2-hours-in-protest.ashx.

177. "Al-mu'tasimoun bi-'Akkar qat'aou al-kahraba' 'an al-baladat alati tataghatha min mahatta Bayt Millat" [Protesters in Akkar cut off electricity from villages that got electricity from Beit Millat station], *Elnashra*, December 19, 2017, https://www.elnashra.com/; "Protesters Cut Electricity in Akkar" December 19, 2017, https://civilsociety-centre.org/sir /protesters-cut-electricity-akkar.

178. "Dispute between ISF and Protesters in Front of Al Jiyeh Factory," Civil Society Knowledge Centre, Conflict Incident Report, July 29, 2016, https://civilsociety-centre.org /sir/dispute-between-isf-and-protesters-front-al-jiyeh-factory. Accessed January 19, 2019.

179. "East Lebanon Residents Protest against Harsh Electricity Cuts: State Media," *Daily Star*, July 8, 2017, http://www.dailystar.com.lb/News/Lebanon-News/2017/Jul-08/412086 -east-lebanon-residents-protest-against-harsh-electricity-cuts-state-media.ashx.

180. "Bekaa Valley Locals Block River with Debris to Protest Pollution," *Daily Star*, May 21, 2017, http://www.dailystar.com.lb/News/Lebanon-News/2017/May-21/406694 -bekaa-valley-locals-block-river-with-debris-to-protest-pollution.ashx.

181. "Jnah Protests Monthlong Water Cutoff," *Daily Star*, September 3, 2018, http://www.dailystar.com.lb/News/Lebanon-News/2018/Sep-03/462115-jnah-protests -monthlong-water-cutoff.ashx.

182. Michal Kranz, "Protesters in North Lebanon Want Tripoli Development to Help Poor," Middle East Eye, September 9, 2018, https://www.middleeasteye.net/news/far -reaching-development-plans-north-lebanon-face-deep-distrust-tripoli-793748499.

183. Misbah al-Ali, "Tripoli Perplexed by Acute Water Shortage," *Daily Star*, April 18, 2016, http://www.dailystar.com.lb/News/Lebanon-News/2016/Aug-18/367730-tripoli -perplexed-by-acute-water-shortage.ashx.

184. "Tripoli Residents protest water and electricity cuts," *Daily Star*, July 8, 2016, http:// www.dailystar.com.lb/News/Lebanon-News/2016/Jul-08/361045-tripoli-residents -protest-water-and-electricity-cuts.ashx.

185. Kranz, "Protesters in North Lebanon Want Tripoli Development to Help Poor."

186. "Protest in Northern Lebanon Demands for Power Supply, Better Healthcare," Xinhua, August 13, 2018, http://www.xinhuanet.com/english/2018-08/13/c_137385484.htm.

187. "Tafh kayl al-Lubnanieen . . . #matat_'abab_al-mustashfa" [It's enough for the Lebanese . . . #she_died_at_the_hospital's_gate], al-Ahed, March 27, 2017, https://www .alahednews.com.lb/.

188. Georgi Azar, "Public Transport Drivers Continue Month of Protest," *An-Nahar*, September 5, 2016, https://en.annahar.com/article/461988-public-transport-drivers -continue-month-of-protest.

189. "Shuban ya'taridouna sayyarat beek ub yaquduha Sourioun 'ala al-tareeq al -duwaliyya bi-Akkar" [Young men stop pickup trucks driven by Syrians on the interna-tional road in Akkar], *Elnashra*, April 26, 2017, https://www.elnashra.com/.

190. "North Lebanon Truck Drivers Decry Competition from Syrian Drivers," *Daily Star*, April 29, 2017, http://www.dailystar.com.lb/News/Lebanon-News/2017/Apr-29 /403896-north-lebanon-truck-drivers-decry-competition-from-syrian-drivers.ashx.

191. "Gridlock as Drivers Briefly Block Roads to Protest 'Illegal Competition,'" *Daily Star*, May 25, 2017, http://www.dailystar.com.lb/News/Lebanon-News/2017/May-25 /407247-gridlock-as-drivers-briefly-block-roads-to-protest-illegal-competition.ashx.

192. "Transportation Drivers Union Goes on Strike, Blocks Roads across Lebanon," Naharnet, July 24, 2018, http://www.naharnet.com/stories/en/248877; "Land Transport Union Closes Down Roads," *Daily Star*, July 25, 2018, http://www.dailystar.com.lb/News /Lebanon-News/2018/Jul-25/457825-land-transport-union-closes-down-roads-across -lebanon.ashx.

193. "Lebanon's Transport Workers Strike Again as Political Uncertainty Persists," For-eign Brief, August 2, 2018, https://www.foreignbrief.com/daily-news/lebanons-transport -workers-strike-again-as-political-uncertainty-persists/; "Land Transport Unions Protest, Press Demands," *Daily Star*, August 3, 2018, http://www.dailystar.com.lb/News/Lebanon -News/2018/Aug-03/458926-land-transport-unions-protest-press-demands.ashx.

194. "Land Transport Unions Stage Nationwide Protest," *Daily Star*, January 10, 2019, http://www1.dailystar.com.lb/News/Lebanon-News/2019/Jan-10/473705-land-transport -union-stages-nationwide-protest.ashx.

195. "Akkar Residents Briefly Block Road to Protest 'Illegal Competition,'" *Daily Star*, April 22, 2017, http://www.dailystar.com.lb/News/Lebanon-News/2017/Apr-22/402951 -akkar-residents-briefly-block-road-to-protest-illegal-competition.ashx.

196. "Iqlim al-Kharoub Residents Protest against 'Illegal' Competition," *Daily Star*, Jan-uary 30, 2017, http://www.dailystar.com.lb/News/Lebanon-News/2017/Jan-30/391582 -iqlim-al-kharoub-residents-protest-against-illegal-competition.ashx.

197. Raed Barhan, "Al-Sultat al-Lubnaniyya: 'tadhiyq al-khinaq' 'ala al-Sourieen bi-faradh shurut jadida lil-istithmar" [Lebanese authorities: "tighten the rope" on Syrians by imposing new conditions for investment], Smart News, May 9, 2017, https://smartnews -agency.com/ar.

198. "Lebanon: General Labor Union Urges Closing Business Hiring Foreigners," MENAFN, August 30, 2018, https://menafn.com/1097362893/Lebanon-general-labor -union-urges-closing-business-hiring-foreigners?src=Rss.

199. "Third Day of Anti-Syrian Labor Protests," *Daily Star*, March 6, 2017, http://www .dailystar.com.lb/News/Lebanon-News/2017/Mar-06/396220-third-day-of-anti-syrian -labor-protests.ashx.

200. Sawsan al-Abtah, "Al-Lubnaniyya ahaq min al-Souri!" [Lebanese are more deserv-ing than Syrians!], Aks Alser, May 15, 2017, https://www.aksalser.com/news/.

201. "Protesters Weather Rain as Parliament Meets," *Daily Star*, March 16, 2017, http:// www.dailystar.com.lb/News/Lebanon-News/2017/Mar-16/397733-protesters-weather -rain-as-parliament-meets.ashx.

202. See AFP, "Lebanese Descend on Capital to Protest Proposed Tax Hikes," *Al -Monitor*, March 19, 2017, https://www.al-monitor.com/pulse/afp/2017/03/lebanon -politics-demonstration-taxes-lebanon-politics-demonstration-taxes-lebanon-politics -demonstration-taxes.html; Ellen Francis, "Hundreds Protest Lebanese Parliament's Pro-posed Tax Hikes," Reuters, March 19, 2017, https://www.reuters.com/article/us-lebanon

-politics-protests-idUSKBN16Q0IG?il=0; Leyal Khalife, "Twitter Explodes as Lebanese Protest the Tax Hike," Step Feed, March 17, 2017, https://stepfeed.com/twitter-explodes -as-lebanese-protest-the-tax-hike-2372; Ghinwa Obeid, "Beirut Tax Hike Protest Gets Heated," *Daily Star*, March 20, 2017, http://www.dailystar.com.lb/News/Lebanon-News /2017/Mar-20/398250-beirut-tax-hike-protest-gets-heated.ashx; "Lebanon: Protests Staged in Beirut against Tax Hikes; Reactions to Al-Hariri Visit to Protest Site," Al-Jadid Satellite Channel (in Arabic, through Open Source Enterprise), March 19, 2017; "Hariri to Anti-Tax Protesters in Riad al-Solh: Corruption Will End," *Daily Star*, March 19, 2017, http://www.dailystar.com.lb/News/Lebanon-News/2017/Mar-19/398185-hundreds-of -lebanese-protest-taxes-to-fund-new-wage-hike-for-fourth-consecutive-day.ashx; Twitter, #laysh_nazil_tatathahir (Why I'm protesting), March 16–18, 2017; Mariam Nabbout, "Lebanon Just Increased Taxes and People Are Really Pissed," Step Feed, March 16, 2017, https://stepfeed.com/lebanon-just-increased-taxes-and-people-are-really-pissed-9377.

203. Ghadir Hamadi, "Protesters Take to Capital's Streets for Various Causes," *Daily Star*, March 20, 2017, http://www.dailystar.com.lb/News/Lebanon-News/2017/Mar-20 /398252-protesters-take-to-capitals-streets-for-various-causes.ashx.

204. Hanan Khaled, "Lebanese Mark Labor Day with Mass Protest," *Daily Star*, May 1, 2017, http://www.dailystar.com.lb/News/Lebanon-News/2017/May-01/404106-lebanese -mark-labor-day-with-mass-protest.ashx; Joseph A. Kechichian, "Lebanese Vent Frustrations over Strained Economy," *Gulf News*, May 1, 2017, https://gulfnews.com/world/mena /lebanese-vent-frustrations-over-strained-economy-1.2020385.

205. Abbey Sewell, "Activists Protest Govt Neglect on Independence Day," *Daily Star*, November 22, 2018, http://www.dailystar.com.lb/News/Lebanon-News/2018/Nov-22 /469858-activists-protest-govt-neglect-on-indepedence-day.ashx.

206. Lisa Barrington, Issam Abdallah, and Imad Creidi, "'No State, No Government': Weary Lebanese Mark 75 years of Independence," Reuters, November 22, 2018, https:// www.reuters.com/article/us-lebanon-independence/no-state-no-government-weary -lebanese-mark-75-years-of-independence-idUSKCN1NR1ME.

207. "Dozens in Beirut Protest Worsening Living Conditions," *Daily Star*, December 26, 2018, http://www.dailystar.com.lb/News/Lebanon-News/2018/Dec-26/472670-dozens-in -beirut-protest-worsening-living-conditions.ashx.

208. "Sabaa Protests Living Conditions, Govt Deadlock," *Daily Star*, December 8, 2018, http://www.dailystar.com.lb/News/Lebanon-News/2018/Dec-08/471245-sabaa-protests -living-conditions-govt-deadlock.ashx.

209. "Thousands of Protesters Decry Lebanon's Economic, Political Situation," *Daily Star*, December 16, 2018, http://www.dailystar.com.lb/News/Lebanon-News/2018/Dec -16/471908-thousands-of-protesters-decry-lebanons-economic-situation.ashx; Hussein Dakroub, "Protests Overshadow Cabinet Deadlock," *Daily Star*, December 24, 2018, http:// www.dailystar.com.lb/News/Lebanon-News/2018/Dec-24/472563-protests-overshadow -cabinet-deadlock.ashx; Anchal Vohra, "Lebanon Protests Grow over Economic Crisis and Political Impasse," *Al Jazeera*, December 28, 2018, https://www.aljazeera.com/news /middleeast/2018/12/lebanon-protests-grow-economic-crisis-political-impasse -181228123503670.html.

210. "Soldiers Assault *Daily Star* Photographer Covering Rally," *Daily Star*, December 24, 2018, http://www.dailystar.com.lb/News/Lebanon-News/2018/Dec-24/472566 -soldiers-assault-daily-star-photographer-covering-rally.ashx.

211. Joe Gamp, "Lebanon Protests: Yellow Vest Anger Hits Middle East as Thousands Call for 'Revolution,'" *Sunday Express*, December 29, 2018, https://www.express.co.uk /news/world/1064752/lebanon-protests-yellow-vest-movement-middle-east-beirut -demonstrations-lebanese-elections; "Lebanese Protest over Economy and Politics, Briefly Closing Some Roads," Reuters, December 23, 2018, https://www.reuters.com/article/us

-lebanon-protest/lebanese-protest-over-economy-and-politics-briefly-closing-some
-roads-idUSKCN1OM0J0; Victorial Yan and Sahar Houri, "'Yellow Vests' Swarm Beirut,
Protest State's Failures," *Daily Star*, December 24, 2018, http://www.dailystar.com.lb/News
/Lebanon-News/2018/Dec-24/472546-yellow-vests-swarm-beirut-protest-states-failures
.ashx; "Overnight Protest in Tripoli Decries Corruption," *Daily Star*, December 22, 2018,
http://www.dailystar.com.lb/News/Lebanon-News/2018/Dec-22/472445-overnight
-protest-in-tripoli-decries-corruption.ashx; "Second Protest in Lebanon Over Economic
Instability," Albawaba, December 27, 2018, https://www.albawaba.com/business/second
-protest-lebanon-over-economic-instability-1231456.

212. "Student Protest Calls for Economic Change," *Daily Star*, January 18, 2019, http://
www.dailystar.com.lb/News/Lebanon-News/2019/Jan-18/474373-student-protest-calls
-for-economic-change.ashx.

213. Sunniva Rose, "Lebanese Protests Simmer amidst Growing Discontent against the
Government," *The National*, January 13, 2019, https://www.thenational.ae/world/mena
/lebanese-protests-simmer-amidst-growing-discontent-against-government-1.812845.

214. Sahar Houri, "Hundreds across Country Protest against Graft, Pollution, Costs,"
Daily Star, January 14, 2019, http://www.dailystar.com.lb/News/Lebanon-News/2019/Jan
-14/473976-hundreds-across-country-protest-against-graft-pollution-costs.ashx.

215. "Nationwide Protests in Lebanon Denounce Corruption," *Daily Star*, January 14,
2019 (updated), http://www.dailystar.com.lb/News/Lebanon-News/2019/Jan-13/473922
-nationwide-protests-in-lebanon-denounce-corruption.ashx.

216. This was a survey commissioned by the International Republican Institute. Sami
Zoughaid, "Lebanon's New Government Must Contend with Citizens' Pessimism," Featured Analysis, Lebanese Center for Policy Studies, February 2019, https://www.lcps
-lebanon.org/featuredArticle.php?id=211. Accessed March 9, 2019.

217. Timour Azhari, "Demonstrators Decry Worsening Living Conditions," *Daily Star*,
January 21, 2019, http://www.dailystar.com.lb/News/Lebanon-News/2019/Jan-21/474560
-demonstrators-decry-worsening-living-conditions.ashx.

218. Timour Azhari, "As Lebanon's Political Class Fails, Beirut's Streets Are Stirring
Once Again," Middle East Eye, January 25, 2019, https://www.middleeasteye.net/news
/lebanons-political-class-fails-beiruts-streets-are-stirring-once-again/.

219. Timour Azhari, "Father Dies after Setting Himself on Fire over School Payments,"
Daily Star, February 9, 2019, http://www.dailystar.com.lb/News/Lebanon-News/2019/Feb
-09/476267-father-dies-after-setting-himself-on-fire-over-school-payments.ashx;
Timour Azhari, "Protesters Demand Reform after Self-Immolation," *Daily Star*, February 12, 2019, http://www.dailystar.com.lb/News/Lebanon-News/2019/Feb-12/476425
-protesters-demand-reform-after-self-immolation.ashx.

220. "'No Confidence in this Government' Protest Staged in Beirut," *Daily Star*, February 12, 2019, http://www.dailystar.com.lb/News/Lebanon-News/2019/Feb-12/476475
-no-confidence-in-this-government-protest-staged-in-beirut.ashx#.

221. As a Palestinian family, UNRWA should have supported their medical care, but
there are disputes on who was responsible for the child's death. Anchal Vohra, "Lebanon:
Palestinian Boy, 3, Dies after 'Hospitals Refuse Care,'" *Al Jazeera*, December 23, 2018,
https://www.aljazeera.com/news/2018/12/lebanon-palestinian-boy-3-dies-hospitals
-refuse-care-181223081520826.html.

222. al-Khalidi, "Jordan Ends Bread Subsidy."

223. Harel, "Protests in Jordan Following Austerity Measures."

224. Interview with former member of parliament and host of political talk show, Amman, September 24, 2018.

225. Interview with Jordan Media Institute, Amman, September 24, 2018.

226. "Fate of Detained Activists to Be Decided by Court—PM," *Jordan Times*, January 15, 2017, http://www.jordantimes.com/news/local/fate-detained-activists-be-decided -court-%E2%80%94-pm.

227. Harel, "Growing Calls in Jordan to Enact Political Reforms."

228. Schwedler, "Routines and Ruptures in Protests and Policing in Jordan."

229. Shibli and Geha, "Critique of the Syrian Refugee Crisis Response," 7.

230. Maya Mikdashi, "War Is Here: The Lebanese Political Elites Unite Again," Jadaliyya, July 25, 2017, http://jadaliyya.com/Details/34451/War-is-Here-The-Lebanese-Political -Elites-Unite-Again?utm_source=Arab%2BStudies%2BInstitute%2BMailing%2BList&u tm_c%E2%80%A6=.

231. Joseph A. Kechichian, "Lebanese Vent Frustrations over Strained Economy," *Gulf News*, May 1, 2017, https://gulfnews.com/world/mena/lebanese-vent-frustrations-over -strained-economy-1.2020385.

232. Timour Azhari, "Power Issue Won't Go out after Vote: Abi Khalil," *Daily Star*, May 1, 2018, http://www.dailystar.com.lb/News/Lebanon-News/2018/May-01/447535-power -issue-wont-go-out-after-vote-abi-khalil.ashx; Thair Ghandour, "Abraz 'ashara mafahiim Lubnaniyya khati'a 'an al-lajieen al-Sourieen" [The 10 most significant Lebanese misconceptions about Syrian refugees], Rasseef22, May 19, 2017, https://raseef22.com/.

233. Ghandour, "Abraz 'ashara mafahiim Lubnaniyya khati'a."

234. "Our Burden Today Is Displaced Syrians: President Aoun," *Daily Star*, March 17, 2017 (March 18 on opensource), http://www.dailystar.com.lb/News/Lebanon-News/2017 /Mar-17/397930-our-burden-today-is-displaced-syrians-president-aoun.ashx; "Hariri: Solve Refugee Issue or Face Disaster," *Daily Star*, March 17, 2017.

235. Hasan Lakkis and Hussein Dakroubi, "Cabinet Set to Draft New Tax Law, Devise Wage Hike Solution," *Daily Star*, September 29, 2017. http://www.dailystar.com.lb/News /Lebanon-News/2017/Sep-29/420954-cabinet-set-to-draft-new-tax-law-devise-wage-hike -solution.ashx; Olivia Alabaster, "Syrian Refugees: Between War and Crackdown in Lebanon," *Al Jazeera*, November 4, 2016, https://www.aljazeera.com/indepth/features/2016/11 /syrian-refugees-war-crackdown-lebanon-161102173130178.html.

236. Victoria Yan, "Uptick in Syrian Refugee Crisis Fake News," *Daily Star*, May 12, 2017. https://www.dailystar.com.lb/News/Lebanon-News/2017/May-12/405477-uptick-in -syrian-refugee-crisis-fake-news.ashx.

237. Ghinwa Obeid, "Beirut Tax Hike Protest Gets Heated," *Daily Star*, March 20, 2017, http://www.dailystar.com.lb/News/Lebanon-News/2017/Mar-20/398250-beirut-tax -hike-protest-gets-heated.ashx; Human Rights Watch, "It's Not the Right Place for Us."

238. "Gov't Cancels Additional Tax on Medicines upon Royal Directives," *Jordan Times*, January 24, 2018, http://jordantimes.com/news/local/gov%E2%80%99t-cancels-additional -tax-medicines-upon-royal-directives.

239. "King Freezes Price Hikes on Fuel and Electricity," *Jordan Times*, June 1, 2018, http://www.jordantimes.com/news/local/king-freezes-price-hikes-fuel-and-electricity.

240. Hana Namrouqa, "Farmers Union, Lawmakers Hopeful for More Tax Exemptions," *Jordan Times*, February 27, 2018, http://www.jordantimes.com/news/local/farmers-union -lawmakers-hopeful-more-tax-exemptions; "Timeline: Jordan Protests Lead to PM's Resignation," *BBC Monitoring*, June 4, 2018, https://monitoring.bbc.co.uk/product/c1dpb96l.

241. "Jordan's King Approves Cabinet Reshuffle to Absorb Discontent over Economy," New Arab, February 26, 2018, https://www.alaraby.co.uk/english/news/2018/2/26/jordan -approves-cabinet-reshuffle-to-absorb-discontent-over-economy.

242. Rana Husseini, "Gov't Reaches Deal with Madaba Town Protesters," *Jordan Times*, June 26, 2016, http://www.jordantimes.com/news/local/gov%E2%80%99t-reaches-deal -madaba-town-protesters.

243. Interview with former member of parliament and host of political talk show, Amman, September 24, 2018.

244. Citizens, however, view this "theft" differently than the government, and often do not consider it wrong, given the items are perceived as public goods and are of inferior quality. Baylouny and Klingseis, "Water Thieves or Political Catalysts?"

245. Mahmoud Al Abed, "Pardoning Water and Electricity Thieves: Destroying Our Home with Our Own Hands (Opinion)," *Jordan Times*, January 23, 2019, http://www.jordantimes.com/opinion/mahmoud-al-abed/pardoning-water-and-electricity-thieves-destroying-our-home-our-own-hands.

246. See, for example, "Gov't Will Respond to Citizens' Demands without Procrastination, Delay—Sarayreh," *Jordan Times*, March 29, 2018, http://www.jordantimes.com/news/local/gov%E2%80%99t-will-respond-citizens%E2%80%99-demands-without-procrastination-delay-%E2%80%94-sarayreh; Hana Namrouqa, "Germany to fund projects to improve water services for host communities," *Jordan Times*, February 29, 2016, http://www.jordantimes.com/news/local/germany-fund-projects-improve-water-services-host-communities; Hana Namrouqa, "New water network scheduled to improve Maan supply—officials," *Jordan Times*, May 31, 2017, http://www.jordantimes.com/news/local/new-water-network-scheduled-improve-maan-supply-%C2%AD%E2%80%94-officials; Laila Azzeh, "Kuwaiti fund grants Jordan $14m for projects to create jobs, improve services," *Jordan Times*, January 29, 2017, http://www.jordantimes.com/news/local/kuwaiti-fund-grants-jordan-14m-projects-create-jobs-improve-services; "World Bank announces $200m project to improve education," *Jordan Times*, December 7, 2017, http://www.jordantimes.com/news/local/world-bank-announces-200m-project-improve-education.

247. Karin Laub, "Jordan Instability Fears as Growth Slows, Unemployment Rises," *AP News*, August 14, 2016, https://apnews.com/de36e6d1c7414d97a4023e57ffe5a2b7.

248. "Lawmakers Vow to Play Significant Role in Country's Advancement," *Jordan Times*, October 25, 2018, http://www.jordantimes.com/news/local/lawmakers-vow-play-significant-role-countrys-advancement.

249. Farah Najjar, "Jordan Protesters: 'Gulf Money Won't Help'," *Al Jazeera*, June 11, 2018, https://www.aljazeera.com/news/2018/06/jordan-protesters-gulf-money-aid-package-180611114422748.html.

250. Osama Al Sharif, "Jordan's Political Elite Warn of More Protests if Reforms Are Ignored," Al-Monitor, June 29, 2018, www.al-monitor.com/pulse/originals/2018/06/jordan-protests-economic-social-contract-razzaz-government.html.

251. "Pardon Law Ratified, Set to be Published in Official Gazette," *Jordan Times*, February 5, 2019, http://www.jordantimes.com/news/local/pardon-law-ratified-set-be-published-official-gazette; Mina Aldroubi, "King of Jordan Issues Decree Approving Royal Pardon," *The National*, February 4, 2019, https://www.thenational.ae/world/mena/king-of-jordan-issues-decree-approving-royal-pardon-1.821819.

252. "Cabinet Convenes in Baabda with Electricity Plan Topping 61-Items Agenda," Lebanese National News Agency Online (through Open Source Enterprise), April 26, 2018.

253. Timour Azhari, "Parliament Committees Look to Revamp Health Care," *Daily Star*, September 11, 2018, http://www1.dailystar.com.lb/News/Lebanon-News/2018/Sep-11/463060-parliament-committees-look-to-revamp-health-care.ashx.

254. Farah-Silvana Kanaan, "Hariri: Govt to Slash Energy Subsidies in 2019," *Daily Star*, December 22, 2018, http://www.dailystar.com.lb/Business/Local/2018/Dec-22/472437-hariri-govt-to-slash-energy-subsidies-in-2019.ashx.

255. Preston, "What's the Deal with Garbage Decentralization?" *Executive Magazine* (blog), March 6, 2018. http://www.executive-magazine.com/economics-policy/whats-the-deal-with-garbage-decentralization.

256. Joseph A. Kechichian, "Lebanese Vent Frustrations over Strained Economy," *Gulf News*, Lebanon, May 1, 2017, https://gulfnews.com/news/mena/lebanon/lebanese-vent-frustrations-over-strained-economy-1.2020385.

CONCLUSION

1. See for example, Alesina, Murard, and Rapoport, "Immigration and Preferences for Redistribution in Europe."

2. Goldstone, "Demographic/Structural Model of State Breakdown," 30.

3. Walsh, "Resource Mobilization and Citizen Protest."

4. Bergstrand, "Mobilizing Power of Grievances."

5. Simmons, "Grievances Do Matter in Mobilization."

6. In addition to others cited in this chapter, Snow et al., "Disrupting the 'Quotidian'"; Walton and Seddon, *Free Markets & Food Riots*.

7. Della Porta et al., *Late Neoliberalism and Its Discontents in the Economic Crisis*; Della Porta, *Social Movements in Times of Austerity*.

8. Bascal Abu Nadir, "Musa'adat istithna'iyya lil-naziheen al-Sourieen fa-matha 'an al-Lubanieen?" [Emergency assistance to displaced Syrians but what about Lebanese?], Saida City Net, July 17, 2014, https://saidacity.net/.

9. "Tafh kayl al-Lubnanieen . . . #matat_'abab_al-mustashfa" [It's enough for the Lebanese . . . #she_died_at_the_hospital's_gate], Alahed News, March 27, 2017, https://www.alahednews.com.lb/.

10. Dionigi, "Rethinking Borders."

11. Rollins, "Syrians Make Easy Scapegoats in Lebanon."

12. Brader, Valentino, and Suhay, "What Triggers Public Opposition to Immigration?"; Shesterinina, "Collective Threat Framing and Mobilization in Civil War." I do not focus on elite discourse of the Syrians as a variable, since it occurred in both states.

13. Rothschild et al., "A Dual-Motive Model of Scapegoating."

14. Gamalerio, "Not Welcome Anymore"; Whitaker and Giersch, "Political Competition and Attitudes towards Immigration in Africa."

15. Hjerm, "Do Numbers Really Count?"

16. In social movement studies, this is called the development of oppositional consciousness. Mansbridge, "Making of Oppositional Consciousness."

17. Economic grievances often turn into political demands historically, in part simply because those in power make the economic policies affecting the country.

18. Stel, "Review Essay"; Mouawad and Baumann, "Wayn Al-Dawla?"

19. Interview with head of municipality on the Syrian border, Beka'a Valley, May 21, 2018.

20. Davis and Silver, "Civil Liberties vs. Security."

21. "Second Wave of Bombings Hits Lebanese Border Village," New Arab, June 27, 2016, https://www.alaraby.co.uk/english/news/2016/6/27/second-wave-of-bombings-hits-lebanese-border-village.

22. Nabih Bulos, "In Lebanon, a Rape and Murder Galvanize Anti-Syrian Fervor," *Los Angeles Times*, October 13, 2017, http://www.latimes.com/world/middleeast/la-fg-lebanon-syria-slaying-2017-story.html.

23. Bassam al-Badareen, "Jadal al-demoghrafiyyan al-Souriyya fil-Urdun yatada'af ba'd thuhur jara'im qatl wa ikhtiraqat 'ameqa li-laji'een wa sa'oud sinario 'al-tawteen' fi Dera'a" [Demographic debate about Syrians in Jordan increase after murders emerged and severe violations by the refugees and the emergence of a nationalization scenario in Dera'a], *Al-Quds al-Arabi* (UK), October 18, 2014, https://www.alquds.co.uk/.

24. Interview with professor, Lebanese University Political Science Department, Beirut, May 24, 2018; AbiYaghi, Catusse, and Younes, "From *Isqat an-Nizam at-Ta'ifi* to the Garbage Crisis Movement."

25. Jacobsen, "Can Refugees Benefit the State?"

26. Duffield, *Global Governance and the New Wars.*

27. EU Bulleting, "Stabilizing Europe's 'Backyard': EU Committed to Support Syrian Refugees in Jordan," December 10, 2018, https://www.eubulletin.com/9304-stabilizing -europes-backyard-eu-committed-to-support-syrian-refugees-in-jordan.html; Arar, "New Grand Compromise," 308.

28. Barnett and Weiss, *Humanitarianism in Question*; Fox, "New Humanitarianism"; Gabiam, "Humanitarianism, Development, and Security in the 21st Century."

29. Collier and Betts, *Refuge.*

30. Ibid., chap. 5.

31. Lenner and Turner, "Making Refugees Work?"

32. Knack, "Building or Bypassing Recipient Country Systems."

33. Batley and Mcloughlin, "Engagement with Non-State Service Providers in Fragile States."

34. Kristoff and Panarelli, "Haiti: A Republic of NGOs?"; Zanotti, "Cacophonies of Aid, Failed State Building and NGOs in Haiti"; Nadene Ghouri, "Liberia Turns to the Private Sector in Controversial Overhaul of Failing Schools," *The Guardian*, August 31, 2016, https://www.theguardian.com/global-development/2016/aug/31/liberia-turns-to-private -sector-controversial-overhaul-failing-schools; "Is Liberia Tired of NGOs?"

35. Naazneen Barma, Naomi Levy, and Jessica Piombo worked on a framework to understand when diverse outcomes result from aid efforts. Barma, Levy, and Piombo, "Disentangling Aid Dynamics in Statebuilding and Peacebuilding."

36. Mcloughlin, "When Does Service Delivery Improve the Legitimacy of a Fragile or Conflict-Affected State?"

37. Brass, *Allies or Adversaries.* Landau documented similar effects. Landau, *Humanitarian Hangover.*

38. Brass, "Blurring Boundaries."

39. Fowler, "Role of NGOs in Changing State-Society Relations."

40. Brass, *Allies or Adversaries.*

41. "Lebanon Freezes UNHCR Staff Permits over Syria Refugees Spat," *Al Jazeera*, June 8, 2018, https://www.aljazeera.com/news/2018/06/lebanon-freezes-unhcr-staff -permits-syria-refugees-spat-180608193601201.html.

42. "Starving Syrian Mother Sets Herself on Fire at Jordan Refugee Camp," *Daily Sabah*, January 14, 2019, https://www.dailysabah.com/syrian-crisis/2019/01/14/starving -syrian-mother-sets-herself-on-fire-at-jordan-refugee-camp#pp; Han and Rossi, "Why the Situation in Rukban Is Deteriorating."

43. Alex Forsyth, "Meeting an Organ Trafficker Who Preys on Syrian Refugees," BBC News Magazine, April 25, 2017, https://www.bbc.com/news/magazine-39272511.

44. Reidy, "Unsafe in Syria, Unwanted in Lebanon," "Desperate Syrians Risk Lives at Sea Escaping Lebanon," *The National*, November 25, 2018, https://www.thenational.ae /world/mena/desperate-syrians-risk-lives-at-sea-escaping-lebanon-1.795737.

45. "Syria War: Displaced Babies Die due to Freezing Weather," BBC News, January 15, 2019, https://www.bbc.com/news/world-middle-east-46880566; "Refugee Homes under War in Lebanon," BBC News, January 13, 2019, https://www.bbc.com/news/av/world -middle-east-46851902/refugee-homes-under-water-in-lebanon.

46. Charlie Dunmore and Rima Cherri, "As Medical Costs Rise, Syrian Refugees Put Health at Risk," UNHCR, https://www.unhcr.org/news/stories/2018/12/5c090f5e4/medical -costs-rise-syrian-refugees-health-risk.html.

47. Human Rights Watch, "Lebanon: Civilians Tried in Military Courts," January 26, 2017; Human Rights Watch, "Our Homes Are Not for Strangers"; Marks, "Pushing Syrian Refugees to Return."

References

SELECTED ELITE INTERVIEWS, FOCUS GROUPS, AND PERSONAL COMMUNICATIONS

Interviews met the requirements of the Institutional Review Board. I erred on the side of caution in protecting individual anonymity. Sources are listed based on the order in which the contacts or events occurred.

Jordan—September 2015

    U.S. Embassy officials
    International Committee of the Red Cross
    UNICEF
    USAID
    Norwegian Refugee Council
    UNFPA
    International Organization for Migration (IOM)
    Danish Refugee Council
    Marwan Muasher, former minister and diplomat, Carnegie
    UNHCR, senior protection official

Lebanon—January 2016 and March 2017

    Conversations with INGO and donor officials, including EU representatives, January 2016
    Halim Shebaya, political analyst, researcher and writer
    Conversations with UNHCR, UNDP, and International Committee of the Red Cross (ICRC) officials
    Discussions with Lebanese Armed Forces officers
    Sahar Atrache, (then) senior analyst, Lebanon, International Crisis Group
    Rabih Shibli, director, Center for Civic Engagement and Community Service, American University of Beirut (AUB)
    Ziad Naboulsi, UNICEF
    Carmen Geha, professor, Political Science Department, AUB
    Mona Fawaz, professor, Urban Studies and Planning Department, AUB, and member, Beirut Madinati
    Bassel Salloukh, professor, Political Science Department, Lebanese American University, Beirut
    Maha Yahya, director, Carnegie Middle East Center
    Roland Riachi, professor, Issam Fares Institute for Public Policy and International Affairs and Faculty of Agricultural and Food Sciences, American University of Beirut
    David Adams, coordinator of Water Projects, UNICEF
    Karam Karam, United Nations Economic and Social Commission for Western Asia and Common Space Initiative

Jordan—September 2017

WANA (West Asia-North Africa Institute), several researchers (two occasions)
U.S. Embassy officials, two occasions
Musa Shteiwi, director, Center for Strategic Studies, University of Jordan (two occasions)
Identity Center official
Mercy Corps, several officials
Zarqa municipality officials
Hikaya Center (NGO)
Ahmad Awad, Phenix Center director
Mohammad Zabi, sheikh and businessman from Ramtha
Afaq Jordan for Development and Training, Mafraq
Action Aid, Mafraq
May Shalabieh, independent consultant and trainer to the UN and NGOs
Young Entrepreneurs Association
Arab Renaissance for Democracy and Development
Baker Hiyari, UNDP
Ghassan Hazboun, former engineer, Mercy Corps
Sheikh and his relatives, Ramtha, northern Jordan
Owner of handicraft workshop, and member of West Irbid municipal council, Irbid
Basim Tweissi, dean of Jordan Media Institute
Rula al-Farra al-Hroub, former minister of parliament, head of al-Urdun Aqwa Political Party, and political talk show host
Marwan Muasher, former minister and diplomat, vice president for studies, Carnegie Endowment for International Peace
Hussam Erhayel, country director, Friedrich Naumann Foundation Jordan

Lebanon—May 2018

Omar Tantawi, Fulbright graduate student, from AUB
Sheikh, Madrasa Iman school, Tripoli
Lawyer in Akkar
Greek Orthodox priest, living on border with Syria
Focus group, eight women, mostly teachers and teenage girls, Aidamoun, Akkar
Assistant to president of municipality, al-Bire
Focus group, four professional men, al-Azm association, Halba
Former Mercy Corps employee specializing in waste projects, Qalamoun, Tripoli
George Antoun, country director and regional program advisor, Mercy Corps
Discussion with military officer
Omar al-Maadarani, tech for food director for Beka'a (NGO)
Assistant to head of Electricite du Liban
President of the municipality, Majd al-Anjar
President of municipality, Beka'a
Qab Elias and Wadi Dalam, assistant, biggest village in central beka'a
President of municipality, Beka'a
Wasim Musbah Shaheen, director of Kayani (a local education NGO)
Teacher and administrator of public school, Beka'a
Director, public school, Beka'a
Hasan, teacher and administrator at public school, Beka'a, Amal
Mukhtar of Fa'our and Delhamiyya, Beka'a
Rabih Shibli, director, Center for Civic Engagement and Community Service, AUB

Bassel el Hassan, professor, Political Science Department, Lebanese University
Mercy Corps officials and employee
Halim Shebaya, political analyst, researcher and writer
Jamil Mouawad, European University Institute
Lea Bou Khater, postdoctoral fellow, AUB

United States and Correspondence

Discussion with Jordanian government official, Washington, DC
E-mail correspondence with various NGO officials
Aysar Hammoudeh, former senior protection assistant, UNHCR-Jordan (2012–
2014), Los Gatos, CA

NEWS SOURCES AND WEBSITES

*News sources are from a wide variety of political persuasions but were used only if the report-
ing could be verified through other sources, including interviews and social media.*

*URLs are included for English sources in endnotes. For Arabic sources, the main site is in-
cluded since URLs are generally extremely long.*

7iber (Jordan)
Ahrar al-Tafileh (Jordanian blog)
Akeed (Jordan Media Credibility
Monitor)
Aks Alser
Al-Ahali
Al Akhbar
Alahed News (Lebanese, Shi'a-leaning)
Al-Alam al-yawm
Al-Anba'
Al-Arab (UK)
Al-Arabi al-Jadeed
Al Bawaba
Al-Binaa
Al-Dustour (Jordanian, official)
Al-Ghad (Jordanian)
Al-Ittihad (Emirates)
Aliwaa
Al-Jadid Satellite Channel
Al Jazeera (Arabic and English)
Al-Kawn News
All of Jordan
Al-Maqar
Al-Serat al-mustaqeem
Al-Rai (Jordanian, official)
Al-Rai Media (Kuwait)
AlSouria (Syrian diaspora)

Al-Watan (Egypt)
Ammon News
Andalou Agency
An-Nahar
Arabi21
Asharq Al-Awsat
Associated Press
The Atlantic
Atlantic Council
BBC News (English and Arabic)
Black Iris (Jordan blog)
Bloomberg News
Business News (Lebanon)
Carnegie
CBC Radio
CCTV Arabic
Christian Science Monitor
CityLab
CNN Arabic
Daily Star (Beirut)
DW (German)
El Dorar
El Nashra (Arabic)
Fair Observer
Fanack Water
Financial Times
Global Citizen

The Guardian (UK)
Huffington Post
The Independent
IRIN
Janoubia
JBC News
Jordan Times (Amman)
Jordan Vista
Jordan Zad
Legal Agenda (English and Arabic,
al-Mufakira al-qanouniyya)
Los Angeles Times
MENAFN
MENASource
Middle East Centre Blog
Middle East Eye
Naharnet
The National (United Arab Emirates)
National News Agency (Beirut)
National Public Radio (U.S.)
New Arab (U.K.)
New York Times

Now Media
O News Agency
Peace Insight
Raseef 22
Reuters
Roya News
Saida City Net (local Lebanese)
Saraya News
Sawaleif
Sky News
Smart News (Syrian opposition)
SMEX
Step Feed
Synaps
Techonomy
The Telegraph
Tripoli Scope (local Lebanese)
Wall Street Journal
Washington Post
World Weekly
Xinhua (China)
Zaman Alwasl

PRIMARY STATISTICS SOURCES

European Bank for Reconstruction and Development
European Union
International Monetary Fund
UNHCR
United Nations
Government of Jordan
Government of Lebanon
World Bank

CITED WORKS

Ababneh, Sara. "'Do You Know Who Governs Us? The Damned Monetary Fund':
    Jordan's June 2018 Rising." Middle East Report Online, June 30, 2018. http://
    merip.org/mero/mero063018.
Ababsa, Myriam. "Gulf Donors and NGOs Assistance to Syrian Refugees in Jordan."
    Amman: UNHCR, June 2014. https://reliefweb.int/report/jordan/gulf-donors
    -and-ngos-assistance-syrian-refugees-jordan.
Abdih, Yasser, Andrea Gamba, and Rafik Selim. "Jordan: Selected Issues." Middle East
    and Central Asia Department, International Monetary Fund, April 14, 2014.
Abdih, Yasser, and Carolin Geginat. "The Economic Impact of the Syrian Conflict on
    Jordan." Economic Window (blog), September 30, 2014, https://www.imf.org
    /external/np/blog/nafida/093014.pdf.
AbiYaghi, Marie-Noëlle, Myriam Catusse, and Miriam Younes. "From Isqat an-Nizam
    at-Ta'ifi to the Garbage Crisis Movement: Political Identities and Antisectarian

Movements." In *Lebanon Facing the Arab Uprisings*, edited by Rosita Di Peri and Daniel Meier, 73–91. London: Springer, 2017.

Abou-Zahr, Sawssan. "Refugees and the Media in Lebanon," *Peace Insight*, August 29, 2017, https://www.peaceinsight.org/blog/2017/08/refugees-and-media-lebanon/.

Abou Zeid, Mario. "A Time Bomb in Lebanon: The Syrian Refugee Crisis." *Diwan, Carnegie Middle East Center* (blog), October 6, 2014. http://carnegie-mec.org/diwan/56857.

Abu-Fadil, Magda. "Lebanon: Mixed Messages as Media Cope with Internal Stress and External Pressure." In *How Does the Media on Both Sides of the Mediterranean Report on Migration? A Study on 17 Countries - by Journalists for Journalists and Policy-Makers*, 88–93. European Union and International Centre for Migration Policy Development, 2017.

Abu-Odeh, Adnan. *Jordanians, Palestinians, & the Hashemite Kingdom in the Middle East Peace Process*. Washington, D.C.: United States Institute of Peace Press, 1999.

Abuqudairi, Areej. "A Tale of Two Za'ataris." *IRIN* (blog), July 26, 2013. http://www.irinnews.org/feature/2013/07/26/tale-two-za%E2%80%99ataris.

Abu-Rish, Ziad. "Doubling Down: Jordan Six Years into the Arab Uprisings." *Jadaliyya* (blog), February 16, 2017. http://www.jadaliyya.com/pages/index/25886/doubling-down_jordan-six-years-into-the-arab-upris.

——. "Garbage Politics." *Middle East Report* 45, no. 277 (Winter 2015). http://www.merip.org/mer/mer277/garbage-politics.

——. "Municipal Politics in Lebanon." *Middle East Report* 46, no. 280 (Fall 2016). http://www.merip.org/mer/mer280/municipal-politics-lebanon.

Abu Sitta, Salman. *The Palestinian Nakba 1948*. London: The Palestinian Return Centre, 2000. http://www.plands.org/en/books-reports/books/the-palestinian-nakba-1948.

Achilli, Luigi. "Syrian Refugees in Jordan: A Reality Check." Migration Policy Centre, European University Institute, 2015. http://cadmus.eui.eu/handle/1814/34904.

Achilli, Luigi, Nasser Yassin, and M. Murat Erdogan. "Neighbouring Host-Countries' Policies for Syrian Refugees: The Cases of Jordan, Lebanon, and Turkey." Working Paper, 2017. http://cadmus.eui.eu/handle/1814/44904.

Adely, Fida. "The Emergence of a New Labor Movement in Jordan." *Middle East Report*, no. 264 (Fall 2012).

AEMS (Advance Engineering & Management Services). "Impact of the Syrian Crisis on the Lebanese Power Sector and Priority Recommendations." Lebanese Ministry of Energy and Water and the UNDP, February 2017. https://www.lb.undp.org/content/lebanon/en/home/library/environment_energy/The-Impact-of-the-Syrian-Crisis-on-the-Lebanese-Power-Sector-and-Priority-Recommendations.html.

Al Ajlouni, Laith. "The Recent Protests in Jordan and the Way Forward: Renegotiating the Social Contract," Middle East Centre (blog), London School of Economics and Political Science, July 16, 2018. http://blogs.lse.ac.uk/mec/2018/07/16/the-recent-protests-in-jordan-and-the-way-forward-renegotiating-the-social-contract/.

Ajluni, Salem, and Mary Kawar. "Impact of the Syrian Refugee Crisis on the Labour Market in Jordan." Beirut, International Labour Organization, 2014. https://www.ilo.org/wcmsp5/groups/public/---arabstates/---ro-beirut/documents/publication/wcms_242021.pdf.

Ajluni, Salem, Mary Kawar, International Labour Organization, and ILO Regional Office for Arab States. *Towards Decent Work in Lebanon: Issues and Challenges in Light of the Syrian Refugee Crisis*. Beirut: ILO, 2015.

Akram, Susan M., Sarah Bidinger, Aaron Lang, Danielle Hites, Yoana Kuzmova, and Elena Noureddine. "Protecting Syrian Refugees: Laws, Policies, and Global

Responsibility Sharing." Boston University School of Law, International Human Rights Clinic, n.d.

——. "Protecting Syrian Refugees: Laws, Policies, and Global Responsibility Sharing: Report Summary." *Middle East Law and Governance* 7, no. 3 (2015): 287–318.

Alami, Mona. "The Impact of the Syria Crisis on Salafis and Jihadis in Lebanon." *MEI Policy Focus (Middle East Institute)* 3 (April 2014).

Alesina, Alberto, Elie Murard, and Hillel Rapoport. "Immigration and Preferences for Redistribution in Europe." Cambridge, MA: National Bureau of Economic Research, February 2019. https://doi.org/10.3386/w25562.

Al-Harahsheh, Sura, Rida Al-Adamat, and Seraj Abdullah. "The Impact of Za'atari Refugee Camp on the Water Quality in Amman-Zarqa Basin." *Journal of Environmental Protection* 6, no. 1 (2015): 16–24.

Ali, Doa, Hussam Da'aneh, Sara Obeidat, Mohammad Hijazi, and Sufian Ahmad. "A Town's Sudden Growth: Jordanians and Syrians Share the Poverty of Mafraq." *7iber* (blog). Accessed February 16, 2018. http://www.7iber.com/2014/08/a-towns-sudden-growth/#.WodI6BPwYch.

Al-Khatib, Bashar, and Katharina Lenner. "Alternative Voices on the Syrian Refugee Crisis in Jordan: An Interview Collection." Rosa Luxemburg Stiftung, 2015. http://www.rosaluxemburg.ps/wp-content/uploads/2015/11/Jordan-Book-ref-English.pdf.

Al-Masri, Muzna. "The Social Stability Context in the Nabatieh & Bint Jbeil Qazas." Conflict Analysis Report. UNDP Peacebuilding in Lebanon Project, March 2016.

Al-Saadi, Yazan. "Examining Curfews against Syrians in Lebanon." Civil Society Knowledge Centre, 2014, http://civilsociety-centre.org/content/examining-curfews-against-syrians-lebanon-0.

Al Shalabi, Jamal. "Jordan: Revolutionaries without a Revolution." *Confluences Méditerranée* 77, no. 2 (2011): 91.

Alsharabati, Carole. "Survey on Perceptions of Syrian Refugees in Lebanon." Beirut: Institut des Science Politiques, Université Saint-Joseph, 2014. https://data2.unhcr.org/en/documents/download/45083.

Amnesty International. "Denied Refuge: Palestinians from Syria Seeking Safety in Lebanon," 2014. https://www.amnesty.org/en/documents/MDE18/002/2014/en/.

——. "Growing Restrictions, Tough Conditions: The Plight of Those Fleeing Syria to Jordan," October 10, 2013. https://www.amnestyusa.org/reports/growing-restrictions-tough-conditions-the-plight-of-those-fleeing-syria-to-jordan/.

——. "Living on the Margins: Syrian Refugees in Jordan Struggle to Access Health Care," March 23, 2016. https://www.amnestyusa.org/files/living_on_the_margins_-_syrian_refugees_struggle_to_access_health_care_in_jordan.pdf.

——. "Pushed to the Edge: Syrian Refugees Face Increased Restrictions in Lebanon," June 15, 2015. https://www.amnesty.org/en/documents/document/?indexNumber=mde24%2f1785%2f2015&language=en.

Anderson, Betty S. *Nationalist Voices in Jordan: The Street and the State.* Austin: University of Texas Press, 2005.

Andoni, Lamis, and Jillian Schwedler. "Bread Riots in Jordan." *Middle East Report*, no. 201 (1996): 40–42.

Aranki, Dalia, and Olivia Kalis. "Limited Legal Status for Refugees from Syria in Lebanon." *Forced Migration Review*, no. 47 (2014): 17.

Arar, Rawan. "Leveraging Sovereignty: The Case of Jordan and the International Refugee Regime—Project on Middle East Political Science." In *Refugees and Migration Movements in the Middle East*, 12–15. POMEPS Studies 25. Project on Middle East Political Science, 2017. https://pomeps.org/2017/03/29/leveraging-sovereignty-the-case-of-jordan-and-the-international-refugee-regime/.

——. "The New Grand Compromise: How Syrian Refugees Changed the Stakes in the Global Refugee Assistance Regime." *Middle East Law and Governance* 9, no. 3 (2017): 298–312.

Asfour, Hana. "Jordan: Local Perceptions on Syrian Refugees (Part 2/2)." *Fair Observer*, March 19, 2014. https://www.fairobserver.com/region/middle_east_north_africa /jordan-local-perceptions-syrian-refugees-62951/.

Atrache, Sahar. "Beirut Bombing Widens Lebanon's Shiite-Sunni Divide." *International Crisis Group* (blog), November 13, 2015. http://blog.crisisgroup.org/middle-east -north-africa/2015/11/13/beirut-bombing-widens-lebanons-shiite-sunni -divide/?utm_campaign=shareaholic&utm_medium=printfriendly&utm _source=tool.

——. "Lebanon's Resilience under the Weight of Syria's War." *Crisis Group* (blog), June 25, 2015. https://www.crisisgroup.org/middle-east-north-africa/eastern -mediterranean/lebanon/lebanon-s-resilience-under-weight-syria-s-war.

——. "Lebanon's Un-Collected Problems." *Crisis Group* (blog), August 27, 2015. https://www.crisisgroup.org/middle-east-north-africa/eastern-mediterranean /lebanon/lebanon-s-un-collected-problems.

Barak, Oren. "Commemorating Malikiyya: Political Myth, Multiethnic Identity and the Making of the Lebanese Army." *History and Memory* 13 (2001): 60–84.

Barham, Nasim. "Is Good Water Governance Possible in a Rentier State? The Case of Jordan." Analysis. Center for Mellemøststudier, Syddansk Universitet, May 2012.

Barjas, Elham. "Municipal Regulation of Syrian Refugees in Lebanon: The Case of Kfar-Rimman." *Legal Agenda* (blog), November 21, 2016. http://legal-agenda .com/en/article.php?id=3204.

Barma, Naazneen H., Naomi Levy, and Jessica Piombo. "Disentangling Aid Dynamics in Statebuilding and Peacebuilding: A Causal Framework." *International Peacekeeping* 24, no. 2 (2017): 187–211.

Barnes-Dacey, Julien. "Syria: The View from Jordan." *European Council on Foreign Relations* (blog), June 17, 2013. http://www.ecfr.eu/article/commentary_syria _the_view_from_jordan138.

Barnett, Michael, and Thomas G. Weiss. *Humanitarianism in Question: Politics, Power, Ethics*. Ithaca, NY: Cornell University Press, 2008.

Batley, Richard, and Claire Mcloughlin. "Engagement with Non-State Service Providers in Fragile States: Reconciling State-Building and Service Delivery." *Development Policy Review* 28, no. 2 (March 2010): 131–54.

Baumann, Hannes. "Social Protest and the Political Economy of Sectarianism in Lebanon." *Global Discourse* 6, no. 4 (October 1, 2016): 634–49.

Baylouny, Anne Marie. "Born Violent: Armed Political Parties and Non-State Governance in Lebanon's Civil War." *Small Wars & Insurgencies* 25, no. 2 (March 4, 2014): 329–53.

——. "Building an Integrated Military in Post-Conflict Societies: Lebanon." In *Building an Integrated Military in Post-Conflict Societies*, edited by Thomas C. Bruneau and Florina Cristiana Matei, 242–54. Routledge Handbooks Online, 2012.

——. "Militarizing Welfare: Neo-Liberalism and the Jordanian Regime." *Middle East Journal* 62, no. 2 (2008): 277–303.

——. *Privatizing Welfare in the Middle East: Kin Mutual Aid Associations in Jordan and Lebanon*. Bloomington: Indiana University Press, 2010.

Baylouny, Anne Marie, and Stephen J. Klingseis. "Water Thieves or Political Catalysts? Syrian Refugees in Jordan and Lebanon." *Middle East Policy* 25, no. 1 (2018): 104–23.

Beck, Martin. "Contextualizing the Current Social Protest Movement in Lebanon." *E-International Relations* (blog), November 10, 2015. https://www.e-ir.info/2015 /10/10/contextualizing-the-current-social-protest-movement-in-lebanon/.

Beck, Martin, and Simone Hüser. "Jordan and the 'Arab Spring': No Challenge, No Change?" *Middle East Critique* 24, no. 1 (January 2, 2015): 83–97.

Beinin, Joel. "A Workers' Social Movement on the Margin of the Global Neoliberal Order, Egypt 2004-2012." In *Social Movements, Mobilization, and Contestation in the Middle East and North Africa*, edited by Frédéric Vairel and Joel Beinin, First ed., 181–201. Stanford University Press, 2011. http://www.sup.org/books/title/?id=23271.

Beirut Research and Innovation Center, Lebanese Center for Studies and Research. "Citizens' Perceptions of Security Threats Stemming from the Syrian Refugee Presence in Lebanon." Background Paper. International Alert, February 2015. http://www.international-alert.org/publications/citizens-perceptions-security -threats-stemming-syrian-refugee-presence.

Bekdache, Nathalie. "Lebanon's Garbage Crisis: A Historical Moment in State-Building?" *International Alert* (blog), September 10, 2015. http://www.inter national-alert.org/blog/lebanons-garbage-crisis.

Bergstrand, Kelly. "The Mobilizing Power of Grievances: Applying Loss Aversion and Omission Bias to Social Movements." *Mobilization: An International Quarterly* 19, no. 2 (2014): 123–42.

Berthier, Rosalie. "Abracada . . . Broke: Lebanon's Banking on Magic." *Synaps* (blog), May 2, 2017. http://www.synaps.network/abracada-broke.

Betts, Alexander, Ali Ali, and Fulya Memisoglu. "Local Politics and the Syrian Refugee Crisis: Exploring Responses in Turkey, Lebanon, and Jordan." Refugee Studies Centre, Oxford Department of International Development, University of Oxford, 2017.

Blanco-Palencia, María. "Jordanian Youth in Collective Action: Structure and Significance of the Jordanian Al-Ḥirāk Al-Shabābī (Youth Movement)." *Revista de Estudios Internacionales Mediterráneos* 19 (2015): 75–90.

Bohra-Mishra, Pratikshya, and Douglas S. Massey. "Individual Decisions to Migrate during Civil Conflict." *Demography* 48, no. 2 (May 2011): 401–24.

Bondokji, Neven, and Erica Harper. "Journey Mapping of Selected Jordanian Foreign Fighters." Amman: West Asia-North Africa Institute, Royal Scientific Society, August 2017.

Borland, Elizabeth. "Quotidian Disruption." In *Wiley-Blackwell Encyclopedia of Social and Political Movements*, 1038–41 (2013).

Bou Khater, Léa. "Public Sector Mobilisation despite a Dormant Workers' Movement." *Confluences Méditerranée*, no. 92 (–Winter 2014–15): 125–42.

Brader, Ted, Nicholas A. Valentino, and Elizabeth Suhay. "What Triggers Public Opposition to Immigration? Anxiety, Group Cues, and Immigration Threat." *American Journal of Political Science* 52, no. 4 (2008): 959–78.

Brand, Laurie A. "Palestinians and Jordanians: A Crisis of Identity." *Journal of Palestine Studies* 24, no. 4, Summer (1995): 46–61.

——. *Palestinians in the Arab World: Institution Building and the Search for State.* New York: Columbia University Press, 1988.

Brass, Jennifer N. *Allies or Adversaries: NGOs and the State in Africa.* Cambridge, UK: Cambridge University Press, 2016.

——. "Blurring Boundaries: The Integration of NGOs into Governance in Kenya." *Governance* 25, no. 2 (2012): 209–35.

Bustani, Hisham. "Jordan—A Failed Uprising and a Re-Emerging Regime." *Your Middle East* (blog), May 6, 2013. http://www.yourmiddleeast.com/opinion/hisham -bustani-jordan-a-failed-uprising-and-a-reemerging-regime_12178.

——. "Jordan's New Opposition and the Traps of Identity and Ambiguity." *Jadaliyya* (blog), April 20, 2011. http://www.jadaliyya.com/pages/index/1303/jordans-new -opposition-and-the-traps-of-identity-a.

Cali, Massimiliano, and Samia Sekkarie. "Much Ado about Nothing? The Economic Impact of Refugee 'Invasions.'" *Brookings* (blog), September 16, 2015. https:// www.brookings.edu/blog/future-development/2015/09/16/much-ado-about -nothing-the-economic-impact-of-refugee-invasions/.

Cammett, Melani. *Compassionate Communalism: Welfare and Sectarianism in Lebanon.* Ithaca, NY: Cornell University Press, 2014.

Cammett, Melani, and Sukriti Issar. "Bricks and Mortar Clientelism: Sectarianism and the Logics of Welfare Allocation in Lebanon." *World Politics* 62, no. 03 (July 2010): 381–421.

Carpi, Estella. "Against Ontologies of Hospitality: About Syrian Refugeehood in Northern Lebanon." Middle East Institute, October 27, 2016. https://www.mei .edu/content/map/against-ontologies-hospitality-about-syrian-refugeehood -northern-lebanon.

——. "The Everyday Experience of Humanitarianism in Akkar Villages." Civil Society Knowledge Centre, Lebanon Support, March 24, 2014. http://civilsociety-centre .org/paper/everyday-experience-humanitarianism-akkar-villages.

Carrion, Doris. "Syrian Refugees in Jordan: Confronting Difficult Truths." Chatham House, Royal Institute of International Affairs, 2015. https://www.chathamhouse .org/publication/syrian-refugees-jordan-confronting-difficult-truths.

Center for Insights in Survey Research. "Survey of Jordan Public Opinion: National Poll #14." International Republican Institute, November 23, 2016.

Center for Strategic Studies. "Istitlaa' lil-rai al-'am hawla ba'dh al-qadaya al-rahina fil-Urdun—Taymouz 2013" [The results of a public opinion poll about some current issues in Jordan—July 2013]. Amman: Center for Strategic Studies, University of Jordan, 2013. http://jcss.org.10-0-0-4.mint.imagine.com.jo /ShowNews.aspx?NewsId=328.

——. "Jordanians Feel Less Safe since Syrian Refugee Crisis Started—Survey." September 14, 2017. http://jcss.org/ShowNews.aspx?NewsId=561.

Chalcraft, John T. *The Invisible Cage: Syrian Migrant Workers in Lebanon.* Stanford, CA: Stanford University Press, 2008.

Cherri, Zeinab, Pedro Arcos González, and Rafael Castro Delgado. "The Lebanese-Syrian Crisis: Impact of the Influx of Syrian Refugees to an Already Weak State." *Risk Management and Healthcare Policy* 9 (July 2016): 165–72.

Chit, Bassem, and Mohamad Ali Nayel. "Understanding Racism against Syrian Refugees in Lebanon." Civil Society Knowledge Centre, Lebanon Support, October 2013. http://civilsociety-centre.org/paper/understanding-racism-against-syrian -refugees-lebanon.

"Chopping up the Tree of State—Lebanon's Political System Leads to Paralysis and Corruption." *The Economist*, April 19, 2018.

Christophersen, Mona. "Educating Syrian Youth in Jordan: Holistic Approaches to Emergency Response." New York: International Peace Initiative, December 2015.

Christophersen, Mona, Jing Liu, Cathrine Moe Thorleifsson, and Åge A Tiltnes. "Lebanese Attitudes towards Syrian Refugees and the Syrian Crisis: Results from a National Opinion Poll Implemented 15–21 May, 2013." Fafo Paper, 2013.

Ciezadlo, Annia. "Sect Symbols." *The Nation*, February 21, 2007. https://www.thenation .com/article/sect-symbols/.

Clark, Janine A. "Field Research Methods in the Middle East." *PS: Political Science & Politics* 39, no. 3 (July 2006): 417–24.

Clark, Janine A., and Bassel F. Salloukh. "Elite Strategies, Civil Society, and Sectarian Identities in Postwar Lebanon." *International Journal of Middle East Studies* 45, no. 4 (2013): 731–49.

Clemens, Michael, and Jennifer Hunt. "The Labor Market Effects of Refugee Waves: Reconciling Conflicting Results." CEP Discussion Paper. London School of Economics and Political Science, Centre for Economic Performance, July 2017. http://www.nber.org/papers/w23433.pdf.

Cochrane, Paul, Sami Halabi, and Tabitha Ross. "Child Labor in Agriculture on the Rise in Lebanon." *Executive Magazine* (blog), June 12, 2016. http://www.executive-magazine.com/economics-policy/child-labor-in-agriculture-on-the-rise-in-lebanon.

Collier, Paul, and Alexander Betts. *Refuge: Rethinking Refugee Policy in a Changing World*. New York: Oxford University Press, 2017.

Connable, Ben. *From Negative to Positive Stability: How the Syrian Refugee Crisis Can Improve Jordan's Outlook*. Research Report, RR-1069-MCIA. Santa Monica, CA: RAND Corp., 2015.

Corbeil, Alexander. "Hezbollah Re-Ascendant in Lebanon." *Carnegie Endowment for International Peace* (blog), August 17, 2017. http://carnegieendowment.org/sada/72856.

Crisp, Jeff, Jane Janz, Jose Riera, and Shahira Samy. "Surviving in the City: A Review of UNHCR's Operation for Iraqi Refugees in Urban Areas of Jordan, Lebanon and Syria." Geneva: UNHCR, 2009.

Darwish, T., T. Atallah, M. El Moujabber, and N. Khatib. "Salinity Evolution and Crop Response to Secondary Soil Salinity in Two Agro-Climatic Zones in Lebanon." *Agricultural Water Management*, Special Issue on Advances in Integrated Management of Fresh and Saline Water for Sustainable Crop Production: Modeling and Practical Solutions, 78, no. 1 (September 15, 2005): 152–64.

Davis, Darren W., and Brian D. Silver. "Civil Liberties vs. Security: Public Opinion in the Context of the Terrorist Attacks on America." *American Journal of Political Science* 48, no. 1 (January 2004): 28–46.

Davis, Rochelle, Grace Benton, Will Todman, and Emma Murphy. "Hosting Guests, Creating Citizens: Models of Refugee Administration in Jordan and Egypt." *Refugee Survey Quarterly* 36, no. 2 (2017): 1–32.

Dawass, Maha. "Poverty in Jordan." Working Paper. Conference of European Statisticians, Geneva, United Nations Economic Commission for Europe, April 9, 2015. https://www.ssrn.com/abstract=3162257.

Della Porta, Donatella. "Late Neoliberalism and Its Discontents: An Introduction." In *Late Neoliberalism and Its Discontents in the Economic Crisis*, edited by della Porta et al., 1–38. Cham, Switzerland: Springer, 2017.

——. *Social Movements in Times of Austerity: Bringing Capitalism Back into Protest Analysis*. Malden, MA: Polity Press, 2015.

Della Porta, Donatella, Massimiliano Andretta, Tiago Fernandes, Francis O'Connor, Eduardo Romanos, and Markos Vogiatzoglou. *Late Neoliberalism and Its Discontents in the Economic Crisis: Comparing Social Movements in the European Periphery*. Cham, Switzerland: Springer, 2017.

Dibeh, Ghassan, Ali Fakih, and Walid Marrouch. "Decision to Emigrate Amongst the Youth in Lebanon: The Role of Socio-Economic Factors." Scientific Paper, #1. Sahwa, 2016. http://www.sahwa.eu/OUTPUTS/Other-publications/Decision-to-Emigrate-amongst-the-Youth-in-Lebanon.

Dickinson, Elizabeth. "Shadow Aid to Syrian Refugees." *Middle East Report* 44, no. 272 (Fall 2014). http://www.merip.org/mer/mer272/shadow-aid-syrian-refugees.

Dionigi, Filippo. "Rethinking Borders: The Dynamics of Syrian Displacement to Lebanon." *Middle East Law and Governance* 9, no. 3 (November 11, 2017): 232–48.

——. "Statehood and Refugees: Patterns of Integration and Segregation of Refugee Populations in Lebanon from a Comparative Perspective." *Middle East Law and Governance* 9, no. 2 (2017): 113–46.

"Do-It-Yourself: Public Services in the Arab World." *The Economist*, August 8, 2015.

Douglas, Tom. *Scapegoats: Transferring Blame*. London: Routledge, 1995.

Duffield, Mark. *Global Governance and the New Wars: The Merging of Development and Security*. 2nd ed. London: Zed Books, 2014.

El-Abed, Oroub. "The Discourse of Guesthood: Forced Migrants in Jordan." In *Managing Muslim Mobilities: Between Spiritual Geographies and the Global Security Regime*, edited by Anita Fábos and Riina Isotalo, 81–100. New York: Palgrave Macmillan, 2014.

El Amine, Yasmina. "Lebanon Water Forum: Rethinking Water Service Provision in Lebanon." Conference Report. Beirut, Issam Fares Institute for Public Policy and International Affairs, American University of Beirut and Oxfam, October 2016.

El Helou, Maya. "Refugees under Curfew: The War of Lebanese Municipalities against the Poor." *Legal Agenda* (blog), December 22, 2014. http://legal-agenda.com/en /article.php?id=3052.

El-Mallakh, Nelly, and Jackline Wahba. "Syrian Refugees and the Migration Dynamics of Jordanians: Moving In or Moving Out?" Working Paper. Economic Research Forum, April 2018.

El Mufti, Karim. "Official Response to the Syrian Refugee Crisis in Lebanon, the Disastrous Policy of No-Policy." Civil Society Knowledge Centre, Lebanon Support, January 10, 2014. http://civilsociety-centre.org/paper/official-response -syrian-refugee-crisis-lebanon-disastrous-policy-no-policy.

El-Sharif, Ahmad. "'Restoring Pride in Jordanian National Identity': Framing the Jordanian National Identity by the National Committee of Retired Army Veterans." *Studies in Literature and Language* 12, no. 5 (May 26, 2016): 40–53.

Errighi, Lorenza, and Jörn Griesse. "The Syrian Refugee Crisis Labour Market Implications in Jordan and Lebanon." Discussion Paper. Luxembourg, Publications Office of the European Union, 2016.

Fafchamps, Marcel, and Forhad Shilpi. "Determinants of the Choice of Migration Destination." *Oxford Bulletin of Economics and Statistics* 75, no. 3 (2013): 388–409.

Fakih, Ali, and May Ibrahim. "The Impact of Syrian Refugees on the Labor Market in Neighboring Countries: Empirical Evidence from Jordan." *Defence and Peace Economics* 27, no. 1 (January 2, 2016): 64–86.

Food and Agriculture Organization of the United Nations (FAO). "Agricultural Livelihoods and Food Security Impact Assessment and Response Plan for the Syria Crisis in the Neighbouring Countries of Egypt, Iraq, Jordan, Lebanon and Turkey: FAO in Emergencies." Food and Agriculture Organization of the United Nations, 2013. http://www.fao.org/emergencies/resources/documents/resources -detail/en/c/173889/.

Farhat, Joumana. "The Repercussions of the Syrian Refugee Crisis on Lebanon: The Challenges of Providing Services and Creating Jobs." Roundtable Report Series. Lebanon, Lebanese Center for Policy Studies, 2016.

Flanigan, Shawn Teresa, and Mounah Abdel-Samad. "Hezbollah's Social Jihad: Nonprofits as Resistance Organizations." *Middle East Policy* 16, no. 2 (June 2009): 122–37.

Fowler, Alan. "The Role of NGOs in Changing State-Society Relations: Perspectives from Eastern and Southern Africa." *Development Policy Review* 9, no. 1 (March 1991): 53–84.

Fox, Fiona. "New Humanitarianism: Does It Provide a Moral Banner for the 21st Century?" *Disasters* 25, no. 4 (2001): 275–89.

Francis, Alexandra. "Jordan's Refugee Crisis." Carnegie International Endowment for Peace, 2015.

Gabiam, Nell. "Humanitarianism, Development, and Security in the 21st Century: Lessons from the Syrian Refugee Crisis." *International Journal of Middle East Studies* 48, no. 2 (May 2016): 382–86.

Gamalerio, Matteo. "Not Welcome Anymore: The Effect of Electoral Incentives on the Reception of Refugees." SSRN Scholarly Paper. Rochester, NY: Social Science Research Network, September 8, 2017. https://papers.ssrn.com/abstract=3035420.

Gaspard, Toufic K. *A Political Economy of Lebanon, 1948–2002: The Limits of Laissez-Faire.* Boston: Brill, 2004.

Gates, Carolyn. *Merchant Republic of Lebanon: Rise of an Open Economy.* New York: I. B. Tauris, 1998.

Geha, Carmen. *Civil Society and Political Reform in Lebanon and Libya: Transition and Constraint.* New York: Routledge, 2016.

——. "Politics of a Garbage Crisis: Social Networks, Narratives, and Frames of Lebanon's 2015 Protests and Their Aftermath." *Social Movement Studies* (October 24, 2018): 1–15.

Ghanem, Nizar. "Dialogue and Local Response Mechanisms to Conflict between Host Communities and Syrian Refugees in Lebanon." Conflict Scan. Search for Common Ground, May 2014. https://www.sfcg.org/wp-content/uploads/2014/06 /Dialogue-and-Local-Response-Mechanisms-to-Conflict-between-Host -Communities-and-Syrian-Refugees-in-Lebanon.pdf.

——. "Local Governance under Pressure: Research on Social Stability in T5 Area, North Lebanon." Report of Findings. Menapolis and Oxfam Italia, 2016.

Goertz, Gary, and James Mahoney. *A Tale of Two Cultures: Qualitative and Quantitative Research in the Social Sciences.* Princeton, NJ: Princeton University Press, 2012.

Goldstone, Jack A. "A Demographic/Structural Model of State Breakdown." In *Readings on Social Movements: Origins, Dynamics, and Outcomes*, 2nd ed., edited by Doug McAdam and David A. Snow, 30–37. New York: Oxford University Press, 2009.

Goldstone, Jack Andrew, and Charles Tilly. "Threat (and Opportunity): Popular Action and State Response in the Dynamics of Contentious Action." In *Silence and Voice in the Study of Contentious Politics*, edited by Ronald R. Aminzade and Jack A. Goldstone, 179–194. Cambridge, UK: Cambridge University Press, 2001.

Gomez, Margarita Puerto, and Asger Christensen. "The Impacts of Refugees on Neighboring Countries: A Development Challenge." Background Note. World Development Report 2011. World Bank, June 29, 2010. http://documents .worldbank.org/curated/en/459601468337158089/The-impacts-of-refugees-on -neighboring-countries-a-development-challenge.

Government of Jordan. "The Jordan Compact: A New Holistic Approach between the Hashemite Kingdom of Jordan and the International Community to Deal with the Syrian Refugee Crisis." London, February 4, 2016. https://reliefweb.int/report /jordan/jordan-compact-new-holistic-approach-between-hashemite-kingdom -jordan-and.

Government of Lebanon and the United Nations. "Lebanon Crisis Response Plan 2015–2016," December 15, 2014. https://www.humanitarianresponse.info/en /operations/syria/document/lebanon-crisis-response-plan-2015-2016.

Grigg, Hannah. "One Year after Jordan's Fuel Protests." *MENASource* (blog), December 4, 2013, Atlantic Council. https://www.atlanticcouncil.org/blogs/menasource /one-year-after-jordan-s-fuel-protests.

Haider-Markel, Donald P., and Mark R. Joslyn. "Gun Policy, Opinion, Tragedy, and Blame Attribution: The Conditional Influence of Issue Frames." *Journal of Politics* 63, no. 2 (2001): 520–43.

Hamdan, Kamal, and Lea Bou Khater. "Strategies of Response to the Syrian Refugee Crisis in Lebanon." Policy Dialogues Series—Lebanon. Common Space Initiative, 2015.

Hameleers, Michael, Linda Bos, and Claes H. de Vreese. "'They Did It': The Effects of Emotionalized Blame Attribution in Populist Communication." *Communication Research* 44, no. 6 (August 1, 2017): 870–900.

Han, Aisha, and Rachel Rossi. "Why the Situation in Rukban Is Deteriorating." *Atlantic Council* (blog), December 5, 2018. https://www.atlanticcouncil.org/blogs/syriasource/why-the-situation-in-rukban-is-deteriorating-2.

Harb, Charles, and Rim Saab. "Social Cohesion and Intergroup Relations: Syrian Refugees and Lebanese Nationals in the Bekaa and Akkar." American University of Beirut and Save the Children, 2014. https://data2.unhcr.org/es/documents/download/40814.

Harb, Mona. "Cities and Political Change: How Young Activists in Beirut Bred an Urban Social Movement." Working Paper No. 20, Power2Youth, September 2016.

Harb, Mona, Ali Kassem, and Watfa Najdi. "Entrepreneurial Refugees and the City: Brief Encounters in Beirut." *Journal of Refugee Studies* 32, no. 1 (2019): 23–41.

Harel, Z. "Protests in Jordan Following Austerity Measures—Including Elimination of Bread Subsidy," Inquiry & Analysis Series, MEMRI, February 21, 2018. https://www.memri.org/reports/protests-jordan-following-austerity-measures-%E2%80%93-including-elimination-bread-subsidy.

Harel, Z. "Growing Calls in Jordan to Enact Political Reforms, Limit King's Powers," Inquiry & Analysis Series, no. 1427, MEMRI, December 10, 2018. https://www.memri.org/reports/growing-calls-jordan-enact-political-reforms-limit-kings-powers.

Harris, Rebecca. "Transforming Refugees Into 'Illegal Immigrants:' Neoliberalism, Domestic Politics, and Syrian Refugee Employment in Jordan." B.A. thesis, Brown University, 2016.

Hashemite Kingdom of Jordan. "Jordan's Way to Sustainable Development: First National Voluntary Review on the Implementation of the 2030 Agenda." September 28, 2015. https://sustainabledevelopment.un.org/content/documents/16289Jordan.pdf.

Hazbun, Waleed. "Assembling Security in a 'Weak State': The Contentious Politics of Plural Governance in Lebanon since 2005." *Third World Quarterly* 37, no. 6 (June 2, 2016): 1053–70.

Hermez, Sami. "When the State Is (n)Ever Present: On Cynicism and Political Mobilization in Lebanon." *Journal of the Royal Anthropological Institute* 21, no. 3 (September 2015): 507–23.

Hjerm, Mikael. "Do Numbers Really Count? Group Threat Theory Revisited." *Journal of Ethnic and Migration Studies* 33, no. 8 (November 1, 2007): 1253–75.

Hourani, Guita. "The Media and the Syrian Refugees in Lebanon: An Overview." Paris: UNESCO, 2016.

Hourani, Guita G. "State Security and Refugees: Operationalizing the 'Ladder of Options' by the Government of Lebanon." *Middle East Journal of Refugee Studies* 3, no. 2 (2018): 101–120.

Hourani, Najib B. "Lebanon: Hybrid Sovereignties and U.S. Foreign Policy." *Middle East Policy* 20, no. 1 (March 2013): 39–55.

Hovil, Lucy. "Self-Settled Refugees in Uganda: An Alternative Approach to Displacement?" *Journal of Refugee Studies* 20, no. 4 (2007): 599–620.

Howard, David M. "Analyzing the Causes of Statelessness in Syrian Refugee Children." *Texas International Law Journal* 52 (2017): 281.

Howden, Daniel, Hannah Patchett, and Charlotte Alfred. "The Compact Experiment: Push for Refugee Jobs Confronts Reality of Jordan and Lebanon." News Deeply: Quarterly Reports, December 13, 2017. http://issues.newsdeeply.com/the -compact-experiment.

Human Rights Watch. "'As If You're Inhaling Your Death'—The Health Risks of Burning Waste in Lebanon." December 1, 2017. https://www.hrw.org/report/2017 /12/01/if-youre-inhaling-your-death/health-risks-burning-waste-lebanon.

——. "'I Just Wanted to Be Treated like a Person': How Lebanon's Residency Rules Facilitate Abuse of Syrian Refugees," January 2016. https://www.hrw.org/sites /default/files/report_pdf/lebanon0116web.pdf.

——. "'It's Not the Right Place for Us': The Trial of Civilians by Military Courts in Lebanon." New York: Human Rights Watch, 2017. https://www.hrw.org/report /2017/01/26/its-not-right-place-us/trial-civilians-military-courts-lebanon.

——. "Jordan: Syrian Medical Workers Deported." *Human Rights Watch* (blog), December 8, 2014. https://www.hrw.org/news/2014/12/08/jordan-syrian-medical -workers-deported.

——. "Jordan: Syrians Blocked, Stranded in Desert." *Human Rights Watch* (blog), June 3, 2015. https://www.hrw.org/news/2015/06/03/jordan-syrians-blocked -stranded-desert.

——. "Lebanon: Civilians Tried in Military Courts." *Human Rights Watch* (blog), January 26, 2017. https://www.hrw.org/news/2017/01/26/lebanon-civilians-tried -military-courts.

——. "Lebanon: Rising Violence Targets Syrian Refugees," September 30, 2014. https://www.hrw.org/news/2014/09/30/lebanon-rising-violence-targets-syrian -refugees.

——. "Lebanon: Syrian Women at Risk of Sex Trafficking." *Human Rights Watch* (blog), July 28, 2016. https://www.hrw.org/news/2016/07/28/lebanon-syrian-women-risk -sex-trafficking.

——. "Not Welcome: Jordan's Treatment of Palestinians Escaping Syria," August 7, 2014. https://www.hrw.org/report/2014/08/07/not-welcome/jordans-treatment -palestinians-escaping-syria.

——. "'Our Homes Are Not for Strangers': Mass Evictions of Syrian Refugees by Lebanese Municipalities," 2018. https://www.hrw.org/report/2018/04/20/our -homes-are-not-strangers/mass-evictions-syrian-refugees-lebanese-munici palities.

Hüser, Simone. "The Syrian Refugee Crisis and Its Impact on Jordan: In Reference to the Regime's Structural Deficits." In *The Levant in Turmoil: Syria, Palestine, and the Transformation of Middle Eastern Politics*, edited by Martin Beck, Dietrich Jung, and Peter Seeberg, 79–99. New York: Palgrave Macmillan, 2016.

Husseini, Jalal Al. "Jordan and the Palestinians." In *Atlas of Jordan: History, Territories and Society*, edited by Myriam Ababsa, 230–45. Contemporain Publications. Beirut: Presses de l'Ifpo, 2014. http://books.openedition.org/ifpo/5014.

IHRC and Norwegian Refugee Council. "Registering Rights: Syrian Refugees and the Documentation of Births, Marriages, and Deaths in Jordan." October 2015. https://hrp.law.harvard.edu/wp-content/uploads/2015/11/Registering-rights -report-NRC-IHRC-October20151.pdf.

International Committee of the Red Cross. "Bled Dry—How War in the Middle East Is Bringing the Region to the Brink of a Water Catastrophe." Report, March 2015.

https://www.icrc.org/en/document/bled-dry-how-war-middle-east-bringing
-region-brink-water-catastrophe.

International Crisis Group. "Arsal in the Crosshairs: The Predicament of a Small
Lebanese Border Town." Middle East Briefing. International Crisis Group,
February 23, 2016. https://www.crisisgroup.org/middle-east-north-africa/eastern
-mediterranean/lebanon/arsal-crosshairs-predicament-small-lebanese-border
-town.

———. "Lebanon's Hizbollah Turns Eastward to Syria." *Middle East Report* 153. May 27,
2014.

———. "Lebanon's Self-Defeating Survival Strategies." International Crisis Group, Middle
East & North Africa. July 20, 2015. https://www.crisisgroup.org/middle-east
-north-africa/eastern-mediterranean/lebanon/lebanon-s-self-defeating-survival
-strategies.

———. "Popular Protest in North Africa and the Middle East (IX): Dallying with Reform
in a Divided Jordan." Middle East/North Africa Report. International Crisis
Group, March 12, 2012. https://www.crisisgroup.org/middle-east-north-africa
/eastern-mediterranean/jordan/popular-protest-north-africa-and-middle-east-ix
-dallying-reform-divided-jordan.

———. "Too Close For Comfort: Syrians in Lebanon." Middle East Report, May 13, 2013.
https://www.crisisgroup.org/middle-east-north-africa/eastern-mediterranean
/lebanon/too-close-comfort-syrians-lebanon.

International Labour Organization (ILO). "The Jordanian Labour Market: Multiple
Segmentations of Labour by Nationality, Gender, Education and Occupational
Classes." Discussion Paper. Regional Office for Arab States Migration and
Governance Network (MAGNET). ILO, July 2015.

International Republican Institute. "IRI Poll: Jordanians Encouraged by Stability;
Concerned about High Prices and Refugee Numbers." IRI: International Republican Institute, March 10, 2014. http://www.iri.org/resource/iri-poll-jordanians
-encouraged-stability-concerned-about-high-prices-and-refugee-numbers.

———. "Survey of Jordan Public Opinion, November 30–December 6, 2013." Decem-
ber 30, 2013. https://www.iri.org/sites/default/files/2014%20March%2010%20
Survey%20of%20Jordanian%20Public%20Opinion%2C%20November%2030
-December%206%2C%202013_0.pdf.

International Rescue Committee (IRC). "Economic Impacts of Syrian Refugees. Existing
Research Review & Key Takeaways." Policy Brief. From Harm to Home, Rescue
.Org. International Rescue Committee, 2016.

———. "Emergency Economies: The Impact of Cash Assistance in Lebanon," August
2014. https://www.rescue.org/sites/default/files/document/631/emergencyecono
miesevaluationreport-lebanon2014.pdf.

———. "Policy Brief: Impact of Syrian Refugees on Host Communities." International
Rescue Committee (IRC), January 1, 2016. https://www.rescue.org/report/policy
-brief-impact-syrian-refugees-host-communities.

IRIN. "The Case That Exposes Jordan's Deportation Double Standards," May 25, 2015.
http://www.thenewhumanitarian.org/fr/node/255330.

IRIN News (now The New Humanitarian). "To Avoid Tensions with Refugees, Lebanese
Hosts Need Support," January 28, 2013. http://www.thenewhumanitarian.org
/analysis/2013/01/28/avoid-tensions-refugees-lebanese-hosts-need-support.

IRIN News (now The New Humanitarian). "Syrian refugees head to Lebanon's Shi'a
south," January 29, 2013. Accessed December 10, 2019. http://www.thenewhu
manitarian.org/news/2013/01/29/syrian-refugees-head-lebanon-s-shia-south.

"Is Liberia Tired of NGOs?" *Global Witness* (blog), March 31, 2014. https://www
.globalwitness.org/en/blog/liberia-tired-ngos/.

Jaafar, Rudy, and Maria J. Stephan. "Lebanon's Independence Intifada: How an
Unarmed Insurrection Expelled Syrian Forces." In *Civilian Jihad: Nonviolent
Struggle, Democratization, and Governance in the Middle East,* edited by Maria
J. Stephan, 169–82. New York: Palgrave Macmillan, 2009.

Jacobsen, Karen. "Can Refugees Benefit the State? Refugee Resources and African
Statebuilding." *Journal of Modern African Studies* 40, no. 4 (2002): 577–96.

———. "Cities of Refuge of the Middle East: Bringing an Urban Lens to the Forced
Displacement Challenge." Policy Note. World Bank, September 14, 2017.
http://fic.tufts.edu/publication-item/cities-of-refuge/.

Jamal, Manal A. "The 'Other Arab' and Gulf Citizens: Mutual Accommodation of
Palestinians in the UAE in Historical Context." In *Arab Migrant Communities in the
GCC: Summary Report,* edited by Zahra Babar et al. Georgetown University School
of Foreign Service in Qatar, 2015. https://papers.ssrn.com/abstract=2840380.

———. "The 'Tiering' of Citizenship and Residency and the 'Hierarchization' of Migrant
Communities: The United Arab Emirates in Historical Context." *International
Migration Review* 49, no. 3 (September 2015): 601–32.

Janmyr, Maja. "The Legal Status of Syrian Refugees in Lebanon." Working Paper. Beirut:
IFI & AUB, 2016.

———. "Precarity in Exile: The Legal Status of Syrian Refugees in Lebanon." *Refugee
Survey Quarterly* 35 (2016): 58–78.

Jarmuzek, Mariusz, Najla Nakhle, and Francisco Parodi. "Lebanon: Selected Issues." IMF
Country Report. Washington, DC: IMF, July 2014.

Jasper, James M. *The Art of Moral Protest: Culture, Biography, and Creativity in Social
Movements.* Chicago: University of Chicago Press, 1997.

Javeline, Debra Lynn. *Protest and the Politics of Blame: The Russian Response to Unpaid
Wages.* Ann Arbor: University of Michigan Press, 2009.

Jawad, Rana. "A Profile of Social Welfare in Lebanon: Assessing the Implications for
Social Development Policy." *Global Social Policy* 2, no. 3 (2002): 319–342.

Johnston, Hank, and John A. Noakes. *Frames of Protest: Social Movements and the
Framing Perspective.* Lanham, MD: Rowman & Littlefield, 2005.

Jones, Katharine, and Leena Ksaifi. "Struggling to Survive: Slavery and Exploitation of
Syrian Refugees in Lebanon." The Freedom Fund, 2016. https://d1r4g0yjvcc7lx
.cloudfront.net/uploads/Lebanon-Report-FINAL-8April16.pdf. Accessed
December 9, 2019.

"Jordan's Gabba3at Moment," *Black Iris* (blog), June 4, 2018. http://black-iris.com/2018
/06/04/jordans-gabba3at-moment/.

Karmel, E. J. "How Revolutionary Was Jordan's Hirak?" Amman: Identity Center, 2014.

Kelberer, Victoria. "Negotiating Crisis: International Aid and Refugee Policy in Jordan."
Middle East Policy 24, no. 4 (2017): 148–165.

Kerbage, Carole. "Politics of Coincidence: The Harak Confronts Its 'Peoples.'" Working
Paper. Issam Fares Institute for Public Policy and International Affairs, American
University of Beirut, February 2017.

Kerbo, Harold R. "Movements of 'Crisis' and Movements of 'Affluence': A Critique of
Deprivation and Resource Mobilization Theories." *Journal of Conflict Resolution*
26, no. 4 (1982): 645–63.

Khawaja, Bassam. "The Gaps in Lebanon's New Refugee Policy." Human Rights Watch,
March 14, 2017. https://www.hrw.org/print/301093.

———. "Growing Up without an Education: Barriers to Education for Syrian Refugee
Children in Lebanon." Human Rights Watch, 2016. https://www.hrw.org/report

/2016/07/19/growing-without-education/barriers-education-syrian-refugee
-children-lebanon.

Khorma, Tamer. "The Myth of the Jordanian Monarchy's Resilience to the Arab Spring:
Lack of Genuine Political Reform Undermines Social Base of Monarchy." SWP
Comments 33. Berlin: Stiftung Wissenschaft und Politik—SWP - Deutsches
Institut für Internationale Politik und Sicherheit (German Institute for Interna-
tional and Security Affairs), 2014. https://nbn-resolving.org/urn:nbn:de:0168
-ssoar-398371.

Kingston, Paul. "Patrons, Clients and Civil Society: A Case Study of Environmental
Politics in Postwar Lebanon." *Arab Studies Quarterly* 23, no. 1 (2001): 55–72.

Kingston, Paul W. T. *Reproducing Sectarianism: Advocacy Networks and the Politics of
Civil Society in Postwar Lebanon*. Albany, NY: SUNY Press, 2013.

Knack, Stephen. "Building or Bypassing Recipient Country Systems: Are Donors
Defying the Paris Declaration?" *Journal of Development Studies* 50, no. 6 (June 3,
2014): 839–54.

Knio, Karim. "Lebanon: Cedar Revolution or Neo-Sectarian Partition?" *Mediterranean
Politics* 10, no. 2 (2005): 225–31.

Kristoff, Madeline, and Liz Panarelli. "Haiti: A Republic of NGOs?" Peace Brief. United
States Institute of Peace, April 26, 2010, https://www.usip.org/publications/2010
/04/haiti-republic-ngos.

Kukrety, Nupur, and Sarah Al Jamal. "Poverty, Inequality and Social Protection in
Lebanon." Oxfam Research Reports. Issam Fares Institute for Public Policy and
International Affairs, American University of Beirut and Oxfam, April 2016.

Lambert, Hélène. "Temporary Refuge from War: Customary International Law and the
Syrian Conflict." *International & Comparative Law Quarterly* 66, no. 3
(July 2017): 723–45.

Landau, Loren Brett. *The Humanitarian Hangover: Displacement, Aid, and Transformation in Western Tanzania*. Johannesburg: Wits University Press, 2008.

Lebanese Center for Policy Studies. "Supporting Municipalities in Responding to the
Refugee Crisis," May 14, 2016. http://lcps-lebanon.org/agendaArticle.php?id=65.

Leenders, Reinoud. *Spoils of Truce: Corruption and State-Building in Postwar Lebanon*.
Ithaca, NY: Cornell University Press, 2012.

Lenner, Katharina. "Blasts from the Past: Policy Legacies and Memories in the Making of
the Jordanian Response to the Syrian Refugee Crisis." Max Weber Red Number
Series. EUI Working Papers. European University Institute, 2016. http://opus
.bath.ac.uk/52658/.

Lenner, Katharina, and Lewis Turner. "Making Refugees Work? The Politics of Integrat-
ing Syrian Refugees into the Labor Market in Jordan." *Middle East Critique* 28,
no. 1 (2019): 65–95.

Le Troquer, Yann, and Rozenn Hommery al-Oudat. "From Kuwait to Jordan: The
Palestinians' Third Exodus." *Journal of Palestine Studies* 28, no. 3 (April 1, 1999):
37.

LHIF. "Background Paper on Unregistered Syrian Refugees in Lebanon." Lebanese
Humanitarian INGO Forum, July 15, 2014.

Lozi, Basem M. "The Effect of Refugees on Host Country Economy: Evidence from
Jordan." *Interdisciplinary Journal of Contemporary Research in Business* 5, no. 3
(July 2013). http://journal-archieves34.webs.com/114-126.pdf.

Mackreath, Helen. "Cosmopolitanism in Akkar? Why the Role of Host Families Is
Significant." *E-International Relations* (blog), June 28, 2015. http://www.e-ir
.info/2015/05/28/cosmopolitanism-in-akkar-why-the-role-of-host-families-is
-significant/.

Madoré, Marianne. "The Peaceful Settlement of Syrian Refugees in the Eastern Suburbs of Beirut: Understanding the Causes of Social Stability." Civil Society Knowledge Centre, 2016. https://civilsociety-centre.org/paper/peaceful-settlement-syrian -refugees-eastern-suburbs-beirut-understanding-causes-social.

Mansbridge, Jane. "The Making of Oppositional Consciousness." In *Oppositional Consciousness: The Subjective Roots of Social Protest*, edited by Aldon Morris, 1–19. Chicago: University of Chicago Press, 2001.

Marks, Jesse. "Pushing Syrian Refugees to Return." *Carnegie Endowment for International Peace* (blog), March 1, 2018. http://carnegieendowment.org/sada/75684.

Martínez, José Ciro. "Bread Is Life: The Intersection of Welfare Politics and Emergency Aid in Jordan." *Middle East Report*, no. 272 (Fall 2014). http://www.merip.org /mer/mer272/bread-life.

——. "Leavened Apprehensions: Bread Subsidies and Moral Economies in Hashemite Jordan." *International Journal of Middle East Studies* 50, no. 2 (May 2018): 173–93.

Masri, Sawsan, and Illina Srour. "Assessment of the Impact of Syrian Refugees in Lebanon and Their Employment Profile, 2013." Beirut, International Labour Organization, Regional Office for the Arab States, 2014.

Mazur, Michael P. *Economic Growth and Development in Jordan*. London: Croom Helm, 1979.

McAdam, Doug, John D. McCarthy, Mayer N. Zald, and Mayer Zald N. *Comparative Perspectives on Social Movements: Political Opportunities, Mobilizing Structures, and Cultural Framings*. New York: Cambridge University Press, 1996.

Mcloughlin, Claire. "When Does Service Delivery Improve the Legitimacy of a Fragile or Conflict-Affected State?" *Governance* 28, no. 3 (July 2015): 341–56.

Mercy Corps. "Analysis of Host Community-Refugee Tensions in Mafraq, Jordan." October 2012. https://reliefweb.int/report/jordan/analysis-host-community -refugee-tensions-mafraq-jordan.

——. "Charting a New Course: Rethinking the Syrian Refugee Response," December 2013. https://www.mercycorps.org/research-resources/charting-new-course -re-thinking-syrian-refugee-response.

——. "Engaging Municipalities in the Response to the Syria Refugee Crisis in Lebanon." Policy Brief. Mercy Corps and British Embassy Beirut, March 2014. https://www .mercycorps.org/sites/default/files/Mercy%20Corps%20Lebanon%20Policy%20 Brief%20Engaging%20Municipalities%20%28English%29.pdf.

——. "From Jordan to Jihad: The Lure of Syria's Violent Extremist Groups." Policy Brief. September 24, 2015.

——. "From Tension to Violence: Understanding and Preventing Violence between Refugees and Host Communities in Lebanon." Beirut: Mercy Corps Lebanon, 2017.

——. "Mapping of Host Community-Refugee Tensions in Mafraq and Ramtha, Jordan." May 2013. https://data2.unhcr.org/en/documents/download/38301. Accessed February 9, 2018.

——. "Seeking Stability: Evidence on Strategies for Reducing the Risk of Conflict in Northern Jordanian Communities Hosting Syrian Refugees," April 14, 201. https://www.mercycorps.org/research-resources/seeking-stability-evidence -strategies-reducing-risk-conflict-northern-jordanian.

——. "Tapped Out: Water Scarcity and Refugee Pressures in Jordan." Amman, 2014. https://www.mercycorps.org/sites/default/files/MercyCorps_TappedOut _JordanWaterReport_March204.pdf. Accessed October 6, 2017.

——. "Things Fall Apart: Political, Economic, and Social Instability in Lebanon," June 2013. https://www.mercycorps.org/sites/default/files/MC%20Lebanon%20 LivelihoodConflict_Assesment_%20Full%20Report%200913.pdf.

Ministry of Environment, Government of Lebanon, and UNDP. "Lebanon Environmental Assessment of the Syrian Conflict and Priority Interventions." September 2014.

Ministry of Planning and International Cooperation. "Needs Assessment Review of the Impact of the Syrian Crisis on Jordan: Executive Summary." Hashemite Kingdom of Jordan, Host Community Support Platform, November 2013.

Mitri, Dalya. "Challenges of Aid Coordination in a Complex Crisis: An Overview of Funding Policies and Conditions Regarding Aid Provision to Syrian Refugees in Lebanon." Civil Society Knowledge Centre, Lebanon Support, May 23, 2014. https://civilsociety-centre.org/paper/challenges-aid-coordination-complex-crisis.

Mokbel, Madona. "Refugees in Limbo: The Plight of Iraqis in Bordering States." *Middle East Report*, no. 244 (Fall 2007): 10–17.

Molnar, Petra. "Discretion to Deport: Intersections between Health and Detention of Syrian Refugees in Jordan." *Refuge: Canada's Journal on Refugees* 33, no. 2 (2017): 18–31.

Moore, Pete. "Jordan's Long War Economy." *Political Economy Project* (blog), September 1, 2017. http://www.politicaleconomyproject.org/2/post/2017/09/jordans-long-war-economy-pete-moore.html.

Moore, Will H., and Stephen M. Shellman. "Whither Will They Go? A Global Study of Refugees' Destinations, 1965–1995." *International Studies Quarterly* 51, no. 4 (2007): 811–34.

Mouawad, Jamil, and Hannes Baumann. "Wayn Al-Dawla?: Locating the Lebanese State in Social Theory." *Arab Studies Journal* 25, no. 1 (2017): 66–90.

Mourad, Lama. "From Conflict-Insensitive to Conflict-Driven Aid: Responding to the Syrian Refugee Crisis in Lebanon." *Middle East Institute* (blog), December 19, 2016. https://www.mei.edu/content/map/conflict-insensitive-conflict-driven-aid.

——. "Inaction as Policy-Making: Understanding Lebanon's Early Response to the Refugee Influx." Project on Middle East Political Science, 2017. https://pomeps.org/wp-content/uploads/2017/03/POMEPS_Studies_25_Refugees_Web.pdf#page=50.

——. "'Standoffish' Policy-Making: Inaction and Change in the Lebanese Response to the Syrian Displacement Crisis." *Middle East Law and Governance* 9, no. 3 (November 11, 2017): 249–66.

Mourad, Lama, and Laure-Hélène Piron. "Municipal Service Delivery, Stability, Social Cohesion and Legitimacy in Lebanon: An Analytical Literature Review." Background Paper. Developmental Leadership Program and Issam Fares Institute for Public Policy and International Affairs, American University of Beirut, 2016.

Nagle, John. "Between Entrenchment, Reform and Transformation: Ethnicity and Lebanon's Consociational Democracy." *Democratization* 23, no. 7 (November 9, 2016): 1144–61.

——. "Ghosts, Memory, and the Right to the Divided City: Resisting Amnesia in Beirut City Centre: Ghosts, Memory, and the Right to the Divided City." *Antipode* 49, no. 1 (January 2017): 149–68.

Najem, Tom. *Lebanon: The Politics of a Penetrated Society*. New York: Routledge, 2012.

Nanes, Stefanie. "Jordan's Unwelcome 'Guests.'" *Middle East Report* 37, no. 244 (2007): 22–24.

Nasser, Razan, and Steven Symansky. "The Fiscal Impact of the Syrian Refugee Crisis on Jordan." USAID, January 5, 2014. https://www.dropbox.com/s/kq74hjhw15gxmkw/The%20Fiscal%20Impact%20of%20Syrian%20Refugees%20on%20GOJ.pdf.

Naufal, Hala. "Syrian Refugees in Lebanon: The Humanitarian Approach under Political Divisions." MPC Research Report. San Domenico di Fiesole, Italy: Migration

Policy Centre, Robert Schuman Centre for Advanced Studies, European University Institute, 2012.

Norton, Augustus Richard. "Hizbullah and the Israeli Withdrawal from Southern Lebanon." *Journal of Palestine Studies* 30, no. 1 (2000): 22–35.

Norwegian Refugee Council. "Consequences of Limited Legal Status for Syrian Refugees in Lebanon: NRC Lebanon Field Assessment Part Two." Information, Counselling and Legal Assistance Programme, NRC Field Assessment—North, Bekaa, South, March 2014. https://www.nrc.no/resources/reports/the-consequences-of -limited-legal-status-for-syrian-refugees-in-lebanon/.

Norwegian Refugee Council and International Human Rights Clinic (IHRC). "Securing Status: Syrian Refugees and the Documentation of Legal Status, Identity, and Family Relationships in Jordan," November 2016. https://www.nrc.no/resources /reports/the-consequences-of-limited-legal-status-for-syrian-refugees-in -lebanon/.

Norwegian Refugee Council and International Rescue Committee. "No Escape: Civilians in Syria Struggle to Find Safety Across Borders," November 13, 2014. https://www .nrc.no/resources/reports/no-escape---civilians-in-syria-struggle-to-find-safety -across-borders/.

Nowrasteh, Alex. "Economics of the Syrian Refugee Crisis." *Cato Institute* (blog), May 2, 2016. https://www.cato.org/blog/economics-syrian-refugee-crisis.

Nucho, Joanne Randa. *Everyday Sectarianism in Urban Lebanon: Infrastructures, Public Services.* Princeton, NJ: Princeton University Press, 2016.

Obeid, Michelle. "Searching for the 'Ideal Face of the State' in a Lebanese Border Town." *Journal of the Royal Anthropological Institute* 16, no. 2 (June 2010): 330–46.

O'Donnell, Kelly, and Kathleen Newland. "The Iraqi Refugee Crisis: The Need for Action." Washington, DC: Migration Policy Institute, 2008.

Orhan, Oytun. "The Situation of Syrian Refugees in the Neighboring Countries: Findings, Conclusions and Recommendations." ORSAM Report. ORSAM, April 2014.

Oxfam International. "Lebanon Looking ahead in Times of Crisis: Taking Stock of the Present to Urgently Build Sustainable Options for the Future." Oxfam Discussion Papers, 2015.

——. "Syrian Refugee Influx Adding to Jordan's Water Worries." *Conflict & Emergencies Blog Channel* (blog), April 2013. https://blogs.oxfam.org/en/blogs/13-03-22-syria -refugees-adding-jordan-water-worries.

Ozaras, Resat, Ilker Inanc Balkan, and Mucahit Yemisen. "Prejudice and Reality about Infection Risk among Syrian Refugees." *Lancet Infectious Diseases* 16, no. 11 (November 2016): 1222–23.

Paler, Laura, Leslie Marshall, and Sami Atallah. "The Fear of Supporting Political Reform." Policy Brief. Lebanese Center for Policy Studies, May 2018.

——. "The Social Costs of Public Political Participation: Evidence from a Petition Experiment in Lebanon." *Journal of Politics* 80, no. 4 (October 2018): 1405–10.

Polanyi, Karl. *The Great Transformation.* Vol. 5. Boston: Beacon Press, 1957.

Polletta, Francesca. "Contending Stories: Narrative in Social Movements." *Quantitative Sociology* 21, no. 4 (1998): 419–46.

Pop, Valentina. "Jordan Prince Pours Cold Water on EU Initiative for Syrian Refugees." *WSJ* (blog), June 1, 2017. https://blogs.wsj.com/brussels/2017/06/01/jordan -prince-pours-cold-water-on-eu-initiative-for-syrian-refugees/.

"Preserving Lebanon's Water before the Wells Run Dry." *World Bank* (blog), September 30, 2014. http://www.worldbank.org/en/news/feature/2014/09/30/preserving -lebanon-s-water-before-the-wells-run-dry.

Proctor, Keith. "Refugee Crisis Draining Jordan's Water Resources." *MENASource* (blog), the Atlantic Council, March 21, 2014. http://www.atlanticcouncil.org /blogs/menasource/refugee-crisis-draining-jordan-s-water-resources.

———. "High and Dry with the Hashemites," *Fanack Water Newsletter*, March 18, 2015. https://water.fanack.com/high-and-dry-with-the-hashemites/.

REACH Initiative. "Access to Water and Tensions in Jordanian Communities Hosting Syrian Refugees," Thematic Assessment Report, June 2014. https://reliefweb.int /sites/reliefweb.int/files/resources/REACH_JOR_Report_HealthandTensionsinJor danianCommunitiesHostingSyrianRefugees.pdf.

———. "Education and Tensions in Communities Hosting Syrian Refugees." Thematic Assessment Report, June 2014. https://reliefweb.int/sites/reliefweb.int/files /resources/REACH_JOR_Report_EducationandTensionsinCommunitiesHosting SyrianRefugees.pdf.

———. "Evaluating the Effect of the Syrian Refugee Crisis on Stability and Resilience in Jordanian Host Communities: Preliminary Impact Assessment." REACH, January 2014. https://www.reach-initiative.org/what-we-do/news/reach -workshop-on-jordanian-communities-hosting-syrian-refugees/.

———. "Livelihoods, Employment and Tensions in Jordanian Communities Hosting Syrian Refugees." Thematic Assessment Report, Amman, Jordan: British Embassy, June 2014. https://reliefweb.int/sites/reliefweb.int/files/resources /REACH_JOR_Report_EmploymentandTensionsinJordanianCommunitiesHostin gSyrianRefugees.pdf.

———. "Social Cohesion in Host Communities in Northern Jordan." Jordan Assessment Report, May 2015. https://reliefweb.int/sites/reliefweb.int/files/resources/reach _jor_report_social_cohesion_in_host_communities_in_northern_jordan_may _2015%20%281%29%20%281%29.pdf.

———. "Understanding Social Cohesion and Resilience in Jordanian Host Communities, Assessment Report June 2014," 2014. https://reliefweb.int/report/jordan /understanding-social-cohesion-and-resilience-jordanian-host-communities -assessment.

REACH and UNHCR. "Livelihoods Assessment of Syrian Refugees in Akkar Governorate." Assessment Report. Lebanon, December 2014. http://orange.ngo/wp content/uploads/2018/01/Livelihoods-Assessment-of-Syrian.pdf.

Reed, Barbara A., and Jean-Pierre Habicht. "Sales of Food Aid as Sign of Distress, Not Excess." *Lancet* 351, no. 9096 (January 10, 1998): 128–30.

Reidy, Eric. "Unsafe in Syria, Unwanted in Lebanon," IRIN, December 11, 2018. https://www.irinnews.org/news-feature/2018/12/11/Syria-refugees-Lebanon -Mediterranean-drowning-Europe-Middle-East-smuggling.

Republic of Lebanon. "London Conference—Lebanon Statement of Intent," February 4, 2016. https://www.gov.uk/government/publications/supporting-syria-and-the -region-london-2016-lebanon-statement.

Riachi, Roland. "Beyond Rehashed Policies: Lebanon Must Tackle Its Water Crisis Head-On." *Lebanese Center for Policy Studies: Featured Analysis* (blog), October 2014. http://lcps-lebanon.org/featuredArticle.php?id=27.

———. "The Private Modes of Water Capture in Lebanon." In *Towards a Peace Economy in Lebanon*, edited by Jessica Banfield and Victoria Stamadianou, 39–45. International Alert, 2015. https://www.international-alert.org/sites/default/files/Lebanon _TowardsPeaceEconomy_EN_2015.pdf.

Ridge, Tom, and Gayle Smith. "Confronting the Global Forced Migration Crisis: A Report of the CSIS Task Force on the Global Forced Migration Crisis." CSIS Task Force on the Global Forced Migration Crisis and the CSIS Project on Prosperity and Development. Washington, DC: Center for Strategic & International Studies, 2018.

Rollins, Tom. "Syrians Make Easy Scapegoats in Lebanon." *IRIN* (blog), July 28, 2016. https://www.irinnews.org/feature/2016/07/28/syrians-make-easy-scapegoats-lebanon.

Rossi, Rachel, Shruti Kumar, and Aisha Han. "Factbox: Jordan's Austerity Protests." *Atlantic Council* (blog), June 7, 2018. https://www.atlanticcouncil.org/blogs/menasource/factbox-jordan-s-austerity-protests.

Rothschild, Zachary K., Mark J. Landau, Daniel Sullivan, and Lucas A. Keefer. "A Dual-Motive Model of Scapegoating: Displacing Blame to Reduce Guilt or Increase Control." *Journal of Personality and Social Psychology* 102, no. 6 (2012): 1148–63.

Ruisi, D., and M. Shteiwi. "Economic and Social Integration of Migrants and Refugees in Jordan and Lebanon." In *Migrants and Refugees: Impact and Future Policies. Case Studies of Jordan, Lebanon, Turkey and Greece*, edited by 5 M. Shteiwi, EuroMesco Joint Policy Study no. 4. European Institute of the Mediterranean, 28–5, 2016. https://www.iemed.org/publicacions-en/historic-de-publicacions/joint-policy-studies/4.-migrants-and-refugees.-impact-and-policies.-case-studies-of-jordan-lebanon-turkey-and-greece.

Ryan, Curtis R. "Identity Politics, Reform, and Protest in Jordan." *Studies in Ethnicity and Nationalism* 11, no. 3 (2011): 564–78.

——. *Jordan and the Arab Uprisings: Regime Survival and Politics Beyond the State*. New York: Columbia University Press, 2018.

——. "'We Are All Jordan' . . . But Who Is We?" *Middle East Report Online*, July 13, 2010. http://www.merip.org/mero/mero071310.

Saadallaoui, Bassem. "Competing for Scarce Resources: The New Concern for Syrian Refugees and Host Communities in Lebanon." *ENN (Emergency Nutrition Network) Field Exchange* (blog), November 2014. https://www.ennonline.net/fex/48/competing.

Saad-Ghorayeb, Amal. "People Say No." *Al-Ahram Weekly Online*, August 3, 2006, Opinion. http://weekly.ahram.org.eg/Archive/2006/806/op33.htm.

Sadaka, George, Jocelyne Nader, and Tony Mikhael. "Monitoring Racism in the Lebanese Media: The Representation of the 'Syrian' and the 'Palestinian' in the News Coverage." Lebanon: Maharat Foundation & UNDP, 2015.

Saghieh, Nizar. "Manufacturing Vulnerability in Lebanon: Legal Policies as Efficient Tools of Discrimination." March 19, 2015. Legal Agenda. http://legal-agenda.com/en/article.php?id=690&folder=articles&lang=en.

——. "The Right to Food Safety: Rights-Based Dialogue as a Springboard towards State-Building." *Jadaliyya* (blog), March 6, 2015. http://www.jadaliyya.com/pages/index/20977/the-right-to-foo.

Salamah, Dalal. "Violations of Professional Principles: Tools Generating 'Hate Speech' . . . Coverage of Syrian Refugees as Example." AKEED, May 3, 2016. http://www.akeed.jo/index.php?option=com_mqal&view=item&id=393&Itemid=141&lang=en&layout=social.

Salemi, Colette, Jay A. Bowman, and Jennifer Compton. "Services for Syrian Refugee Children and Youth in Jordan: Forced Displacement, Foreign Aid, and Vulnerability." Working Paper. Economic Research Forum, April 2018.

Salloukh, Bassel F. "The Syrian War: Spillover Effects on Lebanon." *Middle East Policy* 24, no. 1 (2017): 62–78.

Salloukh, Bassel F., Rabie Barakat, Jinan S. Al-Habbal, Lara W. Khattab, and Shoghig Mikaelian. *The Politics of Sectarianism in Postwar Lebanon*. London: Pluto Press, 2015.

Salti, Nisreen, and Jad Chaaban. "The Role of Sectarianism in the Allocation of Public Expenditure in Postwar Lebanon." *International Journal of Middle East Studies* 42, no. 4 (November 2010): 637–55.

Saroufim, Maya, Khalil Charafeddine, Grace Issa, Haifaa Khalifeh, Robert H. Habib, Atika Berry, Nada Ghosn, Alissar Rady, and Ibrahim Khalifeh. "Ongoing Epidemic of Cutaneous Leishmaniasis among Syrian Refugees, Lebanon." *Emerging Infectious Diseases* 20, no. 10 (October 2014): 1712–15.

Sassoon, Joseph. *The Iraqi Refugees: The New Crisis in the Middle East.* New York: IB Tauris, 2008.

Save the Children. "Too Young to Wed: The Growing Problem of Child Marriage among Syrian Girls in Jordan." 2014. London: Save the Children, https://www .savethechildren.org.uk/content/dam/global/reports/education-and-child -protection/too-young-to-wed.pdf.

Save the Children and UNICEF. "Small Hands Heavy Burden: How the Syria Conflict Is Driving More Children into the Workplace." July 2, 2015. http://childrenofsyria .info/wp-content/uploads/2015/07/CHILD-LABOUR.pdf.

Schwedler, Jillian. "The Political Geography of Protest in Neoliberal Jordan." *Middle East Critique* 21, no. 3 (September 2012): 259–70.

——. *Protesting Jordan.* Stanford, CA: Stanford University Press, forthcoming.

——. "Routines and Ruptures in Protests and Policing in Jordan." Paper presented at the Freeman Spogli Institute for International Studies and Center on Democracy, Development, and the Rule of Law, Stanford University, April 12, 2017.

——. "Jordan's Austerity Protests in Context," *Atlantic Council* (blog), June 8, 2018. https:// www.atlanticcouncil.org/blogs/menasource/jordan-s-austerity-protests-in-context.

Seeberg, Peter. "Jordan's Migration Diplomacy and the Syrian Refugees." News Analysis, Center for Mellemøststudier, Syddansk Universitet, November 2016. https://www .sdu.dk/-/media/files/om_sdu/centre/c_mellemoest/videncenter/artikler/2016 /seeberg+article+nov+16.pdf?la=da&hash=DE6CBFEB956A1322D3D78230AD3B 55BC02A9984F.

Seeley, Maira. "Jordanian Hosts and Syrian Refugees: Comparing Perceptions of Social Conflict and Cohesion in Three Host Communities." Programme Research no. 25. Generations for Peace Institute Research, December 2015, https://www.generations forpeace.org/wp-content/uploads/2016/11/OX-2015-MS-Report-02.pdf.

Seeley, Nicholas. "The Politics of Aid to Iraqi Refugees in Jordan." *Middle East Report*, no. 256 (Fall 2010): 37–42.

Shesterinina, Anastasia. "Collective Threat Framing and Mobilization in Civil War." *American Political Science Review* 110, no. 3 (2016): 411–27.

Shibli, Rabih, and Carmen Geha. "Critique of the Syrian Refugee Crisis Response: The Case of Lebanon." Working Paper no. 28. Middle East and North Africa Regional Architecture (MENARA), December 2018.

Shihab-Eldin, Ahmed. "Jordan First: A King's Modernization Motto Obscures a Palestinian Past and Iraqi Present." *Huffington Post* (blog), January 5, 2009. https://www .huffingtonpost.com/ahmed-shihabeldin/jordan-first-a-kings-mode_b_148589.html.

Simmons, Erica. "Grievances Do Matter in Mobilization." *Theory and Society* 43, no. 5 (2014): 513–46.

Snow, David A., Daniel M. Cress, Liam Downey, and Andrew W. Jones. "Disrupting the 'Quotidian': Reconceptualizing the Relationship between Breakdown and the Emergence of Collective Action." *Mobilization* 3, no. 1 (1998): 1–22.

Staton, Bethan. "Young Reformers Want Debate, Not Protest, to Drive Change in Jordan." *Middle East Eye* (blog), November 7, 2016. http://www.middleeasteye .net/news/jordan-youth-movement-democracy-debate-631139717.

Stave, Svein Erik, and Solveig Hillesund. "Impact of Syrian Refugees on the Jordanian Labour Market: Findings from the Governorates of Amman, Irbid and Mafraq." International Labour Organization Regional Office for the Arab States and Fafo, 2015.

Steinmayr, Andreas. "Exposure to Refugees and Voting for the Far-Right: (Unexpected) Results from Austria." SSRN Scholarly Paper. Rochester, NY: Social Science Research Network, March 21, 2016. https://papers.ssrn.com/abstract=2750273.

Stel, Nora. "Mukhtars in the Middle: Connecting State, Citizens and Refugees." Jadaliyya (blog), December 4, 2015. http://www.jadaliyya.com/Details/32751/Mukhtars-in -the-Middle-Connecting-State,-Citizens-and-Refugees.

———. "Review Essay: Lebanon—The Challenge of Moving Analysis beyond the State." Middle East Policy 20, no. 1 (March 2013): 163–74.

Stevens, Dallal. "Legal Status, Labelling, and Protection: The Case of Iraqi Refugees in Jordan." International Journal of Refugee Law 25, no. 1 (2013): 1–38.

Suleiman, Yasir, and Paul Anderson. "'Conducting Fieldwork in the Middle East': Report of a Workshop Held at the University of Edinburgh on 12 February 2007." British Journal of Middle Eastern Studies 35, no. 2 (August 2008): 151–71.

"Supporting Syria and the Region: Post-London Conference Financial Tracking." London: Department for International Development, February 2017.

Tell, Tariq. "Early Spring in Jordan: The Revolt of the Military Veterans." Beirut: Carnegie Middle East Center, November 4, 2015. https://carnegieendowment.org /files/ACMR_Tell_Jordan_Eng_final.pdf.

———. The Social and Economic Origins of Monarchy in Jordan. New York: Palgrave Macmillan, 2013.

Thibos, Cameron. "One Million Syrians in Lebanon: A Milestone Quickly Passed." Policy Brief. San Domenico di Fiesole, Italy: Migration Policy Centre, Robert Schuman Centre for Advanced Studies, European University Institute, June 2014.

Thompson, E. P. "The Moral Economy of the English Crowd." In Customs in Common, 185–351. New York: New Press, 1993.

Tilly, Charles. "The Blame Game." American Sociologist 41, no. 4 (December 2010): 382–89.

Traboulsi, Fawwaz. A History of Modern Lebanon. London: Pluto Press, 2018.

Tsourapas, Gerasimos. "The Syrian Refugee Crisis and Foreign Policy Decision-Making in Jordan, Lebanon, and Turkey." Journal of Global Security Studies (May 4, 2019). https://doi.org/10.1093/jogss/ogz016.

Turner, Lewis. "Explaining the (Non-) Encampment of Syrian Refugees: Security, Class and the Labour Market in Lebanon and Jordan." Mediterranean Politics 20, no. 3 (2015): 386–404.

United Nations Development Programme (UNDP). "The Syrian Crisis: Implications for Development Indicators and Development Planning—Lebanon." http://www .lb.undp.org/content/lebanon/en/home/library/poverty/the-syrian-crisis.html.

———. "A Profile of Sustainable Human Development in Lebanon." United Nations Development Programme, 1997. http://www.undp.org.lb/programme/gover nance/advocacy/nhdr/nhdr97/index.cfm. Accessed October 6, 2017.

UNHCR and UNICEF. "Vulnerability Assessment of Syrian Refugees in Lebanon." 2017. https://data2.unhcr.org/en/documents/details/61312.

UNICEF. "A Study on Early Marriage in Jordan 2014." Jordan Country Office, 2014. https://www.unicef.org/media/files/UNICEFJordan_EarlyMarriageStudy2014 -email.pdf.

United Nations Population Fund. "New Study Finds Child Marriage Rising among Most Vulnerable Syrian Refugees." January 31, 2017. /news/new-study-finds-child -marriage-rising-among-most-vulnerable-syrian-refugees.

Valenza, Matteo, and Shatha AlFayez. "Running on Empty: The Situation of Syrian Children in Host Communities in Jordan." UNICEF, May 2016.

Van Dyke, Nella. "Threat." In *The Wiley-Blackwell Encyclopedia of Social and Political Movements*, edited by David A. Snow, Donatella della Porta, Bert Klandermans, and Doug McAdam, 1–3. Malden, MA: Wiley-Blackwell, 2013.

Van Dyke, Nella, and Sarah A. Soule. "Structural Social Change and the Mobilizing Effect of Threat: Explaining Levels of Patriot and Militia Organizing in the United States." *Social Problems* 49, no. 4 (2002): 497–520.

Van Vliet, Sam. "Syrian Refugees in Lebanon: Coping with Unprecedented Challenges." In *Lebanon and the Arab Uprisings: In the Eye of the Hurricane*, edited by Maximilian Felsch and Martin Wahlisch, 89–103. New York: Routledge, 2016.

Van Vliet, Sam, and Guita Hourani. "Regional Differences in the Conditions of Syrian Refugees in Lebanon." Civil Society Knowledge Centre, April 23, 2014. http://civilsociety-centre.org/paper/regional-differences-conditions-syrian-refugees-lebanon.

Waddell, Kaveh. "Facebook Vigilantism Is a Scary Thing." *The Atlantic*, March 19, 2018. https://www.theatlantic.com/international/archive/2018/03/the-moral-dilemma-of-civilian-justice-in-lebanon/555251/.

Walsh, Edward J. "Resource Mobilization and Citizen Protest in Communities around Three Mile Island." *Social Problems* 29, no. 1 (1981): 1–21.

Walton, John, and David Seddon. *Free Markets & Food Riots: The Politics of Global Adjustment*. Cambridge, UK: Blackwell, 1994.

Ward, Patricia. "Refugee Cities: Reflections on the Development and Impact of UNHCR Urban Refugee Policy in the Middle East." *Refugee Survey Quarterly* 33, no. 1 (2014): 77–93.

Whitaker, Beth Elise, and Jason Giersch. "Political Competition and Attitudes towards Immigration in Africa." *Journal of Ethnic and Migration Studies* 41, no. 10 (2015): 1536–57.

"Why Lebanon Has Not Passed a Budget for 12 Years." *The Economist*, March 27, 2017. https://www.economist.com/the-economist-explains/2017/03/27/why-lebanon-has-not-passed-a-budget-for-12-years.

"Widespread Middle East Fears That Syrian Violence Will Spread." *Pew Research Center's Global Attitudes Project* (blog), May 1, 2013. http://www.pewglobal.org/2013/05/01/widespread-middle-east-fears-that-syrian-violence-will-spread/.

Wieland, Carsten. "Syrian-Lebanese Relations: The Impossible Dissociation between Lebanon and Syria." In *Lebanon and the Arab Uprisings: In the Eye of the Hurricane*, edited by Maximilian Felsch and Martin Wahlisch, 167–80. New York: Routledge, 2016.

Wimmen, Heiko. "The Long, Steep Fall of the Lebanon Tribunal." *Middle East Report Online*, December 1, 2010. https://www.merip.org/mero/mero120110.

World Bank. "Economic Opportunities for Jordanians and Syrian Refugees- Questions and Answers." Accessed January 19, 2018. http://www.worldbank.org/en/country/jordan/brief/economic-opportunities-for-jordanians-and-syrian-refugees-questions-and-answers.

——. "Lebanon: Economic and Social Impact Assessment of the Syrian Conflict." Washington, DC, World Bank, September 2013. https://openknowledge.worldbank.org/handle/10986/16790.

——. "Municipalities at the Forefront of the Syrian Refugee Crisis." *Feature Story* (blog), August 3, 2016. https://www.worldbank.org/en/news/feature/2016/08/03/municipalities-at-the-forefront-of-the-syrian-refugee-crisis.

——. *Unlocking the Employment Potential in the Middle East and North Africa: Toward a New Social Contract.* Washington, DC: World Bank, 2004.

World Bank Group. *Forcibly Displaced: Toward a Development Approach Supporting Refugees, the Internally Displaced, and Their Hosts.* World Bank Publications, 2017.

Yacoubian, Mona. "Facing the Abyss: Lebanon's Deadly Political Stalemate." *USIPeace Briefing.* United States Institute of Peace, February 2008.

Yassin, Nasser, et al. "No Place to Stay? Reflections on the Syrian Refugee Shelter Policy in Lebanon—UN-Habitat." UN Habitat and Issam Fares Institute for Public Policy and International Affairs, American University of Beirut, September 2015. https://unhabitat.org/wpdm-package/no-place-to-stay-reflections-on-the-syrian-refugee-shelter-policy-in-lebanon/.

Yom, Sean L. "The New Landscape of Jordanian Politics: Social Opposition, Fiscal Crisis, and the Arab Spring." *British Journal of Middle Eastern Studies* 42, no. 3 (July 3, 2015): 284–300.

——. "Tribal Politics in Contemporary Jordan: The Case of the Hirak Movement." *Middle East Journal* 68, no. 2 (April 15, 2014): 229–47.

Zanotti, Laura. "Cacophonies of Aid, Failed State Building and NGOs in Haiti: Setting the Stage for Disaster, Envisioning the Future." *Third World Quarterly* 31, no. 5 (2010): 755–71.

Zelin, Aaron Y. "Jihadism in Lebanon after the Syrian Uprising." In *Lebanon and the Arab Uprisings: In the Eye of the Hurricane*, edited by Maximilian Felsch and Martin Wahlisch, 50–69. New York: Routledge, 2016.

Zetter, Roger, Héloise Ruaudel, Sarah Deardorff-Miller, Eveliina Lyytinen, Cameron Thibos, and F. S. Pedersen. "The Syrian Displacement Crisis and a Regional Development and Protection Programme: Mapping and Meta-Analysis of Existing Studies of Costs, Impacts and Protection." Tana Copenhagen and the Ministry of Foreign Affairs of Denmark, February 4, 2014. http://www.Alnap.Org/Resource/10679.

Index

Abdullah (emir), 23–24, 73

activism: for state solutions responsibility, 84; threats to livelihood and, 6–7, 81, 106

aid. *See* humanitarian aid; international aid

Akeed media watch group, 73–74

Aoun, Michel, 31–32, 74, 132

Arab Uprisings, 19, 28, 35, 89, 133–34, 142

Armenian refugees, Lebanon absorption of, 18, 22

austerity policies, 4, 7, 141

austerity protests, 17, 96–97, 137, 140, 143; in Jordan, 122–24

Azraq refugee camp, 41, 113, 157n65

Baabda Declaration, Lebanon, 43

Baalbek: electricity lack in, 3, 93; security concerns in, 99

bail-out system, for Jordan Syrian refugees, 41, 114

Beirut Is My City movement, 96

benefits: of INGOs, 16, 61; from international aid, 47–48; Jordan state and military employment, 20, 24–25; from Syrian refugees, 16, 47–48, 61–62; for Za'atari refugee camp, 61–62

Black September battle, 24

blame: of INGOs by citizens, 4; psychological satisfaction in, 139–40; of regimes, 17, 123–24; state solutions responsibility and, 6, 7, 66, 135–36; threats to livelihood and solution prioritization, 6. *See also* Syrian refugees blame

borders: international aid restrictions and Lebanon, 115–16; Jordan closures in 2013, 114, 148; Lebanon closing of, 72

bread: Jordan riots over, 25–26, 28; protests over price increase of, 123; subsidy, 25, 28, 97, 132, 137

budget: Jordan civil service cut and international aid, 25; Lebanon 2016–2019 protests over, 129–30; NGOs state and municipalities support of, 107

child labor, 10, 53, 62–63, 148

child marriages, 60, 62–63

Christian Free Patriotic Movement, Hizbollah alliance with, 31–32

citizens: expectations of aid to, 86–88, 140; humanitarian organizations aid to, 80, 111; INGOs blamed by, 4; Lebanon aid requirement to, 113–14; on NGOs and expectations increase, 10–11; protest for rights same as Syrians, 142–43; public services lack for, 10–11, 16, 137–38; refugees separation from, 10; taxation increase for, 136; violence against Syrian refugees, 75–77

civil wars: Lebanon Civil War, 18–21, 31–34; Syrian Civil War, 32–33, 59; Syrian refugees increase of, 38

coercion, in Jordan, 27, 29

conflict: humanitarian organizations concerns for, 107, 111; INGOs prevention of, 76, 110; international aid, leverage and, 109, 112–14; Palestine-Israel, 33. *See also* security

consociational democracy, of Lebanon, 19, 29, 80

corruption, 141; Jordan economic concerns and, 27; in Lebanon, 34, 85, 86; Lebanon protests over, 129; protests over, 17, 96–97, 122–24, 137, 140, 143; state elites charges of, 16, 19, 80, 86–88, 136, 140; Transparency International on Jordan and Lebanon, 19; trash and political, 96

crime: drug-related, 77; increase in, 59–60, 71; media on, 75; Syrian refugees and perception of, 76

crisis mobilization, 7, 11, 14, 137; from increased taxation and decreased subsidies, 13; Lebanon #YouStink movement, 12–13, 93, 94–96; regime criticism through, 12; state regional divisions and, 13; on trash, 12–13, 41, 95–96

culture. *See* social relations and culture

curfews, of municipalities, 59–60, 76, 99, 110, 116

Daesh. *See* ISIS

debt: in Jordan and Lebanon, 21, 68; Lebanon decrease through fees and VAT, 121; of municipalities, 86

CPSIA information can be obtained
at www.ICGtesting.com
Printed in the USA
LVHW092008061221
705418LV00013B/827/J